Mike & Deb...

MW00489220

PARADISE

Family Guides

HAWAI'I:
THE BIG ISLAND

Making the Most of Your Family Vacation

by John Penisten

P PRIMA PUBLISHING
PO Box 1260 STI
Rocklin, CA 95677
PRIMA

In affiliation with Paradise Publications

Hawai'i: The Big Island, A Paradise Family Guide
Copyright © 1992 Paradise Publications, Portland, Oregon

First Edition: May 1989
Second Edition: March 1991
Third Edition: October 1992

Editors: Greg & Christie Stilson
Illustrations: Janora Bayot
Maps: Liane Sing
Layout & Typesetting: Paradise Publications
Cover Design: The Dunlavey Studio
Cover Photograph: Mare Schechter, Hapuna Beach, Hawai'i, Hawai'i

Published by Prima Publishing, Rocklin, California

Library of Congress Cataloging-in-Publication Data

Penisten, John.
    Hawai'i: The Big Island, making the most of your family vacation / John Penisten.
       p. cm. -- (Paradise Family Guide)
    Includes indexes.
    ISBN 1-55958-233-2 : $12.95
    1. Hawai'i Island (Hawai'i)--Guidebooks. 2. Family recreation -- Hawai'i --
Hawai'i Island. I. Title. II. Series.
DU628.H28P45   1992
919.6904'4--dc20   92-23027
                                         CIP

92 93 94 95 RRD 10 9 8 7 6 5 4 3 2 1
Printed in the United States of America

WARNING-DISCLAIMER
Prima Publishing in affiliation with Paradise Publications has designed this book to provide information in regard to the subject matter covered. It is sold with the understanding that the publishers and authors are not liable for the misconception or misuse of information provided. Every effort has been made to make this book as complete and as accurate as possible. The purpose of this book is to educate. The author, Prima Publishing and Paradise Publications shall have neither liability nor responsibility to any person or entity with respect to any loss, damage, or injury caused or alleged to be caused directly or indirectly by the information contained in this book. They shall also not be liable for price changes, or for the completeness or accuracy of the contents of this book.

HOW TO ORDER
Quantity discounts are available from the publisher, Prima Publishing, PO Box 1260 STI, Rocklin, CA 95677; telephone (916) 786-0449. On your letterhead include information concerning the intended use of the books and the number of books you wish to purchase.

"HAWAI'I KUAULI"
(Hawai'i is a verdant countryside)

*This third edition is dedicated to the memory of my father,
James Penisten, who helped me in so many ways and who also
spent lots of time "on the road" over the years.*

ME KE ALOHA PUMEHANA
(With warm Aloha)

This third edition could not have been written without the help of many fine
people in Hawai'i and elsewhere.

A special "Mahalo!" to the many readers who have shared their Big Island travel
discoveries, experiences and perspectives (good and bad!) and added to the
accuracy and content of this book.

I'd like to thank the following people for the various ways in which they assisted
with this project: Robert Salomone, Patti Cook, Adi Kohler, Sheree Moffatt,
Charlene Goo, Charles Park, Diana Reutter, Jeanne Yagi, Ruth Limtiaco, Deborah
Cotter, Elizabeth DeMotte and Tom Hagen. These fine folks provided me with
information and their own unique insight into experiencing the Big Island.

Thanks to Jim Yoshida of Hawai'i Community College in Hilo for his able
assistance and guidance in the operation of computer word processing programs.
He was always there when needed.

Liane Sing, a skilled Big Island graphic artist, did the original and updated maps
for this book and deserves a big thanks for a job well done.

A special thanks goes to my wife, Susan, and my two daughters, Janelle and
Joelle, for sharing their ideas and many of the adventures of traveling around the
Big Island of Hawai'i.

CHANT

Puka mai ka la i kai o Puna
I keauhou ka wana'ao, ke alaula
A pi'i a'e la a kau ka la i ka lolo
Mai kalae i ka mole o Lehua
Hanini ka ua, ko'iawe i ka nahele
E kupu, a mu'o, a liko
A ulu na pulapula o ka 'aina
Ma Waiakea e kahe mai ka wai lani
I ho'opulu i ka 'ili o ka malihini
Ea mai ke 'ala o na pua, lana i ka makani
Halihali ke aloha i na makamaka
Auhea 'oukou, e noho mai i moku ola
A kipa i ka nani o Mauna Kea me Mauna Loa
Loloa ke ola o ka lahui

The sun burst forth over the sea of Puna
The dawn and sunrise at Keauhou,
Ascending higher and higher overhead.
From Kalae to the base of Lehua,
The rain overflows, moving through the forest,
Stirring the new growth, buds and leaves,
Nuturing the seedlings (offsprings) of the land.
At Waiakea the heavenly waters flow,
Drenching the skin of the visitor.
The scent of flowers arises, floating on the wind,
Carrying our love to our dear friends,
Listen you all, come, dwell on Moku Ola, the island of life
In the beauty of Mauna Kea and Mauna Loa
Long live the good people of this nation.

An original Hawaiian chant composed by
Kamuela Chun of Hawai'i Community College
for Commencement, 1991.
Reprinted with permission.

TABLE OF CONTENTS

I.   PREFACE

II. GENERAL INFORMATION
  a. Introduction - Why It's Called The Big Island 11
  b. The Big Island's Best 14
  c. A History of Hawai'i 16
  d. County of Hawai'i 20
  e. Hawaiian Language, Glossary 20
  f. A Few Words About Pidgin English 23
  g. Big Island Place Names 24
  h. Getting to the Big Island 26
  i. What to Pack 29
  j. Traveling with Children 30
  k. Travel Tips for the Physically Impaired 34
  l. Senior Travel 35
  m. Weddings-Honeymoons in Paradise 36
  n. Helpful Information 39
  o. Important Phone Numbers 40
  p. Getting Around 40
  q. A Few Words About Fish and Other Seafood 47
  r. Grocery Shopping 49
  s. Special Big Island Gifts (Omiyage) 50
  t. Souvenirs, Gifts, Antiques 52
  u. Self-Service Laundries 53
  v. Annual Big Island Events 54
  w. Big Island Weather 59
  x. Tsunamis 61
  y. Earthquakes 61
  z. Tropical Photography 61

III. WHERE TO STAY - WHAT TO SEE
  a. Introduction 65
  b. ACCOMMODATIONS INDEX 67
  c. Bed and Breakfast Lodging 69
  d. Private Residences 81
  e. Long Term Stays 82
  f. Military Recreation Center 82
  g. Camping 83
  h. North Kona-South Kona Districts
      1. North Kona, South Kona, Kona's Gold Coast 87
      2. What to Do and See 88
      3. Where to Shop 92
      4. Accommodations 95
  i. South Kohala District
      1. The Kohala Coast 109
      2. What to Do and See 111
      3. Where to Shop 114
      4. Accommodations 115
  j. South Hilo District 121
      1. Hilo: A Look on the Bright Side 121
      2. What to Do and See 123
      3. Where to Shop 127
      4. Accommodations 129
  k. North Hilo and Hamakua Districts 133
  l. North Kohala District 138
  m. The Saddle Road Area 143
  n. Puna District 147
  o. Ka'u District 152
  p. BOOKING AGENTS 158

IV. RESTAURANTS

 a. Introduction/Best Bets 161
 b. Nightclubs and Entertainment 164
 c. ALPHABETICAL INDEX 165
 d. FOOD TYPE INDEX 167
 e. Big Island Drive Ins/Plate Lunch Shops 170
 f. Luaus and Hawaiian Dinner Shows 172
 g. Dinner Cruises 173
 h. Restaurants
  1. South Kona and North Kona 174
  2. South Kohala 189
  3. Hilo 198
  4. South Hilo and Hamakua 211
  5. North Kohala 212
  6. Puna 213
  7. Ka'u 215

V. RECREATION AND TOURS

 a. Introduction/Best Bets 217
 OCEAN ACTIVITIES
 b. Beaches - Snorkeling 218
  1. Water Safety/Best Bets 219
  2. BEACH INDEX 220
  3. South Kona Area 221
  4. North Kona Area 222
  5. South Kohala Area 223
  6. North Kohala Area 225
  7. Hamakua Area 226
  8. North Hilo Area 226
  9. South Hilo Area 227
  10. Puna Area 228
  11. Ka'u Area 229
 c. Booking Agencies/Representatives 230
 d. Sea Excursions and Glassbottom Boat Cruises 231
 e. Snorkeling and Diving Cruises 233
 f. Dive Shops 235
 g. Deep Sea Fishing Charters 237
 h. Windsurfing 243
 i. Jet Skiis/Parasailing 243
 j. Kayaks-Hobie Cats 244
 LAND ACTIVITIES
 a. Land Tours-Booking Agents 245
 b. Bicycle Tours 247
 c. Golf 248
 d. Tennis 251
 e. Public Swimming Pools 252
 f. Hiking/Camping 253
 g. Snow Skiing 255
 h. Horseback Riding 256
 i. Art and Fun 257
 j. Health & Fitness Centers 257
 k. Hunting 258
 AIR TOURS
 a. Small Plane Flightseeing 259
 b. Helicopter Tours 260

VI. HAWAIIANA READING FOR ADULTS AND CHILDREN

VII. INDEX

VIII. READER RESPONSE - ORDERING INFORMATION

ISLAND OF
HAWAI'I
4,038 sq. mi.

**RELATIVE GEOGRAPHIC SIZE: MAJOR
ISLANDS OF THE STATE COMPARED
TO THE BIG ISLAND.**

NORTH

HAWAIIAN ISLANDS

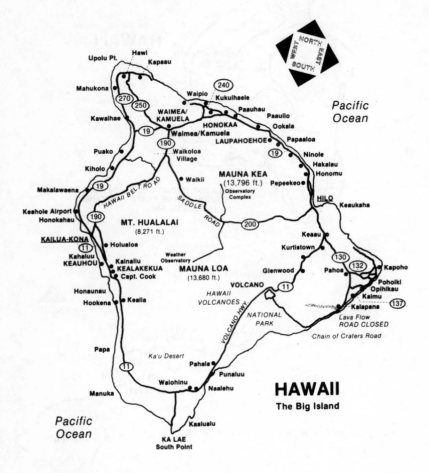

HAWAII
The Big Island

PREFACE

Since the first edition of this book in 1989, Hawai'i Island has grown significantly as a destination for Hawai'i bound visitors. The Big Island's visitor industry continues to grow and expand to meet the demand as more visitors find out about its special charms and attractions.

Visitors are increasingly attracted to the raw starkness of Hawai'i Volcanoes National Park, the verdant rain forests, flower farms and botanical gardens, cascading steams and waterfalls of the Hilo and Hamakua Coast areas, the pastoral beauty of the Waimea and Kohala Mountains ranch country, and the world-class resort facilities, water sports, golf and tennis of the Kona and Kohala Coasts.

As a Big Island resident and photojournalist for over fifteen years, I've had the opportunity to write about and photograph numerous island subjects for various magazines and newspapers. And while I won't claim to know everything about the Big Island, this book hopefully provides the latest most up-to-date information available on accommodations, where to go and what to see, dining and activities around the island.

This edition has an expanded listing of Bed & Breakfast operations, a segment of the visitor industry that continues to grow dramatically. B&B's are proving more popular with visitors seeking a non-resort experience, closer to nature and to local people who can provide a personal perspective on a Big Island visit.

Last year over one million visitors came to the Island of Hawai'i. That's quite an increase over just a few years ago when the Big Island was often the least-visited of Hawai'i's four major islands. It's an indication that the Big Island has developed a reputation for delivering a quality vacation experience.

If you're planning a vacation in Hawai'i, don't confine your trip to just Honolulu and the beach at Waikiki. Get out to the neighbor islands and see the real Hawai'i. And, hopefully, you'll find this book helpful in planning your visit to the Big Island as well as useful during your stay here.

If you are going to Kaua'i and/or Maui, you should definitely get copies of the companion books in the **Paradise Family Guide Series** including **KAUA'I** by Don and Bea Donohugh, and **MAUI** by Greg and Christie Stilson. See ORDERING INFORMATION at the end of the book.

A sincere effort has been made to assure the accuracy of this guidebook at the time of publication, but changes do occur frequently in the transitory travel-visitor industry. Hotels, lodges, B&B's, condominiums, restaurants, menus, car rental agencies, airlines, tour operators, shops, etc. can and do change frequently along with prices and services. For the latest update information on the island, Paradise Publications has available **HAWAI'I - THE BIG ISLAND UPDATE,** a quarterly newsletter which chronicles current changes in the Big Island travel industry scene. To order a complimentary issue or a yearly subscription see ORDERING INFORMATION.

It is hoped that you enjoy this book, that it proves useful to you and that your visit to Hawai'i Island is safe, enjoyable and totally relaxing. And when it's time to go home, you'll leave with pleasant memories of your Big Island vacation and its many wonders and wonderful people.

Aloha!

John Penisten

John Penisten

GENERAL INFORMATION

INTRODUCTION - *WHY IT'S CALLED THE BIG ISLAND*

For a long time it's been known variously as "The Volcano Island," or "The Orchid Island," and perhaps more commonly as "The Big Island." To some, it's been something of a long-standing identity problem, at least to those in business and industry and especially the visitor industry. To most others, and to those who live here, it doesn't really seem to matter. To those who perceive it as a problem, the name "Hawai'i," the name of this island, too often is confused with the name of the state. For it so happens that this island indeed gave the name to the entire archipelago known as "Hawai'i" or the "Hawaiian Islands." In an attempt to avoid confusion between the island and the state of the same name, many have coined labels over the years to clarify, once and for all, its name, its singular identity, and to set it apart from the other islands. Whether it's "The Volcano Island," "The Orchid Island," "The Island of Hawai'i," "Hawai'i Island," "Hawai'i-The Island," "Hawai'i, Hawai'i" (a former mayor's favorite!...like New York, New York!), "The Big Island of Hawai'i," "Hawai'i-The Big Island," by any name, it is purely and simply, "The Big Island."

A few years ago, the Hawai'i Visitors Bureau-Big Island Chapter went through the same struggle to come up with a slogan to promote its visitor industry. After considering all the possibilities, "The Big Island of Hawai'i: Celebrate Great Moments With Us" was adopted. And thus it is, for all practical purposes, The Big Island of Hawai'i. For the record, the telephone company's local directory yellow pages lists some 111 businesses and organizations under the name "Big Island" and some 160 under the name "Hawai'i" or "Hawai'i Island."

So how did it come to be the Big Island. Well, one story has it that a group of World War II soldiers who were stationed on the Big Island were on leave in Honolulu. They were asked where they were stationed and one of them replied, "Well, we're on the island of....uh, island of....oh, you know, that "Big Island" over there!" From then on it came to be the "Big Island." In fact, it is an accurate description of the island, it is a pretty big place, in more ways than one. There's no disputing the fact that the Big Island is biggest in land size of all the Hawaiian Islands. At 4,038 square miles, the Big Island is twice the size of all the other Hawaiian Islands combined. And it's still growing due to the recent eruptions and lava flows of Kilauea Volcano which have added many acres of new shoreline.

The Big Island also has the highest mountain in Hawai'i, 13,796 ft. Mauna Kea (White Mountain in Hawaiian), a dormant volcano which last erupted some 10,000 years ago. Mauna Kea along with its twin peak, 13,677 ft. Mauna Loa

(Long Mountain), an active volcano which erupted as recently as 1984, comprise the bulk of the Big Island. Mauna Kea is, in fact, often called the biggest mountain in the world, Mt. Everest included, when it is measured from its base some 32,000 ft. below the ocean's surface. For many folks from colder climes, the following claim may not be too meaningful, but the Big Island has had the biggest recorded snowfalls of any tropical mountain in the Pacific Basin area. Over 12 feet of snow is not uncommon during severe winter storms at Mauna Kea's nearly 14,000 ft. summit. Snow skiing is a unique seasonal activity available only on the Big Island. And then there is the Mauna Kea Observatory Complex, located at the very summit of Mauna Kea, which is the recognized premier site for optical-infrared-submillimeter astronomy in the entire world. The observatory boasts several "largest" categories: collectively, the telescopes of Mauna Kea have more light gathering power than any other location in the world; in addition, it lays claim to the largest infrared telescope in the world, the 150 inch (3.8 m) United Kingdom Infrared Telescope; the largest optical-infrared telescope in the world, the 144 inch (3.6 m) Canada-France-Hawai'i Telescope; and the two largest submillimeter telescopes in the world, the 410 inch (10.4 m) Caltech Submillimeter Observatory and the 590 inch (15 m) James Clerk Maxwell Telescope; and when it is completed by 1993, the $85 million 394 inch (10 m) W.M.Keck Telescope multi-mirror instrument will be the largest such operational telescope in the world, period. Mauna Kea has some $150 million worth of high tech astronomical telescopes in place and plans are already underway for more telescopes to be built by the year 2000, ensuring Mauna Kea's place as the premier site in the world for astronomical research.

Hawai'i's biggest park is none other than Hawai'i Volcanoes National Park, 229,177 acres. It features the biggest active volcano in the world, 13, 677 ft. Mauna Loa, and an even more active sister peak, Kilauea at 4,077 ft. Two of Kilauea's many vents, Pu'u O and Kupaianaha, have been in an ongoing eruptive stage since January 3, 1983, one of the longest continuous eruptions ever recorded. Hawai'i Volcanoes National Park also has the biggest lava tube in Hawai'i, Thurston Lava Tube, 1494 ft. long, 22 ft. wide, and 20 ft. high. Waipio Valley near the town of Honoka'a on the Hamakua Coast is the state's biggest. The verdant valley runs a huge gap in the coast six miles long and 2000 ft. deep. This lush and fertile valley still produces taro as it did in the days of old Hawai'i. The Big Island boasts numerous waterfalls including the magnificent 422 ft. sheer drop of Akaka Falls State Park on the Hamakua Coast north of Hilo.

In Kohala is the biggest, oldest, and best preserved Hawaiian heiau (a temple where the ancient religion of old Hawai'i was practiced). The temple of Mookini Luakini is near the birthplace of King Kamehameha the Great. Built entirely of waterworn basalt rocks, it is in the shape of an irregular parallelogram, 267 ft. x 135 ft. x 250 ft. x 112 ft. with 30 ft. high walls all around. The walls vary in width from 13 ft. to 15 ft. It is estimated to be 1500 years old.

The port town of Hilo features the biggest annual hula dance celebration, the Merrie Monarch Festival, which is held each spring. This competition draws hula halau (groups) from all over Hawai'i and even the mainland U.S. It is the recognized "Super Bowl" of hula dance competition. It regularly sells out its three night performances well in advance.

Meanwhile over in Kona, one can find two of the biggest sporting events in the world. One is the annual Hawaiian International Billfish Tournament held each August and which attracts fishing teams and media from around the world who take part in the chase for record Kona marlin and yellow-fin tuna. In October, Kona takes on a different sporting mood as it plays host to the annual Ironman Triathlon World Championship. This incredible triple endurance event attracts over a thousand triathletes who take part in a 2.4 mile open ocean swim, a 112 mile bike ride, and a 26.2 mile marathon run. The Hawai'i Ironman Triathlon gave birth to the now worldwide sport of triathlon competitions.

The Parker Ranch at Kamuela is the state's largest ranch and largest individually owned ranch in the U.S. It has over 50,000 head of Hereford cattle roaming over 220,000 acres of rolling green pasture land.

The Big Island has the world's largest anthurium and orchid flower industries. The anthurium industry produced some 1.2 million dozens of the popular blooms in 1990 with a value of $7.4 million. The orchid industry produced millions of orchids of various types: single flowers, sprays, and potted plants with a value of several million dollars. The Big Island floriculture and nursery industries had some $33.7 million in 1990 sales, by far more than any other island in the state.

Data for 1990 reveals that Hawai'i's macadamia nut industry had 690 farms with some 22,600 acres of orchards under cultivation which produced 50 million pounds of the popular gourmet nuts worth over $71 million. The bulk of this industry and production is on the Island of Hawai'i even though orchards are being planted on other islands as well. The world's largest processor of macadamia nut products, the Mauna Loa Macadamia Nut Corporation, is located just outside of Hilo. The company's modern factory and visitors center make it the industry leader not only in Hawai'i but the world.

And in 1990, there were 266 Big Island papaya farms with 2,280 acres in production, which produced 67,045,000 pounds of papaya with a value of $14,282,000, almost all of the state's entire production of $14.8 million of the delectable fruit.

In 1990, Hawai'i's gourmet coffee industry, located almost exclusively on the cool-sunny slopes of Mt. Hualalai in Kona (although coffee groves are now being developed on other islands), had 620 farms on 5,300 acres which produced 2,200,000 pounds of Kona coffee beans valued at over $7 million. Hawai'i is the only place in the U. S. where coffee is grown commercially. The Big Island is the only place where genuine *Kona Coffee* is produced.

In 1990, the Big Island had just 27 banana farms cultivating 400 acres which produced 7,000,000 pounds or the bulk of the state's total production of 11.3 million pounds of bananas. The fruit was valued at $2.4 million.

But beyond all of this, the Big Island of Hawai'i is big on friendliness, scenic beauty, diversity and activities and the casual air of a basically rural lifestyle which is unhurried, unharried, and definitely underrated. Oh yes, I think you're going to like it here. Welcome to the Big Island of Hawai'i!

THE BIG ISLAND'S BEST

Annual Event: The Merrie Monarch Festival, Hilo, each April

Beautiful Beach: Kaunaoa Bay Beach (Mauna Kea Beach)

Beautiful Sunrise: From Mauna Kea overlooking Hilo

Beautiful Sunset: From Mauna Kea overlooking Kona-Kohala

Botanical Garden: Hawai'i Tropical Botanical Garden near Hilo on old Hamakua
Highway scenic route

Scenic Drive: Old Hamakua Highway just north of Hilo

Scenic View: Waipio Valley Overlook

Easy Hike: Across the floor of steaming Kilauea Iki Crater, Hawai'i Volcanoes
National Park

Nature Hike: Akaka Falls State Park, Hamakua Coast

Unusual Tour: Weekly star-gazing astronomy program at the Onizuka Center for
International Astronomy at 9,200 ft. level of Mauna Kea

Dive Tour: An underwater tour on the Atlantis IV submarine to cruise Kona's
reefs

Cruise: Any of the glassbottom snorkel cruises along the Kona Coast to Kealakekua Bay Marine Reserve and Captain Cook monument.

Thrill: Helicopter or small plane ride over Kilauea Volcano eruption and lava
flows

Backroad Adventure Tour: The Mana Road around Mauna Kea's flanks through
forest and ranch country from Saddle Road to Kamuela

Golf Course: The Mauna Kea Beach Hotel course, ranked among "America's
100 Greatest" and "Hawai'i's Finest" by *Golf Digest.*

Snorkeling: Anaeho'omalu Beach which fronts the Royal Waikoloa Hotel on the
Kohala Coast.

Diverse Shopping: Old downtown Hilo is experiencing a rennaisance of sorts
with many new shops, specialty stores, art galleries and boutiques worth
exploring.

Family-style Restaurant: Don's Grill, 485 Hinano Street, Hilo

Meal for the money: Kay's Lunch Center, 684 Kilauea Avenue, Hilo

Splurge Meal: Dinner at the Mauna Kea Beach Hotel's award-winning restaurant, The Batik Room

Splurge Weekend: An oceanfront room at the Mauna Kea Beach Hotel with American Plan (breakfast and dinner included) at any of their award-winning restaurants.

Sweet Bread: Punalu'u Brand from Punalu'u, Ka'u District

Shave Ice: Kawate Seed Shop, 1990 Kinoole St., Hilo, (Food Fair Supermarket Complex)

Macadamia Nuts: Mauna Loa Macadamia Nuts brand, Hilo

Macadamia Nut Chocolates: Big Island Candies brand

Potato Chips: Deguchi Kitch'n Cook'd brand, Kona

Taro Chips: Atebara brand, Hilo

Kim Chee: Kohala Kim Chee brand (hot spicy pickled cabbage), Kohala

Baked Goods and Pastries: Suzanne's Bakeshop, 75-5702 Alii Dr., Kailua-Kona

Malasadas: Tex's Drive In, Honoka'a

Fresh coconut pie: Holy's Bakery, Kapa'au, Kohala

Cookies: Donna's Cookies, Pa'auilo, Hamakua Coast

Buffet Lunch: Mauna Kea Beach Hotel, The Terrace

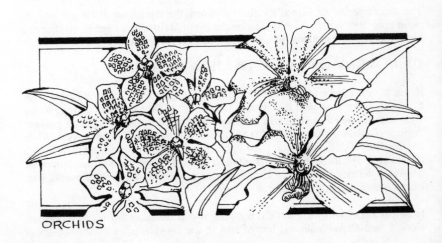

ORCHIDS

A HISTORY OF HAWAI'I

It is somewhat ironic that much of the history of today's Hawai'i is inextricably linked to the Big Island, the youngest and still growing member of the archipelago. And the history of early Hawai'i was affected by one man, Kamehameha the Great, a Big Island native son.

The history of Hawai'i is generally recognized as covering four periods. The first is the ancient pre-historic period before the discovery of the islands by the western world. The Polynesian race that populated Hawai'i migrated across the vast Pacific in simple sailing canoes. Their origin is believed to have been in Southeast Asia via Indonesia. They island-hopped across the Pacific in their great migratory journeys although anthropologists disagree on the routes they took and other details. The fact of all this is that these ancient sea-faring peoples crossed vast stretches of open ocean in simple craft using only their knowledge of the ocean, currents, winds, and stars to navigate. Hawai'i has been settled since about the fourth century A.D., even before Europeans dared to explore beyond their own borders.

The second period spans the discovery of the islands by the great British explorer, Captain James Cook, in 1778. This period also covers the rise to power of Kamehameha and his conquest of all the islands of Hawai'i by 1796 and the coming of traders, missionaries, and settlers. The monarchy established by Kamehameha lasted but a century as the Kingdom of Hawai'i under Queen Liliuokalani was overthrown in 1893.

The third period covers the founding of the Republic of Hawai'i in 1894 and the eventual annexation by the United States in 1898, and its organization as the Territory of Hawai'i in 1900. The period covers the rise of Hawai'i's agricultural economy, its pivotal role in World War II, and its admission into the Union as the Fiftieth State in 1959.

The fourth period of Hawai'i's history covers the time from statehood and its rapid assimilation into the American mainstream to the current age of electronics, high tech communications, jet transportation and mass tourism.

DISCOVERY OF THE HAWAIIAN ISLANDS

It was Captain James Cook, the famed British explorer of the Pacific, who was the first westerner to land in Hawai'i in January, 1778. Cook was enroute to the west coast of North America in search of the fabled Strait of Anian, a passage through North America that would shorten the voyage from Europe to Asia. While enroute from Tahiti, Cook stumbled upon Hawai'i, sighting the islands of Kaua'i and O'ahu. He made his first landfall at Kaua'i. Cook named the group the Sandwich Islands in honor of his friend and patron, the Earl of Sandwich, then First Lord of the British Admiralty.

He spent a fortnight there but did not visit any of the other islands of the group. Cook's men traded nails and bits of iron to the Hawaiians for fresh supplies of pork, fish, fowls, sweet potato, taro, yams, and water. With his ships, Resolution and Discovery, Cook sailed on to North America to continue his explorations.

After spending the next eight months exploring North America's west coast, Cook's party returned to Hawai'i with the intention of wintering there to refit and reprovision. They made the north coast of Maui in November, 1778, and Cook made it a point to sail leisurely through the Hawaiian group during the next few weeks learning what he could about the people of Hawai'i. At the various stops along the way, Cook took several of the Hawaiian chiefs aboard his ship to exchange gifts and courtesies. One of Cook's guests was the then obscure chief Kamehameha from the Big Island. Little did these two men know at their casual meeting then that, between them, they would bring about incredible changes upon Hawai'i that have a lingering impact today.

On January 17, 1779, the two ships anchored in Kealakekua Bay on the Kona Coast of the Big Island. When Cook landed, he was taken to a heiau (temple) where he underwent a religious ceremony recognizing him as the incarnation of Lono, the Hawaiian god of the makahiki (harvest) season. The Hawaiians believed that with Cook's arrival at such an auspicious time, the makahiki, that he indeed was the revered god, Lono.

Having refit and resupplied their ships, Cook's party set sail along the Kona Coast on February 4th. Unfortunately, a storm off the Kohala Coast damaged the mast of the Resolution and the group turned back to the safety of Kealakekua Bay. It was a fateful decision.

On February 13th while Cook's group was tending to repairs, various altercations arose between Cook's men and the Hawaiians. The next morning, it was discovered that a small boat from the Discovery had been stolen. Cook intended to get it back and landed with an armed marine guard. He planned to take the chief hostage until the boat was returned, a plan that had worked in previous such incidents with the Polynesians.

With Cook and his armed guards on the shore, and a large restless crowd of Hawaiians armed with daggers, clubs, and spears, the situation became quite tense. The Hawaiians were alarmed at the hostile intent of Lono and his armed guard. Word came that another chief had been killed by a shot from another boat. The Hawaiians now became visibly angered and made threatening advances toward the Cook party. Cook ordered his men to withdraw to the small boats on the shore. In the heated exchange, a Hawaiian threw his dagger at Cook who in turn fired one barrel of his gun which injured no one but angered the crowd more. Cook fired his second barrel and killed a Hawaiian. At that point, Cook's guards opened fire and a general melee broke out. Cook apparently turned to run to the boats but was struck down with a club and stabbed in the back with a dagger. He fell into the water and died on the spot.

And so, the world's foremost explorer of the Pacific met a tragic and untimely death in a place he introduced to the world. Today, a monument stands on the shore of Kealakekua Bay on the Kona Coast marking the exact spot where Captain James Cook met his fate.

HAWAI'I UNITED UNDER ONE RULE

Kamehameha (The Lonely One) was born in Kohala on the Big Island of Hawai'i about 1758. And although his parents were of noble rank, he was not in a direct line of succession to an alii (leading chief) position. Kamehameha grew up to be a fierce warrior noted for his tenaciousness, strength and intelligence.

The Hawai'i of the period was marked by inter-island civil war among the individual island chiefs and kings. And even on the Big Island, there was civil war among the chiefs who vied for dominance. Some chiefs from the Kona district, fearful of losing their lands under a new leading chief, asked Kamehameha to be their leader. Kamehameha had an ambition to conquer the Big Island and all of Hawai'i and unite the islands under one rule.

The 1780's saw the Big Island embroiled in civil war between Kamehameha of Kona-Kohala, Keawemauhili of Puna, Keoua of Ka'u, and Kahekili, king of neighboring Maui Island. In 1790-91, Kamehameha consulted a prophet from Kaua'i, Kapoukahi, who advised him that he would conquer all the islands if he built a large temple to his family war god, Ku-ka-ili-moku.

And so it came to be that Kamehameha did build his temple, Pu'ukohola Heiau (Hill of the Whale), located on a hill above Kawaihae Bay, Kohala, in 1791 and launched his rendezvous with destiny. Kamehameha's plans to conquer Hawai'i were primarily hindered at this time by his cousin, Keoua Ku'ahu'ula, his last major Big Island rival. Kamehameha invited Ku'ahu'ula to his temple dedication to make peace and Ku'ahu'ula willingly accepted. As Ku'ahu'ula and his companions landed on the beach below the heiau, Kamehameha's warriors swept down and killed them all. Ku'ahu'ula's body was carried up to the temple and was offered as the principal sacrifice to Kamehameha's war god.

After Keoua Ku'ahu'ula's death, virtually all opposition on the Big Island to Kamehameha ended and the prophesy began to be fulfilled. By 1794, Kamehameha had conquered Maui, Moloka'i, and Lana'i, and in 1795, the island of O'ahu. It was little wonder that he became known as Kamehameha the Great and established his kingdom over most of the islands of Hawai'i. In 1796, an attempted invasion of Kaua'i was disrupted by a storm. It wasn't until 1810, through an agreement with its king, that Kaua'i came under Kamehameha's control. Thus Kaua'i and nearby Ni'ihau have the distinction of being the only Hawaiian Islands not conquered in battle by Kamehameha.

However, Kamehameha did fulfill the prophesy and united all the Hawaiian Islands under one kingdom. Kamehameha the Great ruled his realm from Kailua on the Kona Coast until his death in 1819. He strictly observed the ancient religion of the Hawaiians and served as the official guardian of the war god which had brought him success in his conquests of Hawai'i. Upon his death, his son, Liholiho, became Kamehameha II.

However, little did Kamehameha the Great know, prior to his death, of the impending changes that were about to take place in his Hawai'i. Since the discovery of Hawai'i by the western world in 1778, the islands were increasingly exposed to an influx of traders, explorers, settlers, and in 1820 just after Kamehameha's death, the arrival of the first of many New England Congregational and Presbyterian missionaries. All of these westerners were to bring about significant changes over the coming generations as Hawai'i was forced into a world of which it knew nothing when it was "discovered" in 1778.

Soon after Kamehameha the Great's death, his son and successor, Liholiho, overthrew the "kapu" system and belief in the old Hawaiian religion. During this period in the early 1820's, the Christian missionaries, traders, and other foreigners who ventured into the islands did so at an opportune time. They easily established footholds and through their various efforts gained power and influence. Contacts with the western world increased and by the early 1840's, the Kingdom of Hawai'i was recognized by the United States, France, and Great Britain.

Sugar, first grown commercially in Hawai'i in 1835, became the kingdom's principal industry with large tracts of land developed into plantations. In the early years, the cultivation, harvesting, and processing of sugar was labor-intensive and the sugar planters needed laborers. Throughout the nineteenth century the native Hawaiian population declined from about 85,000 in 1850 to some 40,000 in 1890. This was due in part to such things as the introduction of western disease and the loss of many of its youth to the whaling ship industry in the 1840's. In the last half of the nineteenth century, the Hawaiian government began allowing the importation of foreign laborers to support the increasingly important sugar industry. Thus, the great waves of immigration began with large numbers of Chinese, Portuguese, Japanese, Koreans, and Filipinos being brought in to work the plantations, often under harsh conditions and standards. Labor immigration continued on into the early 1900's and to an extent still continues today. From these mixed ethnic groups came Hawai'i's label as a cosmopolitan melting-pot of diverse peoples.

The monarchy begun by Kamehameha the Great survived for a century until Queen Liliuokalani's reign was overthrown in 1893 by a group of primarily American revolutionists, and replaced by a provisional government headed by Sanford B. Dole. On July 4, 1894, the islands became the Republic of Hawai'i and after repeated efforts, in August, 1898, the islands were annexed as a territory of the United States.

The early 1900's in Hawai'i were years of relative peace and development. Hawai'i burst upon the American consciousness once again on the morning of Sunday, December 7, 1941 with the Japanese attack on Pearl Harbor. In one quick change of scene, Hawai'i entered the stage to play a pivotal role in the tragic drama that was World War II in the Pacific. Like the rest of post-war America, Hawai'i was on the threshold of even greater social, cultural, and economic development. The post-war years have seen Hawai'i grow tremendously. Hawai'i's admission to the Union as the Fiftieth State in 1959 was recognition of its achievements and future potential as part of the United States.

COUNTY OF HAWAI'I

The County of Hawai'i is comprised solely of the geographical boundaries of the Big Island. The County of Hawai'i (pop. 122,300) has its seat of government in Hilo (pop. 45,700) the commercial center and main port. The other major population centers are Kailua-Kona (pop. 23,000), the South Kohala District (pop. 9,000) and the South Kona District (pop. 7,900). The rest of the island population is spread among rural villages and small towns. The Big Island has about one-tenth of the total statewide population. The county is governed by a mayor and an elected nine-member county council who set legislative law and policy. The Big Island populace in turn elects its own senators and representatives to the state legislature which convenes annually in Honolulu.

HAWAIIAN LANGUAGE

SPEAKING HAWAIIAN

One of the more positive things the early missionaries did for the Hawaiians was to standardize their Polynesian based language into a written language. Previously, Hawaiian was a spoken language only. Hawaiian is one of the family of languages in the Pacific and shares much similarity to the languages of other Pacific islands. The missionaries organized the Hawaiian language into an alphabet of twelve letters, five vowels (a, e, i, o, u) and seven consonants (h, k, l, m, n, p and w). Every letter of a word is sounded. Syllables end in vowels and many syllables contain only vowels. All Hawaiian words end in a vowel. There are no double consonants in Hawaiian. A vowel always separates consonants.

The five vowels are pronounced as follows:

a	as in father, above	o	as in note, own
e	as in obey, weigh	u	as in rule, true (oo)
i	as in marine (ee)		

In addition, there are some vowel combinations which resemble diphthongs and are pronounced as follows:

ai and ae (eye) as in mile, line
ao and au (ow) as in cow, how
ei (ay) as in day, say
oe (oy) as in boy, toy

The accent generally falls on the next to last syllable, although some words are unaccented. The inverted comma ('), called an "okina," is used in some words to indicate the "glottal stop," a sign that a k sound found in other Polynesian dialects has disappeared in Hawaiian usage. Where this mark appears, the accent falls on the preceding vowel as in the following: Ka'u (Kah'oo), Kapa'au (Kahpah'ow).

The consonants are pronounced as they are in English, with w being the only exception. When w introduces the last syllable of a word, it sometimes is sounded

20

as a v. Examples are the famous Polynesian ceremonial drink, awa, is actually pronounced "ava" and the area on Oʻahu called Ewa is pronounced "Ehva."

Learning and trying to use Hawaiian on your visit will add a new dimension to your travel experience. Learning, listening for, and using some of the local language can also prove useful in interpreting road maps, street signs, and place names. The following is a glossary to give you an introduction to Hawaiian words in common use. You will often hear and see these words and expressions used throughout Hawaiʻi and it will be useful to be familiar with them.

HAWAIIAN GLOSSARY

aʻa - rough, clinky lava
ae - yes
aina - land
akamai - smart, clever, expert
ala - a road or a path
alii - chief, member of chiefly class
aloha - love, affection, farewell, hello
aole - no
auwai - a stream
auwe - alas!, woe is me!
ehu - a red-haired Hawaiian
hala - the pandanus tree from which leaves (lauhala) are used to make baskets and woven mats
hale - a house
hana - work
hao - iron
haole - stranger, foreigner, generally means a white person
hapa - part, sometimes means a half
hapai - pregnant, carry
hauoli - to rejoice
heiau - temple, place of worship
holoholo - to run from one place to another, to visit
holoku - gown, often with a train
holomuu - cross between a holoku and a muumuu, less formal dress or gown with no train
honi - to kiss, a kiss
hoomalimali - take it easy, patience
huhu - angry, upset
hui - a group, union, club, etc. most often referred to business groups who pool their money for investment purposes
hukilau - a communal fishing party in which everyone helps drive the fish into a huge net, pulls it in, and divides the catch
hula - the traditional dance of Hawaiʻi
imu - the underground ovens used in luaus to roast food
imua - forward, in front of
ipo - sweetheart
kahuna - a priest, doctor of old Hawaiʻi having supernatural or spiritual powers
kai - the sea, salt water
kalo - the taro plant root from which poi is made

kamaaina - native born or old timer, refers to those who have lived in the islands a long time

kanaka - a man, male Hawaiian

kane - man, male, used to identify men's restroom, toilet

kapa - the tapa cloth pounded from mulberry tree bark and usually colorfully decorated

kapakahi - crooked, uneven

kapu - forbidden, prohibited, keep out

kaukau - food, to eat

keiki - a child; keikikane - a boy; keikiwahine - a girl

kiawe - algarroba tree, grows in leeward (dry) areas

kokua - help

kona - south, direction from which winds and rain often come

koolau, north, windward

kuleana - homestead, plot of ground, territory, used to denote one's area of interest or primary activity

lanai - porch, terrace, patio

lani - heaven, sky

lauhala - pandanus tree leaf used in baskets and mats

laulau - bundle of food, usually pork, fish, etc. wrapped in taro leaves and ti leaves then steamed

lei - a garland or necklace of flowers

lomilomi - massage

luau - a traditional Hawaiian feast

luna - a plantation foreman or overseer

mahalo - thank you

makai - toward the sea

malihini - a newcomer to the islands

malo - loincloth worn by kane (men)

mana - the spiritual power which old Hawaiians believed existed in all things

manawahi - free, gratis

mauka - toward the mountains, inland

mauna - mountain

mele - song, chant

menehune - Hawaiian dwarf or elf

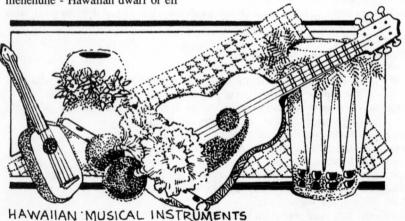

HAWAIIAN MUSICAL INSTRUMENTS

moana - the ocean

moe - sleep

muumuu - gown, Mother Hubbard-type dress the missionaries introduced to enforce modesty on Hawaiian women, now a colorful garment indispensable to any island woman's wardrobe

nani - beautiful

niu - coconut

nui - big, great

oe - you

okole - posterior, used to refer to the buttocks

okolehao - Hawaiian liquor distilled from the ti root

opu - stomach

pake - Chinese

palapala - book, printing, writing

pali - a cliff

paniolo - a Hawaiian cowboy

pau - finished, done

pilau - stench, smelly

pilikia - trouble

pipi - cattle, beef

poi - paste made from pounded taro root, a Hawaiian staple

puaa - pig

puka - hole

pupu - Hawaiian appetizer or hors d'oeuvre

pupule - crazy

wahine - female, woman, often used to identify women's toilet

wikiwiki - to hurry, make quick

A FEW WORDS ABOUT PIDGIN ENGLISH

As the unofficial language of Hawai'i, pidgin English is used everywhere. You will hear it on the streets, at the beaches, in the shopping centers, at offices, and even in the schools. It is the lingua franca of local islanders. Many locals can turn it on and off at will, others use it as their dominant mode of daily speech. It's been influenced by the various ethnic groups that have made Hawai'i home over the years. It takes some getting used to especially for the untrained ear. Visitors are advised to listen and enjoy and try to understand this local "lingo" but leave it to the local folks to actually use. Here's a sample:

any kine - anything

ass why - that's the reason, that's why

brah, bruddah - brother, good friend

buggah - guy, friend, also a pest or nuisance

bumbye - soon enough

chicken skin - goose bumps, when your skin gets the chills

chop suey - all mixed up

cockaroach - to steal or sneak away with something

da kine - a generally used term referring to everything, as in the right thing

fo'real - this is for real, no kidding

garans - guaranteed, for sure

get - used in place of verb "have"
get chance - possibility
heah - here
hele on - get moving
Howzit! - How are you?
ice shave - snow cone
junk - lousy, terrible
li'dat - like that
like - to want or want to
lolo - stupid, dumb
lua - toilet
make ass - to screw up, make a fool of oneself
manini - stingy, cheap
momona - fat
mo'bettah - better
musubi - rice balls
nah, nah, nah - no, just kidding
ni'ele - nosy
no can - cannot
no mo' - none
no shame - don't be shy
not! - you must be kidding, it cannot be
or what? - phrase added to any question
ono - delicious
pau - over, done, finished
plenty - lots, a great number
stink-eye - dirty look
talk story - talk, gossip
whatevah - applied to just about anything

BIG ISLAND PLACE NAMES

Halema'uma'u (Ha'lee'ma'oo'ma'oo) - crater, fire pit, within Kilauea Crater at
    Volcanoes National Park
Hilo (Hee'low) - county seat of Big Island (first night of new moon)

Holualoa (Ho'loo'ah'low'ah) - village in Kona District (long sled course)

Honoka'a (Ho'no'ka'aa) - small town on Hamakua Coast (rolling bay)

Ka Lae (Kah'lie) - southernmost point in Hawai'i (the point)

Kailua (Kai'loo'ah) - resort village in Kona (two seas)

Kapa'au (Kah'paa'ow) - village in North Kohala District (elevated portion of a
    heiau)
Kawaihae (Kah'wai'high) - village and bay on Kohala Coast (water of wrath;
    refers to people who fought over water supply in this arid area)
Kealakekua (Kay'al'lah'kay'koo'ah) - bay on Kona Coast where Captain James
    Cook landed and was killed (pathway of the god)

Kona (Ko'nah) - west coast district of Big Island (leeward side)

Laupahoehoe (Lau'pah'ho'ee'ho'ee) - village on Hamakua Coast (smooth lava flat)

Mauna Kea (Mau'nah Kay'ah) - 13, 769 ft. mountain, highest in Hawai'i (white mountain; often covered with snow in winter)

Mauna Loa (Mau'nah Low'ah) - 13, 677 ft. mountain, second highest in Hawai'i (long mountain; still active volcano, last erupted in 1984)

Na'alehu (Nah'ah'lay'who) - southernmost community in Hawai'i (volcanic ashes)

Onekahakaha (O'knee'ka'ha'ka'ha) - beach in Keaukaha area of Hilo (drawing sand)

Pahala (Pa'hah'la) - village in Ka'u District (cultivation by burning mulch)

Pahoa (Pa'hoe'ah) - village in Puna District (dagger)

Pololu (Po'low'loo) - valley in North Kohala (long spear)

Pu'ukohola (Poo'oo'ko'hoe'lah) - heiau (temple) at Kawaihae Bay (hill of the whale)

Waiakea (Wai'ah'kay'ah) - area of Hilo town near Hilo Bayfront (broad water)

Waiau (Wai'ow) - fresh water lake on Mauna Kea (swirling water)

Wailoa (Wai'low'ah) - river and pond in Hilo town (long water)

Wailuku (Wai'loo'koo) - river in Hilo town (water of destruction)

Waimea (Wai'may'ah) - village in Kohala District ranch country (red water)

Waipio (Wai'pee'o) - valley on Hamakua Coast (curved water)

SPINNER DOLPHINS

GETTING THERE

Your first step in planning a trip to the Big Island should be to visit a professional travel agent. Better yet, if you don't already deal with one exclusively, visit two or three, if possible, regarding your travel plans. The travel industry, especially the airline industry, changes from day to day so much that it is virtually impossible for any travel agent to keep on top of everything. That's why it's important to check with more than just one on availability of flights, airfares, accommodations, tour packages, and all the details. It is also a good idea to do your homework before you consult a travel agent. The fact that you are reading this guidebook is a first step. By making yourself knowledgeable about travel to Hawai'i, and the Big Island, you can help your travel agent do a better job for you. In addition, it is wise to decide ahead how much to allow for expenses on your trip, how long you want to stay, where you want to stay, what you want to see and do, and all the other related details. You may wish to contact the Hawai'i Visitors Bureau and various Big Island resort associations listed in the "Helpful Information" section in this chapter. They'll send you all sorts of information and literature on hotels, attractions, what to see and do, etc. You can also visit your local library or bookstore and browse through some of the books listed in the HAWAIIANA READING FOR ADULTS section of this book.

While most visitors arrive in Hawai'i by air, it is still possible to arrive via elegant oceanliner. In a throwback to a bygone era, American Hawai'i Cruises of San Francisco in the early 1980's began operating occasional west coast to Hawai'i cruises that connect with their week-long, inter-island cruise aboard the *Independence* and the *Constitution*. P & O Lines cruise ships, *Oriana, Canberra*, and *Pacific Princess* sometimes call in at Honolulu on their Pacific cruises as does the Royal Viking Line's *Sagafjord* and *Vistafjord* and well as Cunard's *Queen Elizabeth II*. For the adventurous sailor-types, some freighters also carry small numbers of passengers from west coast ports to Hawai'i and beyond. Check with your travel agent.

American Hawai'i Cruises operate their week-long, inter-island cruises with the *Independence* and the *Constitution*. The ships visit Hilo and Kailua-Kona on the Big Island as well as other ports-of-call in the Hawaiian Islands. The ships generally spend a full day at each port before sailing in the evening. Shore excursions and various tours are available from dockside at each port. Ask your travel agent or contact American Hawai'i Cruises, 550 Kearny St., San Francisco, CA 94108, or call toll free 1-800-227-3666.

Jet planes have put Hawai'i only 5-5 1/2 hours from the West Coast. And with some 6 million visitors arriving in Hawai'i annually, competition among the airlines is fierce. There are all kinds of air fares and your travel agent can readily access the range via computer. Fares change rapidly, even by the minute, as do ticketing requirements and certain restrictions. A good travel agent will be able to help you sort out all the alternatives.There are several foreign airlines that stop at Honolulu International Airport on O'ahu. However, under federal law, they have no U.S. traffic rights, that is they cannot take passengers from one U.S. city to another, including Honolulu. You can fly a foreign airline and stop in Honolulu only if you are continuing on to an overseas destination.

There are presently nine major American air carriers serving Honolulu from several mainland U.S. cities. Telephone numbers are as follows:

AIR AMERICA - Reservations 1-800-247-2475, in Hawai'i 1-808-833-4433

AMERICAN - Reservations 1-800-433-7300, Hawai'i 1-808-526-0044

AMERICAN WEST AIRLINES - Reservations in Hawai'i, 1-800-247-5692

CONTINENTAL AIRLINES - Reservations 1-800-525-0280, in Hawai'i for information, 1-808-836-7730

DELTA AIR LINES - Reservations 1-800-221-1212, Hawai'i 1-808-955-7211

HAWAIIAN - Reservations 1-800-367-5320, Big Island 1-800-882-8811

NORTHWEST - Reservations 1-800-225-2525, Big Island 1-808-935-5275

TWA - Reservations 1-800-221-2000

UNITED AIRLINES - There is no central 800 number but one for each area of the U.S. See the yellow pages in your area. In Honolulu, the number for reservations and information is 1-808-547-2211 and on the Big Island it is 961-2811. United Airlines is the dominant air carrier to Hawai'i with about half of all traffic. They have more flights to more places, foreign and to the U.S. mainland, than any other airline. They currently provide direct mainland to Honolulu service with continuing service to Keahole Airport in Kona.

All United Hawai'i inbound flights (and mainland-bound return flights as well) pass through United's mini-hub at Honolulu International Airport. Their schedule sometimes changes with seasonal demand (Christmas-New Year's for example) when they may add direct flights to the Big Island from the west coast. If your schedule or plans do not allow you to take one of the United Airlines connecting Kona flights, you should have decided ahead of time whether you will enter the Big Island through Kona or Hilo and what local inter-island airline you will fly to get you to your final destination. Be sure to have your baggage checked accordingly for Kona or Hilo. If you didn't have your baggage checked through to your final Big Island destination, you will have to retrieve them at the baggage claim area upon your arrival at Honolulu International Airport. From there, it is about a quarter of a mile walk or longer to the inter-island terminal which is next door to the overseas terminal. There is also a free Wiki Wiki Shuttle. If you walk over and have lots of luggage, rent one of the luggage carts inside the baggage claim area. For $1.50 you can push your luggage over to the inter-island terminal and save yourself some trouble.

A new inter-island terminal is under construction and will hopefully be completed in 1993. When open, it will provide much needed new facilities for Hawaiian Airlines, Aloha Airlines and Aloha Island Air (a subsidiary of Aloha Airlines). Hawaiian and Aloha are generally competitive and offer a variety of fares.

Have your travel agent check into group or family fares, special fares for children, senior citizens, military, and for the first and last flights of the day between islands. If you are planning multiple inter-island flights, you might want to consider buying low-priced coupon tickets from either Hawaiian or Aloha which are sold in books of six. They usually have no expiration date, can be used by anyone, and can save up to 15% on the regular inter-islands fares. Both airlines offer occasional special monthly unlimited air passes for flat rates, inquire about the availability. Hawaiian and Aloha are generally competitive on their jet fares but Hawaiian has an edge with their DASH-7 turbo-prop planes in that they charge slightly less for these flights, if you don't mind taking a little longer to get to your destination.

Hawaiian and Aloha have several flights daily between Honolulu and Kona or Hilo, the Big Island's gateways. Aloha flies all Boeing 737 jets while Hawaiian flies DC-9 jets and DASH 7 turbo-prop planes inter-island. Aloha Island Air flies small DeHavilland commuter turbo-props. Jet flights between Honolulu and Kona take 33 minutes, and between Honolulu and Hilo 40 minutes. The slower turbo-prop planes take about an hour and a half between Honolulu and Kona or Hilo. That includes a brief stop on Maui in either direction as all turbo-prop flights pass through Maui. On its mainland and overseas routes, Hawaiian flies DC-8's and L-1011's. If you came on Hawaiian Airlines from the mainland U.S. or overseas, your inter-island fare was probably already included in your ticket.

One other thing to inquire about are the special inter-island, airfare-room-car packages, that the airlines offer. These vary from season to season but are almost always a bargain for short stays on the neighbor islands compared to purchasing each item separately. Contact information on the inter-island carriers is as follows:

ALOHA AIRLINES - For reservations and information call 1-800-323-3345; in Honolulu, 1-808-833-3219; and on the Neighbor Islands, 1-800-652-6541.

HAWAIIAN AIRLINES - For reservations and information; 1-800-367-5320; in Honolulu, 537-5100, all other Neighbor Islands, 1-800-882-8811.

ALOHA ISLAND AIR (Owned by Aloha Airlines) -This small commuter-tourist airline flies Dehaviland Twin Otters between Honolulu and the small country airport of Kamuela on the Big Island, as well as to other points in the neighbor islands. Their number is 1-800-323-3345; in Honolulu, 1-808-833-3219; and on the Neighbor Islands, 1-800-652-6541.

There are several small air charter and helicopter tour operators on the Big Island and these are listed in RECREATION AND TOURS, the "Air Tours" section.

Both the Keahole Airport in Kona and Hilo International Airport in Hilo provide modern terminal facilities. Although both airports were built in the mid-1970's, the Hilo airport has become something of a white elephant. At the time it was planned, Hilo was seen by tourism officials as a second gateway to Hawaii, providing some relief to congested Honolulu International Airport.

Several of the major airlines were already providing direct mainland to Hilo flights and the prospect of a new airport brought hopes of Hilo becoming a major tourist center. Unfortunately, the oil embargo of the early '70's brought on a crisis that sent Hawai'i tourism in general, and Hilo's hopes in particular, into a tailspin. In the meantime, construction on the new airport began even as the airlines began pulling out of Hilo. United was the last to leave in the early '80's, now centering their Big Island operations in Kona. Thus, Hilo ended up with an airport that is about three sizes too big. It has eight jetway arrival-departure gates but only two or three are used regularly. The cavernous waiting room inside the terminal is pleasant, colorful and comfortable, and conspicuously quiet until a Hawaiian or Aloha flight comes in. It's one airport you don't have to worry about crowds, there aren't any, except on long weekends and holiday periods when it seems like all of Hilo wants to go to Honolulu at the same time.

But the Big Island didn't lose out altogether. What was Hilo's loss was Kona's gain. Now that United Airlines flies from the mainland to Kona via Honolulu, visitor traffic to Kona has increased. In addition, the new resort developments along the Kohala Coast hold promise of further growth in the industry on the Big Island's sunny side. But more on that later.

If you're transiting through Kona's airport, or even driving by on the highway, make sure to stop and see the *Astronaut Ellison S. Onizuka Space Center*. This is a memorial to the Big Island's own native son and astronaut, born and raised on a Kona coffee farm, who was lost aboard the 1986 space shuttle disaster. The museum features memorabilia from Ellison's career in space exploration and includes hands-on displays and a piece of "moon rock" on loan from NASA. Open daily 8:30AM - 4:30PM; admission adults $2, children .50 cents. For information, contact Onizuka Space Center, P.O.Box 833, Kailua-Kona, HI 96745, (808) 329-3441.

WHAT TO PACK

As the golden rule of packing says, "Pack your bags, then remove half of that and you are ready to go." It's probably a fair assessment on the issue of what to take. All rules aside, you won't need too much to be comfortable in paradise. Dress is definitely casual, generally lightweight cotton and blend materials. Permanent press wash-and-wear clothing is best. The accent is on keeping cool in the tropics. Shorts and tee shirts are the mode here. The only evening dresses or coats and ties you might need would be for that elegant evening out at one of the more plush dining rooms at Kona or Kohala resorts. Otherwise keep it casual. The only warmer clothes you might need would be for visits to Waimea-Kohala ranch country, Volcanoes National Park, or Mauna Loa and Mauna Kea. Warm water-repellant jackets for hiking Volcanoes National Park or touring the ranch country would be very useful. Warm clothing suitable for below-freezing temperatures are in order if you plan to visit the summit of Mauna Kea where it can snow anytime of the year. Comfortable walking or hiking shoes are definitely a must for any short hikes in the parks or along the beaches. The local footwear is what mainland folks call "thongs," or rubber slippers. In Hawai'i they are called "zoris" or more simply "slippahs" (to borrow a pidgin word). They are great for wearing anywhere and everywhere, except for more formal occasions. You can buy a pair here for around $2-3. A good sunscreen, a camera and film, and any other items of a personal nature could round out your packing. If you've forgotten something, you'll be able to get it here in the discount stores, supermarkets, drug stores and shopping centers.

TRAVELING WITH CHILDREN

Most youngsters will be able to handle the stress and pressure of traveling quite well if they are adequately prepared ahead of time. If they have never flown before, they need to be told what to expect, what it is like in a plane, what takes place on board a plane inflight. Youngsters have a natural curiosity and some basic information will increase their understanding and excitement about their trip to Hawai'i across the Pacific. One good thing to do would be to visit a library or bookstore together for some background information and reading on Hawai'i. A few children's books can do wonders to increase a youngster's perception and understanding of Hawai'i and the Big Island. See HAWAIIANA READING FOR CHILDREN at the back of this book. And while you're at it, pick up a book or two for yourself. See HAWAIIANA READING FOR ADULTS for suggestions.

GOODY BAGS: Most youngsters take the waiting in airports and riding in airplanes for long hours quite well if they have enough to keep them occupied. While packing your luggage for the trip, include some special surprise goody bags for each youngster. Have enough surprises so that you can hand them out at intervals through the duration of the trip. Suggestions for things to include are small story books appropriate for the youngster, coloring books and crayons, game books, sticker books with sheets of colorful stickers, and even safe toys suitable for use on a plane or in confined places. You can even include snacks, small boxes of their favorite cereal, or even small cartons of juice with straw attached. Use your own imagination and create special goody bags that will keep your youngsters happy and content. The flight attendants on the plane can sometimes provide complimentary gift bags for the kids. But you should come prepared with your own versions. It will all help make your own trip much more pleasant and satisfying.

ESSENTIALS: If you are traveling with an infant, make sure you have enough supplies of diapers, baby food, formula, etc. Soft teething rings and toys can help an infant clear the ears and equalize the air pressure if there is a problem. Older youngsters can do the same with chewing gum. Your carry-on luggage should include essential items, toilet articles, medicines, and even light changes of clothing in case your luggage is delayed or lost. Also, equally distribute important items and even clothing in all bags so the loss or delay of one bag won't be traumatic for one individual. Before you leave on your trip, be sure to check with your pediatrician especially if your child has a cold or is subject to ear problems. Inquire into the use of antihistamines or special medicines for childrens' use.

CAR SEATS: Hawai'i state law requires that all children age three and under must be placed in an infant restraint seat at all times when riding in an automobile. Most car rental companies have child car seats available but charge an $8-12 daily fee for use. Also, during peak travel seasons, demand may be high and reservations for car seats may not be completely reliable. And sometimes the car seat you get may not be that reliable either. So, you may want to consider bringing your own. An extra benefit of bringing your own car seat is that it may be usable on the airplane inflight. Check with your travel agent. If you check the car seat as baggage, put it in a box or use a large plastic bag and be sure to label it clearly.

CRIBS: Most hotels and condos provide infant cribs for a fee of $5-15 per night. Local rental shops also have them available for a few dollars per night if you opt to not bring your own portable crib.

BABYSITTING: Most hotels and condos have a babysitting service or list of available sitters and will help you with arrangements. Fees usually run from $8-10 per hour. There are no organized babysitting services or agencies.

EMERGENCIES/MEDICAL TREATMENT: There are several clinics and hospitals around the Big Island which can handle emergencies or walk-in patients. Your condominium or hotel desk can provide you with suggestions or check the yellow pages. In Kona, the Kaiser Permanente Medical Care facilities are at 75-184 Hualalai Rd. (329-3866); the Keauhou-Kona Medical Clinic is at 78-6780 Alii Dr., Suite 3201 (322-2750). For non-emergency medical care, Kona-Kohala Health Care Center (329-1346) is in the Lanihau Center on Palani Rd. next to Long's Drugs and is open everyday. In Hilo, the Hilo Medical Group is at 1292 Waianuenue Ave. (961-6631). In Waimea/Kamuela, the Lucy Henriques Medical Center is right on Highway 19 near the Parker Ranch Shopping Center (885-7921). The Kona Hospital is in Kealakekua (322-9311) and Hilo Hospital is at 1190 Waianuenue Ave. (969-4111). There are also hospitals in Ka'u in Pahala town (928-8331), in Kohala at Kapa'au town (889-6211), and in Honoka'a town (775-7211). For emergency fire/ambulance service anywhere on the Big Island, call 961-6022. See "Important Phone Numbers" for additional listings.

BEACHES FOR CHILDREN: There are several safe beaches on the Big Island that are ideal for youngsters. In Hilo, Onekahakaha Beach Park in the Keaukaha area has a protected tidal pool enclosed by large rock boulders that slow the action of incoming surf. It is an ideal spot for the keikis (children) to swim, splash, and have a good time. On the west side, Spencer Park at Kawaihae, South Kohala, provides one of the calmest beaches on the Big Island. Its small beach and sparkling clear water are perfect for the small ones. Hapuna Beach State Park near the Mauna Kea Beach Hotel, South Kohala, is a large expanse of open sand great for the kids to run and play. The water is shallow here and the surf moderate but adults must be vigilant with youngsters in the water. Anaehoomalu Beach fronting the Royal Waikoloa Hotel, South Kohala, is a large sweeping crescent

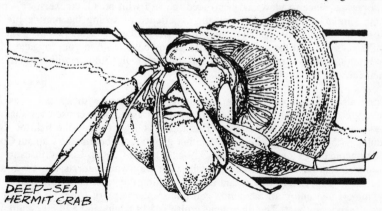

DEEP-SEA
HERMIT CRAB

with fine sand, moderate surf and shallow water. Kamakahonu Beach fronting the King Kamehameha Kona Beach Hotel next to the Kailua-Kona Pier is also a fine small beach with gentle water that seems to have been made just for the keikis. Never leave children unattended in the water because even the calmest of beaches occasionally have a surprise large wave roll in. A children's flotation device is strongly recommended in all cases. Also don't forget to liberally apply a good sunscreen before and after beachtime. And don't let the youngsters stay out in the sun for too long a period. Several short periods are better than one long period of being exposed to Hawai'i's strong sun. The same goes for you too mom and dad!

HOTEL-CONDO POOLS: It is essential to supervise your children at the hotel or condo swimming pool. Most hotel-condo pools usually aren't more than five or six feet at the deep ends and two or three feet at the shallow ends. Several of the newer hotels and resorts have Jacuzzi pools next to the regular pool. Vouching from my own daughters' experience, kids love the Jacuzzi. But be careful to not let them stay in the very warm water too long. Again, even at hotel-condo pools, use of a children's flotation device is highly recommended.

ENTERTAINMENT: Both Hilo and Kona, and even several of the small towns around the island, offer movie theaters showing the latest films. In Hilo, there are two theater complexes: Waiakea Theaters 1-2-3 in the Waiakea Town Plaza and the Prince Kuhio Theaters 1-2 in the Prince Kuhio Plaza. In Kona there are the Hualalai Theaters 1-2-3 and the World Square Theater at Kona Marketplace. Most of the hotels have cable television as well as in-house movies.

Most youngsters will be fascinated with exploring the beach and shores for bits of coral, seashells, and even looking for ocean tide pool life in the shallows. A guidebook to Hawai'i's shells, reef fish, and marine life may help them develop a better understanding of the beach and shore ecosystems. *Hawaiian Reef Animals* by Hobson & Chave, and *Hawaiian Fishwatcher's Field Guide* by Greenberg are two good references. Another excellent book especially for children is *Sand to Sea: Marine Life of Hawai'i* by Feeney and Fielding. A good place to see and feed the myriad schools of Hawai'i's colorful reef fish is at Kahalu'u Beach Park in Keauhou just south of Kailua-Kona. At the beach park next to the Keauhou Beach Hotel, schools of colorful fish swarm about in the shallow calm waters. It is a perfect place to view and hand feed the fish with bread, crackers, or something similar. Children will enjoy the experience of seeing the marine life up close. If they are old enough, they can use a mask and snorkel to gain an underwater view of the colorful reef life. If you have room in your luggage, plan on bringing along a light fishing rod and spinning reel. Children will enjoy trying their luck for some of the reef fish.

Kona also offers some good glassbottom boat cruises with special rates for children. Captain Bob's Kona Reef Tours offers a one hour cruise over shallow reef waters along the Kailua-Kona Coast, and you get to feed the fish too, $15 adults, $7.50 children (322-3102). Another glassbottom boat is the Captain Cook VIII operated by Hawaiian Cruises (329-6411). The Captain Cook cruises to the protected marine life preserve of Kealakekua Bay where guests can swim and snorkel in the pristine waters and enjoy watching the schools of reef fish. Non-swimmers can enjoy all the action and underwater scenery from the comfort of the glassbottom boat. The three hour cruise is $49 adults and $24.50 children.

In Hilo, a good place to check out marine life is at the Richardson Ocean Center located on Kalanianaole Avenue in the Keaukaha area. Here displays and aquariums explain much about the ecosystem and marine life of Hawai'i's beaches, reefs, and ocean. Lots of interesting fish are on display. There are also calm tidal pools to explore for such things as sea cucumbers, sea urchins, starfish, crabs, limpets, and other interesting forms of marine life. Youngsters can swim in the calm water too.

And as for fish, you can't beat the display of the Hilo fishing fleet's daily catch each morning at the Suisan Fish Auction. Here you can see the huge 100+ lb. yellow fin tuna and numerous colorful reef fish and seafood delicacies being sold. The auction is a genuine cross-cultural experience, with the bidding being done in pidgin English. It takes place each morning between 7 - 9AM (except Sundays) at Suisan Fish Market on the Wailoa River, Hilo Bay, adjacent to Banyan Drive hotels and Liliuokalani Park on the bayfront. Don't miss this when you visit Hilo!

Outside Hilo is one of the Big Island's least known attractions, perfect for kids of all ages. The Panaewa Rainforest Zoo is three miles south of Hilo off the Volcano Highway #11 on Mamaki Street. Watch for a sign indicating the turnoff. This facility, operated by the County of Hawai'i, is the only authentic rainforest zoo in the country. On display are animals from around the world representative of rainforest dwellers. Included are a pack of beautiful Bengal Tigers, monkeys, tapir, pygmy hippopotamuses, parrots, and more. It's a pleasant place to stroll and picnic. There are no crowds and it's free!

Most restaurants provide a special keiki (children's) menu. And there are the usual attractions of several McDonald's around the island, some with a playground area. See the RESTAURANTS chapter of this book for dining details.

Finally, check with your hotel or condo desk and the local newspapers community activity file for additional children's activities around the Big Island. Many of the hotels provide special children's activities like hula dancing lessons, lei making, making a coconut leaf hat, playing Hawaiian games, and various other arts and crafts. During the summer and the major holiday seasons, many of the big hotels and resorts provide special supervised children's programs. For details, see the ACCOMMODATIONS sections for the area in which you are staying.

PARROTS

TRAVEL TIPS FOR THE
PHYSICALLY IMPAIRED

When making your travel plans it is best to do so well in advance and to inform the hotels and airlines that you are handicapped and what services or special needs you require. A good travel agent should also be able to assist in planning for your needs. Most visitor industry facilities in Hawai'i are only too happy to accommodate the physically impaired. It would be wise to bring along your medical records in case of an emergency. And it is recommended that you bring your own wheelchair and inform the airlines accordingly.

ARRIVAL AND DEPARTURE: Both the Hilo and Kona airports on the Big Island are easily accessible for mobility impaired persons. Parking stalls are available at both terminals for the handicapped. Restrooms with wheelchair accessible stalls are also found in both terminals. The local airlines are very conscientious in accommodating the handicapped. Special lifts to the aircraft are provided wheelchair passengers, but again be sure to notify them in advance.

TRANSPORTATION: Only two Big Island rental car companies provide hand controls: Avis and Hertz. Avis requires two weeks advance notice and Hertz requires at least seven days. See the Rental Car listing for phone numbers. The Hawai'i County "Hele On" bus system provides a demand-response transportation service with lift-equipped vans within the Hilo and Kona areas only to accommodate individuals unable to utilize the standard transit buses. This "curb to curb" service is available from 7:00 AM to 4:30 PM Mondays through Fridays except County holidays. Requests for service must be made at least a day in advance. For information, call Coordinated Services at (808) 961-3418 in Hilo or (808) 323-2085 in Kona.

MEDICAL SERVICES AND EQUIPMENT RENTAL: As noted in the "Traveling With Children/Emergencies" section, Hilo Hospital telephone is (808) 969-4111, Kona Hospital telephone is (808) 322-9311. Some agencies can assist in providing personal care attendants, companions, and nursing aides while on your visit. Contact: Big Island Center for Independent Living in Hilo at (808) 935-3777; Medical Personnel Pool in Hilo at 961-4621 and in Kealakekua, Kona at (808) 322-2722. Medical Personnel Pool is a national organization with offices in major cities across the country. One can make arrangements for attendants in Hawai'i by calling one of the local offices on the mainland.

The following companies provide medical equipment rentals. Pacific Rent-All in Hilo, 1080 Kilauea Avenue, (808) 935-2974, rents everything from hospital beds to wheelchairs; Medi-Home Care in Hilo, 28 Pookela St., (808) 969-1123, rents a full line of wheelchairs, walkers, crutches, etc.; Kona Coast Drugs, 75-5759 Kuakini Highway, Suite 104, corner of Hualalai & Kuakini, (808) 329-8886, rents a full line of wheelchairs, walkers, crutches, etc. Contact them in advance.

ACCOMMODATIONS: Most of the major Big Island hotels (at least the newer ones) and many of the condominium developments provide handicapped accessible rooms and facilities. However, because some have only a few, request reservations well in advancé. See the WHERE TO STAY chapter listing of hotels/condos and designation for handicapped accessibility.

ACTIVITIES: The Hawai'i Easter Seal Society can provide information on recreational activities for the disabled traveler. Contact them in advance in Hilo at (808) 961-3081. More information and phone numbers can be found in the RECREATION AND TOURS chapter.

Additional information for the disabled traveler in Hawai'i can be obtained by contacting the Commission on the Handicapped, State Department of Health, 1190 Waianuenue Avenue, Hilo, Hawai'i 96720, (808) 935-7257, or the Commission on the Handicapped, Old Federal Building, 335 Merchant St., #215, Honolulu, Hawai'i 96813, (808) 548-7606.

SENIOR TRAVEL

Seniors traveling to and around the Big Island are advised to inquire with all airline, car rental firms, hotels, restaurants and paid attractions/activities as to whether any "Senior Discounts" are available. It's a good rule to always ask for any special discounts, rates, etc. that are provided especially for seniors. Your travel agent can be helpful on this also but don't hesitate to ask yourself if you make your own reservations. Many times there are "unadvertised" special senior rates.

The County of Hawai'i offers seniors a discount of 1/3 off the regular bus fares on its "Hele On" bus system. The bus system serves the entire Big Island with regularly scheduled services. For complete information and the latest fares, contact the "Hele On Bus," County of Hawai'i Transit Agency, 25 Aupuni St., Hilo, HI 96720, (808) 935-8241.

When making inquiries about senior discounts with travel agencies, tour operators, airlines, car rental firms, restaurants and the like, be ready to provide a valid photo/age I.D.

The University of Hawai'i at Hilo, through its Continuing Education and Community Services Division, operates an annual program for the nationally-known "Elderhostel Program." In the Elderhostel Program, seniors have the opportunity to spend a week or more each summer on campus at UH-Hilo taking various courses and workshops in Hawai'i-Pacific culture, history, language, astronomy, vulcanology, oceanography, marine science and more. Fees cover tuition, room and board. Inquire with Elderhostel Program Director, University of Hawai'i at Hilo, CCECS, 523 W. Lanikaula St., Hilo, HI 96720-4091; phone (808) 933-3555.

On the Big Island, additional senior information can be obtained from the County of Hawai'i's Elderly Information & Referral Office, (808) 961-3418.

WEDDINGS AND HONEYMOONS IN PARADISE

A honeymoon on the Big Island can be "Paradise Found." And to make a romantic experience even more intimate, you can have your wedding here too. Many couples have chosen such settings as a Kona beach at sunset, the lush beauty of Liliuokalani Gardens in Hilo, on board a yacht sailing the majestic Kohala Coast, or for the traditional setting, any number of the Big Island's lovely little country churches. One is the beachside St. Peter's Church at Kahalu'u, in Keauhou-Kona.

Obtaining a marriage license is relatively easy. The legal age is eighteen for both parties and proof of age such as a certified birth certificate copy or baptismal record is required for those nineteen and under. The bride must have a rubella blood test and have the results certified by the lab,and physician ordering the test, using the prescribed form from the State of Hawai'i Department of Health. This form, along with an information packet, can be obtained from the Marriage License Section, Department of Health, State of Hawai'i, 1250 Punchbowl St., Honolulu, Hawai'i 96813 (808) 548-5862. Providing the proper form is used, the rubella test may be done by any government-approved laboratory on the mainland and signed by a physician licensed in any state. You can bring the test results with you to Hawai'i. Once the test results are approved, you can obtain a marriage license from any authorized agent in Hawai'i. On the Big Island, call the Department of Health at 961-7327 for the name/address of a licensing agent in the area where you are staying. The license fee is $16.00. Both parties must appear in person and there is no waiting period once the license is issued. The license is valid for thirty days anywhere in Hawai'i.

WEDDING CHAPELS/SERVICES

The following is a listing of wedding chapels and services that can provide everything from a traditional church wedding to a lavish beachside exchange-of-vows at sunset at your choice of locations. Various packages are available and include such things as flowers, photography, video, music, champagne and even limousine. Costs will vary with how lavish and extravagant one wants a wedding to be.

Aloha Baptist Church of Honoka'a, Kou Street, Honoka'a, HI 96727; (808) 775-9978

Aloha Weddings in Paradise, 78-261 Manukai, #1601, Kanaloa at Kona, Kailua-Kona, HI 96740; (808) 322-6577

Rev. B. R. Bates, Kamuela, HI 96743; (808) 885-7222; non-denominational wedding packages

Kinoole Baptist Church, 1815 Kinoole Street, Hilo, HI 96720; (808) 959-8012

Kona Baptist Church, 78-7156 Puuloa Rd, Kailua-Kona, HI 96740; (808) 322-9119

Living Waters Assembly of God, 89 Maikai, Hilo, HI 96720; (808) 959-9524

Paradise Weddings Hawaii ★, P.O.Box 383433, Waikoloa, HI 96738; 1-800-428-5844, (808) 883-9067, FAX (808) 883-8479; a full service wedding coordination operation which can arrange everything on the Big Island from location, minister, flowers, photos and wedding champagne and cake.

Rev. Patrick Thompson, Kailua-Kona, HI (808) 322-3116

In addition, most of the major hotels and resorts have a social director who can often assist with your plans. Check with your travel agent on the various wedding-honeymoon packages currently offered by the hotels-resorts. There are usually different packages to fit different budgets. (Prices are subject to change without notice.)

Hyatt Regency Waikoloa, One Waikoloa Beach Resort, Kohala Coast, HI 96743; 1-800-772-0011, (808) 885-1234, FAX (808) 885-7592. The Hyatt has a 4 night honeymoon "Romance" package that includes oceanfront room, champagne on arrival, one dinner and one breakfast and a sunset catamaran cruise. $1650 per couple.

Keauhou Beach Hotel, 78-6740 ALii Drive, Kailua-Kona, HI 96740; 1-800-367-6025, (808) 322-3441, FAX (808) 322-6586. The Keauhou Beach has various rooms and facilities for large and small weddings/receptions. Ceremonies can be held under a lattice arch by the sea, in the Kuakini Gardens or in the Coconut Grove, for groups of a few up to 500. Various wedding packages include every-thing from minister and photographer to flowers and wedding cake.

Kona Hilton Beach & Tennis Resort, 75-5852 Alii Drive, P.O.Box 1179, Kailua-Kona, HI 96740; 1-800-452-4411, (808) 329-3111, FAX (808) 329-9532. The Hilton has a standard 4 day/3 night honeymoon package for $490, extra nights are $130. This includes full American breakfast every day, nightly orchid turndown service, champagne and chocolates upon arrival and a honeymoon remem-mbrance gift.

Kona Surf Resort, 78-128 Ehukai Street, Keauhou-Kona, HI 96740, 1-800-367-8011, (808) 322-3411, FAX (808) 322-3245. The Kona Surf has a staff wedding coordinator who can assist with all the necessary arrangements. Their wedding packages are named after the fragrant seasonal flowers of the island, Gardenia, Jasmine and Ginger. The packages include various amenities such as flowers, champagne, photography or video, minister/justice of the peace, and wedding site of Keauhou Gardens, Wedding Gazebo or Kona Royal Chapel. The Ginger is $250, the Jasmine is $675 and the Gardenia is $1050. A standard honeymoon hotel package includes oceanfront room, rental car and champagne for $120 per night per couple.

HIBISCUS & PALM

Kona Village Resort, P.O.Box 1299, Kaupulehu-Kona, HI 96745, 1-800-367-5290, (808) 325-5555, FAX (808) 325-5124. The Honeymoon Hideaway package includes accommodations in a private thatched "hale" (bungalow) for 5 days/4 nights at $2025 or 8 days/7 nights at $3465 per couple, extra nights for $480. Also included are airport transportation, flower lei greeting on arrival, champagne in the "hale" and choice of snorkeling sail or therapeutic body massages. Honeymooners enjoy full American Plan breakfast, lunch and dinner as well as unlimited use of tennis courts, sailboats, outrigger canoes, snorkeling gear and glass-bottom boat cruises.

The Island Wedding package includes the complete 4 or 7 night Honeymoon Hideaway plus a marriage license issued right at the resort, and the minister to perform the ceremony. There are fresh flower bridal leis and decorations, champagne, music and a wedding cake, plus photographer to record it all and produce a 24 page photo album for the couple. The complete 5 day/4 night package is $3405 and the 8 day/7 night package is $4845, extra nights for $480.

Mauna Kea Beach Hotel, P.O.Box 218, Kamuela, HI 96743; 1-800-882-6060, (808) 882-7222, FAX (808) 882-7657. The Mauna Kea Beach offers a standard 6 day/5 night honeymoon package for $1,990. It includes deluxe ocean view or beach front room, champagne and fruit basket on arrival, matching his/hers yukata robes, limo transfer to/from airport, daily breakfast and optional dinner ($99 extra per couple) in the hotel's award-winning dining rooms. Various wedding ceremony packages are also available and include different amenities from flowers, to champagne to photos. Rates range from $715 to $1650.

Mauna Lani Bay Hotel and Bungalows, P.O.Box 4000, Kohala Coast, HI 96743-4000, 1-800-367-2323, (808) 885-6622, FAX (808) 885-4556. Mauna Lani has a 4 day/3 night honeymoon package featuring luxurious oceanview accommodations with private lanai, breakfast and dinner daily, airport limousine service, a bottle of fine champagne upon arrival, a basket of fresh island fruit and a special remembrance amenity. The cost per couple is $1695 with extra nights available at $365 per couple. A deluxe ocean front package is available for $1895 per couple, $415 per extra night.

Ritz-Carlton Mauna Lani, One North Kaniku Drive, Kohala Coast, HI 96743; 1-800-845-9905, (808) 885-2000, FAX (808) 885-8886. The Ritz-Carlton has a basic 3 night "Time for Romance" honeymoon or anniversary package. It includes limousine airport transfer, luxury oceanview room, champagne, plush terry robes and daily breakfast. Guests can also use the fitness center and tennis pavilion facilities. The 3 night package is $999 per couple.

HELPFUL INFORMATION

INFORMATION COUNTERS: Official State of Hawai'i information counters are located in the arrival areas of both the Hilo (935-1018) and Kona (329-3423) airports. They have lots of brochures and information of all sorts and can help answer questions on Big Island travel.

HAWAI'I VISITORS BUREAU OFFICES: Maintains two offices on the Big Island: 250 Keawe Street, Hilo, Hawai'i 96720; (808) 961-5797, FAX (808) 961-2126; and 75-5719 W. Alii Drive, Kailua-Kona, Hawai'i 96740; (808) 329-7787, FAX (808) 326-7563. They provide additional literature and information on hotels, condos, tours, activities, etc.

BIG ISLAND RESORT ASSOCIATIONS: These organizations can provide further information relative to their resort area: Destination Hilo, P.O. Box 1391, Hilo, HI 96721; 808/935-5294. Kohala Coast Resort Assoc., P.O. Box 5000, Kohala Coast, HI 96743-5000; (808) 885-4915. Keauhou Visitors Assoc., 78-6831 Alii Dr., Suite 234, Kailua-Kona, HI 96740-2413; (808) 322-3866.

BIG ISLAND GROUP (BIG): This organization is composed of the County of Hawai'i, the Hawai'i Visitors Bureau and various hotels, resorts and visitor industry businesses who have joined together to promote the entire Big Island as a destination. Contact this group for information about the Big Island as well: Big Island Group, HCO2 Box 5900, Kamuela, HI 96743; (808) 885-5900.

BIG ISLAND NEWSPAPERS: Prior to your visit, you may want to subscribe to one or the other daily to get information on upcoming events and to learn more about the Big Island in general. For the best wrap-up on local events and activities, it's recommended that you subscribe to both the Sunday and daily editions if you choose to subscribe at all. Hawai'i Tribune-Herald, 355 Kinoole St., Hilo, HI 96720;(808) 935-6621; West Hawai'i Today, 75-5629R Kuakini Highway, Kailua-Kona, HI 96740; (808) 329-9311

TELEVISION: Most hotels and condos have TV's in-room. The major networks have Honolulu stations that telecast to the Big Island. These are KGMB (CBS) Channel 9, KHON (NBC) 11, KITV (ABC) 13, and KHET (PBS) 4. In addition, there is Hilo Channel 2-Community Resource Channel and all major cable networks including NGN/Fuji Channel 16, a Japanese language network that carries a good mix of Japanese television programs with English sub-titles.

RADIO: Stations KKON-790 AM and KOAS 92.1-103.1 FM fill the air waves in Kona while KBIG-98 FM, KHLO-850 AM, KIPA-620 AM, KPUA-670 AM, and KWXX-95 FM do the same for the Hilo side. Maui and O'ahu (Honolulu) stations are picked up occasionally.

PERIODICALS: Many free publications are available at shopping centers, hotels, supermarkets, etc. around the island. They are usually directed to visitors with lots of related advertising. They can be helpful in providing information on places to see and things to do. These publications often have discount coupons on everything from meals to tours to clothing. Some to look for are *This Week Big Island*, *Hawai'i Island Guide* and *Big Island Drive Guide*.

IMPORTANT PHONE NUMBERS:

EMERGENCY:
- Police - Hilo 935-3311
- Police - Kailua-Kona 323-2645
- Police - Kohala 889-6225
- Ambulance - Fire anywhere on Big Island 961-6022
- Otherwise dial "0" for operator who will assist you.

Poison Control Center 1-800-362-3585
Crisis/Help Line island wide 329-9111
Sexual Assault Crisis Line 935-0677
Family Crisis Shelter 959-8400
American Red Cross 935-8305
Hawai'i Island Chamber of Commerce 935-7178
Hawai'i Visitors Bureau
- Hilo 961-5797
- Kona 329-7787

Hilo Hospital 969-4111
Kona Hospital 322-9311
Hawai'i Volcanoes National Park Headquarters 967-7311
Volcano Eruption Message/Information 967-7977
Hawai'i State Parks Division 961-7200
Hawai'i County
- Parks & Recreation 961-8311
- Information 961-8316
- Office of Complaints 961-8223
- Research & Development 961-8366

Weather Forecast
- Island of Hawai'i 961-5582
- Hawaiian Waters 935-9883

GETTING AROUND

FROM THE AIRPORT

Upon your arrival in Hilo or Kona, and after getting your luggage from the baggage claim area, you need to arrange transportation to where you are staying. Your options are a rental car, bus/limo hotel shuttle, or a taxi cab. Unfortunately, due to a strong political lobbying effort from the Big Island taxi cab companies, the County of Hawai'i does not allow its own "Hele On" public bus system to service the airports.

Some of the local tour bus/limo companies do, however, provide airport to hotel service on a pre-arranged basis. Try Grayline of Hawai'i (Kona, 329-9337; Hilo, 935-2835), Roberts Hawai'i (Kona, 329-1688; Hilo, 935-2858), Hawai'i Resorts Transportation Co. (Kohala-Mauna Lani Hotel, 885-7478; Honoka'a, 775-7291) or Big Island Limousine Service (Kona, 325-1088). Reservations should be made at least a day in advance or through your travel agent.

There is a new shuttle service serving the Kona-Kohala area. Kona Speedishuttle began door-to-door airport shuttle service in 1991. Rates from the Kailua-Kona area to the Kona airport are $7 per person. Rates from other West Hawai'i locations vary by distance. Call Kona Speedishuttle at 329-5433. Approximate airport-hotel per person one way bus fares are: Kona Airport to Kailua-Kona or Keauhou area hotels $8-10; to the Kohala Coast resorts as follows, Royal Wai-koloan Hotel $15, Hyatt Regency Waikoloa Hotel $16, Mauna Lani Bay Hotel $17, Ritz-Carlton Mauna Lani Hotel $17, Mauna Kea Beach Hotel $18. Hilo Air-port to Banyan Drive hotels in Hilo $5.

Taxis from both the Hilo and Kona airports are expensive. Big Island taxis are metered but they practically double the transportation fare over buses and even make renting a car attractive, at least from the Kona airport. In Hilo, from the airport to Banyan Drive hotels, a distance of two and a half miles, the standard charge is about $7. Hilo's taxi services include ABC Taxi (935-0755), Ace Taxi (935-8303), A-1 Bob's Taxi (935-4800), Aloha Taxi (935-1600), Hawai'i Taxi (959-6359), Hilo Harry's Taxi (935-7091), Ke-akea-Lani Wahine Taxi (935-9207) and Uncle George Taxi (935-2489).

From the Kona Airport to Kailua-Kona area hotels, a distance of seven to ten miles, the fare is $15-17; to Keauhou area hotels, a distance of 12 to 14 miles, the fare is $26-28; to the Kohala Coast hotels which are spread out along the coast for 20 to 30 miles, the fares are as follows: Royal Waikoloan Hotel $32, Hyatt Regency Waikoloa Hotel $33, Mauna Lani Bay Hotel $38, Ritz-Carlton Mauna Lani Hotel $38, Mauna Kea Beach Hotel $45. Kona-Kohala taxi services include Alpha Star Taxi (885-4771), C & C Taxi (329-6388), Island Cruise Taxi-Limo (885-8687), Island Taxi (325-5381), Kona Airport Taxi (329-7779), Marina Taxi (329-2481), Paradise Taxi (329-1234/326-1234) and Waimea Taxi (885-7040).

Other distances on the Big Island from Kona Airport: to Hilo via the north route Highway 19 is 86 miles; to Kamuela via Highway 19 is 34 miles; to Volcano via Highway 11 is 100 miles; to South Point via Highway 11 is 60 miles; to Honoka'a via Highway 19 is 49 miles; and to Hawi in North Kohala via High-ways 19/270 is 44 miles. From the Hilo Airport to Kailua-Kona via Highway 19 is 97.5 miles; to Honoka'a via Highway 19 is 42 miles; to Hawi in North Kohala via Highways 19/250 is 76 miles; to Kamuela via Highway 19 is 54.6 miles; to Volcano via Highway 11 is 28 miles; and to South Point via Highway 11 is 73 miles. The distance between Hilo and Kailua-Kona via the south route Highway 11 is 125 miles.

LOCAL BUSSES

Once settled in your hotel, you still need local transportation to get around. Taxis provide Hilo and Kailua-Kona area service and even standard tours, but again expense is a factor. In the Kailua-Kona and Keauhou areas, you can catch the "Alii Shuttle" bus which serves the entire length of Alii Drive from Kailua-Kona to Keauhou. The shuttle runs daily and takes 45 minutes in each direction. Its turn around points are the Lanihau Shopping Center in Kailua-Kona and the Kona Surf Resort in Keauhou. The shuttle makes stops along Alii Drive enroute at all major hotels and shopping centers. The fare is $1 each way; hours of operation are 7:45AM - 10PM, daily. Look for the red, white and blue bus.

The other transportation alternative is the "Hele On" bus system operated by the County of Hawai'i. The public buses provide both Hilo and Kailua-Kona as well as island-wide service. Standard fare for short distances is $.75 within Hilo or Kailua-Kona, and gradually increases depending on how far you are going or to what town around the island. The around the island fare, Hilo to Kona, is a reasonable $6.00 one way.

Bus tickets are sold by the sheet at a 10% discount from the regular fare. Ten tickets per sheet cost $6.75. Certified senior citizens, handicapped and students are entitled to a special discount and can purchase ticket sheets for $5.00. Bus tickets are available at various stores, shops, and businesses around the island displaying the Hele On bus poster. There is a $1.00 per piece charge for luggage and back-packs. For bus schedules, contact County of Hawai'i, Mass Transportation Agency, 25 Aupuni Street, Hilo, HI 96720, (808) 935-8241.

LIMOUSINE SERVICE

If you want to splurge on transportation, you can arrange for a personalized limousine for everything from airport-hotel service to a complete private around the island tour. Try A Touch of Class Limousine, Kona, 329-0603; Aloha Aina Limousine, Waikoloa, 883-8687; Big Island Limousine, Kona, 325-1088; Carey Limousine, Kona, 1-800-548-8490; Island Cruise Taxi-Limo, Kamuela, 885-8687; Limo's Hawai'i, Waikoloa, 883-8499; Luana Limousine Service, Kona, 326-5466; Robert's Hawai'i, Kona, 329-1688, Hilo, 935-2858; The cost is obviously expensive, but generally first-class for those who can afford it.

RENTAL CARS, VANS, 4-WHEEL DRIVES, EXOTIC CARS

The Big Island has some 1500 miles of paved county and state roads and highways. And those roads and highways pass through some of the loveliest and most diverse scenery in Hawai'i. The best ways to see it all is by hiring your own car. There are several rental car companies located on the Big Island and most have stations in Hilo and Kona. A few have desks at major hotels and resorts. Some are national chains while others are local. One thing is certain: they all have a variety of cars available at a variety of rates, with special low-season, weekly discount, and holiday package deals. You can check out the following list and contact them yourself (many have toll free numbers) or you can have your travel agent do it.

Rental cars are your best bargain for transportation since they give you the independence and mobility to come and go as you please and to see and do what you want. Rates vary greatly among the car rental agencies as well as by season so it's wise to shop around. On the Big Island the daily rate for a compact-size automatic is $30-35 with no mileage charge. For a mid-size car, the daily rate is $40-55, no mileage charge. Full-size cars are generally $60 and up. Seven passenger vans go for $50-90 daily, no mileage charge, with larger vans up to $130 daily. Various luxury cars are also available and they command premium rental rates. Many of the agencies offer special seasonal weekly rates and its always good to check on these. There are also special hotel room/car packages that are good values. Keep in mind that these figures are only approximate. They represent averages from a survey of rental car agencies. Things like air conditioning increase the rate. Special rates may apply during the "low" season in Hawai'i, usually from Labor Day until about Thanksgiving and again from Easter until about June 1. Hawai'i's peak season from December 1 until March 30 or so, finds demand and prices high on rental cars. The summer season although not as strong as winter generates a fair amount of demand and rates seem to fluctuate.

One thing that affects car rental rates is the extra charges for insurance coverage. These rates can run anywhere from $7-15 per day and more. This increases the daily rate drastically and most agencies strongly encourage you to buy the coverage. However, it is suggested that you check with your own insurance company at home to verify exactly what your policy covers. In fact, bring along your insurance company's address and telephone number just in case. Hawai'i is a no-fault state and without the insurance, if there is an accident, you are required to take care of all the damages before leaving the island.

Most of the car rental agencies have similar policies. They require a minimum age of 21 to 25 and a major credit card for a deposit or to hold your reservation. Most feature no mileage charges with you paying for the gas (from $1.65-1.90 per gallon). There is also a 4% sales tax.

For the adventurous who want to see some of Hawai'i's back roads and byways, you should consider renting a 4-wheel drive Jeep, Geo Tracker or similar vehicle. Alamo, Harper, Sunshine, Dollar and some of the others rent them with daily rates ranging beginning at $60. These vehicles are approved for traversing such roads as Highway 200, the Saddle Road, between Hilo and Waikoloa which passes over the plateau between Mauna Kea and Mauna Loa. The Saddle Road is off limits to regular rental cars and driving on it is a violation of the rental car agreement. You would need a 4-wheel drive vehicle to reach such places as the summit of 14,000 ft. Mauna Kea, and other inaccessible back road locations, which are also off limits to regular rental cars.

If your car rental preferences lean toward something out of the ordinary, and your budget allows for it, you can even rent an "exotic car," the latest thing in rentals. Exotic cars are just that, wheels that are a cut above the rest and come with names like Lamborghini, Ferrari, Porsche, BMW, Maserati, Corvette and many more. Rates? I thought you'd never ask. Sample daily rates are as follows, insurance, etc. is extra: Lamborghini $1100, Ferrari $495, Maserati $275, Porsche $250-350, Jaguar $295, BMW $175, Masda Miata $195, Corvette $199-500. Most of these "exotics" are convertibles and are available on the Big Island from Aloha Exotic Rentals, Ciao Exoticar Rentals and Kona Convertibles. See following listing.

One final note on renting a car on the Big Island. If you pick up your car at one airport, say at Kona, and drop it off at Hilo, most car rental agencies will charge you what is called a "drop" charge. This can run as high as $30-40. That's why it is usually best to pick up and return a rental car at the same location.

WARNING: Even paradise has its share of thieves so *never* leave your automobile unlocked at the beach, park, scenic site or parking lot. Also, take personal valuables with you. Secure your car and your valuables. And don't leave the keys in your car.

RENTAL CAR COMPANY LISTING:

ALAMO RENT A CAR
1-800-327-9633
Hilo 961-3343
Kona 329-8896

ALOHA EXOTIC RENTALS
Kona 329-2202

AVIS RENT A CAR
1-800-831-8000
Hilo 935-1290
Kona 329-1745

BUDGET RENT A CAR
1-800-527-7000
Hilo 961-0661
Kona 329-8511

CIAO EXOTICAR RENTALS
Kona 326-2426
Waikoloa 326-CIAO

DOLLAR RENT A CAR
1-800-342-7398
Hilo 961-6059
Kona 329-2744

HARPER CAR & TRUCK
Rentals of Hawai'i
Hilo 969-1478

HERTZ RENT A CAR
1-800-654-3131
Hilo 935-2896
Kona 329-3566

KONA CONVERTIBLES
Waikoloa 885-4329

NATIONAL CAR RENTAL
1-800-227-7368
Hilo 935-0891
Kona 329-1674

RENT & DRIVE INC.
Kailua-Kona 329-3033

SUNSHINE OF HAWAI'I
Rent A Car
Hilo 935-1108
Kona 329-2926

THRIFTY CAR RENTAL
1-800-367-2277
Hilo 935-1936
Kona 329-1730

TROPICAL RENT A CAR
Hilo 935-3385
Kona 329-2437

V.I.P. CAR RENTAL
Kona 329-7328
or 326-9466

WORLD RENT A CAR
Kona 329-1006

MOPEDS, MOTORSCOOTERS, MOTORCYCLES, BICYCLES

Mopeds and motorscooters can be rented in Kona. Try Rent Scootah in Kona, across from King Kam Hotel, 326-4821; or Ciao Activities in Kona, 75-5663A Palani Road, 326-4177; or Budget Rent a Car in Kona, 329-8511. In addition to motorscooters, Ciao also has a couple of 150cc-250cc motorcycles for rent in Kona. Check for the latest half and full day rates.

Bicycles can be rented in Kona at Dave's Triathlon Shop, 74-5588M Pawai Place, 329-4522, B & L Bike & Sports, 74-5576B Pawai Place, 329-3309, or either of the Ciao Activities locations in Kona or Waikoloa.

DRIVING ON THE BIG ISLAND

You'll find that driving on the Big Island is really no different than anywhere else, with one small exception. Big Island drivers are generally the most courteous and congenial among all the islands of Hawai'i. The majority of Big Island drivers drive with "Aloha" and will yield to others, allow others to make left turns in front of them, wave others through intersections and generally display other forms of courteous driving. But like everywhere too, there are a few who don't know how to drive courteously. You'll pick up fast on Big Island driving courtesy, but likewise, drive defensively at the same time.

You can drive completely around the Big Island, from Hilo to Kona, in a day, but it is a very tiring drive and not really practical for sightseeing and leisurely exploring. The circle drive is around 225 miles or so. The best thing to do would be to drive one leg between Kona and Hilo, say the northern route through Kamuela and Honoka'a, and then spend a night or two in Hilo taking in the sights of that area. Then the drive back to Kona could be completed another day via the southern route, through Volcanoes National Park and the Ka'u District to take in those sights. This routing could just as easily be reversed. The distance from Hilo to Kona around the north side through Kamuela is just about 100 miles. Around the south side through Ka'u it is about 125 miles. For an excellent road map of the Big Island, *Hawai'i, The Big Island* by cartographer James A. Bier is highly recommended. The cost is $2.50 at local bookstores or it can be ordered from Catalog Order Desk, The University of Hawai'i Press, Honolulu, Hawai'i 96822. If you're traveling with youngsters, plan on stopping at some of the town parks along the way to let the children stretch their legs and run off excess energy. Most of the parks have a playground area with swings, climbing bars, carousels, etc. It's a request I get frequently from my "backseat gang."

Hawai'i Warrior Markers: While driving around the Big Island, be on the lookout for the distinctive red and yellow cloaked Hawaiian Warrior marker-signs along the road. These signs have been erected by the Hawai'i Visitors Bureau to note special historic sites, places of interest to visitors, and scenic attractions. They are very easy to recognize and will help lead you to discover many additional interesting things while touring around the island.

GINGER

45

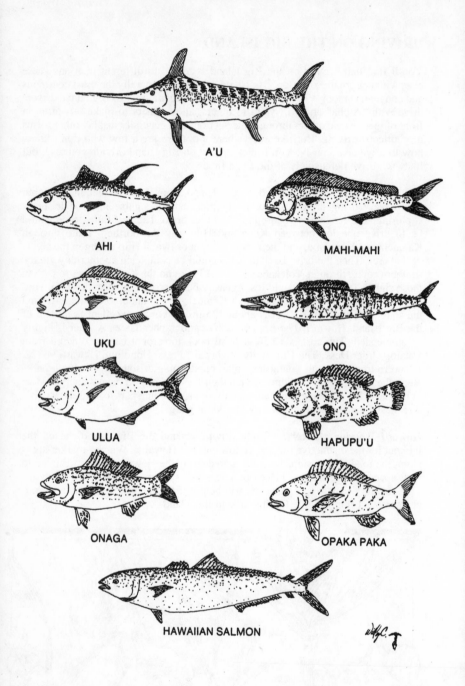

A'U

AHI

MAHI-MAHI

UKU

ONO

ULUA

HAPUPU'U

ONAGA

OPAKA PAKA

HAWAIIAN SALMON

46

A FEW WORDS ABOUT FISH
AND OTHER SEAFOOD

About the only things harder for visitors to pronounce properly than the names of towns and streets are the names of fish. And whether you are dining out or buying fresh fish at the market, Hawaiian fish names can be confusing. Among the more common fish caught commercially and that you'll see at the market and on restaurant menus are Ahi (yellow fin tuna), Aku (blue fin tuna), Ono (wahoo), Mahimahi (dolphin fish), and several species of marlin. Other popular table fish include Opakapaka (pink snapper) and Onaga (red snapper) which provide delicate white flaky meat.

A short list of Hawai'i's more popular seafood delicacies follows:

A'AMA - A small black crab that scurries over rocks at the beach. A delicacy required for a Hawaiian luau.

A'U - The broadbill swordfish averages 250 lbs. in Hawai'i. The broadbill is a rare catch, hard to locate, difficult to hook, and a challenge to land.

AHI - The yellow fin tuna (Allison tuna) is caught in deep waters surrounding the Big Island. The pinkish red meat is firm yet flaky. This fish is popular for sashimi (raw, sliced thin, dipped in mustard-soy sauce) and costs $15-20 per lb. at New Year's when it is most in demand. They can weigh over 200 lbs.

ALBACORE - This smaller version of the Ahi averages 40-50 lbs. and is lighter in both texture and color.

AKU - This is the blue fin tuna, usually averaging 5-15 lbs.

EHU - Orange snapper

HAPU - Hawaiian sea bass

IKA - Hawaiian squid, used for many dishes

KAMAKAMAKA - Island catfish is a very tasty and popular dish, however, a little difficult to find at most restaurants.

LEHI - The Silver Mouth is a member of the snapper family with a stronger flavor than Onaga and Opakapaka and a texture resembling Mahimahi.

MU'U - A very mild white fish which is seldom seen on menus because it is very difficult to catch

MAHIMAHI - Also called dolphin fish but unrelated to the mammal of the same name. Ranges from 10-65 lbs. It is a seasonal fish and commands a high price when fresh. Traditionally one of Hawai'i's most popular seafoods, it is often imported from other Pacific and Far East areas to meet the demand. If it's on your dinner menu, ask if it is fresh (caught in Hawai'i) or frozen (imported). Excellent eating fresh and almost as good even if frozen, if prepared well.

ONAGA - Red snapper, considered a bottom fish as it is caught in quite deep water. Bright pink scales, tender white meat.

ONO - This one is a member of the barracuda family but the meat is flaky, moist, and "very good," which is what Ono means in Hawaiian.

'OPAE - Shrimp

OPAKAPAKA - Pink snapper has very light, flaky, delicate meat.

OPIHI - Single shell limpet, mollusc that clings to rocks on the shore. Dangerous and difficult to gather as hazardous surf can sweep pickers into the ocean. Many have been drowned this way. But opihi are a must for an authentic Hawaiian luau.

PAPIO - This is a baby Ulua which is caught in shallow waters and weighs 5 - 25 pounds.

TAKO - Better known as octopus. This a is very popular seafood prepared numerous ways and used in various dishes.

ULUA - Also known as Pompano, this fish has firm and flaky white meat. Often caught along the Big Island's steep rocky coastline. Ulua can weigh up to 100 lbs. A Papio is a young ulua usually under 25 lbs.

WANA - Otherwise known as the sea urchin, many consider this a real delicacy. Simply scoop out the contents of the wana shell and enjoy!

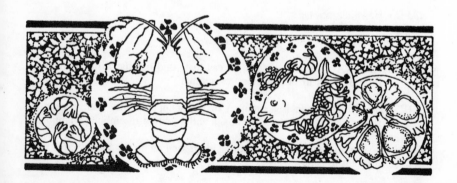

GROCERY SHOPPING

You can expect to pay quite a bit more on the average for groceries on the Big Island compared to what you pay on the U.S. mainland. In fact, in a 1991 study done by the University of Hawai'i at Hilo in conjunction with the American Chamber of Commerce Researchers Association, a market-basket survey of 59 items revealed Hilo's prices an average of 37% higher than other mainland cities. And, like on the mainland, island stores vary in price so it pays to shop around. Weekly advertised specials can change prices considerably. The following sample prices are averages only and may vary from store to store around the island. These prices were quoted a few months prior to publication so expect them to be higher as you read this.

> Blue Bonnet margarine, 1 lb. - $2.07
> Kraft American cheese slices, 12 oz.-$3.67
> Oscar Mayer beef hot dogs, 1 lb. - $3.69
> Wheaties cereal, 12 oz. - $3.49
> Lay's potato chips, 7 oz. twin pack-$2.33
> whole fresh chicken - $.89-1.19 lb.
> bread, 1 lb. loaf - $1.65-2.39
> Skippy Peanut Butter, 18 oz. - $3.13
> Nabisco crackers, 1 lb. - $1.93
> hamburger, 30% fat - $1.97 lb.
> chuck roast, 7 bone - $2.17 lb.
> New York steak - $6.87 lb.
> Sirloin tip steak - $4.87 lb.
> Pork chops - $2.77 lb.
> head lettuce - $.99 lb.
> 1/2 gal. milk - $2.15
> 1/2 gal. orange juice - $3.33
> Eggs-Grade A large, doz. - $1.75, medium-$1.63
> Bathroom tissue, 4-roll pack - $1.59
> 12-pack Natural Light Beer - $7.49
> 12-pack Pepsi or Coke - $6.45

You'll find the range of grocery stores on the Big Island from simple Mom n' Pop country stores to modern convenient supermarkets. In Hilo, the major supermarkets are KTA Super Stores, Safeway, Sure Save, Food Fair, and Sack n' Save. In Kona, the major supermarkets are KTA Superstores, Sure Save, Foodland, Food 4 Less and Kamigaki Market. In Waimea, the major stores are KTA and Sure Save while in Waikoloa it is Waikoloa Village Market. Most of them advertise in the local newspapers, offering weekly specials and coupons.

Around the island, each town has a market or two and there are a number of stop and shop convenience stores such as 7-Eleven food stores. The Safeway and Food Fair stores in Hilo and the KTA stores in Hilo/Puainako, Waimea, Kailua-Kona and at Keauhou-Kona feature the latest in full service deli counters, ready to eat foods and bakeries.

On your trips around the island and through the towns, be on the lookout for one of the nondescript Mom n' Pop stores. These are the old fashioned small town family run stores, usually with grandma or grandpa still tending store and not infrequently by one of the younger members of the family who have returned to take over the family enterprise. With their homey country atmosphere, simple furnishings and fixtures, old ad displays on the walls, and ancient water coolers that keep beer and soda chilled, these old town stores allow you to step back into an earlier era of Hawaiian history. And often too you might luck out and get there as the homemade cookies, fresh sushi, or other country goodies are just out of the kitchen. And if nothing else, you might be able to get a "shave ice."

SPECIAL BIG ISLAND PRODUCTS

It's an island tradition that when you go traveling, you bring back some special gifts and goodies from the place you visit for friends and relatives back home. The Japanese call these special gifts "omiyage." For local folks from other parts of Hawaii, their Big Island visit wouldn't be complete without several extra boxes of goodies to take home. That's why at the airport baggage check in areas you'll see all manner of boxes and containers full of Big Island products destined for friends and relatives back home.

The Big Island doesn't disappoint when it comes to supplying local products for those back home to enjoy. These products are all grown or produced right here on the Big Island and are easily available at local supermarkets and gift stores around the island. Some of these products have already been mentioned in the "Best Bets" or other sections of this book. Naturally, most of these are edible food products with the exception of flowers. And while some of these products can be transported easily, a few are perishable and will require refrigeration and special handling.

One more note: pineapple isn't grown commercially on the Big Island but you can obtain it in local supermarkets and gift shops for shipping home. The pineapples come from either O'ahu or Maui.

Look for these special Big Island products:

Atebara Taro Chips from Hilo
Deguchi Kitch'n Cook'd Potato Chips from Kona
Miriam's Cookies from Kona
Puna Papaya from the Puna District
Donna's Cookies from the Hamakua Coast
Harrie's Lavosh from Hilo
Frank's Foods or Miko Meats Portuguese Sausage from Hilo
Kulana Foods Brand Dried Beef Jerky from Hilo
Mauna Loa brand macadamia nuts and chocolates from Hilo
Big Island Candies brand macadamia nut chocolates from Hilo
Mountain View Stone Cookies from Mountain View
Amano fish cake and tempura (surimi) from Hilo
        (an essential ingredient for saimin noodles)

Hilo Macaroni Factory crackers from Hilo
    (sorry they don't make macaroni anymore)
Niolopa brand tropical fruit jams and jellies from Hilo
Hawaiian Macadamia Plantations brand macadamia nuts, chocolates, cookies and
    other goodies from Honoka'a
Pure Kona Coffee (several brands available in local supermarkets) from Kona
Punalu'u Sweetbread from Punalu'u, Ka'u District
Anthuriums and orchids from Big Island flower farms and florist shops
Oshiro Tofu Products brand tofu from Hilo
Kelly Boy's sweetbread and cinnamon rolls from Hilo
Robert's Bakery macadamia nut cookies from Hilo
Pueo Poi Factory laulau and poi from Hilo
The Chocolate Bar chocolate sushi from Hilo
Ishigo's Bakery breads and pastries from Honomu on the Hamakua Coast
Holy's Bakery frozen fruit pies from Kapa'au in North Kohala
2 lb. bags of fresh raw (brown) sugar from Hamakua Coast fields
Kohala Kim Chee from Hawi, Kohala
Big Island Taro Chips from Kalaoa on the Hamakua Coast
Hakalau Honey from Ouye Apiaries in Hakalau
Busy Bees Honey from Pahoa, Puna District
Orchid Island Cheure and Feta goat milk cheeses, Kurtistown

KONA COFFEE

SOUVENIRS - GIFTS - ANTIQUES

Visitors to Hawai'i have no end of local souvenir and gift shops at shopping centers and resorts from which to choose mementos from their vacation in paradise. See the WHERE TO STAY - WHAT TO SEE chapter for details on each area of the island. However, for authentic local made-in-Hawai'i items, you need to be selective. Much of the souvenir and gift items in many of the shops are not made in Hawai'i but imported, mostly from the Far East, and passed off as "local." So, be selective. If in doubt as to a product's origin, ask the shop clerk. After all, it's your money.

If you are an antique buff, you'll find some interesting antique shops around the island that are worth a browse. You'll find all sorts of antiques, collectibles and old attic items like vintage Aloha shirts and muumuus (women's dresses), soda and milk bottles, plantation-era items, ethnic-related things and lots more. The following is a listing of antique shops. If you're planning a stop at a particular shop, you might want to call ahead to check on their hours of business as they vary.

Country Store Antiques - in Captain Cook, Kona next to Manago Hotel (323-3005)

Flamingo's - 75-5744 Alii Dr., Kona Inn Shopping Village, Kailua-Kona (329-4122)

Flamingo's Tropical Silks - in the Hyatt Regency Waikoloa Hotel, Kohala Coast (885-5504)

Honoka'a Trading Co. - Mamane Street, Honoka'a (775-0808)

Hula Heaven - 75-5744 Alii Drive, Kona Inn Shopping Village, Kailua-Kona (329-7885)

Mid Pacific Store - 76 Kapiolani St., Hilo, opposite Lyman Museum (935-3822)

Northern Lights - 118 Ponahawai Street, Hilo (935-9800)

Odd Varieties Shop - 164 Kilauea Avenue, Hilo (961-5141)

Seconds to Go Inc. - in Honoka'a (775-9212)

Shibuya Station - 73-1204 Ahikawa, Kona (325-5226)

The Home Place - 43 Haili Street, Hilo (935-7494)

Tinny Fisher's Antique Shop - on Highway 19, Mountain View (968-6011)

SELF-SERVICE LAUNDRIES

Most hotels and condo units have a laundry service available, either the commercial send-out type or in-house coin-operated machines. Check with your front desk. For those in need of self-service laundries, there are a few located around the island. Hours of operation may vary, so call first.

Heli Mai Laundromat, Kailua-Kona, Palani Road and Kuakini Highway a block above the King Kam Hotel, North Kona Shopping Center, 329-3494; open daily 5AM - 11PM.

Hilo Quality Cleaners Coin Laundry, 210 Hoku, Hilo, 961-6490; open Monday through Saturday only, 5AM - 10PM.

Jupiter Cleaners & Laundry, in the village of Kainaliu, Kona, 322-2929; open daily 6AM - 9PM.

Lole Wai Laundry, in the heart of Waimea across from the Waimea Shopping Center, 885-4696; open daily 5AM - 12 midnight.

Motherload Washerette, Honoka'a, just off the main street of town next to the Dairy Queen, 775-9788; open daily 6AM - 10PM.

Na'alehu Shopping Center Laundromat, in Na'alehu, Ka'u District, just off Highway 11.

Tyke's Laundromat, 74-5583 Pawai Place, Kailua-Kona, 326-1515; open daily, 6AM - 10PM; and at 1454 Kilauea Avenue, Hilo, 935-1093.

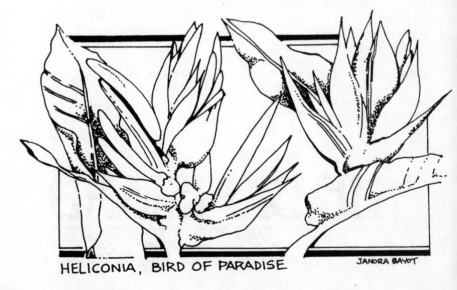

HELICONIA, BIRD OF PARADISE   JANORA BAYOT

53

ANNUAL BIG ISLAND EVENTS

The following is only a partial listing of the many social, cultural, community, and sporting events that take place around the Big Island annually. The events are listed monthly only since the exact dates change yearly. Many events have numerous related activities like the annual Merrie Monarch Hula Festival in April which features hula dance and music, a parade, and arts and crafts demonstrations and displays of Hawaiiana. The same is true for many of the holiday celebrations, cultural fairs, and other events. For more specific information on dates, locations, etc., contact the Hawai'i County Research & Development Office at (808) 961-8366 in Hilo, or the Hawai'i Visitors Bureau-Big Island Chapter in Hilo at (808) 961-5797 or in Kona at (808) 329-7787. For additional listings of events see the local Big Island newspapers and visitor periodicals where you are staying.

JANUARY
"Hauoli Makahiki Hou" (Happy New Year celebrations) - Islandwide
Saddleroad 100K Relay & Ultra-Marathon - Hilo/Waimea
Keauhou Open Pro-Am Golf Tourney - Kona
Hawai'i County Band Jazz Concert - Hilo
Kilauea Wilderness Marathon & Rim Run - Volcano
"Kung Hee Fat Choy" (Chinese New Year celebrations) - Island-wide

FEBRUARY
La Pa'ani (Hawaiian Sports Day) - Kona
Annual University of Hawai'i at Hilo Homecoming - Hilo
Free Style Ski Meet - Mauna Kea ski slopes
Keauhou-Kona Half Triathlon - Kona
Hawai'i County Band Guest Conductor Concert - Hilo
Big Island High School Basketball Tournament - Hilo

MARCH
Kona Marathon - Kona
Big Island Auto Show - Hilo
Big Island Plant Show/Sale - Hilo
International Hawai'i Ski Cup Meet - Mauna Kea ski slopes
Haili Men's Volleyball Tournament - Hilo
Kona Stampede Rodeo - Kona
Miss Aloha Hawai'i Pageant - Hilo
Hawai'i County Band Concert - Hilo
Prince Kuhio Day Holiday

THE BIG ISLAND
OF HAWAII
Celebrate great moments with us!

APRIL
Moku-O-Hawai'i Volleyball Tournament - Hilo
Big Island School Band Festival - Hilo
Buddhist "Hanamatsuri" Festival - Island-wide
Boy Scout "Makahiki" Show - Island-wide
Hawai'i County Band Concert - Hilo
Paniolo Ski Meet - Mauna Kea ski slopes
Easter Sunrise Services - Island-wide
Merrie Monarch Hula Festival - Hilo
Pu'ukohola Educational Festival - Kawaihae

MAY
May Day-Lei Day Observances - Island-wide
John Kekua, Sr. Canoe Regatta - Hilo Bay
Kawaihae Canoe Regatta - Kawaihae
Kona Gold Jackpot Fishing Tournament - Kona
Flores De Mayo Celebration - Hilo
Kona Mauka Troller's Wahine Fishing Tournament - Kona
Visitor Industry Charity Walk - Kona
Kona Iki Troller's Jackpot Fishing Tournament - Kona
Hawai'i County Band Concert - Hilo
Golden Goddess Fishing Tournament - Hilo
Annual Western Week Celebration - Honoka'a
Miss Filipina Hawai'i Pageant - Hilo
"I Luna Lilo" Mauna Loa Hike to summit - Volcanoes National Park
Annual Keauhou-Kona Triathlon - Kona
Judi's Polynesian Dance Studio Recital - Hilo
Queen Liliuokalani Canoe Regatta - Kona
Memorial Day Observances - Island-wide

JUNE
King Kamehameha Holua Ski Special - Mauna Kea ski slopes
Big Island Shoreline Fishing Tourney - Island-wide
Kamehameha Celebration Canoe Regatta - Kona
King Kamehameha Day Celebrations/Parades - Island-wide
Lei-draping of King Kamehameha statue, Kapa'au, Kohala
Wee Guys Fishing Tournament - Kona
Kauikeaouli Canoe Regatta - Kona
Kona Iki Trollers Fishing Tournament - Kona
Andy Levin Run for Charity - Hilo
Volcano Dance Retreat - Volcano
Wailani Canoe Regatta - Hilo Bay
Vintage Years Triathlon & Relay Run - Kona
4-H Beef Steer Show - Hilo
Big Island Massed Band Concert - Hilo
Miss Jr. Sampaguita Pageant - Hilo
Buddhist Obon Festivals - Island-wide Buddhist temples
Hawai'i Quarterhorse Show - Waiki'i Ranch, Kohala

JULY
Hapuna Rough Water Swim - Hapuna Beach, Kohala
Moku-O-Hawai'i Big Island Canoe Regatta Championship - TBA
Hawai'i County Band July 4th. Concert - Hilo
Annual July 4th. Naalehu Town Carnival & Rodeo - Naalehu
Annual Fourth Fest - Hilo and Island-wide
Pu'uhonua O Honaunau Cultural Festival - Honaunau, Kona
Buddhist Obon Festivals - Island-wide Buddhist temples
Annual Big Island Bonsai Show - Hilo
Annual Hilo Orchid Society Show - Hilo
Parker Ranch Rodeo and Horse Races - Waimea
Kona Mauka Trollers Fishing Tournament - Kona
Big Island Marathon and Half Marathon - Hilo
Royal Waikoloa Hotel Benefit Tennis Tournament - Waikoloa
Mauna Kea Beach Hotel Annual Pro-Am Golf Tournament - Kohala
Keaukaha Canoe Race - Hilo Bay
Kona Ahi Jackpot Fishing Tournament - Kona
International Festival of the Pacific - Hilo
Plantation Days Festival - Hilo
Keauhou-Kona Women's Golf Tourney - Kona
Kilauea Iki Run - Volcano
Hawai'i Light Tackle Tournament - Kona
Kona Hawaiian Billfish Tournament - Kona
Annual Hawai'i Anthurium Association Show - Hilo

AUGUST
Dan Nathaniel Sr. Canoe Race - Hilo
Hawaiian International Billfish Tournament - Kona
Hawai'i County Band Concert - Kona
Buddhist Obon Festivals - Island-wide Buddhist temples
Greater Mana to Kamuela Footrace 10K Run - Waimea
Noenoe Seamountain Women's Golf Tournament - Ka'u
Richard Smart Canoe Race - Kawaihae
Kona Mauka Trollers Fall Fishing Tournament - Kona
Kona Fil-Am Women's Fast Pitch Softball Tourney - Kona
Great Waikoloa Open Golf Tournament - Waikoloa
Kona A'lure Women's Fishing Tournament - Kona
A.J. McDonald Canoe Race - Kona
Pu'ukohola Heiau Establishment Day Cultural Festival - Kawaihae
YWCA Women's Triathlon - Hilo
Senior Citizens Softball Tournament - Hilo
Macadamia Nut Harvest Festival - Honoka'a
Lydia Kamakaeha Canoe Race - Kawaihae
Kona Iki Trollers "Keiki" Fishing Tourney - Kona
Sand Castle & Sculpture Contest - Kona
Big Island Badminton Tourney - Hilo
Miss Latina Pageant - Hilo
Queen Liliuokalani Canoe Race - Kona
Horseshoe Pitching Championship - Kona

AUGUST (con't)
Kauikeaouli/Kona Gardens Canoe Race - Kona
Admissions Day Holiday Celebrations - Island-wide
Okinawan Cultural Fest & Hari Boat Races, Wailoa River, Hilo

SEPTEMBER
Hawai'i County Fair - Hilo
Big Island Aloha Week Festivals - Island-wide
Parker Ranch Roundup Rodeo - Waimea
Hilo Trollers Championship Fishing Tourney - Hilo
Senior Citizens Fishing Derby - Hilo, Kona
Keiki Deep Sea Fishing Tourney - Kona
Golden Marlin Jackpot Fishing Tourney - Kona
Puna Canoe Race - Kalapana
Duke's Kona Classic Fishing Tournament - Kona
Sure Save Charity Walk/Run - Hilo
Concert in the Park - Hilo
Iwalani O Ke Kai Jackpot Fishing Tourney - Kona
Senior Citizens Hawai'i Friendship Festival - Hilo, Kona
Chuck Machado Luau's Jackpot Fishing Tourney - Kona
Chuck Machado Luau's Golf Tourney - Kona
Kona Nightingale Donkey Race - Kona
Okoe Bay Rendezvous Marlin Fishing Tournament - Ka'u
Hawai'i Country Fair - Kailua-Kona
Big Island Polo Tournaments - Waiki'i Ranch, Kohala

OCTOBER
Mauna Loa Macadamia Nut Festival & Parade - Hilo
Ironman World Triathlon Championship - Kona, Kohala
Octoberfest Harvest Festival - Hilo
Bario Fiesta - Hilo
Great Waikoloa Golf Tourney - Waikoloa
Kohala Coast Senior's Golf Classic - Waikoloa
Kohala Country Fair - Kohala
North Kohala Biathlon - Kohala

OCTOBER (con't)
Annual Kohala Club Rodeo - Waimea
Big Island Dog Show - Hilo
Big Island "Karaoke" Singing Contest - Hilo
Concert in the Park - Hilo
Big Island Cat Show - Hilo
Aloha Big Island Bike Trek - Hilo/Volcanoes National Park
Big Island Polo Tournaments - Waiki'i Ranch, Kohala

NOVEMBER
LPGA-PING Golf Tourney - Kona
Festival of Trees - Kona
Run for Hunger 10K Run - Waimea
Kona Coffee Festival and Parade - Kona
Veteran's Day Observances - Island-wide
Kupuna Hula Competition - Kona
La Pa'aui (Hawaiian Sports Day) - Kona
Hawai'i Cattlemen's Bull and Horse Show Sale - Waikoloa
Pop Warner Shriner's Football
University of Hawai'i-Hilo Vulcans Basketball Classic - Hilo
Christmas in the Country - Volcano
Kilauea Lei Making Contest - Volcanoes National Park
Big Island Ultraman Triathlon - Island-wide
Botengo Classic (Bowling-Tennis-Golf) - Hilo, Ka'u
Christmas Arts and Crafts Fair - Kamuela
Christmas Parade - Kona
Concert in the Park - Hilo
YWCA Festival of Trees - Hilo
Big Island Polo Tournaments - Waiki'i Ranch, Kohala

DECEMBER
Christmas Parades - Island-wide towns
Christmas Arts and Crafts Shows - Kona, Hilo
Mauna Lani Bay Hotel Golf Tourney - Kohala Coast
Paniolo Golf Tourney - Kona
Christmas Fantasy - Honoka'a
Festival of Trees - Kona
Lyman House Museum's "A Christmas Tradition" - Hilo
"Christmas Singing Tree" - Hilo
Christmas Concert in the Park - Hilo
Mauna Kea Beach Hotel Golf Tourney - Kohala Coast
Annual Christmas Concerts - UH-Hilo Theatre, Hilo
Japanese New Year's Mochi (Good Luck) Rice Pounding - Island-wide

BIG ISLAND WEATHER

The Big Island's weather is a case of variety and extremes. The Big Island claims both the driest locality in the State as well as the wettest population center in the islands.

Hawai'i lies well within the belt of northeasterly trade winds generated by the semi-permanent Pacific high pressure cell to the northeast. The climate of the island is greatly influenced by terrain. Its outstanding features are the marked variations in rainfall by elevation and from place to place, the persistent northeasterly trade winds in areas exposed to them, and the equable year around temperatures in localities near sea level.

Over the island's east windward slopes, rainfall occurs principally in the form of showers within the ascending moist trade winds. Mean annual rainfall, except for the semi-sheltered Hamakua district, increases from 100 inches or more along the coasts to a maximum of over 300 inches at elevations of 2000-3000 ft. and declines to about 15 inches at the summits of Mauna Kea and Mauna Loa. In general, the southern and western leeward areas are sheltered from the trades by the high mountains and are therefore drier. Mean annual rainfall may range from 20-30 inches along the coasts to 120 inches at elevations of 2500-3000 ft.

DRESSING FOR THE WEATHER: Comfortable summer type wear is suitable all year round on the Big Island. Dress is casual. However, a warm sweater or jacket would be useful for cool evening breezes or for visits to cool areas like Volcanoes National Park or Waimea ranch country. And if you plan hiking excursions, you may find light raingear useful. For treks to Mauna Kea or Mauna Loa, resort wear is definitely out. It can snow at any time of the year on either mountain and very cold weather can be experienced at any time at high elevations. Appropriate dress is in order.

KOHALA AND KONA: The driest area on the Big Island, and in the State with an average annual rainfall of less than 10 inches, is the coastal strip just leeward of the southern portion of the Kohala Mountains and of the saddle between the Kohalas and Mauna Kea. This is the area surrounding Kawaihae Bay on the Kohala Coast. Not long ago, the Hawai'i State Planning and Economic Development Department did a "Sunshine Map" study and found that the Kohala Coast has the highest sunshine rating in the state - even higher than such noted resorts as Ka'anapali on Maui and Waikiki on O'ahu. Kohala also maintains a near constant 78 degrees F. the year around. The Kailua-Kona and Keauhou resort areas average about 20 inches of rainfall annually. With such consistent sunny dry weather it is easy to see why the Kona and Kohala areas have become such popular destinations.

HILO: And then we have Hilo. Poor Hilo! It has been the butt of more jokes about its rain than there are umbrellas to sell. It seems that down through the years, people have taken a special delight in maligning Hilo for its rather damp atmosphere. They make up stories about how you don't tan in Hilo, you rust! They even say it rains all the time in the City of Rainbows. That is definitely not true. There was one day, oh a couple of years ago, when it didn't rain at all.

All kidding aside, it does rain an awful lot in Hilo, more than any other population center in the Hawaiian archipelago. Within the city of Hilo average rainfall varies from about 130 inches a year near the shore to as much as 200 inches in mountain sections. The wettest part of the island, with a mean annual rainfall exceeding 300 inches, lies about 6 miles up-slope from the city limits. Rain falls about 280 days a year in the Hilo area. In fact, Hilo is recognized as the rainiest city in the United States by the U.S. Census Bureau's *County and City Data Book*. Hilo has the highest average annual rainfall, 128.15 inches, of any of the nation's cities with a population of 25,000 or more. Interestingly, Hilo's total rainfall in 1990 surpassed all previous records when 211.22 inches of rain were recorded. Needless to say, even Hiloans were in awe of Nature's abundance.

Auwe! With such a soggy reputation like that, one certainly doesn't need any more detractors. In fact, it really isn't as bad as one would think. Many of the showers are brief passing ones and according to statistics, three-quarters of Hilo's rain falls at night. Thus it doesn't spoil most daytime visitor activities. Also, the number of clear to partly sunny days far surpasses the number of totally cloudy-rainy days annually.

Another thing about Hilo's infamous rain is that it is equally distributed throughout the year. There is no distinct wet or dry season. Hilo's temperatures remain fairly constant also, averaging a high of 81 degrees F. and a low of 66 degrees F. the year round. And although the relative humidity in Hilo is in the moderate to high range as would be expected, the weather is seldom oppressive and uncomfortable due to the natural ventilation and cooling provided by the prevailing ocean breezes.

And like the Kona-Kohala climate that has provided such marvelous conditions for resorts and the visitor industry, Hilo's climate has created special conditions also. Only in Hilo and the surrounding area will you find the lush tropical beauty of the rainforest jungle, breathtaking waterfalls cascading down green gulches, and acres of gorgeous tropical flowers like anthuriums, orchids, bird-of-paradise, ginger, and others. The ample tropical rain makes Hilo and the windward side of the Big Island a real paradise. Even with its sodden reputation as a rainy old town, Hilo indeed is a special place for many people.

TRADE WINDS: Trade winds are an almost constant wind blowing from the northeast through the east averaging 5-15 mph and are caused by the Pacific anticyclone, a high pressure area. The cell remains fairly stationary in the summer (May through October) causing the trades to blow steadily 90% of the time bringing cooling relief for the generally warmer temperatures. In winter (November through April), interruptions diminish the winds constancy and they blow 40%-60% of the time with competing weather fronts, storms, etc.

KONA WEATHER: Hot, humid, and muggy weather is called Kona weather and is often due to an interruption of the trade winds. The trades are replaced by light variable winds and are most noticeable during the warmer summer months. Kona winds may also bring storm fronts and rain from the southwest, the opposite direction from which storms generally approach the islands. Kona storms are noted for their ferocity, bringing high winds, surf, and rain and have occasionally caused property damage.

HURRICANES: Hawai'i lies in the hurricane belt and is susceptible to these tropical cyclones from June through December. These storms carry severe winds of between 75 and 150 mph and are often marked by rain, thunder, and lightning. Most are spawned along the coast of Mexico and follow the trade winds in a westerly direction across the Pacific. Some are born close to the equator and move north. Since 1950, over a hundred hurricanes have been recorded in Hawaiian waters. Of these, only a few have passed nearby or directly struck parts of the Hawaiian Islands. Only Hurricane Dot in 1959 and Hurricane Iwa in 1982 did extensive damage and that was mostly confined to the island of Kaua'i and to a lesser extent on O'ahu.

TSUNAMIS

Hawai'i is susceptible to tsunamis or tidal waves. Over the last century and a half, nine major tsunamis have caused moderate to severe damage and numerous deaths along affected coastlines. Although some tidal waves are locally generated from earthquakes, most of Hawai'i's tidal wave threats originate in South America or Alaska's Aleutian Islands. On the Big Island, Hilo is particularly vulnerable to tsunamis due to the funnel shape of Hilo Bay allowing an already speeding tidal wave to concentrate its force upon reaching land. An Aleutian Islands tsunami in 1946 rolled into Hilo pushing the water to 10 meters above sea level in some places. The death toll reached 83 and property damage was extensive. In 1960, a Chilean generated tsunami struck Hilo at a speed of 65 kilometers per hour and wreaked havoc along Hilo's bayfront destroying a major residential and business section. The water rolled in 11 meters high and 61 people were killed. There have been a few tidal waves generated by Big Island earthquakes as well. There is a statewide Tsunami Warning System in place and the Hawai'i Civil Defense System also coordinates disaster programs. Warning sirens and TV-radio broadcasts indicate approaching danger around all the islands. If you are on a beach or low lying coastal area when you receive such a warning, you must immediately seek higher ground as far away from the coast as possible.

EARTHQUAKES

Because of its volcanic origins, earthquakes are part of Hawai'i's geosystem. Volcanic eruptions on the Big Island are often preceded and accompanied by earthquakes. Few of these are generally strong enough to be felt or cause any damage. Major earthquakes are the result of fault action. Some of these faults are on the ocean floor while others are volcano related. Volcanic earthquakes are caused when sections of a volcano's inner works shift prior to erupting. It is usually associated with the inflation or deflation of a lava reservoir beneath the mountain as the lava swells or drains away.

TROPICAL PHOTOGRAPHY

Most folks who come to Hawai'i to vacation bring a camera to record some of those memorable and exciting scenes and experiences to enjoy again when they get back home. If nothing else, they take a lot of pictures to show off to their friends and relatives and to help them relive their dream vacation in Hawai'i.

And among the exotic places around the world in which to practice travel photography, Hawai'i certainly ranks among the best for beauty, adventure, and cultural attraction. Your picture taking journey through Hawai'i will be greatly enhanced with an awareness of some special factors that affect photography in the tropics. Good travel photographs are the result of forethought, organization, and good judgement before and during the trip. For those contemplating some photography while in Hawai'i, this is a good time to discuss some ideas garnered from several years of work in travel-photojournalism in paradise. Regardless of whether you use a sophisticated SLR (single lens reflex) camera, a compact "point and shoot" automatic type camera, or an instant picture camera such as a Polaroid, a little careful thought and planning will help you get travel pictures of which you'll be proud. The end results will be memorable pictures that will allow you to relive again and again the adventure and excitement of your visit to Hawai'i.

EQUIPMENT: Before you leave home on your trip, you should be intimately familiar with your camera's basic operations. You should run through a roll or two of film just prior to your trip to make sure that all systems are go. Be familiar with all the settings on your camera and install a fresh set of batteries. The majority of camera failures are due to dead batteries. There's nothing worse than being in the field ready for that picture of a lifetime only to have your camera fail due to a $3 set of batteries. Take along an extra set as well.

If you are using a single lens reflex camera (Nikon, Canon, Pentax, Minolta, etc.) you have a choice of lenses for your particular equipment. The standard lens is the normal 50mm which is a general purpose lens for most photographic situations. For those situations where you need more horizontal depth and width, such as panoramic scenes, you will need a wide angle lens. These lenses range from very wide 13-20mm to more narrow scope 24-35mm. For candid portrait shots or scenes and action that are far away, you will need a telephoto lens. Telephoto lenses allow you to bring the scene or action closeup without moving closer to the subject. Telephotos are both medium, 85-105mm, and long range, 180mm to over 1000mm, in focal length. Zoom lenses cover several combined focal lengths, allowing one lens to replace several. There are wide angle zooms, 28-45mm to 43-86mm, and telephoto zooms ranging from 35-105mm to 360-1200mm. Closeup capability can also be achieved with an inexpensive set of screw-in closeup lenses which look very much like filters that fit over the front of a regular lens. Or you can invest in a macro lens built especially for extreme closeup work. For most practical purposes you'll probably find that a normal 50mm, a medium wide angle 24mm or a wide angle zoom, and a telephoto zoom of 75-200mm will cover most of your picture taking situations adequately. But, lens choice is a matter of what kind of photos you're after, personal taste, and budget.

FILM: There is a wide choice of films available. If you plan to shoot color - and what other way is there to capture the essence of Hawai'i? - you have a choice of color negative and color positive films. For snapshot prints to put in an album, you will want to choose a brand name film that ends with the suffix *-color*. These films produce negatives from which prints or enlargements are made. If you plan on projecting your photos using a slide projector, then you will want to use a brand name film with the suffix *-chrome*. These films produce a positive/-transparency image directly on the film, the so-called "what you see is what you get" image as you look through your camera's viewfinder. Films have varying

ASA/ISO ratings, or film speeds, for varied light conditions and applications. The newer color print films range from 100 up to 1000 for average daylight to dim low light conditions. For positive/transparency films, the ASA/ISO ratings range from 25 up to 400 for average to low light conditions. A good choice for all purposes would be a *-color* film rated at 100-200 and a *-chrome* film rated at 64-100. If you choose to shoot your pictures in black and white to make enlargements, a good choice would be ASA/ISO 100 or 400 speed film. These negative films will give good results with natural or artificial lighting. A final thought on film is in order. How much do you bring with you? Well, like everything else, film is more expensive in Hawai'i, probably about 25% more than on the US mainland. You'd be better off to bring your own supply, however, you'll have no problem in buying film once here. Compared to airfare, lodging, and meals, film is cheap, so load up and shoot away!

ACCESSORIES: For taking pictures in extremely low light situations include a flash unit in your equipment. Besides providing general lighting when the available natural lighting is insufficient, flash allows you to fill in and highlight shadow areas on otherwise normal subjects. Flash units for SLR cameras are inexpensive and easy to use. Many automatic compact cameras have built in flash units, virtually taking the guesswork out of flash photography.

The most frequently used filters are the UV (ultra violet) and Skylight. These filters are designed to cut haze and reduce blue tones in some scenes. Professional photographers often keep them on lenses permanently to provide protection for the lens surface. The filters require little exposure adjustment and if your camera has a through-the-lens meter it will adjust automatically. In tropical photography, the Polarizing filter helps darken blue sky, makes clouds stand out more dramatically, and most importantly reduces reflections and glares from bright shining surfaces such as glass, water, sand, etc. For sky scenes, the Polarizing filter must be used at right angles to the sun. Another way to achieve this effect, without a Polarizer, is to increase the ASA/ISO film speed setting of your camera. If you are using ASA 64 slide film, for example, increase the setting to ASA 80. This will allow the camera aperture to compensate its exposure accordingly. For black and white films, red, orange, or yellow filters also produce varying degrees of enhancement.

Other accessories you should have are a sturdy camera bag, a light-weight tripod for telephoto and closeup shots, a cable release, a can of compressed air for dust removal, a soft lens brush, liquid lens cleaner, and tissues. An optional item would be a lead-lined film bag for carrying your film through airport security x-ray machines. Better yet, to avoid the cumulative effect of airport x-rays which can damage films, request a visual inspection of your film and camera equipment as you pass through security checkpoints. Most security personnel will cooperate if you request a hand-inspection.

SHOOTING ON LOCATION: Once you are finally in Hawai'i on location, you can begin to take advantage of all its unique and wondrous natural and geographic features to produce some excellent photographs. The dazzling colors and contrasting scenes of tropical flowers, golden beaches, puffy white clouds, cobalt blue sky, mystic jungles, stark lavaflows, green hills, blue-green ocean, dramatic sunsets, and multi-ethnic peoples will provide plenty of opportunity for picture taking. And because Hawai'i's sun is very strong, especially during the hours it is directly overhead, there are deep shadows and bright glare that interfere with photography. If you are shooting in heavily shadowed areas, use your flash to fill in dark areas, especially on people's faces. Be aware of shadows creeping into the composition as you look through the viewfinder to compose your shot. Use your flash indoors as well as outdoors under the shade of trees or on your shaded hotel lanai and even in shady areas of attractions you visit. If you are shooting a sunset with people in the foreground facing the camera, use your flash again to fill in otherwise the people will appear as silhouettes.

SPECIAL FACTORS: In Hawai'i you will be faced with two climatic extremes that can be hazardous to photography: rain and hot sun. Depending on the season and locale, rain can be frequent and heavy. However, with adequate raingear and plastic camera covers you can still shoot pictures even in the rain. One good point about rainy pictures is that soft subtle lighting can create special effects on your subjects and give your pictures a different accent and mood. Rainy days can also cause you to look inside for interesting subjects you may otherwise pass up.

At the other extreme is the glaring hot sun. The usual mid-day tropical sun is harsh, brilliant, and bright. In this light, as mentioned earlier, heavy shadows almost always creep into photographs. Be aware of them and learn to compensate for them. If your camera has a built-in light meter, take a reading for both light and shadow areas of your scene and then average it out. Bracket your pictures one aperture stop above and below what the camera meter reads out to ensure that one of your photos will be perfect. Keep in mind that the early morning and early evening hours are best for picture taking because the light is usually soft, mellow, and golden, allowing dramatic picture opportunities.

Other potential problem sources for photographers in Hawai'i are the infamous three "S's:" sun, sand, and salt spray. Any one of these can wreak havoc with your camera and film. The sun produces heat very fast in Hawai'i, especially in enclosed locked cars where folks often leave cameras and film unattended for long hours. Too much heat can ruin the emulsions of your film and adversely affect your camera's mechanism. The car will actually act like an oven and "bake" your film and equipment. So avoid leaving your camera equipment and film in a closed up car in the hot sun.

Sand from the beach is another problem. Fine gritty sand can get into the camera's mechanism, on the mirror, and lens. Sand can scratch and damage very easily. Protect your camera when you're on the beach. Don't put it down in direct contact with sand.

Finally, the fine misty salt spray from ocean surf is very corrosive to camera bodies and lenses. After shooting on or near the beach and ocean, thoroughly clean your camera with a soft cloth, lens cleaner and tissues.

Hawai'i provides unlimited picture taking possibilities. Go after them wherever they may be. But remember to use good judgement and be aware of the special factors that affect photography in the tropics. As time goes by you will be glad that you took the time to think, plan, and organize properly for your photography before and during your visit to this splendorous land called Hawai'i.

WHERE TO STAY
WHAT TO SEE

INTRODUCTION

The Big Island has some 6800 hotel and motel rooms and 2100 condominium units available in rental programs. The hotel-motel room count includes standard resort and visitor center hotels as well as several small lodges, motels, inns, and bed and breakfast accommodations in outlying towns and villages in the country. The range includes inexpensive to very expensive, from simple rooms with a shared kitchen and cooking privileges, to plush suites with inclusive meal packages. The Big Island has three major visitor centers: the Kona Coast including Kailua-Kona and the Keauhou area, the Kohala Coast, and Hilo. Other accommodations are located in the Hamakua, North Kohala, Puna and Ka'u districts. This section contains a list of condominiums that are in rental programs as well as hotels and related accommodations. In addition, there is a section on park campgrounds and cabins.

HOW TO USE THIS CHAPTER: To make it easy to locate information on accommodations, the various properties are first indexed alphabetically following this introduction. The listings are then arranged by geographic area beginning with the Kona Coast (including both the Kailua-Kona and Keauhou areas), followed by the Kohala Coast, and then Hilo, and the outlying country areas of Hamakua, North Kohala, Puna and Ka'u. Each geographic section begins with a description of the area, sights to see, shopping information, and then a listing of the accommodations. For each there is the local address, telephone and/or toll free number, and booking or rental agent(s) handling units at that property.

The Big Island, as does the rest of Hawai'i, has a summer off season (low) and a winter peak season (high) that affects supply and demand in accommodations, etc. The off season (low) is generally May 1 to November 30 and the peak season (high) is from December 1 to April 30. Within the low season, there are also two periods that are traditionally quite slow for Hawai'i's visitor industry. These are the times from Easter to approximately June 1 and from Labor Day to December 1. These "slack" periods are good times to take advantage of discounts on hotel rooms, car rentals, etc. The off season usually brings lower prices, discounts, special rates and room-car packages while peak season demand will keep room rates at a premium at most hotels and condominiums. Hilo hotels are not as prone to fluctuations in seasonal demand for accommodations as are the Kona and Kohala area hotels. However, room rates may vary somewhat by high and low season. Check to see what rates apply when booking your reservations as many properties' high-low seasons vary slightly. For properties having high-low pricing, the rates are listed with a slash dividing them. The first price listed is the high season rate, the second price is the low season rate. Some have a flat year around rate so there is only one rate given.

Rates quoted for the hotels are the standard industry "rack rates" and most current available at the time of publication and are, of course, subject to change without notice. However, hotel "rack rates" are something that are seldom paid by guests since the majority of reservation bookings are done at discounted rates of one type or another. If you're doing your own booking, be sure to ask for the lowest possible rate quote or special discount being offered. A good travel agent can also assist in obtaining discounted rate quotes or specials. There are all sorts of special room/car packages, golf packages, tennis packages, honeymoon packages, "returning guest" packages, etc. So inquire before you confirm your rate. If you are a senior citizen, ask for "Senior Citizen Discounts," as more hotels and condos are offering such discounts for those 55 years and over.

Accommodation rates listed in this section are for double occupancy (2 people) unless otherwise specified. Additional persons are charged from $10-15 per night at most places except the first-class properties where the extra person rate may be from $25-35 per night. All properties have a swimming pool unless otherwise noted. Condos have kitchens and parking unless otherwise noted. The abbreviations o.f., o.v., g.v., and f.v. refer to oceanfront, oceanview, gardenview and fairway view units. Additional listing codes are as follows: S-Studio, BR-Bedroom, PH-Penthouse, KF-Kitchen Facilities, Condo-Condominium unit, Cott.-Cottage, (W)-Accommodate wheelchairs.

Note: All hotels, motels, inns, condominiums, etc. in Hawai'i will add on a 9% tax on all accommodations charges. This includes a 4% sales tax and 5% hotel room tax.

Hotels and condominium listings marked with a ★ indicate a property that is an exceptional value due to location, cleanliness, services and amenities available, and general comfort, and not necessarily luxury. In the "What to See and Do" sections, a ★ indicates a worthwhile attraction or activity.

GENERAL POLICIES: All hotels and bed & breakfast operations are identified as such, while all the rest are condominiums even though some don't use the term "condominium" in their name. Condominiums and rental agents usually require a reservation deposit equal to one or two night's rental to secure a confirmed reservation and some also require a security deposit. Some charge higher deposits during winter or peak season holidays like Christmas-New Year's. Generally a 30 day notice of cancellation is needed to receive a full refund although some charge a cancellation fee. Most condos and agents require payment in full either 30 days prior to or upon arrival and the majority *do not* accept credit cards. Hotels on the other hand almost always accept credit cards. Most condos also require a minimum stay of 3 nights and some have 5 and even 7 night minimums or longer in the winter and during peak holiday seasons. The peak winter season brings heavy demand for condo units and the restrictions, cancellation policies, and payment policies are much more stringent. It is not uncommon to book as much as two years in advance for the Christmas-New Year's season. If a condominium listing does not show a rental agent, you can address your correspondence to the manager. Some condo resident managers do not handle reservations and thus you should contact the rental agents listed for those properties. See the individual condo listings and/or the list of BOOKING AGENTS.

NOTE: The Big Island has experienced a housing shortage over the last few years, especially in the Kona and Kohala areas. Because of this the real estate market is in a very fluid state. This affects the availability of short term "vacation rental" units at condominiums as many are being changed to long term residential. Thus, the prices/rates for condo rentals in this section are subject to change at any time as are the availability of "vacation rentals" at any condominium.

ACCOMMODATIONS INDEX

A Bed at Baldy's B & B 77
Adrienne's B & B 70
Alii Villas 98
Aloha B & B 77
Aloha Sunny Branch 77
Arnott's Lodge B & B 75
Aston Royal Sea-Cliff Resort ... 98
Banyan Tree Condominium 98
Becky's B & B 80
Belle Vue B & B 71
Bougainville B & B 80
Carson's Volcano
   Cottage B & B 77
Casa De Emdeko 98
Chalet Kilauea B & B 77
Champagne Cove B & B 77
Country Club Hotel 131
Country Club Villas 99
Doc Boone's B & B 70
Dolphin Bay Hotel 131
Dragonfly Ranch 70
Durkee's Coffeeland B & B 70
Hale Honua Ranch 70
Hale Ho'onanea B & B 75
Hale Kai B & B 75
Hale Kai O Kona 99
Hale Kipa O Kiana B & B 78
Hale Kona Kai 99
Hale Ohia Cottage B & B ... 78,152
Hale O Panaewa B & B 76
Hale Paliku B & B 76
Hale Pohaku 99
Hale Wailea 71
Hale Waipio 72
Hamakua Hideaway 137
Hawai'i Country Cottage 72
Hawai'i Naniloa Hotel 131
Hawai'i Volcanoes B & B 78
Hawai'i Best B & B 72

Hilo Bay Hotel 131
Hilo Hawaiian Hotel 132
Hilo Hotel 131
Hilo Seaside Hotel 132
Holmes' Sweet Home B & B ... 76
Holua at Mauna Loa Village 99
Holualoa Inn B & B 70
Hotel Honoka'a Club 137
Hyatt Regency Waikoloa Hotel . 117
Hydrangea Cottage 78
Island's End B & B 72,141
Kahana Country Cottage 74
Kailua Bay Resort 100
Kailua Plantation House 71
Kalanikai Condominiums 100
Kamuela Inn 72
Kamuela's Mauna
   Kea View B & B 72
Kanaloa at Kona 100
Kealakekua Bay B & B 71
Keauhou Akahi 100
Keauhou Beach Hotel 100
Keauhou Kona
   Surf/Racquet Club 101
Keauhou Palena 101
Keauhou Punahele 102
Keauhou Resort Condominiums . 102
Kilauea Cabins 78
Kilauea Lodge B & B 78,152
King Kamehameha Kona
   Beach Hotel 102
Koa Lane Cottage 73
Kona Alii 102
Kona Bali Kai 102
Kona Bay Hotel 103
Kona B & B 71
Kona Billfisher Condominium .. 103
Kona By The Sea 103
Kona Coast Resort 103

WHERE TO STAY - WHAT TO SEE
Index

Kona Hilton Hotel 103
Kona Hotel 104
Kona Islander Inn 104
Kona Isle Condominium 104
Kona Luana 104
Kona Magic Sands 104
Kona Makai 105
Kona Mansions 105
Kona Nalu 105
Kona Onenalo 105
Kona Palms 105
Kona Plaza 105
Kona Reef 105
Kona Riviera Villa 106
Kona Seaside Hotel 106
Kona Surf Resort Hotel 106
Kona Tiki Hotel 106
Kona Village Resort 106
Kona West 107
Kona White Sands Hotel 107
Makai Hale 73
Malama Llama B & B 71
Malia Kai 108
Maluhia Hale 81
Manago Hotel 108
Mauna Kea Beach Hotel 117
Mauna Lani Bay Hotel/Condos . 118
Mauna Lani Point 119
Mauna Lani Terrace Condos . . . 119
Maureen's B & B 76
Merryman's B & B 71
Morningside B & B 76
Mountain Meadow
   Ranch B & B 73
My Island B & B 78
Orchid Land B & B 79
Our Place Papaikou's B & B . . . 74
Paauhau Plantation House 74
Paradise Place B & B 79

Parker Ranch Lodge 119
Puako Beach Apartments 119
Puu Manu Cottage 73
Rainforest Retreat B & B 79
Ritz-Carlton Mauna Lani 120
Royal Kahili Condominium . . . 108
Royal Waikoloan 120
Seamountain at
   Punalu'u-Colony I 157
Sea Village 108
Shirakawa Motel 157
Shores at Waikoloa 120
South Point B & B 80
Suds' Acres 74
The Country Goose B & B 79
The Guesthouse
   at Volcano B & B 79
The Log House Inn B & B 74
The Nutt House B & B 80
Third Voyage B & B 73
Three Bears B & B 71
Treetops B & B 79
Vista Waikoloa 121
Volcano B & B 79
Volcano Comfort B & B 80
Volcano House Inn 157
Volcano Vacations B & B . . 80,152
Waiakea Villas Hotel 132
Waikoloa Villas 121
Waipio Ridge Vacation Rentals . . 82
Waipio Tree House 137
Waipio Valley Hotel 138
Waipio Wayside B & B 74
White Sands Village 108
Waikii Cottage 73
Waimea Countree B & B 73
Waimea Garden Cottage 73
Wild Ginger Inn B & B 76
Wood Valley B & B 80

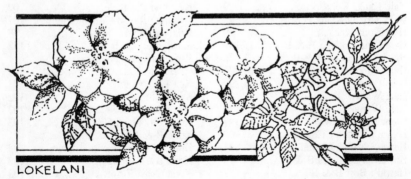

LOKELANI

68

BED AND BREAKFAST LODGING

Bed and Breakfast operations have expanded rapidly over the last couple of years on the Big Island. These popular accommodations are an alternative to the usual resort condominium and hotel room, and often less costly. B & B's, as they're often called, provide a range of accommodations from clean simple rooms to, in some cases, luxurious well-appointed suites. On the Big Island, B & B's offer the chance to stay in everything from a renovated 1930's-era sugar plantation home, a historic old missionary-era home, a log house in cool quiet upcountry forest land, ranch homes and cottages in Parker Ranch country, or a modern cedar mansion with lovely coastal views as well as more traditional family residences of Big Islanders. In most cases, B & B's provide visitors a more homey atmosphere and a chance to get to know local folks more personally. They usually include, as the name implies, a continental-style breakfast which varies with each individual operation. B & B's generally appeal to adventurous travelers who want a different lodging experience apart from the usual excitement of the hotel or resort center.

For directories, information and reservations at B & B operations in Hawai'i, contact the following reservations services:

All Islands B & B
823 Kainui Drive
Kailua, O'ahu, HI 96734
1-800-542-0344 or
(808) 263-2342

Bed & Breakfast Hawai'i
1105 Kuhio Highway #C19
Kapa'a, Kaua'i, HI 96746
1-800-733-1632 or
(808) 822-7771

B & B Honolulu
3242 Kaohinani Drive
Honolulu, HI 96817
1-800-288-4666 or
(808) 595-7533 (all islands)

B & B Pacific-Hawai'i
19 Kai Nani Place
Kailua, O'ahu, HI 96734
(808) 254-5030
(Private homes and cottages)

B & B Reservations
  and Vacation Rentals
1-800-347-6548 or
(808) 742-7187
(all islands in Hawai'i)

Go Native...Hawai'i B & B
65 Halaulani Place
P.O.Box 11418
Hilo, HI 96721
1-800-662-8483 (all islands)

Hawai'i's Best B & B
P.O.Box 563
Kamuela, HI 96743
1-800-262-9912, (808) 885-4550
FAX (808) 885-0550
(Big Island only)

Hawai'i Island B & B Association
P.O.Box 726
Volcano, HI 96785
(No phone-provides listing of member
B & B's on Big Island only)

My Island B & B
P.O.Box 100
Volcano, HI 96785
(808) 967-7110 (Big Island only)

Volcano Reservations
P.O.Box 998
Volcano, HI 96785
1-800-736-7140
(808) 967-7244 (Big Island only)

The following is a listing of individual B & B operations by geographic area:

Kona

Adrienne's B & B ★, R.R. 1, Box 8E, Captain Cook, HI 96704; (808) 328-9726. This Kona cedar home is located 18 miles south of Kailua-Kona on the slopes above the Pu'uhonua O Honaunau National Historic Park, the old Hawaiian place of refuge. The home has an unobstructed view of the ocean and Kona Coast easily seen from the comfort of the lanai hot tub. Accommodations include an oceanview room with king and queen beds, garden room with double and queen beds, and main level room with queen bed. All guests have kitchen and hot tub privileges and each room has color TV/VCR. *Rates: Standard $50-60, Deluxe $70, Weekly $420-490, Monthly $1800-2100, Extra person $15*

Doc Boone's B & B, P.O.Box 666, Kealakekua, HI 96750; (808) 323-3231. This home sits amidst tropical fruit trees above the quiet upcountry Kona town of Captain Cook. It's a short drive to beaches, shopping, restaurants, resorts and Kailua-Kona. 3 rooms and 1 self-contained apt. unit. *Rates: $60 and up nightly.*

Dragonfly Ranch, P.O. Box 675, Honoaunau, HI, 96726; 1-800-487-2159, (808) 328-2159/328-9570. This private country estate is only three minutes from Honaunau Bay on Highway 160, about 20 miles south of Keahole Airport, Kona. The ranch is situated just above the Pu'uhonua O Honaunau National Historic Park. The main house offers two bedrooms with indoor bath and outdoor shower; there is an outdoor waterbed suite with private indoor room, kitchenette and bath; also a separate redwood cottage. Other features include fireplace, massage chair, cable TV/VCR, sundeck and nice views of Kona Coast.
Rates: Standard $70 nightly, Suites $100-140 nightly, Extra person $10

Durkee's Coffeeland, P.O.Box 596, Holualoa, HI 96725; (808) 322-9142. This mountain side home nestles among coffee trees, palms, ferns, tropical fruit trees and flowers. It is in the heart of macadamia nut and coffee orchard country seven miles south of Kailua-Kona above scenic Keauhou Bay. Three rooms and one self-contained apartment available. Lanai views of the beautiful Kona Coast. Enjoy fresh Kona coffee from their own trees and roaster. *Rates: $55-75 nightly.*

Hale Honua Ranch, P.O.Box 347, Kealakekua, HI 96750; (808) 328-8282. This is a private estate with panoramic views of ocean and rolling hills. Tennis, basketball, volleyball, badminton, pool and croquet available. Room for up to 14 people. Facilities include bar-be-que, covered picnic area and the great Hawaiian outdoors. *Rates: $50 and up nightly.*

Holualoa Inn B & B ★, P.O. Box 222, Holualoa, Kona, HI 96725; Phone/FAX (808) 324-1121; reservations through Hawaii's Best B&Bs, 1-800-262-9912, (808) 885-4550 or FAX (808) 885-0550. This attractive cedar home is on a 40 acre estate, a former cattle ranch and coffee farm, in the small, quiet village of Holualoa on the cool slopes of Mt. Hualalai in Kona. The house features a rooftop gazebo providing magnificent views of the surrounding countryside, the Kona Coast, and incredible sunsets. There is a very quiet, relaxing atmosphere. Three guest rooms are available, all with private bathroom and Polynesian/Oriental themed decor. Minimum stay 2 days. *Rates: Deluxe $100-150 nightly.*

Kailua Plantation House ★, 75-5948 Alii Drive, Kailua-Kona, HI 96740; (808) 329-3727; reservations through Hawaii's Best B&Bs, 1-800-262-9912, (808) 885-4550 or FAX (808) 885-0550. This is a luxurious upscale B&B accommodation with individually decorated ocean front or ocean view suites with private lanai. Outdoor pool and spa overlook the ocean. Located within walking distance of Kailua-Kona town. Five rooms available, all have private bath, TV, refrige, phone, etc. *Rates: $120-175 nightly.*

Kealakekua Bay B & B, P.O.Box 1412, Kealakekua, HI 96750; (808) 328-8150. This beach area home has two rooms available that will sleep four people. Rooms have refrige, toaster oven, cable TV, ceiling fans and phones. Home overlooks Kealakekua Bay, mountain and Captain Cook monument. Five minutes to beach. *Rates: $65-75 nightly.*

Kona B & B, 78-6934 Walua Road, Kailua-Kona, HI 96745-2302; (808) 324-0627 or toll free 1-800-657-7704. This operation offers a secluded, quiet, tropical setting with pool, hot-tub, private baths and entrances and cool elevation with 180 degree sunset and ocean views just minutes from beaches and shopping. Room/car packages available; free airport pickup. *Rates: $40 and up nightly.*

Malama Llama B & B ★, located 15 minutes from Kailua-Kona at the 2,000 ft. elevation on Mt. Hualalai. Reservations through Hawai'i's Best B&Bs, 1-800-262-9912, (808) 885-4550. This is a secluded 5-acre farm with a garden-level apartment with private patio. Nice sunsets over the Kona Coast while llamas graze nearby. Sleeps up to five. *Rates: $75 nightly, $15-25 extra person.*

Merryman's B & B ★, P.O.Box 474, Kealakekua, HI 96750; 1-800-545-4390, (808) 323-2276. This is a hillside upcountry home cooled by Kona breezes. The spacious rooms are beautifully and comfortably furnished and offer either ocean or garden view. Two rooms share a bath, one suite has private bath. Large open living room and front-back lanais provide lots of room. Large open yard has lots of tropical plants and greenery. *Rates: $50-80 nightly.*

Three Bears' B & B, 72-1001 Puukala St., Kailua-Kona, HI 96740; (808) 325-7563. Nice ocean views from the lanai of this cedar home. Located above Kona's Keahole Airport at 1600' elevation. Rooms have private baths, cable TV, micro oven, refrige and coffee maker. *Rates: $50-55 nightly, $10 extra person.*

Kohala

Belle Vue B & B ★, reservations through Hawai'i's Best B&Bs, 1-800-262-9912, (808) 885-4550 or FAX (808) 885-0550. This is a spacious two-story cottage bordering open pasturelands of famous Parker Ranch in Waimea. There is a complete kitchen and cozy fireplace. Sleeps four; 3-night minimum stay. Walking distance to restaurants and shopping. *Rates: $115 nightly, $15 extra person.*

Hale Wailea ★, reservations through Hawai'i's Best B&Bs, 1-800-262-9912, (808) 885-4550 or FAX (808) 885-0550. This is a private home on a beach along the Kohala Coast near the luxury resorts. Located just 15 minutes from upcountry Waimea and restaurants/shopping. Sleeps up to four; 3-night minimum stay. *Rates: $150 nightly, $20 extra person.*

Hale Waipio ★, reservations through Hawai'i's Best B&Bs, 1-800-262-9912, (808) 885-4550 or FAX (808) 885-0550. This country home is just a minute's walk from Waipio Valley Lookout on the Hamakua Coast and has expansive ocean views. Surrounded by pastures and sheltered by trees, the 2BR home has kitchen, fireplace and deck. Just 20 minutes from Waimea restaurants/shopping. Sleeps six; 3-night minimum stay. *Rates: $110 nightly, $20 extra person.*

Hawai'i Country Cottage ★, reservations through Hawai'i's Best B&Bs, 1-800-262-9912, (808) 885-4550 or FAX (808) 885-0550. This apartment is an attached wing of a country home and has its own entry, fireplace, paned windows and room to sleep four. *Rates: $80 nightly, $15 extra person.*

Hawai'i's Best B & B ★, P.O. Box 563, Kamuela, HI 96743; (808) 885-4550, U.S. 1-800-262-9912, FAX (808) 885-0550. This booking service caters exclusively to upscale B&B's on the Big Island. The island's best lodgings, ranging from the most traditional host-home rooms to private country cottages, have been selected for inclusion in the "Hawai'i's Best" collection. Each home or cottage has been chosen for its distinctive personality, inspired attention to detail, and for the warm hospitality offered by its hosts. Each offers a beautiful setting, tasteful and comfortable accommodations, attentive service and a relaxed atmosphere. Host accommodations are available around the island in Kamuela, Hilo, Volcano, Kona and on the Kohala Coast. *Daily rates range from $65-150 double, with weekly rates available at most properties.*

Island's End Bed & Breakfast, P.O.Box 1234, Kapa'au, HI 96755; (808) 889-5265. This is an old plantation era home situated in a secluded well-landscaped area. Comfortable accommmodations include two rooms/share bath and a detached studio. Near King Kamehameha' statue and birthplace.
Rates: $50 nightly, kids under age-12 free.

Kamuela Inn ★, P.O. Box 1994, Kamuela, HI 96743, (808) 885-4243, FAX (808) 885-8857. This country inn features 31 comfortable standard and kitchenette rooms all with TV. A new Mauna Kea Wing opened a last year added several comfortable, spacious, well-decorated rooms, two executive suites and a bright breakfast bar room. The original wing's rooms are smaller and a little more simple but very well kept and clean. Located in a quiet cool setting across from Edelweiss Restaurant off Highway 19 in Kamuela town. Near shopping, restaurants, area attractions, etc. and only 15 miles from Kohala Coast resorts and beaches. Reservations should be made well in advance.
Standard $54, Deluxe $67,
Suite (max 3) with kitchen $83, Suite (max 4) with kitchen $93,
Penthouse Suite $93.
Mauna Kea Wing: King Beds $72-79, Two Twins $72, Executive Suites $165.

Kamuela's Mauna Kea View B & B, P.O.Box 6375, Kamuela, HI 96743; (808) 885-8425. This home offers wide open pastoral ranchland views backdropped with Mauna Kea. Rooms include a 2BR unit with living room and kitchen and two separate rooms with shared bath. All have queen beds, color TV and phone. Convenient to area attractions and Kohala Coast resorts.
Rates: $65 nightly, $15 extra person.

Koa Lane Cottage ★, reservations through Hawai'i's Best B&Bs, 1-800-262-9912, (808) 885-4550 or FAX (808) 885-0550. This is a one bedroom cottage with European country decor set in the open pasturelands of Parker Ranch with great views of Mauna Kea. Sleeps four; 2-night minimum stay. *Rates: $80 nightly, $15 extra person.*

Makai Hale ★, reservations through Hawai'i's Best B&Bs, 1-800-262-9912, (808) 885-4550 or FAX (808) 885-0550. This country home is near Kawaihae on the Kohala Coast and offers consistently sunny weather. Four miles to area beaches. The two guest rooms have access to pool/jacuzzi deck. Sleeps five; 2-night minimum stay. *Rates: $65-95 nightly*

Mountain Meadow Ranch B & B ★, P.O.Box 1361, Kamuela, HI 96743; 1-800-535-9376, (808) 775-9376. Located halfway between Kona and Hilo in romantic Ahualoa above Honoka'a. Scenic pastures and majestic trees provide lots of country charm and atmosphere on this seven-acre estate. Enjoy area scenics like Waipio Valley, Parker Ranch, Manua Kea and Waimea town. There are 2 bedrooms, which can sleep up to three people each and a sofa sleeper in the outer room. TV/VCR, sauna, spa (solar powered). *Rates: $55 nightly, $350 weekly.*

Puu Manu Cottage ★, reservations through Hawai'i's Best B&Bs, 1-800-262-9912, (808) 885-4550 or FAX (808) 885-0550. This is a secluded country cottage located in open pastureland 3 miles from Waimea town. A converted horse barn, it has a cozy fireplace and French doors that open to large deck and views of Mauna Kea. A peaceful and romantic getaway. Sleeps four; 3-night minimum stay. *Rates: $105 nightly, $15 extra person.*

Third Voyage B & B, P.O. Box 2155, Kamuela, HI 96743; (808) 885-6858. This operation offers Hawaiian hospitality in an authentic early New England dwelling. Located in the hills above Kamuela town in Parker Ranch country. The home has quiet privacy of a country setting and a lovely view of Mauna Kea. Guests can relax in the cool evening country air by the fireplace and enjoy morning breakfast with fresh Kona coffee. It is only 20 minutes to the Kohala Coast beaches and 1 hour to Kailua-Kona or Hilo. Accommodations are two bedrooms, one queen bed and the other twin beds. *Rates: $45 nightly.*

Waikii Cottage ★, reservations through Hawai'i's Best B&Bs, 1-800-885-4550 or FAX (808) 885-0550. This country cottage is in a rural area at the 4,700 ft. elevation on Mauna Kea, 12 miles from Waimea on Highway 20. A cozy fireplace takes the chill out of the brisk mountain air and lovely English-style gardens grace the grounds. Sleeps four; 3-night minimum stay. *Rates: $95 nightly, $25 extra person.*

Waimea Countree B & B ★, reservations through Hawai'i's Best B&Bs, 1-800-262-9912, (808) 885-4550 or FAX (808) 885-0550. This private home is located in Waimea town and has two bedrooms, each with private bath. Guests enjoy landscaped grounds and heirloom koa furniture. Accommodates four. *Rates: $60 nightly.*

Waimea Gardens Cottage ★, reservations through Hawai'i's Best B&Bs, 1-800-262-9912, (808) 885-4550 or FAX (808) 885-0550. This streamside cottage has two private units on 1 1/2 acres. The cottage's Kohala and Waimea Wings have antique furnishings, patio French doors and decor which lend a pleasant country atmosphere. Each unit sleeps three; 3-night minimum stay. *Rates: $90-95 nightly, $15 extra person.*

North Hilo - Hamakua Coast

Kahana Country Cottage, P.O.Box 1435, Honoka'a, HI 96727; (808) 775-0220. This is a spacious 2BR cottage, one queen bed and two twins sleep four, with full kitchen, fireplace, deck with ocean and mountain views. Located on the rural Hamakua Coast three miles above Honoka'a town.
Rates: $110 nightly, $90 two or more nights.

Our Place-Papaikou's B & B ★, P.O.Box 469, 3 Mamalohoa Highway, Papaikou, HI 96781; 1-800-245-5250, (808) 964-5250. Located four miles north of Hilo on Highway 19. There are 4 bedrooms in a cedar home. Common open lanai to each bedroom, overlooks a stream and tropical vegetation; also has library, fireplace, grand piano, cable TV/VCR. *Rates: $45-65 nightly.*

Paauhau Plantation House ★, P.O.Box 1375, Honoka'a, HI 96727; (808) 775-7222. This is an old sugar plantation manager's estate set amid rolling yards, gardens and lovely trees all surrounded by acres of sugar cane lands. There are three self-contained cottages: Hale Kona and Hale Mauna Kea sleep 4 each and Hale Hilo sleeps up to 6. The rambling main house has a Master Suite that sleeps 4 and two Garden Rooms that sleep 2 each. *Rates: Garden Rooms $105, Master Suite $140, Hale Kona (max 4) $75, Hale Mauna Kea (max 4) $90, Hale Hilo (max 6) $90, Extra person $15.*

Suds' Acres, P.O.Box 722, Paauilo, HI 96776; (808) 776-1611/776-1592. This is a guest cottage on a macadamia nut farm at 1800' elevation on the slopes of Mauna Kea with a Hamakua Coast view. The 2BR cottage has bath, kitchen and living room and is just 5 miles from Honoka'a and 20 miles from Waimea. Sleeps up to 5 people. *Rates: $55 nightly, $10 extra person.*

The Log House Inn B & B ★, P.O. Box 1495, Honoka'a, HI 96727; reservations through Hawai'i's Best B&B's 1-800-262-9912, (808) 885-4550 or FAX (808) 885-0550. This rustic log-construction country inn is located in the cool climate of Ahualoa three miles from Honoka'a town on the Hamakua Coast. It is ten miles from Kamuela and in the heart of the island's ranch country. This elegant country lodge is for guests seeking a different Hawaiian experience, away from the usual hotel/tourist scene. The inn has five comfortable and tastefully-furnished bedrooms, two with private baths, and all are attractively furnished. Guests will enjoy the living room complete with fireplace for those cool ranch country evenings and an upstairs library with TV.
Double, queen bed/share bath $45, $295/week, $1000/month
Double, 2 twin or 1 king bed/private bath $55, $360/week, $1250/month
Master room $65, $425/week, $1500/month

Waipio Wayside B & B, P.O. Box 840, Honoka'a, HI 96727; 1-800-833-8849, (808) 775-0275. This is a refurbished 1938-era sugar plantation home. There are lots of tropical plants around the grounds and deck-gazebo for relaxation. There

are five bedrooms: Moon Room with full-size bed and share bath; Plantation Room with twin beds and share bath; Chinese Room with full-size bed and half-bath; Garden Room with full-sized bed and share bath; Bird's Eye Room with full-size bed and private bath. Easy access to Waipio Valley, Waipio Ridge Walk, Kalopa Park, the Hamakua Coast and Kamuela.
Rates: $50-85 nightly, Extra person $15.

South Hilo - Hilo Town

Arnott's Lodge B & B, 98 Apapane Road, Hilo, HI 96720; (808) 969-7097, FAX (808) 961-9638. This lodge utilizes former apartment units in a B & B operation and is located in the Keaukaha area of Hilo near the beach parks. Private and bunk rooms share a common kitchen and TV room. Some units have private kitchen and bath.
Two bedroom with kitchen/bath $80 night.
Double private room $36 night; single private room $26 night.
Bunk rooms $15 per person per night.

Hale Ho'onanea, 159 Halai Street, Hilo, HI 96720; (808) 961-5446. This Hilo hale is located above town with Hilo Bay and cityscape views. Each room has ocean or garden view, private bath and entry. There is also a sitting room with TV/VCR and library. *Rates: $70/night, $65 2 or more nights, $10 extra person.*

Hale Kai ★, 111 Honolii Pali, Hilo, HI 96720; (808) 935-6330; reservations through Hawaii's Best B&Bs, 1-800-262-9912, (808) 885-4550 or FAX (808) 885-0550.. This home perches on a bluff facing the ocean and Hilo Bay just two miles from downtown Hilo. There are four rooms with private baths and a guest cottage. All rooms face the ocean except the loft room which has a side ocean view. Guests enjoy the pool, jacuzzi and patio. Rooms have king or queen beds and cable TV. Cottage has living room, kitchenette, queen bed, bath, TV. Easy access to area attractions. *Rates: Rooms $75-85/night (3 night minimum), cottage $95/night (5 night minimum), $15 extra person.*

POINSETTIA

Hale O Panaewa, HCR 1, Box 1-A, Hilo, HI 96720; (808) 959-7432/966-7455. This secluded 1BR guest cottage is situated on a nine acre macadamia nut orchard just four miles from Hilo and 25 miles from Volcanoes National Park. Enjoy cable TV, fireplace, king bed and petite kitchen. *Rates: $75 nightly.*

Hale Paliku, 40 Hina Street, Hilo, HI 96720; (808) 969-7153, reservations through Hawaii's Best B&Bs, 1-800-262-9912, (808) 885-4550 or FAX (808) 885-0550. This is a 1930's era home just three blocks from downtown Hilo and two blocks above historic Lyman Museum. The living room offers a nice view of Hilo Bay and town area. Two guest rooms are available. The Mauka (mountainside) room has two twin beds while the Makai (oceanside) room has a king bed. Rooms have a shared bath; linens provided. Easy access to Hilo's restaurants, shopping and attractions. *Rates: Mauka room $50 nightly, Makai room $60 nightly; both rooms $90 nightly.*

Holmes' Sweet Home B & B, 32 Kahoa Road, Hilo, HI 96720; (808) 961-9089. This home is located on the cliffs of Alae Point overlooking Hilo Bay just four miles north of Hilo. There are two rooms, one with twin beds and one with a queen. Both rooms have private entry but share a bath. Shared guest refrige on lanai. *Rates: $55 nightly, $50 for 3 or more nights.*

Maureen's B & B ★, 1896 Kalanianaole, Hilo, HI 96720; (808) 935-9018. This lodging is the old Saiki family mansion (c. 1932) located in the Keaukaha area of Hilo, opposite James Kealoha Beach Park some four miles from town. It's located just past the Mauna Loa Shores condo highrise. The home is lovely redwood and cedar finished with a huge open-beam cathedral ceiling in the living room. Arched doorways and windows give this home a touch of New England. The home has dual staircases winding up to open balconies and guest rooms. Quaint antique furniture pieces, bookcases and artwork make this inviting lodging seem almost like a gallery. Five guest rooms accommodate 2 singles and 4 doubles, a total of 10 guests. With the beach right across the street, swimming, snorkeling and sunning are steps away. There is also cable TV/VCR. Children under 5 years old not accepted due to high stairs and balcony areas. *Rates: $50 nightly.*

Morningside B & B, 486-B Akolea Road, Hilo, HI 96720; (808) 961-3577. Located in the foothills of Hilo, this home has 1BR with private bath, TV, VCR and refrige. Just 15 minutes from Hilo Airport and a short drive to downtown Hilo restaurants, shops and attractions. The Hamakua Coast, flower farms and Volcanoes National Park within easy driving distance.
Rates: $45 nightly, $10 extra person.

Wild Ginger Inn, 100 Puueo Street, Hilo, HI 96720; 1-800-882-1887, (808) 935-5556. Strictly for budget travelers, this old inn dates from 1947 when it was the Palm Terrace Hotel and more recently the Lanikai Hotel. Over the years the old place faded and grew a bit moldy. A coat of bright tropical pink paint has made the wood-frame building stand out. The 40 or so rooms provide only simple spartan accommodations, nothing fancy, great for budget travelers. Coin-operated laundry machines are available. Conveniently located just across the Wailuku River two blocks from downtown Hilo. *Rates: $39-59 nightly.*

Puna

A Bed at Baldy's B & B, P.O.Box 1324, Pahoa, HI 96778; (808) 965-7015. This home has a tropical garden setting and fresh fruit comes right from the garden. There are two spacious guest rooms available. Hosts are knowledgeable about the local area. Most recent volcanic activity is just 8 miles away.
Rates: $40 nightly, $10 extra person, but kids are free.

Aloha B & B, 13-3591 Luana, Leilani Estates, HI 96778; (808) 965-9898. This Hawaiian country home is located between Lava Tree Park and the Kalapana area near recent volcanic activity. The units are equipped with queen bed, refrige, coffeemaker, etc. It's a peaceful, quiet acreage nicely landscaped and has a large covered courtyard and pool. *Rates: $65 nightly.*

Aloha Sunny Branch, 13-1139 Leilani Avenue, Pahoa, HI 96778; (808) 965-7516. This is a completely self-contained 1 BR cottage with full bath and kitchen in the quiet Leilani Estates area located about 20 minutes from Hilo Airport. Sleeps up to 3 people. *Rates: $60 nightly.*

Carson's Volcano Cottage B & B, P.O.Box 503, Volcano, HI 96785; 1-800-845-LAVA, (808) 967-7683. Accommodations at this quiet secluded location include one studio cottage and a three room-cottage. All have private bath, entrances and decks, and two have kitchenettes. Electric blankets and a heater are provided for cool Volcano evenings. Room decor reflects Polynesian, Oriental, Country and Southwest themes. A hot tub on the main house deck is available for all guests. Easy access to national park activities, golf course, restaurants. Deposit required to confirm reservation. *Rates: $50-75 nightly.*

Chalet Kilauea at Volcano B & B, P.O.Box 998, Volcano, HI 96785; 1-800-937-7786 or (808) 967-7786. This home is located on Wright Road in Volcano. Choose from rooms inspired by Pacific, African and European themes, a Treehouse suite or three separate nearby cottages: Ohia Holiday Cottage, Hapu'u Forest Cabin and Hoku Hawaiian House which sleep up to 6 people. Relax in the hot tub, enjoy the fireplace, peruse the library and wake up to a gourmet breakfast in the art deco dining room. The home is at the cool 3800 ft. elevation and just minutes away from Hawai'i Volcanoes National Park, village store and restaurants. Parle francais.
Rates: $75 nightly, Treehouse Suite $95 nightly, cottages $65-100 nightly.

Champagne Cove at Kapoho Beach, 1714 Lei Lehua Street, Hilo, HI 96720; (808) 959-4487. This home is located at Kopoho Beach in the quiet secured Lyman Subdivision 45 minutes south of Hilo. This is a private home consisting of two 3 BR units, one upstairs and one down. Suitable for a couple or larger group. Fully furnished kitchen with linens; TV. There is a large, heated private pool with two shallow areas for toddlers or older persons. The beach is black lava rock and black sand. There is a warm tide pool in the ocean, sheltered from the surf. Whales are often seen offshore in winter. Enjoy swimming, snorkeling and shore fishing. Minimum of one week stay and deposit required.
Rates: $75 nightly, $10 extra person.

Hale Kipa O Kiana, RR2 Box 4874, Kalapana Shores, HI 96778; (808) 965-8661. The beach house has two guest rooms with private entries. Both rooms have ocean views and use of a guest kitchen and healing/massage room. Decorated in simple Hawaiiana style. Lumi Ahi room has in-room sink with bath adjoining healing room and has a double bed. Lumi Kai room has full bath and direct access to kitchen with one double and one twin bed. *Rates: Lumi Ahi $50 nightly, $250 weekly; Lumi Kai $60 nightly, $300 weekly*

Hale Ohia Cottage, P.O.Box 599, Volcano, HI 96785, (808) 967-7986. This country cottage offers 3 BR and sleeps up to 5 people. There is a full kitchen, large living room and one tub-shower bath. Bedrooms have 1 double, 2 singles and a sleeping punee (sofa) in living room. A large covered deck has table, chairs and barbeque for cookouts. Located one mile from national park entrance, near hiking trails, picnic areas, golf course, volcano observatory, etc.
Rates: $50 nightly, $300 weekly, 2 day minimum .

Hawai'i Volcanoes B & B, P.O. Box 28, Volcano, HI 96785, on Kilauea Road; (808) 967-7591/967-8662. This operation is centered in Hale Kilauea. The home is located in the heart of Volcano Village surrounded by the quiet serenity of towering pines and ohia trees. Close by are the entrance to Hawai'i Volcanoes National Park, park attractions and the visitors center, country stores and restaurants. The guest rooms are furnished with a king-size bed or two full-size beds and private bathroom. One room can accommodate four persons comfortably. Relax in the evening in front of a crackling fireplace after a day's outing to area attractions. Golf, orchid gardens, hiking and helicopter rides are easily accessible. Deposit required. *Rates: $65 nightly, $15 extra person.*

Hydrangea Cottage ★, reservations through Hawai'i's Best B&Bs, 1-800-262-9912, (808) 885-4550 or FAX (808) 885-0550. This country cottage is on a 3-acre estate in the Volcano forestlands landscaped with pink and blue hydrangeas (summer blooms) and other plants. The cottage has fireplace, full kitchen and sleeps four. Minimum stay of 2 nights. *Rates: $95 nightly, $15 extra person.*

Kilauea Cabins, P.O.Box 605, Volcano, HI 96785, (808) 967-7448. There are four cabins available each with private bath, refrige, toaster oven and coffeemaker. Two units have complete kitchens. *Rates: $55-65 nightly.*

Kilauea Lodge B & B ★, P.O. Box 116, Volcano, HI 96785; (808) 967-7366. A rustic old YWCA camping lodge and dormitory built in 1938 offers luxurious accommodations and an excellent restaurant with a full American-Continental dinner menu Tuesdays through Sundays. Set amidst the quiet cool country air of Volcano Village near Hawai'i Volcanoes National Park headquarters and visitors center. A new building set in the lush forest near the main lodge provides several comfortable beautifully decorated rooms with private baths. The main lodge offers rooms with private baths and fireplaces. Guests have breakfast in the dining room while enjoying the crackling warmth of the "Friendship Fireplace."
Rates: $75 and up nightly; a separate cottage is $95 per night

My Island B & B ★, P.O. Box 100, Volcano, HI 96785; (808) 967-7216/967-7110, FAX (808) 967-7719. This secluded operation is located in the pleasant cool climate of Volcano Village, not far from Hawai'i Volcanoes National Park visitors center. The house is a historic century-old missionary-style home set amidst a rambling botanical garden and fern forest jungle. The grounds have a fine collection of exotic plants from around the world. Rooms are neat, comfortable, and cozy with various bed arrangements: singles, doubles, triples, and families. Color TV and a library of Hawaiiana are available for entertainment. All the mac nuts you can eat. *Rates: $30-70 nightly.*

Orchid Land B & B, SR-5614, Keaau, HI 96749; (808) 966-7287. This is a solar-powered 4,000 sq. ft. country home with 4 spacious bedrooms, private baths, pool table and ping-pong. Quiet setting off the main highway and one mile from convenience store, midway between Hilo and the Kalapana area. *Rates: $50/night.*

Paradise Place B & B, HCR 9558, Keaau, HI 96749-9318; (808) 966-4600. This home is in rural setting 1/2 mile from the ocean with views of Mauna Kea, the steaming volcano and tropical gardens. Rooms have private entrances and baths, kitchen with refrige, washer/dryer, TV room, pation and hammock. Centrally located to Volcanoes National Park and Hilo area attractions. *Rates: $55 nightly, $10 extra person. Stay six nights, get seventh night free.*

Rainforest Retreat, HCR 5655, Keaau, HI 96749; (808) 966-9671/966-7712, FAX (808) 966-6898. This private home is surrounded by native ohia forest, orchids and horse pastures. A Garden Studio has private entry and bath, king bed, TV, kitchenette and laundry facilities. The Ohia House is a separate cottage with a king and queen beds, TV, deck hot tub, etc. Located just off Highway 130 and 20 minutes from Hilo. *Rates: $55-75 nightly, $10 extra person.*

The Country Goose, P.O.Box 597, Volcano, HI 96785; 1-800-238-7101, (808) 967-7759. This home has 1BR with private bath and entry, king size bed and double futon quilt. Electric baseboard and heat-electric blankets take the chill off the crisp Volcano air. Very peaceful and quiet setting. *Rates: $60-65 nightly.*

The Guesthouse at Volcano, P.O.Box 6, Volcano, HI 96785; (808) 967-7775. This rustic home in the quiet cool fern forest is a mile off the Volcano Highway and three miles from the national park entrance. There is room to sleep six, 2 twins and a queen upstairs and a double sofa bed downstairs. Full kitchen, phone, TV, electric heaters, linens, etc. *Rates: $60 nightly, $10 extra person.*

Treetops B & B, SR 4638, Keaau, HI 96749; (808) 966-6327. This large two-story house has ample parking underneath and provides wide garden and ocean views. Close to Highway 11 and attractions such as Lava Tree Park, Volcanoes National Park, Nani Mau Gardens, etc. 2 guest rooms share a bath. *$45-65 nightly.*

Volcano B & B, P.O. Box 22, Volcano, HI 96785; 1-800-733-7713, (808) 967-7779; FAX (808) 967-7619. This is a peaceful country home located in the heart of cool lush Volcano Village, a mile from the entrance and visitors center of Hawai'i Volcanoes National Park. The house provides three single/double rooms with shared bath. The renovated 1935-vintage three story home is on 3/4 acre landscaped site with fireplace, sunroom, reading room, piano, cable TV/VCR; bicycles available. Access to national park provides year around hiking, biking, sightseeing and other recreational activities. Near village stores and restaurants. *Rates: $45-55 nightly, $10 extra person.*

Volcano Comfort, P.O.Box 605, 3753 Ala Ohia Street, Volcano, HI 96785-0605; (808) 967-7448. This 2BR cottage is located in a quiet secluded garden setting surrounded by tropical rain forest. Completely furnished with private bath, full kitchen, fireplace, and more; up to 6 guests. *Rates: $65/night, $10 extra person.*

Volcano Vacations, P.O.Box 608, Kailua-Kona, HI 96745, (808) 325-7708. This operation offers a 2 BR/1 bath cottage in the cool and quiet Volcano area. The cottage has sauna room, fireplace, fully equipped kitchen, washer-dryer and a 1/2 acre yard. Cottage can sleep four people. Guests can play golf at nearby Volcano golf course, hike Volcanoes National Park trails and take in all the scenic splendor of the area plus enjoy the cool crisp climate. One day's rate required for deposit within 10 days to confirm reservation. *$70 nightly, $430 weekly, $1290 monthly.*

Ka'u

Becky's B & B, P.O.Box 593, Naalehu, HI 96772; (808) 929-9690. This is a fifty year old plantation home in the southernmost community of the USA. Green sand and black sand beaches nearby, South Point and near Volcanoes National Park. Located halfway between Hilo and Kona in the rural Ka'u countryside.
One large room with two double beds and private bath, two other rooms with one queen bed, share bath. *Rates: $55-65 nighlty, $10 extra person.*

Bougainville B & B, P.O.Box 6045, Captain Cook, HI 96704; (808) 929-7089 or 929-9221. Features a pool, hiking, biking, ocean views and South Point and quiet country of rural Ka'u. Operators eager to share Hawaii and relaxing friendly atmosphere. Two guest rooms have private bath and entry. *Rates: $50 nightly.*

South Point B & B ★, P.O. Box 6589, Captain Cook, HI 96704; (808) 929-7466. Located near mileage marker 77 on Highway 11 south from Kona or Hilo. Turn into Donala Street near marker 77, go 50 feet and turn right to first driveway on right. This home offers guests quiet rooms all with private entrance and bath. Guests can enjoy breakfast on the wrap-around lanai while admiring the flowers and view of South Point vista and ocean. Nearby attractions include Ka Lae (South Point) where the first Polynesians landed in Hawai'i, hiking to remote Green Sands Beach, golf at Discovery Harbor or Seamountain courses, and Volcanoes National Park, an easy 45 minute drive away.
Rates: $55/night double occupancy, 3 nights/$150.

The Nutt House, P.O. Box 89, Pahala, HI 96777; (808) 929-9940. Located 1/4 of a mile from Highway 11 in the small village of Waiohinu on the Discovery Harbor road; this private home accommodates up to 4 people in two double rooms. Good naturedly advertised as "A Sane Place to Stay," the lodging offers privacy and seclusion on a private macadamia nut estate. The rooms have private bath with hot tub available. Nearby to tennis, golf, beaches and South Point; Volcanoes National Park an easy 40 minute drive. *Rates: $55 double per night.*

Wood Valley B & B, P.O.Box 37, Pahala, HI 96777; (808) 928-8212. This an old remodeled plantation home on 12 acres of pastureland with gardens and an outdoor bath with woodburning steamhouse. This isolated home gives a unique glimpse of old Hawaii. Best for adventurous budget-minded travelers. One guest room available. *Rates: $45 nightly.*

PRIVATE ESTATES - HOMES - VILLAS

INSIDE HAWAI'I, INC., 3848A Pahoa Avenue, Honolulu, HI 96816; 1-800-722-5771, (808) 737-7313, FAX (808) 735-8857. This reservation service has over 50 units available ranging from 2-8BRs including private estates, beachfront homes and elegant resort condo units. *Rates: $200-2,000 daily.*

KONA SUNSET REALTY, P.O.Box 3540, Kailua-Kona, HI 96745, (808) 329-8329, FAX (808) 329-8864. This property management firm has a variety of vacation rental homes available at varied rates.

KONA VACATION RESORTS, 77-6435 Kuakini Highway, Kailua-Kona, HI 96740, US 1-800-367-5168, Canada 1-800-423-8733 ext. 329, Hawai'i (808) 329-6488 or FAX (808) 329-5480. This service has a wide range of vacation rental homes available at various rates.

MALUHIA HALE, 77-6486 Akai Street, Kailua-Kona, HI 96740; reservations, 170 Emigrant Lake Road, Ashland, OR 97520; call collect (503) 488-2826. This private home is just two blocks from White Sands Beach and has TV, swimming pool. 3 day minimum stay, can accommodate up to 8 people. *Rates: $190 nightly.*

PACIFIC ISLAND ADVENTURES, 4218 Waialae Avenue, Suite 203-A, Honolulu, HI 96816, 1-800-522-3030 or (808) 735-9000. Offers a limited number of homes on all the islands. Most require a seven day minimum stay. 3BR, 4BR, 5BR and 6BR homes available. *Rates: $200-1,500 daily.*

PREMIER CONNECTION, 33 Maruea Street, Suite 200, Wailuku, Maui, HI 96793, (808) 244-4877. Privacy, elegance, and the ultimate in luxury for your Big Island vacation can be provided with a variety of exceptional hotel suites, homes, or mansion-like dwellings, available for short or long term stays. Prices reflect the quality of the accommodations and location. Agency can also arrange transportation, tours, flowers, and all details. *Rates: $200-2,000 daily.*

RESERVATIONS HAWAI'I, Paradise Management Corporation, Kukui Plaza #C-207, 50 South Beretania St., Honolulu, HI 96813; 1-800-367-5205, (808) 538-7145. They have over 700 listings on the Big Island ranging from condo units to vacation homes at a variety of rates available by day, week, month or longer.

SOUTH KOHALA MANAGEMENT, P.O.Box 3301, Waikoloa, HI 96743, 1-800-822-4252, in Hawai'i (808) 883-8500. Choose a home for your ultimate luxury vacation from a select number of private estates. Listings include the exclusive Fairways at Mauna Kea Resort and Puako Beach Oceanfront homes and private villas on the Kohala Coast. Homes feature private swimming pools and jacuzzi, luxurious furnishings and many special amenities. Each home is fully equipped to satisfy even the most discriminating traveller. There is also easy access to golf, tennis and a white-sand swimming beach at the Mauna Kea Beach Hotel, in addition to award-winning dining. Varied rates.

TRIAD MANAGEMENT REALTORS, 75-5629 Kuakini Highway, Kailua-Kona, HI 96740, (808) 329-6402. This property management service has a variety of vacation rental homes available at varied rates.

VACATION LOCATIONS-HAWAI'I, Parker & Co. Realty, P.O. Box 1689, Kihei, Maui, HI 96753, (808) 874-0077. Specializing in beachfront homes, golf course homes and estates around the Big Island. Write directly or call for locations, rates, and amenities. *Rates: $150-2,000 daily.*

VILLA VACATIONS IN HAWAI'I, 4218 Waialae Avenue, #203, Honolulu, HI 96813; 1-800-682-1999, (808) 735-9000, FAX (808) 735-9895. This reservation service has a select list of privately owned beach homes, fairway villas and exclusive estates ranging from 1BR to 8BR. *Rates: $200-2,000 daily.*

WAIPIO RIDGE VACATION RENTALS, P.O.Box 5039, Kukuihaele, HI 96727; (808) 775-0603. This renter has a 1BR home, fully furnished with refrige, microwave oven, coffee maker, fans, TV, etc. Located near the Waipio Valley. *Rates: $70 first day, $60 additional days.*

LONG TERM STAYS

Almost all condo complexes and rental agents offer the long term visitor moderate to substantial discounts for stays of one month or more. Long term rentals can be booked through the agents listed in the above section on PRIVATE ESTATES, HOMES, VILLAS or in the BOOKING AGENTS section.

MILITARY RECREATION CENTER

The Big Island is unique among Hawai'i's Neighbor Islands in that it has an official armed forces recreation center. This is the Kilauea Military Camp located at Hawai'i Volcanoes National Park. KMC, as it is called, has 55 rental cabins available. The rustic well-kept cabins are 1BR, 2BR, 3BR, and 4BR units fully equipped with fireplace, TV, full bath and some have kitchen facilities. The cabins are, however, available only to active duty regular military, reserve or national guard or retired personnel or Department of Defense civilian personnel.

The KMC "Mess Hall," actually a rustic cafeteria which serves standard but ample military chow, is open to any ID card carrying active or retired military personnel. The dining hall like the lodgings are not open to the public. The cabin rentals are very reasonable and are based on rank and grade of the personnel. Advance reservations are required. Current rates are as follows:
Ranks E1-5: Standard 1 or 2BR $23, Deluxe 1BR $26, 2BR w/kitchen $33, Standard 3 or 4BR $33.
Ranks E6-9, W1-3, O1-3: Standard 1 or 2BR $31, Deluxe 1BR $35, 2BR w/kitchen $41, Standard 3 or 4BR $41.
Ranks W4, O4-10, Civilian: Standard 1 or 2BR $39, Deluxe 1BR $44, 2BR w/kitchen $49, Standard 3 or 4BR, $49.

KMC guests can enjoy a full range of recreation activities and programs in the national park including daily tours to various scenic attractions around the island of Hawai'i. Rental equipment is available including tennis rackets, bicycles, back packs, sleeping bags for camping, snorkeling gear and more. KMC also has billiards, ping-pong, video games, mini-golf and a fully equipped six-lane bowling alley. There are also Hawaiian music and hula, Hawaiian story-telling, lei making, and much more. There is a full service cafeteria-dining hall and a PX available. KMC is only about one mile from the national park visitors center and headquarters and Volcano House Hotel and restaurant. Volcano Country Club Golf Course is just across the highway.

For reservations contact Reservations Desk, Armed Forces Recreation Center, Kilauea Military Camp, Hawai'i Volcanoes National Park, Hawai'i 96718, or call (808) 967-8333 or FAX (808) 967-8343. From Honolulu, O'ahu, call locally 438-6707. When making reservations, you can also arrange a free shuttle bus pick-up at the Hilo Airport unless you want to rent your own car for the 40 minute trip to the camp. KMC guests must pay the standard national park entry fee of $5 per vehicle or $2 per person when entering the park.

CAMPING

The Big Island has numerous public parks in both coastal and inland areas. The parks are county, state, or federal operated and several are maintained as camp-grounds for those with their own tents and camping gear. Some also have varied housekeeping cabins or shelters that can be rented overnight or longer. There are no commercial camper or motorhome rental agencies on the Big Island.

County of Hawai'i Parks

The County of Hawai'i maintains a number of parks around the island of which thirteen are designated as campgrounds for those with their own tents and camping gear. The County has no cabins on these campgrounds. Facilities vary at the parks with some having full restrooms, showers and drinking water, while others may have more primitive pit latrines and no drinking water available. Check ahead on what facilities are available. Permits are required for camp-grounds and for use of the pavilions, if available. Campsites are on a first-come, first-served basis, no reservations. Camping permits are issued for one week per park in summer months and two weeks per park in other months.

Camping fees at County parks are Adults - $1 per day, Juniors (13-17) - $.50 per day, Children (12 and under) - no charge. For permits and complete information regarding County of Hawai'i parks, contact: Department of Parks and Recreation, County of Hawai'i, 25 Aupuni Street, Hilo, HI 96720, (808) 961-8311, or in Kona (808) 323-3046.

BIG ISLAND CAMPGROUNDS

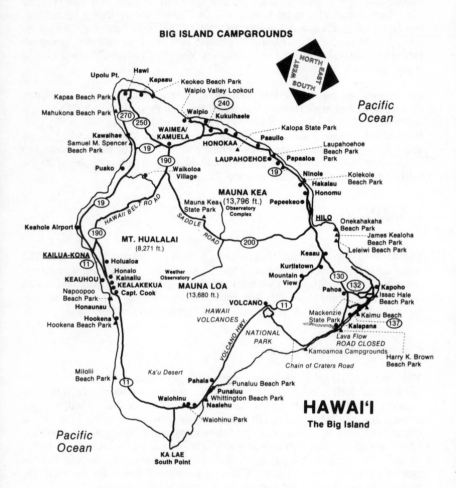

State of Hawai'i Parks

The State of Hawai'i maintains a system of parks around the Big Island and six of them are designated for use as campgrounds. The parks have either a developed campground, camping shelters, housekeeping cabins, or group accommodations (barracks type) housing available for campers. There are no entrance, parking, picnicking, or camping fees. However, permits are required for camping and lodging in the parks where these are available. The maximum length of stay allowable under each permit for camping or lodging in any park is 5 nights.

Hapuna Beach State Recreation Area - on Queen Kaahumanu Highway 19, 2.3 miles south of Kawaihae on the Kohala Coast. Picnic pavilions and A-frame cabins available. This is one of best stretches of white sand beach on the island.

Kalopa State Recreation Area - at 2000 ft. elevation on Kalopa Road, 3 miles upland of Highway 19 about 5 miles south of Honoka'a on the Hamakua Coast. There are picnic pavilions, campgrounds and group lodges available. Nature hiking trails in native forest area.

Kilauea State Recreation Area - at 3700 ft. elevation on Kalanikoa Street off Highway 11 in Volcano Village, 29 miles south of Hilo and 1/2 mile east of entrance to Hawai'i Volcanoes National Park. One housekeeping cabin available. Near hiking trails and attractions of the national park.

MacKenzie State Recreation Area - on Kalapana-Kapoho Road, Highway 137, 9 miles northeast of Kaimu Black Sand Beach. Picnic pavilions available; primitive campground, no drinking water.

Manuka State Wayside - on Highway 11, 19.3 miles west of Na'alehu in southern Ka'u district. This is a place to stop and rest and to picnic among a collection of native and exotic trees and plants. Open shelter camping and picnic pavilion; restrooms available but no drinking water.

Mauna Kea State Recreation Area - at 6500 ft. elevation on Saddle Road, 35 miles upland west of Hilo. Open picnic tables (can be windy here), housekeeping cabins and group lodges available. Dry shrub-land environment, good views of Mauna Kea and Mauna Loa, dry clear weather with cool nights. Near to Pohakuloa military training camp with sometimes busy military traffic.

Lodging fees for the accommodations available are as follows: A-frame Shelters, $7 flat rate per night, maximum of 4 persons can be accommodated in a shelter. A-frames provide basic shelter and consist of single rooms with wooden sleeping platforms and a picnic table. A centrally located pavilion with cooking stove, refrigerator, tables and restrooms-showers are shared by all shelter users. House-keeping cabins consist of single units and duplex cabins which can accommodate up to 6 persons each. Rates are on a per person per night sliding scale:
1 person   - $10.00,   2 persons - $7.00,   3 persons - $6.50
4 persons   -   6.00,   5 persons -   5.50,   6 persons -   5.00

Housekeeping cabins have a kitchen-living room, a bathroom and one to three bedrooms. Each unit is completely furnished with bedroom and kitchen furniture, electric range, refrigerator, hot shower, bathroom, bedding, linen, towels, dishes, and cooking and eating utensils. Fireplaces or electric heating are provided in cold mountain areas.

Group accommodations are available only at the Mauna Kea State Recreation Area and the Kalopa State Recreation Area. A maximum of 64 persons can be accommodated in group cabins at Mauna Kea and 32 persons at Kalopa. Rates are on a per person per night sliding scale and range from 1 person - $8, 4 persons - $5, 8 persons - $3.50, 24 persons - $3, up to 64 persons - $2. Group accommodations consist of 8 person units provided with beds, bedding, linen, toilet facilities, hot shower, and fireplaces. Centrally located is a recreation-dining hall fully equipped for cooking and serving the entire group. Furnishings include a gas range, water heater, refrigerator, freezer, dishes, cooking and eating utensils, tables and chairs, as well as restrooms and a fireplace.

Keys for reserved cabins available from park caretaker or Division of State Parks office in Hilo. Check in time is 2PM, check out time is 10AM. For complete information on obtaining a camping and lodging permit, contact: Department of Land & Natural Resources, Division of State Parks, Hawai'i District Office, P.O. Box 936, Hilo, HI 96720-0936, (808) 961-7200.

Hawai'i Volcanoes National Park

The national park maintains three drive-in campgrounds within Volcanoes National Park for campers with their own tents and gear. Each has pavilion-shelters with picnic tables and fireplaces but you need to bring your own wood or fuel supply. Check the discount stores in Hilo or Kona for camping supplies. No permit is needed and there is no charge for camping. No reservations are taken, as all camping is on a first-come, first-served basis. Stays are limited to 7 days per campground per year. The park service also maintains three simple back-country cabins for hikers but you must register at park headquarters for overnight stays. No reservations are taken for the back-country cabins as use of them is first-come, first-served. However, these cabins are not heavily used and hikers can usually be accommodated. It is necessary to check on trail conditions and water supplies before undertaking a back-country hike. The cabins are located in remote desolate areas, some at high elevations where severe weather can occur, especially in winter. Check with park rangers for information.

One campground, Namakani Paio, also has simple A-frame cabins that can accommodate 4 people in one double bed and two singles. The cabins all share a central restroom and shower facility. Outside each cabin is a picnic table and an outdoor barbeque grill. You must provide your own charcoal and cooking utensils. Nightly rates, January-June $24, July-December $31. Rates include bed linens, towel, and blanket. It's recommended you bring extra blankets or sleeping bags (especially in winter) as the cabins are not heated. Reservations can be made through Volcano House Inn, P.O. Box 53, Hawai'i Volcanoes National Park 96718, (808) 967-7321.

For complete information on visiting, hiking, and camping Hawai'i Volcanoes National Park, contact: Superintendent, Hawai'i Volcanoes National Park, Volcano, HI 96718, (808) 967-7311.

NORTH KONA -
SOUTH KONA

AN INTRODUCTION

This section covers the two districts of West Hawai'i called North and South Kona, which take in some of the most stunning coastline of the Big Island, many important historic sites, and some of its most popular resorts. Since most Big Island visitors arrive at the Kona Airport, this area serves as their introduction to the Island of Hawai'i.

The North and South Kona Districts cover about two-thirds of the West Hawai'i coastline. From north to south, the two districts together stretch along some 60 miles of coastline. From the town of Kailua-Kona, located about mid-coast, the roads follow mostly coastal areas where possible. Highway 19 in the north and Highway 11 in the south pass through extremes in geographic terrain and climate. The roads are all paved and in excellent condition generally. It takes less than two hours to leisurely drive the 60 mile length of the North and South Kona Districts.

North Kona

North Kona takes in vast sweeps of plateau, mountain slopes, vast lava flows, and dry scrubland. The area is foothill country leading up to Mount Hualalai (8271 ft.) and Mauna Loa (13,679 ft.). It is rolling rocky countryside and very dry. The average rainfall is below 10 inches along coastal areas to 20-30 inches and more in inland upslope areas. The climate ranges from arid desert to tropical.

North Kona's main center is Kailua-Kona which is in fact the center for all of West Hawai'i. Other small villages and settlements include Holualoa, Honalo, and Kainaliu. These are coffee growing areas on the slopes of Mount Hualalai. Keauhou is an adjacent resort area just south of Kailua-Kona. The population of North Kona is not really concentrated in any one area, rather it is spread out in subdivisions and around the countryside on small ranches, farms, acreage, and homesites.

South Kona

South Kona hugs the southwestern coastal slopes and flanks of the huge towering volcano, Mauna Loa. The district's one main road, Highway 11 from Kailua-Kona town, passes through upslope areas rather than following the rugged cliffs of the coast, although some coastal areas are accessible. It's generally rolling hilly country, marked by an arid climate along the coast to tropical rainforest in the inland upper slopes. Rainfall varies by elevation. Highway 11 is generally a good road although some short stretches tend to be narrow and very winding. Caution is advised when traveling through South Kona.

South Kona's commercial center is the town of Captain Cook. Other villages include Kealakekua, Honaunau, Keokea, Napo'opo'o, and the Hawaiian fishing village of Miloli'i. Like North Kona, South Kona's population is spread out among the hills and slopes on small ranches, farms, acreage, and homesites.

The area is marked by lush rainforest in upland areas including beautiful tropical trees, plants, and other vegetation all along the road. Macadamia nuts, papaya, bananas, and Kona coffee are some of the products grown in orchards of the area. Lovely tropical flowers abound everywhere. In this sense, South Kona is more colorful and "tropical" than the more arid North Kona District.

Kona's Gold Coast

While it's been billed as the "Gold Coast" of the Big Island, the famed Kona Coast is still centered in the somnolent little fishing village of Kailua. Officially known as Kailua-Kona, it's just plain Kona to local folks. The Kona Coast covers 60 miles of rugged tropical coastline indented with numerous coves and isolated beaches, jutting fingers and towering cliffs of black lava rock and lush mountain slopes. Its some of the most splendid Hawaiian country you'll find anywhere in the islands. For a long time it was *the* resort destination for the Big Island before the rise of the magnificent South Kohala resorts just up the road.

In the old days, pre-1960 or thereabouts, Kona was a very quiet place. It was small and rural and tourists were few and far between. The old Kona Inn was the only real tourist hotel in the area and Kona could hardly be called a resort in those days. But the 60's and 70's brought tourism development and Kailua-Kona rapidly changed from a quiet fishing village to bustling tourist center in a few short years. A construction boom in Kona in the 70's followed by the rise of the nearby Kohala Coast luxury resorts in the 80's attracted many people and created demands for housing, roads, public services, etc. As a result, real estate values skyrocketed along with just about everything else. However, despite its tourist town image, Kona still has a Hawaiian country ambiance about it. Kona's allure rests in its verdant mountain slopes covered with coffee plantations, a deep blue sea filled with hungry marlin and tuna, and a strong tie to old Hawai'i as evidenced by the small town Mom & Pop general stores, old coffee plantation shacks and a relaxed laid-back atmosphere.

The lure of Kona has grown tremendously, thanks in part to a variety of media events and colorful celebrations. The most notable among these are the Hawaiian International Billfish Tournament held each August and the Ironman Triathlon World Championship held each October. These two events alone attract hundreds of participants and media types as well as thousands of spectators from around the world. Local festivals are held throughout the year and create much interest in and attraction to Kona. These include the Kona Coffee Festival held each autumn to highlight the coffee harvest, King Kamehemaha Day Celebrations in June to honor Hawai'i's first monarch, and Admissions Day in August to honor Hawai'i's admission to the union as the fiftieth State. These and other celebrations all generate a number of parades, parties, and performances of local entertainment.

WHAT TO DO AND SEE

The Kona Coast has a reputation for generally consistent fine sunny weather with daytime temperatures averaging in the high 70's and low 80's F. year around. Rainfall along the Kona Coast varies by elevation but averages from 10-40 inches per year. It is no wonder that Kona is well known to sun and fun worshippers. The area abounds with a variety of activities ranging from the sedate to vigorous.

For adventurous history buffs, the fascinating heiau (temples) of old Hawai'i are a must. These sacred temples are the remnants of the old Hawaiian religion. They have been rebuilt with wood frame and grass thatched huts and fearsome looking carved tiki idols to lend an air of authenticity. In the old days, some of these temples were sites for human sacrifices to the gods. In Kona, there are two of these poignant reminders of the old way of life. One is *Ahuena Heiau* ★, located next to Kailua Pier and directly in front of the King Kamehameha Hotel. A walkway in front of the hotel leads directly to it. This site and the surrounding area is where Kamehameha the Great ruled his realm after he united the islands under one kingdom. The other is *Pu'uhonua O Honaunau National Historic Park* ★ (formerly called the City of Refuge), the best preserved heiau in the islands, is located about 20 miles south of Kailua at Honaunau Bay. This shouldn't be missed as it represents so much of Hawai'i's ancient history and culture. National Park Service personnel are on duty to provide information and maps for a self-guided tour through the complex. The site has a restored temple, wooden tiki images, and canoe sheds. At various times of the year, local Hawaiian cultural groups put on authentic arts and crafts demonstrations highlighted during the Fourth of July period with a spectacular three day cultural festival. Call the park visitors center at 328-2288 for information.

Other historic attractions right in Kailua-Kona are *Hulihe'e Palace* ★ built in 1838 and used as a summer residence by Hawaiian royalty and *Mokuaikaua Church* ★, built in 1837 and the oldest church in the islands. These two historic buildings are opposite each other on Alii Drive in the heart of town. A $4 admission fee is charged at the palace to assist the Daughters of Hawai'i in maintaining the building and museum. The palace has some lovely antique Hawaiian furniture, original bedroom furnishings, and antique handmade Hawaiian quilts. It's open daily from 9AM-4PM.

The *Fuku-Bonsai Center* ★ (322-9222) at 78-6767 Mamaloha Highway (old #180 in upper Keauhou area) is a new visitor attraction for Kona. Located in an old quarry, it is an interesting display of bonsai (miniature) plants and features nine different "themed" gardens. Bonsai plants are also for sale here; shipping available. Admission is adults $5, children $2.50. Open daily 8 AM - 5 PM.

PUUHONUA O'HONAUNAU NATIONAL PARK

Holualoa Village, located on Mamalahoa Highway (old #180) and off Hualalai Road just minutes above Kailua-Kona town, is quiety emerging as Kona's leading arts and crafts center. The serene little coffee village boasts a considerable working artisans colony. There is the renowned *Kona Arts Center* ★ which showcases local art works and offers classes through its *Coffee Mill Workshops*. Visitors will enjoy exploring eight art galleries and studios producing everything from raku-fired ceramics to original paintings to hand-crafted jewelry. Two of the better known are *Holualoa Gallery* featuring prints, sculpture, glasswork, ceramics and paintings of Matt and Mary Lovein, and *Studio 7 Gallery*, which showcases mixed-media work by Hiroki Morinoue. *Kimura Lauhala Shop* in Holualoa is the place to shops for a fine selection of woven pandanus creations such as hats, purses and baskets plus other local authentic handicrafts. These are genuine Hawaiian-made articles, not imports. There are also some rustic village stores, shops and a couple of lodgings, the family-owned *Kona Hotel* and *Holualoa Inn B&B*.

One of Kailua-Kona's more popular recreation spots is *Magic Sands Beach* (or Disappearing White Sands Beach) so called for the winter storms which often wash the sand away exposing the rocky coast, only to bring the sand back later. The beach provides good body surfing when sandy but the surf is tricky and dangerous for novices and non-swimmers.

Another popular activity is snorkeling and hand feeding the colorful reef fish at *Kahalu'u Beach Park* just five miles from Kailua town in the Keauhou area. Tiny and picturesque *St. Peter's Catholic Church* sits right on the beach here also.

For the sailor types, glassbottom cruise boats and sailing or diving cruises operate daily trips over Kona's fabulous coral reefs to view the living undersea world. Check your hotel activity desk for cruise schedules and reservations. And of course, if you want to seriously try your skills (and luck!) at hauling up one of the denizens of the deep for which Kona is justly famous, you can easily book a charter boat for a fishing trip. You can try your skill at landing a marlin, ahi (tuna), mahimahi (dolphin fish), ono (wahoo), or any number of other gamefish which abound in Kona's waters. For charter boat bookings, see your hotel activity desk or check the RECREATION AND TOURS chapter.

Along the coast south from Kailua town is *Kealakekua Bay* where Captain James Cook landed and met his fate at the hands of the Hawaiians in 1778. A monument across the bay, accessible by boat, marks the exact spot where Captain Cook fell mortally wounded. The Cook monument is also reached by a very rough hiking trail from Highway 11 at Kealakekua town. *Hikiau Heiau* is a restored temple site and located near the bay in the village of Napo'opo'o.

Going south out of Kailua-Kona on Highway 11, are the small towns of Honalo, Kainaliu, Kealakekua, and Captain Cook. At Kealakekua on Halekii Street is *Mrs. Fields Macadamia Nut Factory* where you can enjoy free samples of the cookies and candy. The *Kona Historical Society Museum*, P.O.Box 398, Captain Cook, HI 96704 (808) 323-3222 is housed in the historic Greenwell Store located on Highway 11, one-half mile south of Kealakekua. Museum hours are 9AM - 3PM weekdays, closed holidays. The museum has regular historic displays featuring early Kona history and maintains a growing reference library and archives. The museum is part of the old Greenwell Ranch. Open to the public, admission by donation. Just south of Captain Cook, look for a sign to the *Amy B.H.Greenwell Ethnobotanical Garden*, P.O.Box 1053, Captain Cook, HI 96704, (808) 323-3318. This 10-acre botanical garden is being developed by the Bishop Museum of Honolulu as a living museum of traditional Hawaiian ethnobotany. The garden is open free to the public, 9AM - Noon daily for self-guided tours. Docent guided tours given on second Saturday of each month.

Look for the *Kealakekua Art Center* ★ which features several art galleries, art shops and boutiques including *Na'Nea Gallery, Pacific Clipper Collections, Potters Den* and others plus *Peacock House Chinese Restaurant* and *The Gallery Cafe.* Just outside of Kealakekua, look for the original *Little Grass Shack at Kealakekua* ★ right on the highway. Here is a fine collection of Hawaiiana, gifts, and arts and crafts. The Kealakekua Bay Road from Highway 11 passes the *Royal Kona Coffee Mill and Museum* ★. Stop here for a free sample of freshly brewed Kona coffee. The museum shop has many gift packs and Kona Coffee souvenirs worth browsing. A little further on is the turnoff at Highway 160 which leads down to the *Pu'uhonua O Honaunau National Historic Park* ★ at Honaunau Bay which was described earlier in this section. A side road from Highway 160 leads to *St. Benedict's Church*, which is Kona's famous "Painted Church." The church's interior is elaborately painted in religious scenes.

At the village of Captain Cook, look for the old country *Manago Hotel* where room rates are reasonable and local-style family meals are still served in the dining room. Just two doors away is the new home of *Deguchi's Kitch'n Cook'd Potato Chips*, a long-time Kona favorite. Highway 11 continues south into the Ka'u District and on to Hawai'i Volcanoes National Park, a distance of 97 miles and approximately a 2 hour and 45 minute drive. The route continues on to Hilo, another 28 miles or 40 minute drive.

KAILUA-KONA CHURCH

WHERE TO SHOP

For those with shopping in mind, Kona has many possibilities. On Palani Road just above Kuakini Highway and the King Kamehameha Hotel are two shopping centers. On the north side is the *Kona Coast Shopping Center*, anchored by *KTA Superstore* and *Pay n' Save* discount store, along with several other specialty shops and some local-style eateries. Opposite this on the south is the *Lanihau Center* featuring *Long's Drugs* and *Food 4 Less Supermarket*. There is also *Penguin's Frozen Yogurt*, *Royal Jade Garden* (Chinese food), *Yuni Special Korean Barbeque*, and a bakery-deli with the amusing name of *Buns in the Sun*.

Below the Lanihau Center in the *Kopiko Plaza*, there are several new shops and restaurants including *Cynthia's Hawaiian Kitchen, Kaminari Japanese Restaurant, Lida's Pasta & Salad Buffet and Kona Mixed Plate*.

Just below the shopping center is *Hilo Hattie's* at 75-5597A Palani Road, 329-7200, a factory which produces colorful Aloha wear including those bright Aloha shirts, muumuus, pareaus, swimsuits, etc. They have free factory tours and a large inventory of garments from which to select at factory prices.

Kamehameha Square is a small shopping complex on Kuakini Highway near the intersection with Palani Road. It is located behind the Hotel King Kamehameha. In this center are *Papagayos Mexican Grill* for Mexican and other international specials and *Rosies Kitchen* for local-style fare. *Dave's Bike & Triathlon Shop* and *Ecoscapes Dive Shop* are also located here.

King Kamehameha Kona Beach Resort has a large shopping mall adjacent to its lobby. Anchoring this mall is a small branch of *Liberty House*, Hawai'i's chain department store. This one features mostly resort wear and Aloha wear fashions, Hawaiiana, souvenirs, etc. Also in the mall are *Traders Hawaiian Gifts* featuring wood carvings and general Hawaiiana merchandise, *The Shellery* for everything under the sun in shells, *Kona Edibles* for Kona coffee, chocolates and macadamia nut products, *Safari*, a boutique of elegant fashions for women, *Kailua Village Artists Gallery, Local Logos, Island Togs,* and other shops. Also in the mall are *Atlantis Submarine Booking Office* and *King Kamehameha Divers*.

On Alii Drive across from the King Kamehameha Hotel and the Kailua-Kona Pier there are a number of small shopping centers and arcades with numerous shops. The *Seaside Shopping Mall* features *Bubi's Sportswear Center of Kona*, *Hawai'i Isle Perfumes, Kona Gift Galley, Goldfish Jewelry, Sandal Stop, Ciao Mopeds* for moped and motorbike rentals and *Kona Activities Booking Center*. Upstairs is the *Cafe Calypso* with nice views of the pier and Kailua Bay.

In the *Kona Square Shopping Center* directly opposite the pier, try *E-Z Discount Store* for sundries, *Kailua Candy Co.* for chocolate and macadamia nut goodies, *Kona Coast Sunglass Co.* for eyewear and *Island Silversmith* for jewelry gifts. *Kona Amigos Restaurant* is located upstairs.

In the *Kona Banyan Court Center*, you'll find *Unison Kona* for T-shirts and official Ironman Triathlon wear, *Kona's Finest Woods* for local woodcraft and gifts, *Big Island Jewelers* and *South Sea Silver* for jewelry, *Pearl Gallery* for pearl jewelry and *Kona Water Sports* for water sports activities rentals. You'll also find *Sibu Cafe*, one of Kona's best international eateries, specializing in Indonesian cuisine.

In the *Kailua Bay Inn Shopping Plaza* just opposite Hulihee Palace and the seawall, check out *Something Different Glass Blower* for unusual glassware items, *Diamonds of the Sea Pearl Shop*, *Kona Jog & Gift Shop* and others. On the lower level are *McGurk's Fish and Chips* and *Guiseppe's Italian Cafe* eateries, while upstairs with a nice view of Kailua Bay is *Marty's Steak and Seafood*. Just behind the complex across the alley is *Suzanne's Bake Shop* for some of the Big Island's best pastries, and *Kona Gift Shop*, *Kona Arts & Crafts*, *ABC Store* for sundries and *The Discovery Gift Shop* for all sorts of gift ideas.

In the *Kona Plaza Shopping Arcade* behind the Rusty Harpoon wing of *Kona Marketplace*, there are *Marlin Casuals* boutique and *Middle Earth Bookshop*. The *Hawai'i Visitors Bureau-Kona Office* is also located here and *Rueben's Mexican Food* restaurant. Out front along Alii Drive is *Kona Marketplace* and *Crown Pearls International* for jewelry and *Crazy Shirts* for T-shirt fashions. Upstairs is the *Rusty Harpoon Restaurant*. *Kona Marketplace* next-door wing also has a number of interesting shops worth exploring, including *Aloha from Kona*, *Kona Bazaar*, *Alii Nexus*, *Island Salsa*, *Kona Shirt Hut*, *Paradise Clothing*, *Kona Flea Market*, *Island Touch*, *Goodies of Hawai'i* and several others.

There are also many interesting shops in the *Kona Inn Shopping Village*. Besides retail shops the center features such restaurants and snack shops as *Fisherman's Landing*, *Kona Inn Restaurant*, *Mrs. Barry's Kona Cookies* and *Don Drysdale's Club 53*. Take some time and stroll through this complex and browse such places as *Dragon Fly Hawaii*, *Alley Gecko's*, *Crystal Visions*, *Glynwood Rogers Originals*, *Golden Orchids*, *The Treasury*, *Hawaiian Fruit & Flower Co.*, *Flamingo's*, *Hula Heaven Hawaiiana*, *Kona Inn General Store* and many more.

Down Alii Drive, a block or so south of Kona Inn Shopping Village, is *Waterfront Row*, a new complex that is a combination dining-shopping center. The food arcade features *The Chart House*, *Jolly Roger*, *Hot Diggity Dog*, *Coffee Pub of Kona* and *Yu Sushi* on the lower level and *Phillip Paolo's Italian Restaurant* upstairs. The shops include *Kona Jack's Fishing Supplies*, *Pacific Vibrations* for swimwear, *Alapaki's* for unique authentic hand-crafted Hawaiiana gifts, *Coconut Joe's Basket Weaving* for genuine handmade basketry and *Lei Aloha Flowers*. There is validated underground parking available. The *Alii Sunset Plaza* is a new mall next to the Kona Alii Condo. While several spaces are vacant, *King Yee Lau Chinese Restaurant* and *Thai Rin Restaurant* are open along with *Breyer's Ice Cream* and others.

South of Kailua-Kona at Keauhou, *Keauhou Shopping Village* is located off Highway 11 at the intersection of Kamehameha III Road and Alii Drive. This complex houses a number of interesting shops and boutiques. It is anchored by *KTA Supermarket*. The shops include *Alapaki's* for fine Hawaiian gifts, handmade originals, wood carvings, etc. *Small World* is a store for children featuring toys and clothes; *Collectors Cottage* features fine ceramics and gifts; *Showcase Gallery* represents the work of noted local artists; *Keauhou Village Book Shop* has a full range of books; and *Possible Dreams* is a complete card and gift shop.

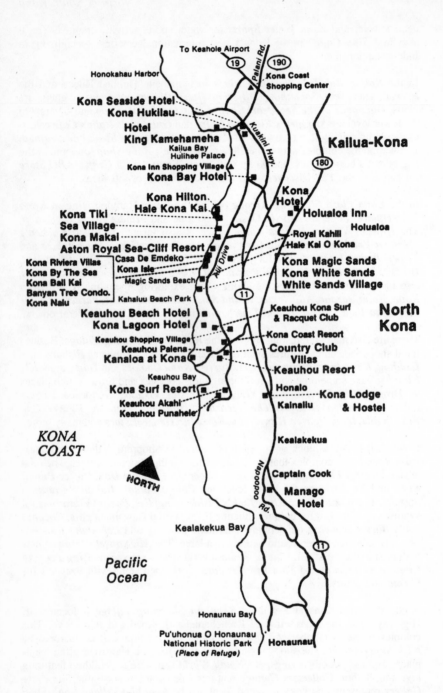

ACCOMMODATIONS -

NORTH AND SOUTH KONA

INTRODUCTION: The resorts and hotels of the Kona Coast are primarily located in the immediate Kailua-Kona town area and spread out along Alii Drive for five miles south leading to a cluster of hotels and condos in the Keauhou area. The accommodations range from first-class hotel and luxury condominiums, to standard budget hotels, to an exclusive hideaway South Seas-style beach resort featuring individual island "hales" (cottages). Unlike other resort areas of Kaua'i, O'ahu, and Maui, Big Island resorts generally don't have broad sandy beaches due to the fact that Hawai'i is still a young island and has not yet developed many fine sandy beaches. At least this is the case on the Kona Coast, where many properties listed as being on the "beach" or "beachfront," are not necessarily on a nice sandy beach. In fact, it is often the exact opposite with the "beach" being very rough rugged lava rock interspersed with sandy areas. However, there are some good beaches in the area. See the RECREATION AND TOURS chapter for details on area beaches.

Whether you decide to stay right in Kailua-Kona town, or in one of the condos along Alii Drive, or even in the nearby Keauhou area, you will still be close to all of the Kona Coast's attractions, dining options, and shopping. Most of the activities and resort attractions are within a 10 mile radius of Kailua-Kona or no more than a short ride away, regardless of where one stays. The lone exception to that rule would be the Kona Village Resort, located in North Kona, twelve miles north of Kailua-Kona town. This exclusive resort is quite secluded on the coast and most visitors who choose to stay there usually do so for the privacy, seclusion, and complete relaxation which this resort provides. By staying in the Kailua-Kona or Keauhou areas, you have easy access to all the activities, attractions, dining, and shopping opportunities of these resort centers. The dining experiences available along the Kona Coast vary considerably. There is a good selection of resort dining rooms and family restaurants in town as well as a variety of local-style eateries featuring ethnic favorites. See the RESTAURANTS chapter for details.

The Kailua-Kona area offers a distinct resort-town atmosphere and attracts the majority of Big Island visitors. With its multitude of hotels, shopping arcades and centers, varied restaurants, shops, historic sites, and busy charter fishing boat harbor, it is the Big Island's preeminent tourist center. There is a lot of hustle and bustle along Alii Drive which is the main street of the town and follows the Kailua Bay coastline and continues south to the Keauhou area.

Kailua-Kona evolved from a quiet country village that became noted for its excellent marlin and tuna fishing into the busy resort town of today. And while the town has changed considerably, it still has that special Hawaiian quality of embracing and respecting the past, enjoying the present and not rushing too fast into the future. It's a resort town true enough but it's still small enough to appreciate and enjoy. And yet it offers visitors those things they want most of a in a vacation in Hawai'i: good choice and value in accommodations, a wide range of restaurants, numerous opportunities for shopping and activities galore.

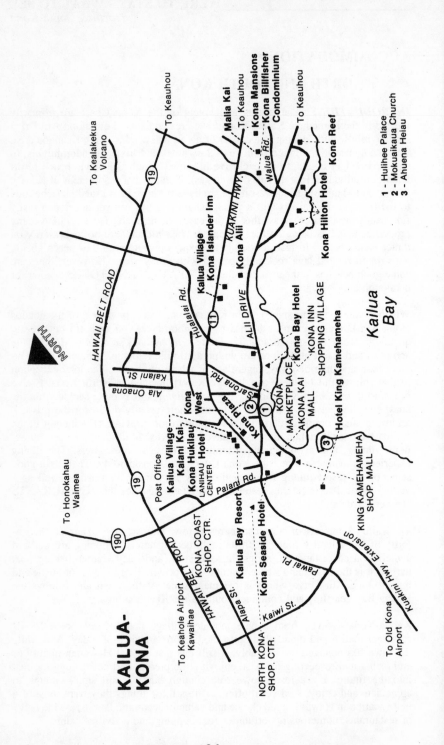

The Keauhou area is somewhat different than Kailua-Kona town. It is a cluster of hotels and condominiums located five miles south of town at the end of Alii Drive. The properties are either on the "beach" (again, no real sandy beach but rather rocky lava rock coastline here) or are situated around the golf course at the Kona Country Club. Keauhou has the quiet ambiance and casualness one would expect of a resort. The generally good accommodations and facilities of the area make it a desirable vacation destination whether one is interested in golf, tennis, sightseeing, shopping or just getting away from it all. And other than resort shops in the hotels, the only other shopping in the immediate area is at the *Keauhou Shopping Village* noted earlier.

BEST BETS

King Kamehameha Kona Beach Resort - This is a good standard quality hotel right on a small sand beach (perfect for kids) on Kailua Bay, in the heart of Kailua-Kona resort town and near to everything.

Kanaloa at Kona - A very nicely maintained condo complex with well furnished, spacious, and comfortable units with beachfront location but no sand beach.

Keauhou Beach Hotel - This is one of the more underrated of Kona's hotel properties, yet its rooms are very clean, comfortable, and it has a relaxing atmosphere. Renovations in the lobby and dining room areas have improved appearances.

Kona Coast Resort - This is a lovely condominium complex on a slope overlooking a Kona Country Club fairway and the ocean just beyond; it offers privacy, seclusion and genuine Hawaiian hospitality from its attentive staff.

Kona Hilton Beach and Tennis Resort - Even though the "Beach" in its name is something of a misnomer (there is no real beach here other than a tiny manmade sand cove), the Kona Hilton is a very nice place to stay. The rooms are nicely furnished and quite comfortable. It is also just a short walk to the center of Kailua-Kona town.

Kona Village Resort - If you want privacy, seclusion, and just plain old peace and quiet, this is for you. A South Seas atmosphere pervades the village with its authentically-styled island cottages reflecting the architecture of Fiji, Samoa, Tonga, Tahiti, the New Hebrides, and other Pacific Islands.

Note: Kona and Kohala resorts and hotels have varied rates by low season (approximately May 1 to November 30) and high season (December 1 to April 30). High/low season rates are listed with a slash dividing them where they apply. Check what rates apply when booking your reservations.

KONA COAST ACCOMMODATIONS

Alii Villas
Aston Royal
  Sea-Cliff Resort
Banyan Tree Condo
Casa De Emdeko
Country Club Villas
Hale Kai O Kona
Hale Kona Kai
Hale Pohaku
Holua at Mauna Loa
King Kamehameha
  Kona Beach Resort
Kailua Bay Resort
Kanaloa at Kona
Keauhou Akahi
Keauhou Beach Hotel
Keauhou Kona Surf
  & Racquet Club
Keauhou Palena Condo

Keauhou Punahele
Keauhou Resort
Kona Alii Condos
Kona Bali Kai
Kona Bay Hotel
Kona
  Billfisher Condos
Kona By The Sea
Kona Coast Resort
Kona Hilton Hotel
Kona Hotel
Kona Islander I
Kona Isle Condo
Kona Luana
Kona Magic Sands
Kona Makai
Kona Mansions
Kona Nalu
Kona Onenalo

Kona Palms
Kona Plaza Condo
Kona Reef
Kona Riviera
Kona Seaside Hotel
Kona Surf Resort
  Hotel
Kona Tiki Hotel
Kona Village Resort
Kona West
Kona White Sands
  Apartment Hotel
Malia Kai
Manago Hotel
Royal Kahili Condo
Sea Village
White Sands Village

ALII VILLAS
75-6016 Alii Drive, Kailua-Kona, HI 96740, (808) 329-1288
Agent: Kona Vacation Resorts, US 1-800-367-5168, Canada 1-800-423-KONA,
FAX (808) 329-5480. This condo has only ten units in rental programs. It is a
beachfront location with palm trees, flowers and garden setting less than a mile
from town. Units are generally clean and well kept although this is strictly a
budget-condo operation. *1 BR g.v. $70 dy, $420 wk; 1 BR o.v. $85 dy, $510 wk;
2 BR o.f. (2,max 4) $115 dy, $690 wk.*

ASTON ROYAL SEA-CLIFF RESORT ★
75-6040 Alii Drive, Kailua-Kona, HI 96740, (808) 329-8021. Agent: Aston
Hotels Hawai'i 1-800-922-7866 , FAX (808) 922-8785. This 148 unit condo-hotel
is completely air conditioned with TV, kitchen, and tennis courts, on the beach.
Studio $135-155, 1 BR (2,max 4) $150-190, 2 BR (2,max 6) $170-425

BANYAN TREE CONDOMINIUM
76-6268 Alii Drive, Kailua-Kona, HI 96740, (808) 329-4220. This small 20 unit
condo has just 10 units available for rental. All are 2 bedroom/2 bath oceanfront
units that will accommodate up to four people. Some units may accommodate up
to six, $10 per extra person. Covered parking, heated swimming pool for winter,
ceiling fans, no air-conditioning. Minimum stay of four days required.
2 BR $115-135 day, $700-810 week

CASA DE EMDEKO ★
75-6082 Alii Drive, Kailua-Kona, HI 96740, (808) 329-6488. Agents; Kona
Vacation Resorts, US 1-800-367-5168, FAX (808) 329-5480; Village Realty (808)
329-1577; Knutson & Associates (808) 326-9393; Golden Triangle Real Estate
(808) 329-1667.

This lovely three story white-washed building is located on the water although there is no sand beach here. The 25 available units are spacious, comfortable, and well-appointed. The central garden-courtyard is well maintained with tropical plants. The oceanside swimming pool features a "sandy beach" surrounding the pool. *1 BR g.v. $75 day, $450 week; 1 BR o.v. $85 day, $510 week; 2 BR o.f. $135 day, $810 week*

COUNTRY CLUB VILLAS (W)

78-6920 Alii Drive, Kailua-Kona, HI 96740, (808) 322-2501
Agents: Hawaiian Apt. Leasing Ent. U.S. 1-800-854-8843, Calif. 1-800-472-8449, Canada 1-800-824-8968, FAX (714) 497-4183; Keauhou-Kona Realty, Inc. 1-800-367-8047 ext.246; Kona Vacation Resorts, US 1-800-367-5168, Canada 1-800-423-8733 ext. 329; Ron Burla & Associates (808) 329-2421.

This condominium is located on the Kona Country Club golf course and has only a few units in rental programs. Amenities include TV, private lanai on each unit, 2 tennis courts, and on request maid service. All units have golf course views with Kona Coast beyond. Minimum 5 nights.
Suite only, 2 BR o.v. (2,max 4) $100-110 day, $600 week

HALE KAI O KONA (W)

76-6204 Alii Drive, Kailua-Kona, HI 96740.
Agents: Hawaiian Apt. Leasing Ent. 1-800-854-8843, Calif. 1-800-472-8449, Canada 1-800-824-8968, FAX (714) 497-4183; Kona Vacation Resorts, US 1-800-367-5168, Canada 1-800-423-8733 ext. 329; Ron Burla & Assoc. (808) 329-2421.
Ocean front townhouse units all with rattan furnishings, washer/dryer, dishwasher, full kitchen, lanais and TV. *Suite only, 4 BR (2,max 8) $200, $1200 week*

HALE KONA KAI ★ (W)

75-5870 Kahakai Road, Kailua-Kona, HI 96740. 1-800-421-3696, (808) 329-2155. Agents: Triad Management 1-800-345-2823, (808) 329-6402; Hawai'i Resort Management 1-800-553-5035 or (808) 329-9393. This 39 unit condo is air-conditioned with on request maid service, TV, BBQ facility. No room telephones. Corner units are larger with bigger lanai area but all units are very nicely furnished. Minimum stay required is three days. Located right on the water and immediately next door to the Kona Hilton Hotel, but there is no sand beach. It is within walking distance to the village. *1 BR (2,max 4) $75-85, extra person $10*

HALE POHAKU

76-6194 Alii Drive, Kailua-Kona, HI 96740. Agents: Kona Vacation Resorts, U.S. 1-800-367-5168, Canada 1-800-800-KONA, or (808) 329-6488, FAX (808) 329-5480; West Hawaii Property Services, Inc., (808) 322-6696. This small 6 unit complex offers oceanfront privacy, individual lanais, ceiling fans, full kitchens, swimming pool, paddle tennis and entertainment area.
2 BR (2,max 4) $130-135, $780-800 week, $2340-2800 month

HOLUA AT MAUNA LOA VILLAGE ★

78-7190 Kaleopapa Road, Keauhou-Kona, HI 96740, (808) 322-9603. Agent: Colony Hotels and Resorts, Inc. 1-800-367-6046. This is a new development in the Keauhou area, located just above the Kona Surf Hotel and Keauhou Bay.

The 469 unit complex is arranged in hexagonal pod-like clusters. Lovely tropical color schemes accent the tasteful decor and contemporary furnishings of each unit. The grounds are well landscaped with numerous bubbling streams and pools, fountains, gardens and a swimming pool for every 18 units. Easy access to Holua Tennis Center, golf at next door Kona Country Club, Players Restaurant on grounds and other resort activities and attractions.
1 BR (2,max 4) $145, 2 BR (4,max 6) $175, 3 BR (6,max 8) $215

KAILUA BAY RESORT
75-5669 Kuakini Highway, Kailua-Kona, HI 96740, (808) 329-2260. This 15 unit condo does not have air-conditioning. In room TV and swimming pool with spa are available. Located one long block from the rocky beach of Kailua Bay and near the center of Kailua-Kona town shopping, restaurants, etc. Minimum 3 months lease. *1 BR $780-850, 2 BR $850-1000*

KALANIKAI CONDOMINIUMS
75-5681 Kuakini Highway, Kailua-Kona, HI 96740, (808) 329-5241. Agents: West Hawai'i Property Services, Inc. (808) 322-6696; Vacationland Sales & Rentals (808) 329-5680; Paradise Management 1-800-272-5252. This condominium is located in the heart of the village and within walking distance of resort activities, shopping, and restaurants. Amenities include air-conditioning and BBQ facilities. Units have mountain views. *1 BR $80 day, $520 week, $1650 month*

KANALOA AT KONA ★
78-261 Manukai St., Kailua-Kona, HI 96740, 1-800-777-1700, (808) 322-9625, FAX (808) 322-3818. Agents: Colony Hotels and Resorts, Inc. 1-800-657-7872; Keauhou-Kona Realty Inc. 1-800-367-8047 ext.246, Hawai'i (808) 322-9555.

This 118 unit condo is located oceanfront in Keauhou but there is no sandy beach. The luxurious units are spacious and fully equipped including lanai wet bar, Koa wood interiors, ceiling fans, and TV. Kanaloa is bordered on one side by the sparkling blue Pacific with a secluded bay for snorkeling and sunning and on the other by the Kona Country Club golf course. Tennis courts, The Terrace Restaurant, cocktail lounge, BBQ facilities, and recreation-meeting room are available. *1-2-3BR $120-215, extra person $15*

KEAUHOU AKAHI
78-7030 Alii Drive, Kailua-Kona, HI 96740, (808) 322-2590. Agents: Triad Management (808) 329-6402; Village Realty (808) 329-1577; Golden Triangle Real Estate (808) 329-1667; Kona Vacation Resorts, US 1-800-367-5168, Canada 1-800-423-8733, ext. 329, FAX (808) 329-5480.

This 48 unit complex is located on the Kona Country Club golf course with far ocean views. There are laundry facilities in each unit, full kitchens and on-property swimming pool. It is 7 miles from the village. Minimum one week stay. *1 1/2 BR o.v. $550/400 week, $1650/1200 month*

KEAUHOU BEACH HOTEL ★
78-6740 Alii Drive, Keauhou-Kona, HI 96740, (808) 322-3441, 1-800-367-6025, local 1-800-446-8990, FAX (808) 322-6586. This fine first-class 310 room property is located next to the rocky coastline. There is a very small sand beach

and lovely tidal pools for youngsters to explore for marine life at low tide. The hotel features air-conditioning, TV, sauna, exercise room, room refrigerators, tennis courts, and Kuakini Terrace Restaurant for casual ala carte and daily buffet dining. Rooms are very clean, spacious, and comfortable and most have nice views of Keauhou coastline. The property has a most relaxing and pleasant ambiance. *Standard $91-115, Deluxe $135-155, Suites $225-395, extra person $13*

KEAUHOU KONA SURF & RACQUET CLUB ★
Alii Drive, Kailua-Kona, HI 96740, (808) 322-9231. Agents: Keauhou-Kona Realty 1-800-367-8047 ext.246, Hawai'i (808) 322-9555; Golden Triangle Real Estate (808) 329-1667; Ron Burla & Associates (808) 329-2421; Village Realty (808) 329-1577; West Hawai'i Property Services, Inc. (808) 322-6696; Kona Vacation Resorts, US 1-800-367-5168, Canada 1-800-423-8733, ext. 329, FAX (808) 329-5480.

This is a large complex of 190 units which are very nicely furnished with TV's plus great views of the golf course fairways or ocean. The complex has wonderful recreation facilities including 3 lighted tennis courts and a poolside community center. *1-2-3 BR $95-140 nightly, $630-900 weekly, $1850-2900 monthly*

KEAUHOU PALENA CONDOMINIUM
78-7054 Kamehameha III Road, Kailua-Kona, HI 96740, (808) 322-3620. Agents: Keauhou-Kona Realty 1-800-367-8047 ext.246, Hawai'i (808) 322-9555; Village Realty (808) 329-1577; West Hawai'i Property (808) 322-6696; Kona Vacation Resorts, US 1-800-367-5168, Canada 1-800-423-8733, ext. 329, FAX (808) 329-5480.

This condo is on the eleventh fairway of the Kona Country Club golf course with easy access for golfing visitors. Units are fully equipped including ceiling fans and TV. The den makes into an extra bedroom enabling these units to sleep four comfortably. It's located near the end of Alii Drive in the Keauhou area. *1 BR (2,max 4) $95 day, $570 week, $1710 month*

KEAUHOU PUNAHELE CONDOMINIUM ★

78-7070 Alii Drive, Kailua-Kona, HI 96740, (808) 322-6585, reservations (206) 742-2440. Agents: Keauhou-Kona Realty 1-800-367-8047 ext.246, Hawai'i (808) 322-9555; Village Realty (808) 329-1577; West Hawai'i Property Services, Inc. (808) 322-6696; Golden Triangle Real Estate (808) 329-1667; Century 21 1-800-255-8052; Kona Vacation Resorts, US 1-800-367-5168, Canada 1-800-423-8733, ext. 329, FAX (808) 329-5480.

This large complex (93 units) has only a few available in rental programs. It is the last complex at the end of Alii Drive in the Keauhou area and on the Kona Country Club golf course with ocean view across golf course. Units are not air-conditioned but are roomy and generally well-appointed with high ceilings keeping units cool and breezy. The units are clean and well-kept and the grounds are well-groomed. Located 7 1/4 miles from the village but Keauhou Shopping Center is only half a mile away. *2 BR $85-120, 3 BR $130, $510-800 weekly*

KEAUHOU RESORT CONDOMINIUMS (W)

78-7039 Kamehameha III Rd, Kailua-Kona, HI 96740, (808) 322-9122; 1-800-367-5286. This condo has just 28 units available with TV, nearby golf course, and maid service. Minimum stay of five days.
1 BR $65-75, deluxe $75-85; 2 BR $85-95, deluxe $95-115

KING KAMEHAMEHA KONA BEACH RESORT ★ (W)

75-5660 Palani Road, Kailua-Kona, HI 96740, (808) 329-2911; toll free US/Canada 1-800-367-2111; FAX (808) 329-4602. This 458 room hotel is one of Kailua-Kona's landmark hotels, located on sandy calm Kamakahonu Beach on Kailua Bay behind the pier at the head of the town's main street, Alii Drive. All rooms are air-conditioned with TV. Restaurants, cocktail lounges, tennis courts, lobby shopping mall, and meeting rooms are available. Extra persons $10 each. *Standard $105-115, Deluxe $180-195, 1-2-3 BR Suites $ 300-500*

KONA ALII CONDOMINIUMS

75-5782 Kuakini Hwy., Kailua-Kona, HI 96740, (808) 329-2000. Agents: Hawai'i Resort Management 1-800-553-5035, Hawai'i (808) 329-9393; West Hawai'i Property (808) 322-6696; Hawai'i Apt. Leasing US 1-800-854-8843, California 1-800-472-8449, Canada 1-800-824-8968; Paradise Management 1-800-272-5252.

Units are fully furnished with private lanai and major appliances. Bedding for up to 4 persons. Tennis court, top floor sun deck, private sandy beach, bar-b-que area. Short two minute walk into Kailua village for shopping, restaurants and resort activities. *1 BR (2,max 4) $80-100, $520-700 weekly, $1700-2100 monthly*

KONA BALI KAI (W)

76-6246 Alii Drive, Kailua-Kona, HI 96740, (808) 329-9381; Agents: Colony Resorts Inc., 1-800-777-1700, FAX (808) 322-3818; Kona Vacation Resorts, US 1-800-367-5168, Canada 1-800-423-8733, ext. 329, FAX (808) 329-5480. This condo has 75 units available on Holualoa Bay, Kona. All units have kitchen and TV, some with air-conditioning, plus sauna, jacuzzi and health club are available. *Studio g.v. $60, 1BR g.v. $65, Studio o.v. $75, 1BR o.f. $90-110, 2BR o.f. $125-135, 3BR o.f. $140*

KONA BAY HOTEL (W)

75-5739 Alii Drive, Kailua-Kona, HI 96740; (808) 329-1393, US/Canada 1-800-367-5102, FAX (808) 935-7903. This older hotel has 145 guest rooms available, all air-conditioned. In room TV, swimming pool, Banana Bay Cafe, cocktail lounge, and shops all available. Located across from the Kona Inn Shopping Village only one block from Kailua Bay. *Standard $62-72, superior g.v. $69-79, deluxe g.v. $74-84, oceanview $84-94, extra person $10*

KONA BILLFISHER CONDOMINIUM

75-5841 Alii Drive, Kailua-Kona, HI 96740, (808) 329-9277. Agent: Hawai'i Resort Mgmt. 1-800-553-5035, Hawai'i (808) 329-9393; FAX (808) 326-4137. This condo has 20 units in rental programs, all air-conditioned with TV and bar-b-que area. It is located across the street from the Kona Hilton Hotel and Kanazawa Tei Japanese restaurant is just next door. It's also within easy walking distance to center of town. *1 BR (2,max 4) $75/60, 2 BR (2,max 6) $95/80*

KONA BY THE SEA

75-6106 Alii Drive, Kailua-Kona, HI 96740, (808) 327-2300. Agent: Aston Hotels & Resorts 1-800-922-7866, Hawaii 1-800-342-1551, FAX (808) 922-8785. 78 units available for guest accommodation and all units are fully air-conditioned with TV and kitchen. The Beach Club Restaurant for fine dining is on grounds. Located on a rocky beach. *1 BR (2,max 4) $160-195, 2 BR (2,max 6) $175-215*

KONA COAST BEACH RESORT ★

78-6842 Alii Drive, Kailua-Kona, HI 96740, (808) 324-0412. Agent: Keauhou Property Management, 1-800-745-5662, FAX (808) 322-3573. This beautiful development has only a few 2BR rental units available. They are spread out among several small complexes on a lovely slope above a fairway of the Kona Country Club with the ocean just beyond. The units are luxuriously furnished with plush furniture, bedding, and overall very tastefully appointed. There is a recreation area, with tennis, jacuzzi, gas BBQ area, and wet bar. Weekly rates only. *2 BR $700-800 weekly, $3,000 monthly.*

KONA HILTON BEACH & TENNIS RESORT HOTEL ★

75-5852 Alii Dr., Kailua-Kona, HI 96740, (808) 329-3111; FAX (808) 329-9532. Agent: Hilton Hotels 1-800-HILTONS. This 445 room hotel is a well-known Kona landmark which sits on a rocky precipice jutting into Kailua Bay and affords a commanding view of the town and bay area. The rooms are very neat, clean and air-conditioned with TV, refrigerators (not stocked) and complimentary coffee-tea making facility. Amenities include the Hele Mai Restaurant and Lanai Terrace Coffee Shop, plus cocktail lounges, tennis courts, shops, and meeting rooms. *Standard $120-130, Deluxe $160-170, Suite $250*

KONA HOTEL ★

P.O. Box 342, Holualoa Road, Holualoa, Kona, HI 96725, (808) 324-1155. Located approximately 7 miles from Kailua-Kona town in a prime coffee farming area on the slopes of Mount Hualalai. This charming upcountry 11 room hotel has been run by the Inaba family for many years. It is one of Kona's original lodgings and is still run with an old fashioned family atmosphere. Nothing fancy but basic accommodation for guests wanting budget accommodations. Guests share a community bathroom and entertain themselves in the small lobby-TV room. This hotel has a quiet and sedate old-fashioned Hawaiian country ambience. *Standard $15-23*

KONA ISLANDER INN
P75-5776 Kuakini Highway, Kailua-Kona, HI 96740, (808) 329-3181. Agents: Aston Hotels & Resorts 1-800-922-7866, Hawai'i 1-800-342-1551, FAX (808) 922-8785; Kona Vacation Resorts, US 1-800-367-5168, Canada 1-800-423-8733, ext. 329, FAX (808) 329-5480.

This condo has just 59 rental units available. Air-conditioning and TV in all rooms. Located on Kuakini Highway two blocks from Kailua Bay. *Standard $74-94, Deluxe $89-109*

KONA ISLE CONDOMINIUM
75-6100 Alii Drive, Kailua-Kona, HI 96740, (808) 329-2241, FAX (808) 326-2401. Agents: Knutson & Assoc. (808) 326-9393; Ron Burla & Associates (808) 329-2421; Hawai'i Resort Management 1-800-553-5035 or (808) 329-9393.

This is an oceanfront complex, some units with oceanview. The beautifully manicured grounds are very spacious and pleasant. There are BBQ facilities and tables poolside and lounge chairs near the oceanfront seawall. There is no sand beach here, it is too rocky. Laundry facilities are in each unit. Located 2 1/4 miles from the village. One week minimum stay.
1 BR g.v. $475/375 weekly, 1 BR o.f. $575/475 weekly $1125-1725 monthly

KONA LUANA
75-5958 Alii Dr., Kailua-Kona, HI 96740, (808) 329-6488. Agent: Kona Vacation Resorts 1-800-367-5168, Canada 1-800-423-8733, ext. 329, FAX (808) 329-5480. This is a small complex but offers full ocean front views over the Pacific with full furnishings, laundry facilities, big screen TV, lanai and wet bar.
2 BR o.f. $125/day, $750/week, $2250/month

KONA MAGIC SANDS
77-6452 Alii Dr., Kailua-Kona, HI 96740, (808) 329-6488. Agent: Kona Vacation Resorts 1-800-367-5168, FAX (808) 329-5480. Located next to famous Magic Sands Beach Park with swimming and body-surfing available. There are just 18 1BR and studio units available. Features TV, Jameson's By the Sea Restaurant, cocktail lounge, and on request maid service. Some rooms have telephones. 3 day minimum stay. *Studios $65-75/day, 1BR $85/day*

KONA MAKAI
75-6026 Alii Drive, Kailua-Kona, HI 96740, (808) 329-6488. Agents: Golden Triangle (808) 329-1667; Village Realty (808) 329-1577; Kona Vacation Resorts 1-800-367-5168, FAX (808) 329-5480; West Hawai'i Property Services, Inc. (808) 322-6696; Hawai'i Apartment Leasing 1-800-854-8843, California 1-800-472-8449, Canada 1-800-824-8968; Paradise Management 1-800-272-5252.

This complex has just 25 units in rental programs. Amenities include jacuzzi, BBQ, tennis courts, sauna and exercise room. Oceanfront but no sandy beach. 3 day minimum stay.
1 BR g.v. $80, o.v. $90-100, 2 BR (2,max 4) g.v. $115, o.v. $125, o.f. $135

KONA MANSIONS (W)

75-5873 Walua Road, Kailua-Kona, HI 96740, (808) 329-2374. Agents: Hawaiian Apt. Leasing 1-800-854-8843, Canada 1-800-824-8968, California 1-800-472-8449, FAX (714) 497-4183; Triad Management (808) 329-6402.

This complex is located across from the Kona Hilton Hotel and within walking distance of the village. There are no good views from this complex. Units do have TV and on request maid service available. Minimum stay of five days required. Easy access to all other resort town activities. There are only a few units in rental programs. 5 day minimum stay. *1 BR Suite (2,max 4) $70*

KONA NALU

76-6212 Alii Drive, Kailua-Kona, HI 96740; (808) 329-6488; Agents: West Hawai'i Property Services, Inc. (808) 322-6696; Kona Vacation Resorts, US 1-800-367-5168, Canada 1-800-423-8733 ext.329, FAX (808) 329-5480. This small complex is located on the waterfront midway between Kailua-Kona and the Keauhou area at the end of Alii Drive. Units are completely furnished and well maintained. *2 BR o.f. $145/day, $870/week, $2610/month*

KONA ONENALO

77-6516 Alii Dr., Kailua-Kona, HI 96740, (808) 329-6488. Agent: Kona Vacation Resorts 1-800-367-5168, Canada 1-800-423-8733 ext. 329, FAX (808) 329-5480. This comfortably furnished condo comes complete including microwave in kitchen, washer/dryer, lots of living area and many other conveniences. Oceanside pool and jacuzzi. *2 BR o.f. (2,max 4) $150/day, $900/week, $2700/month*

KONA PALMS

77-6311 Alii Dr., Kailua-Kona, HI 96740, (808) 329-6488. Agent: Kona Vacation Resorts 1-800-367-5168, Canada 1-800-423-8733, ext. 329, FAX (808) 329-5480. This property is about 3 1/2 miles south of Kailua-Kona town and offers an unobstructed view of the ocean. Units have ceiling fans, washer/dryer and are fully furnished. Building also has an elevator.
1 BR o.v. $90/day, $540/week, $1620/month

KONA PLAZA CONDOMINIUMS

Alii Drive, Kailua-Kona, HI 96740, (808) 329-1132. Agents: West Hawai'i Property (808) 322-6696; Century 21 1-800-255-8052, FAX (808) 329-6693. 75 air-conditioned units right in the heart of the village on Alii Drive across from the Kona Inn Shopping Village. Everything is within walking distance. Guests have access to a rooftop sundeck. *1 BR $60-75, 2 BR o.v. $75-85*

KONA REEF

75-5888 Alii Drive, Kailua-Kona, HI 96740, (808) 329-4780. Agents: Hawaiiana Resorts 1-800-367-7040, Canada 1-800-877-7331, FAX (808) 537-3701; Knutson & Assoc. (808) 326-9393; Kona Vacation Resorts, US 1-800-367-5168, Canada 1-800-423-8733, ext. 329, FAX (808) 329-5480

This condo has 55 units available as vacation rentals. All rooms are air-conditioned with TV. It is nearby to shopping and restaurants. Minimum stay of two nights required. Oceanfront location but no sandy beach.
1 BR g.v. $95-105, 1 BR o.v. $105-115, 1 BR o.f $115-125, 2 BR o.f. $150-185

KONA RIVIERA VILLA CONDOMINIUMS ★

75-6124 Alii Drive, Kailua-Kona, HI 96740, (808) 329-1996. This condo is located on the beach with private lanai on each unit, nearby to tennis courts, golf, snorkeling, plus village shopping and restaurants. Units can accommodate up to four persons. Minimum stay of 3 nights required.

1 BR g.v. $70/60 night, $420/350 week, $1500/1200 month
1 BR o.v. $80/70 night, $490/420 week, $1800/1300 month
1 BR deluxe o.v. $90/80 night, $560/490 week, $2000/1800 month
1 BR o.f. $100/90 night, $630/560 week, $2400/2000 month

KONA SEASIDE HOTEL

75-5546 Palani Road, Kailua-Kona, HI 96740, (808) 329-2455.
Agent: Sands, Seaside and Hukilau Hotels, 1-800-367-7000,
Canada 1-800-654-7020, Hawai'i 1-800-451-6754, FAX (808) 922-0052

This 228 room property recently incorporated the Kona Hukilau Hotel into its operation. The two were owned by the same company and the old Hukilau is the wing fronting Kailua Bay. Most rooms are air-conditioned and all have TV. Stan's Oceanview Restaurant, cocktail lounge, and meeting rooms available. This is in the heart of the village with shopping and restaurants all within walking distance. Kailua Pier is one block away. This is a good budget hotel with clean rooms and simple decor. *Standard $49, Deluxe $59, extra person $10*

KONA SURF RESORT HOTEL   (W)

78-128 Ehukai St., Keauhou-Kona, HI 96740, (808) 322-3411, 1-800-367-8011, FAX (808) 322-3245. This 530 room hotel, one of Keauhou Resort's major properties, sits handsomely on a peninsula bluff above Keauhou Bay and overlooks the fabulous Kona Coast. The rocky coastline has no sand beach but the hotel has fresh and saltwater pools. Spacious rooms are air-conditioned and have TV. Restaurants include The Makee Dining Room and Pele's Court plus cocktail lounges. Other amenities include the adjacent Kona Country Club golf course, tennis courts, shops, and Kona's most complete convention facilities. Lovely tropical botanical gardens surround the hotel grounds, highlighted by a lovely wedding chapel and pond. Extra person $15.

Std. $99-109, g.v. $120-130, o.v. $150-160, o.f. $175-185, suites $375-925

KONA TIKI HOTEL

P.O. Box 1567, Kailua-Kona, HI 96745, (808) 329-1425. This small apartment hotel has just 17 total units with parking, swimming pool, and ceiling fans. No room telephones. Strictly for the budget minded traveler who wants no frills. *Standard $50, Deluxe with kitchenette $55, extra person $5*

KONA VILLAGE RESORT ★ (W)

P.O. Box 1299, Kaupulehu-Kona, HI 96745, (808) 325-5555, U.S. 1-800-367-5290, FAX (808) 325-5124. Agent: John A. Tetley Co. Inc. 1-800-421-0000, Calif. 1-800-252-0211; Canadian Agent: Muriel Fleger, Toronto 416-598-2693, rest of Canada 1-800-268-9051.

This unique resort is a re-creation of a Polynesian village with 125 thatch-roofed hales (houses) for guest rooms. The huts reflect the design and decor of the South Pacific Islands: Hawai'i, Tahiti, Tonga, Fiji, New Caledonia, New Hebrides,

Samoa, Palau, and the Marquesas, with modern conveniences. This is a no-nonsense escapist resort for those seeking complete relaxation, solitude, and the feel of a South Seas Paradise. No room phones, no radios, no TV.

Room rates reflect Full American Plan with all meals included for two people. The weekly luau is unrivaled for quantity and diversity of authentic Hawaiian luau food including roast pig cooked in an earth oven. Located 15 miles north of Kailua-Kona on the beach at Kaupulehu. The Kona Village has a complimentary program for children during school holiday periods and in the summer.
Standard $360-390, moderate $435-475, superior $480-515, deluxe $550-585, Royal oceanfront $530-615. Extra person $140

KONA WEST
75-5680 Kuakini Hwy., Kailua-Kona, HI 96740, (808) 329-6488. Agent: Kona Vacation Resorts 1-800-367-5168, Canada 1-800-423-8733, ext. 329, FAX (808) 329-5480.

This is a small complex near the heart of town on the Kuakini Highway within walking distance of shopping, restaurants, etc. Units are furnished with stove top burners, small refrige and air-conditioning. There are on-site laundry facilities, swimming pool and jacuzzi. *Studio g.v. $60 day, $360 week, Studio o.v. $75 day, $450 week*

KONA WHITE SANDS APARTMENT HOTEL
P.O. Box 594, 77-6467 Alii Drive, Kailua-Kona, HI 96745, (808) 329-3210. Agent: Hawai'i Resort Management 1-800-553-5035, FAX (808) 326-4137.

This small 10 unit apartment-hotel has just 5 units available in rental programs. Full kitchens and TV, ceiling fans and individual private lanai in all units, but no room telephones. This complex is directly across from White Sands Beach. Strictly a no-frills budget-class lodging. 3 day minimum stay. *Standard $55-60 day, $385 weekly, $1,540 monthly   Extra person $6*

KONA VILLAGE RESORT

MALIA KAI ★

75-5855 Walua Road, Kailua-Kona, HI 96740, (808) 329-1897.
Agent: Triad Management (808) 329-6402. This complex is very conveniently
located, about 2 blocks from the center of the village. It is across the street from
the Kona Hilton Hotel. The central courtyard is a profusion of tropical plants and
flowers with a small relaxing swimming pool. It is a very quiet comfortable
location. Units are simply furnished with ceiling and table fans, no air-conditioning. The only negatives of this property are the narrow stairway leading up to
each unit's split-levels and kitchens that show some age and wear.
1 1/2 BR $80/65 day, $480/390 weekly, $1440/1170 monthly

MANAGO HOTEL ★ (W)

P.O. Box 145, Captain Cook, HI 96704, (808) 323-2642. This is another old-
fashioned family hotel operated by the Manago family since its founding in 1917.
There are 64 rooms, some with shared bathroom facilities. The hotel features a
homey family-type environment and the restaurant serves local family-style meals.
Cocktail lounge on grounds. No room telephones. Located right on Highway 11
eight miles from Kailua-Kona in the busy town of Captain Cook at 1400 ft.
elevation above the Kona Coast overlooking Kealakekua Bay and Pu'uhonua O
Honaunau National Historic Park. The Manago enjoys sunny days and cool quiet
evenings. *Standard $23, deluxe $35, extra person $3*

ROYAL KAHILI CONDOMINIUM

78-6283 Alii Drive, Kailua-Kona, HI 96740, (808) 329-2626. Agent: Triad
Management (808) 329-6402, FAX (808) 326-2401. This complex is across the
street from the ocean but has a private oceanfront picnic area and barbeque area.
Laundry facilities are in each unit. It is located 3 miles from the village. The
rental units are in the B-wing with no views.
2 BR $90/75 daily, $600/450 weekly, $1900/1300 monthly

SEA VILLAGE ★

75-6002 Alii Dr., Kailua-Kona, HI 96740, (808) 329-1000. Agents: Paradise
Mgmt. 1-800-367-5205, FAX (808) 533-4621; Knutson & Assoc. (808) 329-9393,
FAX (808) 533-4621; Kona Vacation Resorts 1-800-367-5168, FAX (808) 329-
5480.

This 131 unit condo has 50 guest units available. TV, kitchen, tennis court, maid
service are available but no room telephones. Minimum stay of three days. Units
are very nicely furnished, clean, spacious, and comfortable. The central grounds
are beautifully maintained and landscaped. Pool area with BBQ facilities is right
on water's edge but there is no beach here as it is too rocky. Nice views of Kailua
Bay and the village. 3 day minimum stay.
*1BR g.v. $90-106, 1BR o.v. $102-118, 1BR o.f. $110-126, 2BR g.v. $114-130, 2BR
o.v. $126-142, 2BR o.f. $134-150*

WHITE SANDS VILLAGE ★ (W)

74-6469 Alii Drive, Kailua-Kona, HI 96740. Agents: Hawaiian Apt. Leasing, 1-
800-854-8843, Calif. 1-800-472-8449, Canada 1-800-824-8968, FAX (808) 497-
4183; Triad Management (808) 329-6402; Kona Vacation Resorts 1-800-367-5168,
Canada 1-800-800-KONA, FAX (808) 329-5480.

This 108 unit condo complex has just a few units available in rental programs. The units are air-conditioned with beautiful furnishing and nicely coordinated color schemes. Tennis courts, TV, and on request maid service are available. Minimum stay of five nights required. The central courtyard has a complete kitchen and BBQ area near the pool. The complex is across the street from White Sands Beach Park. 3 day minimum stay. *2 BR g.v. (2,max 4) $100, $600 week, 2 BR o.v. $125, $750 week*

SOUTH KOHALA DISTRICT

THE KOHALA COAST

The *South Kohala District* embraces parts of the Kohala Mountains, the plateau and plains of Parker Ranch, and extends west to the Kohala Coast. The district includes the towns of Kamuela, Waikoloa Village, Kawaihae, and the resorts of the Kohala Coast. Highway 19, the Hawai'i Belt Road that circles the Big Island, connects Kamuela from Honoka'a and continues on down to Kawaihae and the Kohala Coast's Queen Ka'ahumanu Highway. Going south out of Kamuela, Highway 190 is a scenic route which passes through rolling upcountry ranchlands on its way to Kailua-Kona. Some 15 miles out from Kamuela on Highway 190 is the Waikoloa Road turnoff which passes through Waikoloa Village and on down to the Kohala Coast.

It is necessary to clarify some confusion surrounding the town of Kamuela, or Waimea as it is also called. Kamuela is the name for the Waimea post office. It was named, according to some anyway, for Samuel Parker, son of the founder of Parker Ranch. Kamuela is Hawaiian for Samuel. However, the town itself is named Waimea which in Hawaiian means red water. The two names, Kamuela and Waimea, refer to the same place on the Big Island: the home of the famous Parker Ranch. To make matters even more confusing, there is a town on Kaua'i also named Waimea. That's why the post office people, anyway, prefer the name Kamuela for the Big Island town. However, many Big Islanders use the two names interchangeably when talking of the same place. And being a Big Islander myself, I may do it in this book too. Easy isn't it?

Kamuela town lies at the foot of the Kohala Mountains. It is also on the edge of a large plain or plateau that stretches to the base of towering Mauna Kea. The plateau also slopes, gradually, to both the east and west. Driving through this typically Hawaiian ranch country, you'll be amazed at how lush and green the pastures and gardens are. Naturally, there are lots of cattle and horses roaming the large open pasture lands. The rolling grasslands with the forested hills in the distance will remind you of many areas of the great American West such as Wyoming or Colorado. Kamuela is also a truck-farming community and much of the produce consumed in the state is grown here. The cool climate produces many varieties of vegetables such as lettuce, cabbage, carrots, beans, etc.

Most of the rest of the South Kohala District is a virtual desert or near desert. Lying in the lee of Kamuela and the Hamakua Coast tradewinds to the east, most of the downslope district receives very little rain. It is one large tract of dry brown scrubland from the mid-island plateau of 3000 ft. elevation running down to the bone-dry Kohala Coast. The land is mostly hot, dry, windy and rolling grassland with little vegetation other than drought-resistant kiawe and haole-koa trees. Old lava flows disrupt the landscape here and there. Most folks are surprised at this landscape in Hawai'i as they are totally unprepared for it.

The road system through South Kohala is generally excellent. The Kohala Coast Highway 19, the Queen Ka'ahumanu Highway, which connects Kailua-Kona with the Kohala Coast and Kamuela, was completed only in the mid-1970's. At a cost of many millions, the road has returned its investment many times over as it has allowed the development of the famed Kohala Coast super-resorts which we'll be discussing shortly. Highway 19 in this area is a generally straight highway with fairly unobstructed views of the sloping uplands of Kohala and many vast old lava flows through which it passes. And because of its nearness (less than a mile) in most places to the coast, it is quite warm on the road most of the time. In the area just above the Kona Village Resort, about 14-15 miles north of Kailua-Kona, be on the lookout for yellow road signs with the silhouette of a donkey. This area is frequented by the small herds of "Kona Nightingales" as they are called locally. These beasts are the descendants of the donkeys used in the old days to pack supplies and goods up and down the old coastal trail. They were also used to carry bags of coffee harvested from the coffee farms on Kona's steep mountain slopes. They now roam wild in this area and can sometimes be seen near the highway.

The old scenic upcountry route, Highway 190, passes through rolling ranch country and is still used by many since it offers a different panorama on a drive between Kailua-Kona and Kamuela. And because it is at a higher elevation, it is a much cooler drive that the coastal Highway 19. This road is narrower with more hills and curves but it is definitely more scenic for a casual sightseeing drive. Beautiful scenic views of the South Kohala Coast are frequent along this route. On either route, the distance between Kailua-Kona and Kamuela is approximately 40 miles or a driving time of 1 hour. The distance between Kamuela and the Kohala Coast resorts is anywhere from 12 to 20 miles as the resorts are spread out along the coast.

A few years ago, the State of Hawai'i's economic development department produced a statewide "Sunshine Map" and study. That project confirmed what the old Hawaiians knew long ago: the Kohala Coast has the highest sunshine rating in the islands - even higher than such sun resorts as Ka'anapali on Maui and Waikiki on O'ahu. Kohala Coast weather is consistent: average annual rainfall is 8.7 inches over the last 35 years records were kept. Temperatures average in the mid-60's for lows and mid to upper 80's for highs with 78 degrees the average year around. It's no wonder that Kohala lays claim to, and rightfully so, the title of the "sunniest coast" in Hawai'i.

Kohala is one of the least pretentious but most elegant resort destinations in Hawai'i. What first looks like an apparent developers mirage at long range reveals itself on close inspection to be a stunning oasis of luxury resorts, golf courses, tennis complexes, and all the amenities of a palatial playground in the middle of a vast dry inhospitable lava desert.

This lonely desolate stretch of land combines golden beaches, rugged lava flows, hot dry desert, incredibly blue sea, and luxury resorts, all the stuff of dreams. And so it is that the Kohala Coast has become Hawai'i's leading destination with its complex of plush super-resorts. But more on that shortly.

South Kohala has a pastoral side that is best observed in the upcountry town of Waimea, or Kamuela as it is also called. This quiet, cool town (3000 ft. elevation) is the center of paniolo (cowboy) country. Waimea is the headquarters for the famous Parker Ranch, owned by Richard Palmer Smart, the state's largest ranch and the largest individually owned ranch in the United States. Over 50,000 head of Hereford cattle are raised on over 220,000 acres of pastureland. Each year Parker Ranch produces 10 million pounds of beef, more than one-third of Hawai'i's total. Waimea is a ranch town and its atmosphere reflects a country lifestyle. Located on the flatlands of the Waimea plateau and surrounded by rolling hills, the area is a welcome contrast to the warm sunny skies of the Kohala Coast.

WHAT TO DO AND SEE

Visitors to Waimea will find a lot to explore in this cool green upcountry town. A major attraction is the *Parker Ranch Visitor Center* ★ located in the *Parker Ranch Shopping Center*. Here visitors can discover the fascinating history and operations of Parker Ranch and the Hawaiian paniolo (cowboy) lifestyle still in existence today. A large screen video presentation highlights day-to-day ranching activities of the 100 or so ranch hands and cowboys employed by Parker Ranch. Visitors can also browse through the museum which depicts the six generations of the Parker family and see items used during 140 years of ranching history. The visitor center is open daily except Sunday, 9AM-5PM. Admission is $5 for adults, $3.75 for children 4-11 years. Phone: (808) 885-7655.

Another ranch attraction is the historic Parker Ranch homes at *Pu'uopelu* ★. Just outside Waimea on Highway 190 is the entrance to Pu'uopelu, the residence of the present ranch owner. It is the setting for *Mana*, the quaint 140 year old restored New England-style house built by John Palmer Parker I. The interior is

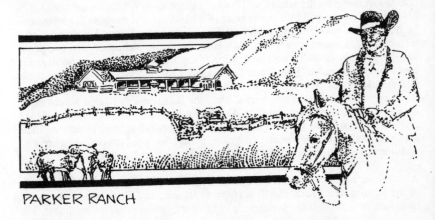

PARKER RANCH

made entirely of native Hawaiian koa wood. *Pu'uopelu*, the 100 year old main ranch residence, features an outstanding art gallery with an impressive collection of original paintings by Degas, Pissarro, Renoir, and Chagall plus many other objets d'art and antiques. Pu'uopelu is open daily except Sunday, 9AM-4:30PM. $7.50 adult admission, $5.00 for children 4-11 years. Phone: (808) 885-5666.

Of interest to World War II/Pacific War vets and history buffs is a large stone marker on Highway 190 near the entrance of Pu'uopelu. The marker notes the surrounding grounds of Parker Ranch which were used as "Camp Tarawa 1943-45" by the 2nd and 5th U.S. Marine Divisions which trained here.

Another Kamuela attraction with ties to Parker Ranch is **Hale Kea** (885-6095), located on the Kawaihae Road just two miles west of town. Hale Kea (White House) was originally built in 1897 and served as the manager's residence for Parker Ranch. The property was later owned by Laurance Rockefeller, developer of the Mauna Kea Beach Hotel. The property was later sold and in 1989, after restoration work, the rambling old home and its 11 acres of gardens and cottages were opened as a visitor attraction. Hale Kea features several specialty shops and boutiques and *Hartwell's Restaurant*. The restaurant features dining in various rooms of the home including the main dining room, veranda, parlor, library and sitting room. The property's gardens have been carefully restored to their former glory and throughout there are reminders of Waimea's rich ranching tradition. Hale Kea is open daily from 9:30AM - 8PM.

The *Kamuela Museum* (885-4724) in Waimea is at the intersection of routes 19 and 250 (Kohala Mountain Road). It is the largest privately owned museum in Hawai'i. Interesting collections of ancient Hawaiian weapons, World War II relics, furniture of Hawaiian royalty, and many other antiques and art objects are on display. Open daily, 9AM-5PM. The admission fee is adults $5, children under age 12, $2.

On the *Kohala Coast*, at Kawaihae Bay is *Pu'ukohola Heiau National Historic Site* ★, well worth a visit. This massive heiau (temple) was built by Kamehameha the Great in 1791 upon the advice of a priest who told Kamehameha that he would conquer all the islands of Hawai'i if he did so. By 1795, Kamehameha did conquer in battle all the islands of Hawai'i except Kaua'i, which later acceded to his rule and recognized him as the ruler of all Hawai'i. At the time Kamehameha built his heiau, his chief Big Island rival was his cousin, Keoua Ku'ahu'ula, also a chief. Kamehameha invited Ku'ahu'ula to his temple dedication to make peace and Ku'ahu'ula fatefully accepted. As Ku'ahu'ula and his party landed at the beach below the heiau, Kamehameha's warriors swept down and killed them all. Ku'ahu'ula's body was carried up to the temple and was offered as the principal sacrifice to Kamehameha's war god. Thus the heiau was dedicated according to ancient Hawaiian religious custom. Just below the heiau site is *Spencer Beach Park*, a popular place for camping, swimming, snorkeling, and picnicking. The beach has calm quiet water and fine sand perfect for youngsters. There are also restrooms, a pavilion, picnic tables, basketball court, and showers.

About three miles south of Kawaihae on Highway 19 and just past the entrance to the *Mauna Kea Beach Hotel*, is *Hapuna Beach State Park*, one of the area's nicer beaches. Restrooms, pavilions, picnic tables, and showers are available. The beach has moderate surf and shallow water good for body surfing but not for board surfing. At the north end of the beach on the hills overlooking the area, a the new *Hapuna Beach Prince Hotel* is under construction. The new 350-room luxury property, part of the Mauna Kea Resort, is to be completed by spring 1994. Next door in front of the Mauna Kea Beach Hotel is *Mauna Kea Beach* on *Kauna'oa Bay*, one of the loveliest white sand crescents on the Big Island. Limited public parking is available at the Mauna Kea Beach Hotel but public access to this lovely beach is maintained.

A mile south of Hapuna Beach on Highway 19 is the *Puako Road* turnoff. Two miles down this narrow winding road through the beach residences lies a trail to the *Puako Petroglyph Fields*. Here visitors can see detailed rock carvings of human figures, mythical figures, and symbols done by the old Hawaiians on the lava rocks. Five miles further south on Highway 19 is the turnoff to *Anaeho'omalu Beach Park* and the *Royal Waikoloan Hotel* and the fabulous *Hyatt Regency Waikoloa Hotel*. Anaeho'omalu Beach is a lovely sweeping wide crescent of golden sand fronting a fishpond. There is good snorkeling and swimming at this beach as the water is generally not too rough. Picnic tables and restrooms are available. The hotel sits behind the beach and fishpond areas but with easy access. Segments of the *King's Highway* ★, the centuries old footpath that winds along the Kohala Coast, can still be walked in this area. Many additional petroglyph fields lie scattered throughout the area. Just north of the Waikoloa Resort area is the *Mauna Lani Resort* which is home to the *Ritz-Carlton Mauna Lani Hotel* and the *Mauna Lani Bay Hotel and Bungalows*. The ancient fishponds at *Kalahuipua'a* next to the Mauna Lani Bay Hotel are being restored and can be seen on a walk through the hotel grounds. This beautiful site is now operated as a working aquaculture preserve stocked with mullet fish.

The Waikoloa Road intersects Highway 19 (Queen Ka'ahumanu Highway on the Kohala Coast) and connects the old Waimea to Kailua-Kona upcountry road, Highway 190. At *Waikoloa Village*, there is a riding stable, restaurant, village store, post office, and a golf course. The Waikoloa Highlands Center, a full-service shopping center, has recently opened. The village is growing as a retirement and vacation community for sunseekers and golfers as well as a residential community for employees of Kohala Coast resorts. Its near proximity of 7-10 miles to the Kohala Coast resorts makes it a popular spot. The distance between Kamuela and Waikoloa is approximately 18 miles.

Five miles north of the Waikoloa Road, Highway 19 intersects with Highway 200, the "Saddle Road" which connects Hilo with West Hawai'i via the plateau between Mauna Kea and Mauna Loa. About six miles above this intersection on the Saddle Road is *Waiki'i Ranch* nestled in the rolling hills at 4,500 ft. elevation. This is the home of the Waiki'i Ranch Polo Club which hosts an annual series of polo competitions each fall.

WHERE TO SHOP

Presently, South Kohala is not noted for its shopping. In fact, at the Kohala Coast resorts, there is little beyond the standard pricey resort shops. Each of the major hotels, Mauna Kea Beach, Mauna Lani Bay Hotel, Ritz-Carlton Mauna Lani, Hyatt Regency Waikoloa and the Royal Waikoloan all have their own resort wear, jewelry, photo, and general gift shops on premises.

At Waikoloa Resort, the *King's Shops* complex opened in early 1992 and when complete (in late '92 or '93) will provide a full-range of first-class resort shops and eateries. Among the tenants are *Benetton, Kula Bay Tropical Clothing, Endangered Species, Kalama Beach, Noa Noa, Island Shells* and others. There will also be restaurants such as *Hama Yu Japanese Restaurant, Ocean Club and Kona Coolers Restaurant & Bar.* The complex also features museum exhibits showcasing the area's cultural history. Up the road at the Mauna Lani Resort, there is also a major shopping center complex under construction as of 1992.

For most shopping needs on the Kohala Coast, one has to go all the way upcountry, from 10-20 miles, to Kamuela. The other alternative is to drive the 25-35 miles south into Kailua-Kona. However, Waimea doesn't disappoint serious shoppers. It has a surprising variety of fine shops and goods available for a small ranch town.

The *Parker Ranch Shopping Center* in the center of town has a number of interesting local shops. First, there is of course the ranch's own *Parker Ranch Store* for official Parker Ranch T-shirts and westernwear accessories. There is also *Alihi Creations* which features Hawaiiana and special gifts from all over, *Keep In Touch* for T-shirts and gifts, *Tropical Daze* for clothing, *Fiberarts Gallerie* for arts and crafts, *Mountain Goldsmiths* for jewelry, *Paniolo Hawaiian Art* and others. Also located here are *Aunty Alice's Restaurant and Bakery, Morelli's Pizza* and *Parker Ranch Broiler.*

Just across Highway 19, is the new *Waimea Center* anchored by *KTA Superstore* for groceries, along with several eateries, *McDonald's, TCBY Yogurt, Subway, Great Wall Chop Suey*, and *Yong's Kal-Bi.* The center also has *Capricorn Bookshop* and several other clothing, boutiques and general shops.

On Highway 19 out toward the west edge of town is *Parker Square Shopping Center*, a shopping complex with an old ranch motif. The complex houses the *Waimea General Store* (885-4479) a general gift shop that also carries arts and crafts, kitchenware items, and all sorts of unique gifts. *Gallery of Great Things* (885-7706) pretty much lives up to its name. It's more like strolling through a museum, or an archeologist's lab. There are numerous antiques and art pieces from all over the Pacific area including Hawai'i, Micronesia, New Guinea, the Solomon Islands, Bali in Indonesia, and more. It is a fascinating collection of authentic Pacific art: tribal masks, wood carvings, primitive weapons, paintings, and more. It's all beautiful and with prices to match! For art lovers and collectors this shop is a must! *Bentley's* (885-5565) is a general gift shop and feature decorative home furnishings and accessories. *Gifts in Mind* carries general gift items and customized Hawaiian jewelry. *Parker Square Cafe* is also located here serving lunch and light snack fare.

Also near the west edge of Kamuela town on the Kawaihae Road is **Opelu Plaza**, a small shopping and commercial development which features **Kamuela Bread Depot** (885-6354) a bakery-deli specializing in wonderful French bread, pastries, sandwiches, soups, salads, and more. They are open daily except Sunday, 6:30AM-5:30PM. **Merriman's**, a gourmet dining room that has won wide acclaim, is also located here. They are open for lunch Monday-Friday 11:30AM - 1:30PM; dinner nightly 5:30 - 9PM; and Sunday brunch 10:30AM - 1:30PM.

ACCOMMODATIONS-SOUTH KOHALA DISTRICT

South Kohala's accommodations are located along the famed Kohala Coast and in the town of Waimea (Kamuela) or at Waikoloa Village. The Kohala Coast resorts are of course where all the excitement and activity are: luxurious hotels and condos, fabulous golf courses, complete tennis facilities, and all the amenities of world-class super-resorts. The Kohala Coast is celebrated for its resort properties which include the Mauna Kea Beach Hotel, the Mauna Lani Bay Hotel and Bungalows, the Ritz-Carlton Mauna Lani, the Hyatt Regency Waikoloa, the Royal Waikoloan Hotel and resort condominiums.

Waimea, boasts a couple of clean comfortable motel-type accommodations in the Parker Ranch Lodge and the Kamuela Inn. Both places offer good value accommodations at reasonable rates. In addition, there are some good quality B & B operations as well. Waikoloa Village has condo rentals in the growing retirement-vacation community only a few minutes drive from the Kohala Coast resorts.

For those wanting to experience the ultimate in luxury, comfort, and sumptuousness, any of the Kohala Coast resorts will fit the bill. These resorts cater to every whim and fantasy and can make your dream vacation a reality. They are the ultimate in resorts in Hawai'i and will provide a memorable experience. The cost of course will be considerable. Among these are the Big Island's all time leading and renowned resort, its newest, its most expensive as well as its largest. The Kohala Coast resorts are simply some of the most splendid playgrounds in Hawai'i. Dining and restaurant options on the Kohala Coast are strictly limited to resort facilities. However, the resorts boast several award-winning restaurants and dining rooms noted for their culinary expertise, diversity of cuisine and personal service. Away from the resorts, one can find local-style favorites and some fine American-Continental cuisine in Kamuela and Kawaihae restaurants. See the RESTAURANTS chapter for details.

BEST BETS

Hyatt Regency Waikoloa - For those seeking an ultimate Hawaiian fantasy resort that incorporates touches of Disneyland and Las Vegas, this is the place.
Mauna Lani Bay Hotel and Bungalows - This elegant sophisticated hotel provides a regal vacation experience for those who like to indulge in the good life.
Mauna Lani Point Condominiums - These units are part of the Mauna Lani Resort and are highly recommended for a first-class vacation experience.
Mauna Lani Terrace Condominium - This luxurious complex has spacious comfortable units in the heart of Mauna Lani Resort surrounded by lagoons, fish ponds and golf course fairways.

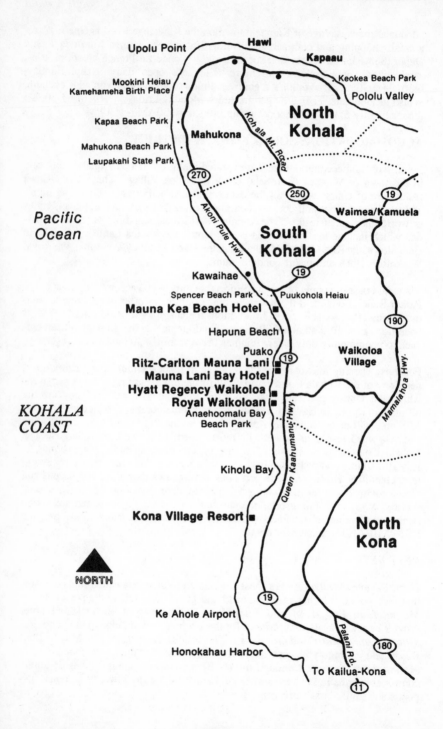

Parker Ranch Lodge - If you are seeking a haven away from the gaudiness of tourist resorts, you'll find it here in quiet cool Kamuela town.

Royal Waikoloan Hotel - This property has about the best beach location of any of the Kohala Coast resorts and is a class act overall.

Mauna Kea Beach Hotel - This is the "grande dame" of the Kohala Coast hotels, having been the first property on the Sunshine Coast over a quarter-century ago. It is an ageless and accommodating property and continues to be one of Hawai'i's finest.

The Shores at Waikoloa - This luxurious complex has spacious units and full amenities that make any stay a totally enjoyable experience.

KOHALA COAST ACCOMMODATIONS

Hyatt Regency Waikoloa Hotel	Puako Beach Apartments
Mauna Kea Beach Hotel	Ritz-Carlton Mauna Lani
Mauna Lani Bay Hotel	Royal Waikoloan
Mauna Lani Point	Shores at Waikoloa
Mauna Lani Terrace Condo	Vista Waikoloa
Parker Ranch Lodge	Waikoloa Villas

HYATT REGENCY WAIKOLOA ★

One Waikoloa Beach Resort, Kohala Coast, Waikoloa, HI 96743, (808) 885-1234, 1-800-233-1234, FAX (808) 885-7592. The Hyatt Regency Waikoloa is the most expensive resort ever built in Hawai'i. It was built at a cost of $360 million and is a unique brand of Polynesian opulence that redefines the notion of a "fantasy resort" forever. This incredible resort is carved out of 62 jagged lava acres on the shores of Waiulua Bay on the famed Kohala Coast. It features 1,241 guest rooms. With the opening of the Hyatt four years ago, the Kohala Coast arrived as Hawai'i's resort of the '90's.

No expense was spared to make this the ultimate of resorts. There is a huge saltwater lagoon teeming with tropical fish and tame dolphins that guests can swim with, an acre-sized swimming pool, waterfalls, and a canal with boats that ferry guests over a mile of waterways to their rooms. This in addition to space-age tram trains and a mile-long open-air museum walkway filled with art treasures from the Orient and Pacific and a wildlife collection. Throw in several different "themed" restaurants, cocktail lounges, a nightclub, complete recreational facilities from golf, to tennis, to deep-sea fishing and diving, and the Hyatt Regency Waikoloa caters to every whim, every need, every vacation fantasy. The Hyatt has a daily program for children, "kamp waikoloa," available for a rate of $35 per child. Extra person age 13 and over $25, children under 12 free. *Standard $235-335, Deluxe $370-395, 1BR suites $575-875, 2BR suites $575-3,000*

MAUNA KEA BEACH HOTEL ★ (W)

One Mauna Kea Beach Drive, Kohala Coast, HI 96743-9706. (808) 882-7222. Reservations: 1-800-882-6060, FAX (808) 882-7657.

This 310 room property is located on the beach on Kauna'oa Bay and is the original Kohala Coast resort. Developed by Laurance Rockefeller in the mid-1960's as Hawai'i's foremost luxurious hotel, it remains the standardbearer for fine resort hotels not only in Hawai'i but worldwide. There's not much more to be said about the resort which has consistently won acclaim and distinction from various organizations and the travel-hospitality industry and the media for its high standards of service and recreational facilities. The American Automobile Association has awarded the Mauna Kea Beach Hotel the coveted AAA Five Diamond Award for excellence two years running. The hotel has been voted "America's Number 1 Favorite Resort" for four consecutive years in a national independent poll of 15,000 CEO's and leading U.S. business executives by *Andrew Harper's Hideaway Report*. In addition, *Travel-Holiday Magazine* has recognized the hotel's exceptional cuisine and service with a rare "blanket" award of excellence which covers all four of its dining rooms. The Mauna Kea's golf course was ranked among "America's 100 Greatest" in 1991 and among "America's 75 Best Resort Courses" by *Golf Digest*. This is along with the *Golf Magazine* rating as one of the "Top 12 Golf Resorts in America." And Mauna Kea's tennis facilities were rated among the "50 Greatest U.S. Tennis Resorts" by *Tennis Magazine* in 1990. Suffice it to say that the Mauna Kea provides the ultimate in luxury, dining, recreational facilities and activities, and a complete vacation experience for the most discerning of travelers. The Mauna Kea has a complimentary "Childrens' Program" during the Easter and Christmas-New Year's holiday seasons and from mid-June through Labor Day.

The hotel boasts the award-winning Batik Room, The Pavilion, The Garden, The Terrace, The Teppan Yaki and The 19th. Hole restaurants, plus weekly Hawaiian luau and a sumptuous clam bake at the Hau Tree Terrace guaranteed to please seafood lovers. In addition there are cocktail lounges, water sports and the lovely crescent of Kaunaoa Beach, golf course, tennis courts, shops, and meeting rooms.

Mountain View $260, Mountain View (8th Floor) $310, Beach Front $380, Ocean View $390, Ocean View (8th Floor) $450
Rates quoted are European Plan (no meals). A Modified American Plan (MAP) including full breakfast and dinner daily is available for following additional rates: guests 13 years and older $68, 5-12 years $40.75, under 5 years no charge when adults on meal plan.

MAUNA LANI BAY HOTEL AND BUNGALOWS ★ (W)
P.O. Box 4000, Kohala Coast, HI 96743-4000, (808) 885-6622.
Reservations 1-800-367-2323, FAX (808) 885-4556.

This sleek and elegant 350 room property sits amidst a stark black lavaflow on beautiful Makaiwa Bay Beach on the Kohala Coast. All rooms are very spacious and luxuriously appointed with oversize TV, refrigerator, air-conditioning, mini-bar, double sink bathrooms and many other features. Le Soleil, The Bay Terrace, and The Canoe House restaurants provide superb dining, and there are cocktail lounges, tennis courts, golf course, shops, and meeting rooms all on grounds. Le Soleil has won recognition for exceptional cuisine from *Travel-Holiday Magazine*. The Mauna Lani Golf Course has received wide acclaim for excellence and an entire new 18-hole layout was added in 1991. The links now include the North and South courses. The fairways wind through lavaflows and along the rugged coastline and are almost too spectacular to believe. One sports editor said of it, "If they ever put a golf course in the Smithsonian, this will be it." It's been designated one of the ten most beautiful golf courses in the world by *Travel*

Weekly; the South course 17th hole was designated as one of three "Pearls of the Pacific" by *Golf Digest*. With the ultimate in luxury and service in mind, the Mauna Lani has five private bungalow suites available, each with its own swimming pool and spa. These private bungalows come complete with limousine, personal butler and concierge staff to cater to the guest's every whim. The Mauna Lani has a complimentary childrens' program, "Camp Mauna Lani," which is offered from late June through Labor Day.
Standard $260-415, Deluxe $450, Suites $725, Bungalow $3,000

MAUNA LANI POINT CONDOMINIUMS ★
2 Kaniku Drive, Mauna Lani Resort, Kohala Coast, HI 96743. Reservations: Classic Resorts 1-800-642-6264, (808) 885-5022, FAX (808) 661-0147. Agents: Hawai'i Apt. Leasing 1-800-854-8843, CA 1-800-472-8449, Canada 1-800-824-8968.

This super luxurious vacation condo has 55 units available, all located on the Mauna Lani Golf Course. The units are plush and feature private lanai, complete kitchens, laundry facilities, air-conditioning and many other amenities. Guests have resort privileges such as private beach and beach club, special tennis and golf rates, health club facilities, and more. Three day minimum stay required.
1 BR $325/190, 2 BR $410/250, 3 BR $480-400, extra person $15

MAUNA LANI TERRACE CONDOMINIUM ★
Mauna Lani Resort, Kohala Coast, HI 96743. (808) 882-1066, FAX (808) 882-7676. Agent: South Kohala Mgmt. 1-800-822-4252, (808) 883-8500. These magnificent luxury units are located adjacent to the Mauna Lani Bay Hotel at Mauna Lani Resort. The large spacious units are sparkling and well maintained throughout with the tasteful decor and furnishings expected of a luxury unit. The units are incredibly large and roomy, providing lots of space to move around, relax and enjoy the special luxurious ambiance of Mauna Lani. All units are air-conditioned with ceiling fan in living room, private lanais, wet bars, and complete laundry facilities. There is easy access to the resort's world class golf and tennis, health club, and water sports. Minimum stay of five nights in high season, three nights in low season.
1 BR (2,max 4) $280/240, 2 BR (2,max 6) $365/310, 3 BR (2,max 8) $475/400

PARKER RANCH LODGE ★
P.O. Box 458, Highway 19, Kamuela, HI 96743, (808) 885-4100, FAX (808) 885-5602. This small 20 unit country motel features spacious rooms all with king or queen beds. Clean pleasant furnishings, TV, and phone with nice meadow and mountain views of Kamuela ranch country. Located right in heart of Kamuela town adjacent to Paniolo Country Inn Restaurant and near shopping, other restaurants, area attractions, etc. It's only a 15 mile drive to the Kohala Coast resorts and beaches. *Standard $68, Deluxe with kitchen $78, extra person $10*

PUAKO BEACH APARTMENTS (W)
3 Puako Beach Drive, Kamuela, HI 96743. (808) 882-7711. This 38 unit condo has 19 units available for vacation rental. The condo is located in the quiet Puako Beach area near Hapuna Beach Park on the Kohala Coast. Rooms have TV and kitchen and there is twice weekly maid service. Extra person $5.
1 BR $55-59, 2 BR (2,max 4) $80-84, 3 BR (2,max 6) $95-99, 4 BR $134-150

RITZ-CARLTON MAUNA LANI HOTEL ★

One North Kaniku Drive, Kohala Coast, HI 96743. (808) 885-2000, 1-800-845-9905, FAX (808) 885-1064. This luxury-class hotel is located next door to the Mauna Lani Bay Hotel at Mauna Lani Resort and is surrounded by fairways of the North Golf Course. It has 550 guest rooms and features The Cafe, The Grill and The Dining Room restaurants plus lounges and an entire range of luxury guest amenities and services. The hotel has a small white sand beach, swimming lagoon and pool, jacuzzi, 15 tennis courts including grass and exhibition courts and a health and fitness center. There are also extensive conference facilities. The "Ritz Kids Program" is a hands-on activities program offered for youngsters.
Standard $260, Superior $295, Deluxe o.v. $365, Ocean Front $415, Ritz-Carlton Club $450, Suites $550-2,800, extra person $35

ROYAL WAIKOLOAN HOTEL ★

P.O. Box 5300, Waikoloa Beach Drive, Kohala Coast, HI 96743-5000. (808) 885-6789. Reservations: US and Canada, 1-800-537-9800, FAX (808) 885-7280; The Grande Collection of Hotels, 1-800-223-0888.

This 550 room hotel is located directly behind the beautiful 1/2 mile crescent shaped Anaeho'omalu Bay Beach and lagoon amidst a stark black lava flow. The rooms are attractively furnished, air-conditioned and have TV. There is also a separate 20-room Royal Cabana Club at the edge of the beach lagoon, operated as an upscale or concierge section of the hotel with a separate staff and special services such as complimentary continental breakfast and sunset cocktails. The lobby is spacious and opens out onto a lanai overlooking the pool and gardens. The hotel features the Garden Cafe, Royal Terrace, and Tiare Room Restaurants, cocktail lounges, tennis courts, access to Waikoloa Resort golf courses, shops, and meeting rooms. With Anaeho'omalu Beach and its lovely fishponds fronting the hotel, this is one of the loveliest settings along the Kohala Coast. It is a natural for varied water-sports activities which are readily accessible to guests through *Ocean Sports Waikoloa*, located on the beach. A special free childrens' program, "Keiki's Hoolaulea," is offered during summer. The Royal Waikoloan has received the 1991 AAA Tour Book 4-Diamond rating. *Extra person $20*
Garden View $ 99, Mountain View $135, Ocean View $160
Ocean Front $195, Royal Cabana $250, Suites $350-750

SHORES AT WAIKOLOA ★

HC02 Box 5460, Waikoloa, HI 96743. (808) 885-5001. Agents: ASTON Hotels & Resorts 1-800-922-7866, Hawai'i 1-800-342-1551, FAX (808) 922-8785; South Kohala Mgmt. 1-800-822-4252, Hawai'i (808) 883-8500, FAX (808) 883-9818; Hawai'i Apt. Leasing 1-800-854-8843, CA 1-800-472-8449, Canada 1-800-824-9868. There are 72 units available in rental programs. These are 1-2-3BR, all fully air-conditioned, full kitchens, TV, washer/dryer, private lanai and wetbar as standard features. The units are very spacious and well furnished with lots of extra room and large bathrooms. Perfect for families. Guests have easy access to pool, barbecue facilities, tennis courts and adjacent Waikoloa Beach and King's Golf Courses. Guests can enjoy dining at any of several resort restaurants at the Royal Waikoloan or Hyatt Regency. Golf course fairway location in Waikoloa Beach Resort.
1 BR (2,max 4) $190/160, 2 BR (2,max 6) $220/185
2 BR (2,max 6) $275/240 Golf Villa, 3 BR (2,max 8) $340/305

VISTA WAIKOLOA ★
Waikoloa Beach Drive, Waikoloa Beach Resort, Waikoloa, HI 96743; Agent:
South Kohala Management, 1-800-822-4252, (808) 883-8500, FAX (808) 883-
9818. This luxurious new development was completed in early 1992 and at
publication time had very few of its 122 total units available in vacation rental
programs. The multi-building complex is located right on Waikoloa Beach Drive
between the Royal Waikoloan and Hyatt Regency Waikoloa and next to the golf
course fairways. The units are completely furnished with full kitchens, a/c and
access to pool, spa and resort recreational facilities.
2 BR (2,max 6) $220/185, 2 BR (2,max 6) $275/240 Golf Villa,
3 BR (2,max 8) $340/305

WAIKOLOA VILLAS
P.O. Box 3498, Lua Kula Drive, Waikoloa, HI 96743; (808) 883-9144. Agent:
Hawaiian Island Resorts, 1-800-367-7042, FAX (808) 544-1868. This condo has
41 units available in rental programs. Units have kitchens, telephones, TV,
meeting room, weekly maid service. Golf course is nearby. Minimum stay of 2
days required. *1 BR $115-135, 2 BR $125-150, 3 BR $165-185,   extra person $10*

SOUTH HILO DISTRICT

HILO: A LOOK ON THE BRIGHT SIDE

Mention has already been made of Hilo and its notorious rainy reputation ("Big
Island Weather"). Granted, it's probably Hawai'i's most underrated and least
glamorous place. It has what public relations experts call "an image problem."
Even though it does rain a lot - some 130 inches annually - its sordid reputation
is really undeserved as there is so much more to the Big Island's county seat
(pop. 45,000) and gateway to lush and lovely East Hawai'i than its jaded rainy
reputation. Of course, I admit, I am biased. I live here, by choice and good
fortune. Hilo has had so many jokes made about its rain and more stories
fabricated about its wet climate that even some Hilo folks believe them! But
whatever is said about their fair town, Hilo folks remain decidedly cheerful, open,
friendly, and optimistic. Afterall, these are the people who have endured every-

BOUGAINVILLEA   J. BAYOT

thing Mother Nature has thrown at them: earthquakes, tidal waves, and threatening eruptions and lava flows from Mauna Loa. They are not about to let a little rain get them down, or other folks' unfair jokes about their town. When you've survived all of these, you know a good thing when you have it and for them Hilo is it, rain or shine.

Known informally to some as Bay City or Crescent City (for its curving beach on Hilo Bay) and even the City of Rainbows (an obvious attempt to brighten its image) Hilo dates back to early Hawai'i. It was long the government and commercial trade center of the island and serviced the sugar plantations that were the main industry of early Hawai'i. The abundant rains still produce lush fields of sugar cane but, in spite of it, the industry is withering. Several plantations have gone out of business in the last twenty years and former cane lands are being planted in macadamia nuts, papayas, bananas, and tropical flowers which hold more economic promise and are more environmentally sound.

Today's Hilo remains a colorful small town that attracts the island's country folks and still provides shave ice (snow cones), sodas, and Saturday movies for island youngsters just as it did a generation or two ago. It remains as the governmental, commercial, and social hub of the island's east side. Though it is a generally conservative town, as small towns are inclined to be, it is learning to cope with an ever changing economy and lifestyle, however some might argue that point.

And while Hilo's once-promising tourist industry has given way to the booming Kona-Kohala resort areas on the west side, Hilo has not given up entirely. As mentioned, the area's agriculture is learning to diversify with the exit of sugar and Hilo is gaining recognition as a residential small college town with the growth and expansion of the state supported University of Hawai'i at Hilo and adjoining Hawai'i Community College. The schools share a lovely campus and a cosmopolitan enrollment of some 4000 students from around the islands of Hawai'i, the U.S. mainland and all over the Pacific Rim.

The United Kingdom Infrared Telescope organization, which operates two observatories on Mauna Kea, has its world headquarters near the university campus in Hilo. Along with the multi-million dollar Prince Kuhio Plaza shopping center and other local development like the Hilo Main Street renovation of old downtown Hilo, there is a reflection of confidence in the business community in Hilo's future.

With its distinctly tropical climate, Hilo has become the center for the world's largest tropical flower industry. Anthuriums, those heart-shaped long-lasting blooms that fetch $2-3 each in winter, are marketed by the thousands worldwide from numerous farmer co-ops and flower farm exporters. The orchid industry features numerous varieties of lovely cut flowers, sprays, and potted plants that are exported worldwide also.

Old downtown Hilo is a conglomeration of vintage wood frame and stucco finished buildings, many dating from the turn of the century. A walk through town reveals an interesting collection of general retail shops, offices, flower and fruit stalls, seed shops, fish markets, butcher shops, old fashioned soda fountains, barber shops, lunch shops, and Mom & Pop stores. Many of these places give the impression of it still being the 1930's. You can sample everything from a bag of cracked seed (delectable Chinese preserved and dried fruits and fruit seeds, a sort of Oriental candy), to a local gourmet plate lunch, to a bag of fragrant tropical fruits or a bouquet of tropical blooms. In addition, you may chat with the friendly Hilo folks who make old downtown Hilo a rich cross-cultural experience. And where else can you get a haircut for $6.00 these days? Or use parking meters that still take nickles, dimes and pennies?

The last few years have seen much improvement and change in downtown Hilo as new businesses have renovated old shop buildings. Several new restaurants and coffee shops, gift shops, art galleries, boutiques and more have added new life to a once decaying downtown. Even the venerable Palace Theater on Haili Street is undergoing a facelift with plans to serve as a cultural and performing arts center. Added to such attractions as the East Hawai'i Cultural Center and the twice-weekly Farmers Market at the corner of Mamo and Kamehameha Streets and its easy to see why people are rediscovering downtown Hilo. Much of the change and renovation has been brought about through the efforts of downtown merchants, new businesses moving in and the Hilo Main Street Program which has assisted with various development projects. While making downtown Hilo more attractive to people, great care has been placed on preserving its unique historical tradition.

And after experiencing the real Hilo and its notorious rain, perhaps you'll come to see that Hilo does indeed have its place in the sun to soothe and comfort those with tortured soul and psyche who seek relief in a slower pace of life. With its warm showers, lush tropical splendor, and friendly caring folks, Hilo is indeed a balm for troubled souls and aching hearts. You see, the old line about Hilo's rain is really relative. It's all in how you look at it. Hilo's rainy reputation has kept the visitor counts to a minimum which some folks don't mind. Because of it, Hilo has been slow to change. And perhaps that's good. It has helped Hilo to retain its essential hometown charm and personality, a valuable asset these days. Yes, there is a bright side to Hilo. And you really need to discover it for yourself. Oh, and when you come, bring your umbrella. It looks like a shower today!

WHAT TO DO AND SEE

Hilo and vicinity receive little attention from the visitor industry as a destination. However, a locally organized group is working to publicize the area's attractions. **Destination Hilo**, can be reached at P.O. Box 1391, Hilo, Hawai'i 96721; telephone 808/935-5294. And partly because of Hilo's anonymity, it presents an "unspoiled paradise" image, if there is such a thing. There is so much to see, experience, and enjoy in this perennial Hawaiian hometown that you'll need more than a day or two to see it all. A description of some of the major attractions follows.

Liliuokalani Park ★ is located on Banyan Drive in the Waiakea Peninsula adjacent to the hotels and on the shore of Hilo Bay. This authentic Japanese garden park was named in honor of Hawai'i's last reigning monarch, Queen Liliuokalani. It was built in the early 1900's as a memorial to the immigrant Japanese who developed the old Waiakea Sugar Plantation. The park features several magnificent Japanese stone lanterns, pavilions, an arching footbridge, a tea house, and reflecting lagoons. It is one of Hawai'i's loveliest cultural parks. Free. This is a must see place in Hilo.

Banyan Drive Trees line Hilo's hotel row and give it the name "Banyan Drive." Most of these handsome spreading trees were planted fifty or more years ago by such VIPs as President Franklin D. Roosevelt, Britain's King George V, Amelia Earhart, Babe Ruth, Fannie Hurst and other notables of the era. There's even one planted by a then-aspiring politician named Richard Nixon. Each tree is marked accordingly.

Coconut Island in Hilo Bay is a small island just offshore from Liliuokalani Park. A footbridge just opposite the Hilo Hawaiian Hotel leads to it. It is a great place for watching local fishermen angling and the kids swimming and diving from an old bridge platform. There are picnic tables and shelters available. Coconut Island is often used for cultural events by local groups. Worth a stroll in evening at sunset if you are staying at a nearby hotel.

Old Mamalahoa Highway Scenic Drive ★ is just five miles north of Hilo at the intersection with Kalanianaole School. Old Highway 19 follows the rugged rainforested Hamakua Coast for four miles before linking back with the newer Highway 19. The scenic route takes in numerous gulches and coves as it winds through lovely coastal country with scenic views of the rugged Hamakua Coast and lush rainforest jungles. Shower trees, royal poinciana, breadfruit, coconut, African tulip, and royal palms line the route much of the way. The old route passes through aged sugar plantation villages with melodious names such as Papaikou, Onomea, Pepeekeo, and Kawai Nui. It's definitely an easy and scenic drive well worth taking.

Rainbow Falls and Boiling Pots are above old downtown Hilo and just off Wainuenue Avenue on Rainbow Drive at Wailuku River State Park. This small park features walking trails, restrooms, and magnificent views of Rainbow Falls, best viewed early in the morning when the sun strikes the falls, sending rainbows over the spray and pool. A little further up the road, above Hilo Hospital, the Wailuku River is marked by giant holes and recesses, called Boiling Pots, in the lavarock gorge. The Pots create a series of deep swirling pools, falls, and rapids during heavy rain periods. There is no safe swimming in this treacherous and deep gorge. There are restroom facilities, picnic tables, and a scenic overlook of the Wailuku River Gorge. Free.

Suisan Fish Market Auction ★ is located on Hilo Bay at the mouth of the Wailoa River on Lihiwai Street and within walking distance of the Banyan Drive hotels. The auction is a colorful cultural experience and a must for Hilo visitors. Laid out is the fishing tuna fleet's catch of 50-100 lb. yellow fin tuna (ahi), plus numerous colorful tropical fish, squid, and other seafood delicacies. The auction is conducted in a spirited multi-lingual pidgin-English that gives an exotic atmosphere to the scene. The auction begins at 7:00 A.M. Mon. through Saturday. Closed Sunday. Free. Don't leave Hilo without first experiencing this activity!

University of Hawai'i at Hilo and Hawai'i Community College Campus is located between Lanikaula and Kawili Streets in Hilo. The University and Community College, which share a common campus have a combined enrollment of some 4000, offer two and four year degree programs. The University utilizes its special geography and resources to offer programs of study in such unique fields as Hawaiian Studies, Pacific Islands Anthropology, Marine Science, Oceanography, Aquaculture, Volcanology, Geothermal Energy, Astronomy and others. The Community College specializes in the Liberal Arts, Business Education and vocational-technical trades. The serene campus is landscaped with many species of tropical trees and plants. Its theatre hosts numerous public performances, concerts, shows, and plays throughout the year and the Campus Center art gallery has ongoing displays. The campus annually hosts several Elderhostel Program senior citizen courses for U.S. mainland visitors as well as a broad range of summer session offerings. Visitors are welcome. For information, contact the Office of College Relations, UH-Hilo (808) 933-3568, or HCC Provost's Office, (808) 933-3611, 523 W. Lanikaula St., Hilo, Hawai'i 96720-4091.

Lyman Museum and Mission House ★ is an old New England style missionary home built in 1839 for the Rev. David and Sarah Lyman, the first Christian missionaries to arrive in Hilo. In addition to the original Lyman House, the Museum next door holds a unique collection of memorabilia of early Hilo and Big Island life. Included are items from the pre-western old Hawaiian era, the Hawaiian Monarchy era of the 1800's, and the early 1900's. Numerous artifacts from the different cultures that populated Hawai'i are also on display. Museum hours are Mon.- Sat., 9:00AM to 5:00PM, at 276 Haili Street, 935-5021. Admission fee is $3.50 for adults, $2.50 for children ages 13-18, $1.50 for children ages 6-12. Mission House tours are given several times daily beginning at 9:30AM.

Downtown Hilo Walking Tours with Kalakaua Park as the town center are the focus of a free tour scheduled for the third Saturday of each month at 9AM. The tours are sponsored by the Lyman Museum and American Association of University Women. Kalakaua Park, in the center of downtown Hilo, was originally conceived as a civic center by King Kalakaua. The park has roots to one of the first missionary stations as early as 1825. Other nearby places of historical interest included in the walking tour are Niolopa (the present Hilo Hotel), the old and new library buildings, the old federal building, Lyman Musuem and others. Reservations can be made through Lyman House Museum (808/935-5021). Tours begin at the museum, 276 Haili Street, Hilo.

LYMAN HOUSE MUSEUM

East Hawai'i Cultural Center is located in downtown Hilo at 414 Kalakaua Street, opposite Kalakaua Park and the Post Office. The center is housed in the Old Police Station, a historic building constructed in 1932 and placed on the National Register of Historic Buildings and Places. It resembles a Hawaiian "hale" (house) of the 1800's with its hipped roof. The Center is dedicated to culture and the arts in East Hawai'i. Ongoing art gallery shows and exhibits are free and open to the public. Community theater performances are sponsored by the Center throughout the year as well as special events and activities. For information, call 961-5711. Open daily except Sunday, 9AM - 4PM.

Panaewa Rain Forest Zoo ★, located a couple of miles south of Hilo just off the Volcano Highway 11 on Mamaki Street, is one of Hilo's least known and most delightful free attractions. It is one of the few natural tropical rainforest zoos in the United States. The small facility is operated by the County of Hawai'i and features several rainforest species in natural environment enclosures. Among the animals on display are a family of African pygmy hippopotamuses, a variety of rainforest monkeys, a tapir, various jungle parrots, a family of gorgeous rainforest tigers, and endangered Hawaiian birds like the Nene Goose, Hawaiian 'Io (hawk), Pueo (owl) and Hawaiian Stilt. The zoo is a pleasant walk through natural Hawaiian rainforest with numerous flowering trees and shrubs. Colorful peacocks strut openly. The zoo is adjacent to the Panaewa Equestrian Center, horse stables, and racetrack-rodeo grounds. Open daily, 9:00 AM to 4:30 PM, 959-7224. Free.

Mauna Loa Macadamia Nut Factory ★ is located three miles south of Hilo on the east side of Volcano Highway 11 and back in through the orchards a couple of miles. Look for road signs marking the entrance. A visitors center provides free samples of Hawai'i's popular gourmet nut and a wide variety of macadamia nut products are available for purchase, and there is a free narrated factory tour. Open daily from 9:00 AM to 5:00 PM. Call 966-8612 for information.

Wailoa State Park-Wailoa Center is adjacent to Suisan Fish Market on the Wailoa River and behind Kamehameha Avenue and the Hilo Bayfront. Wailoa Park comprises the lands surrounding the Wailoa River and Waiakea Fish Pond. There are lots of picnic tables and several covered pavilions. Fishermen in rowboats are often seen floating around the pond angling for the abundant mullet fish. There are also a Vietnam Veterans War Memorial and a Tsunami (Tidal Wave) Memorial in the park. The Wailoa Center in the park features various free art exhibits, seasonal showings, and cultural displays by local artisans. Check the schedule at the Center for current show. Wailoa Park is a good place for a pleasant picnic lunch.

Flower farms and botanical gardens are numerous in the Hilo area and many welcome visitors. Farm and nursery visits are usually free, but private botanical gardens charge admission. Check your hotel desk or the visitor brochures and newspapers for listings of Hilo area orchid and anthurium farms. The following are a few of my favorite places to see Hawai'i's tropical beauty up close:

Hawai'i Tropical Botanical Garden ★, just north of Hilo on the four mile scenic drive (old Highway 19). Nature trails meander through tropical rainforest, cross streams and waterfalls, and follow the rugged coast. Extensive collections of palms, bromeliads, gingers, exotic ornamentals, and rare plants. Open daily 8-5.

Phone 964-5233. Adult admission is $12, children under 12 are free. Well worth the ticket price when you see what they have created out of former overgrown wild jungle. A garden of joy for nature photographers.

Nani Mau Gardens ★, 421 Makalika Street, Hilo, just south of town off Volcano Highway. You can't miss the turn off the highway, just look for beautiful floral beds and displays on both sides of Makalika Street. From the highway, it's a half-mile to the gardens. There are some 20 acres of tropical foliage, flowers, trees and plants along with a waterfall, pond and Japanese Garden. Visitors can stroll on their own or opt for a tram tour through the grounds. The orchid greenhouse is spectacular with many varieties of orchids in bloom. There is a large gift shop also. Open daily, 8-5. Phone 959-3541. $5.00 admission fee.

Paradise Orchid Gardens, 575 Hinano Street, Hilo. Open Monday through Saturday, 9-5, Sunday 10-2. Phone 935-4043. Free.

Rainbow Tropicals ★, on Mamaki Street just off Volcano Highway 11 just south of Hilo, Open daily 8:30-5. Self-guided tour of ochid, anthurium, and tropical plant gardens. Phone 959-4565. Free.

Hirose Nurseries, 2212 Kaneolehua Ave., Hilo. Open daily 7:30-4:30. Stroll through rainforest gardens of orchids, anthuriums, and tropical plants. Phone 959-4561. Free.

Hilo Tropical Gardens, 1477 Kalanianaole, Hilo, Open daily 8:30-5. Stroll through gardens of exotic tropical flowers including orchids, anthuriums, gingers, etc. Phone 935-4957. Free.

WHERE TO SHOP

Hilo can be a great place to explore and shop for special mementos or gifts. It has everything from modern shopping centers with the latest boutiques, fashion shops, and department stores, to nondescript little arts and crafts and specialty shops in old downtown Hilo. Some of the shopping centers and specialty shops worth checking are listed below.

Shopping Centers in Hilo have everything from major department stores (Sears, Penny's, Liberty House), to discount stores (Longs Drugs, Pay n' Save, Woolworths, Ben Franklin), to fashion stores, shoe stores, bookstores, jewelry stores, etc. Many fashion and department stores carry Hawaii-made Aloha clothing for those who want to get into colorful Aloha shirts and muumuus. Shopping centers are the newer *Prince Kuhio Plaza* at intersection of Kanoelehua (Volcano Highway 11) and Puainako Streets; *Hilo Shopping Center* at corner of Kekuanaoa and Kilauea Avenue; *Kaiko'o Mall* on Kilauea Avenue; and *Puainako Town Center* on Kanoelehua opposite Prince Kuhio Plaza.

Sugawara Lauhala & Gift Shop, 59 Kalakaua Street, 935-8071, and *Maile's Hawai'i*, 216 Kamehameha Avenue, 935-8944, are two places to visit if you are looking for authentic Hawaiian handicraft items. Look for genuine locally made Hawaiian lauhala (pandanus) woven slippers, hats, baskets, handbags, mats, and related goods.

Hawaiian Handcraft Shop Factory, 760 Kilauea Avenue, 935-5587, is the place to go for fine handcrafted wood products. Check out the carvings, bowls, platters, trays, and other items made from local koa, monkeypod, milo, breadfruit, and other Hawaiian woods.

Hilo Hattie's Fashion Center, Prince Kuhio Plaza, 961-3077, is the original Aloha-wear factory. Features all locally made Hawaiian Aloha shirts, shorts, dresses, and muumuus. Showroom, factory tours, purchases directly from factory.

In old downtown Hilo on Keawe Street between Waianuenue and Kalakaua, the "Keawe Collection of Shops" provide some interesting browsing and gift ideas. *The Potter's Gallery*, corner of Waianuenue and Keawe, serves as the outlet for the Big Island Artists & Craftsmen group and has many beautiful and functional works of art, as does *Da Ceramic Shop*, just around the corner on Waianuenue.

Next door on Keawe is *The Chocolate Bar*, which is an attractive sweet shop offering many unusual hand-made chocolate confections and treats, ice cream, and other goodies. *Futon Connection* has a fine collection of varied oriental home furnishings, pillows, lounge items, etc. *Bear's Coffee* offers a wide choice of coffees and special treats to enjoy at sidewalk tables. *The Most Irresistible Shop in Hilo* (also in Prince Kuhio Plaza) is just that. It is loaded with all sorts of specialty items for every room in your house as well as many gift ideas and local items.

Finishing out the Keawe Collection of Shops are *Cunningham Gallery* and *The Picture Frame Shop* which can fix you up with a lovely Hawaiian work of art to decorate that empty wall space at home.

In the Hilo Shopping Center, corner of Lanikaula and Kilauea, *Oriental Designs* is a specialty T-shirt shop with lots of local designs and other take home gift ideas. Try *Pickle Barrel* for a bento (box) lunch, sandwich, saimin or other local-style goodies. *The Orient Connection* is an oriental food store for those with a fancy to take home some of the local and imported oriental products.

On Kamehameha Avenue downtown, you'll enjoy exploring such restored landmarks as the *S. Hata Building* with its handsome bell tower. This carefully restored facility now houses a number of shops and offices and the Cafe Pesto restaurant. Kam Avenue has many old and new shops and small businesses representing a revitalization of old downtown. *Mo'oheau Park and Bandstand* and *Mo'oheau Bus Terminal* are also located here on the bayfront.

And for those with a flair for adventure, in old downtown Hilo each Wednesday and Saturday, take in the *Hilo Farmers' Market*, a fresh produce and general flea market operation on the corner of Mamo Street and Kamehameha Avenue across from Mo'oheau Park. It's a colorful gathering that will give you a glimpse of local folks at their best, just being themselves. You might even find some bargains!

ACCOMMODATIONS - HILO

Most of Hilo's hotels are located along Banyan Drive on the Waiakea Peninsula which extends out into Hilo Bay. These hotels are on the bay but there are no sandy beaches as the lavarock coastline is too rough and rugged. The Hilo Hotel is located in old downtown while the Dolphin Bay Hotel is located on a quiet street in an older residential area not far from downtown. The Waiakea Villas Hotel is located adjacent to Wailoa State Park and Waiakea Fishponds in a relatively quiet secluded garden location a mile from the Banyan Drive area hotels.

For great views of Hilo town, Hilo Bay, and the twin towers of Mauna Kea and Mauna Loa, you should stay at one of the Banyan Drive hotels. For the best views, the Hawai'i Naniloa or the Hilo Hawaiian are tops. The Banyan Drive hotels also offer the best values in accommodations for visitors considering their amenities, facilities, and location. For pre-arranged sightseeing coach/bus tours, pick-ups are easiest at Banyan Drive hotels, although arrangements can be made at the other hotels as well. If you have your own car, it doesn't matter where you stay in Hilo as you can easily find your way around to the important sites. And even the public "Hele On" bus service can take you to points around town. As for shopping and dining, again wherever you stay in Hilo, you won't be far from shopping centers and/or dining options. Hilo is not a large town. Banyan Drive provides several hotel restaurants and local restaurants and eateries are not far away. See the RESTAURANT chapter for details.

BEST BETS: Dolphin Bay Hotel - This is a budget-class lodge with clean simply furnished rooms near downtown Hilo. *Hawai'i Naniloa Hotel* - This is Hilo's landmark property. There has been a "Naniloa" hotel in Hilo for, well, almost as long as there have been visitors to Hawai'i. It is still a fine place to stay while in Hilo. *Hilo Hawaiian Hotel* - This lovely building faces directly onto Hilo Bay and Coconut Island. It has a relaxing Hawaiian ambiance and is just a nice place for a visit. *Hilo Hotel* - If you're on a budget and looking for clean simple rooms without resort frills, the Hilo Hotel is a real value. It's downtown location puts you into the heart of old town Hilo's shops. In addition, its Restaurant Fuji has the best Japanese cuisine on the island. Room rate includes continental breakfast.

HILO BAY WITH MAUNAKEA

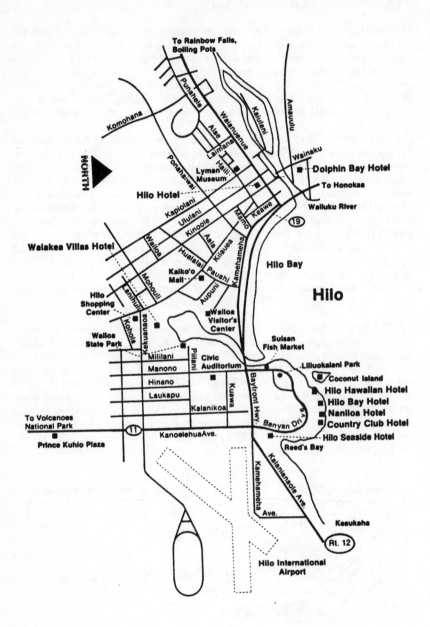

HILO ACCOMMODATIONS

Country Club Hotel   Dolphin Bay Hotel
Hawai'i Naniloa Hotel   Hilo Hawaiian Hotel
Hilo Bay Hotel   Hilo Seaside Hotel
Hilo Hotel   Waiakea Villas Hotel

COUNTRY CLUB HOTEL (W)
121 Banyan Drive, Hilo, HI 96720; Phone/FAX (808) 935-7171. All 130 units are air conditioned, some with TV. Stratton's Restaurant, cocktail lounge, and meeting room are on premises. Located across the street from Naniloa Country Club golf course and on shores of Hilo Bay. However, there is no beach as the shoreline is rugged lavarock. Within walking distance of Coconut Island, Liliuokalani Park, and Suisan Fish Auction. *Standard $50, Deluxe $65, extra person $7*

DOLPHIN BAY HOTEL ★
333 Iliahi Street, Hilo, HI 96720. (808) 935-1466. This small 18 unit hotel is located in a quiet old residential area of Hilo four blocks from the downtown area and three blocks from Hilo Bay. There are few amenities other than fans and TV; no room telephones. Kitchen facilities are included in all units. The rooms are bright, airy, spacious, and very clean. Extra persons $7.
Standard $46, Deluxe $57, Suite $67-77, Weekly $300-500, extra person $8

HAWAI'I NANILOA HOTEL ★ (W)
93 Banyan Drive, Hilo, HI 96720; (808) 969-3333, 1-800-367-5360, FAX (808) 969-6622. This lovely 325 unit tower is a Hilo landmark overlooking Hilo Bay, and across from the Naniloa Country Club golf course and in heart of Banyan Drive hotel area; walking distance to Coconut Island, Liliuokalani Park, Suisan Fish Auction. The spacious rooms are 100% air conditioned with TV. The hotel features the Sandalwood Restaurant for continental-regional dining, Shokoen Restaurant for Chinese cuisine and Nihon Saryo for Japanese cuisine. There is a cocktail lounge and karaoke bar, complete health spa and fitness center and resort pool. There is no beach as the shoreline is rugged lavarock. This is one of Hilo's nicest hotels. *Standard $96, Deluxe $154, Suite $189-574, extra person $15*

HILO HOTEL ★
P.O. Box 726, 142 Kinoole St., Hilo, HI 96720. (808) 961-3733, FAX (808) 935-7836. This small, homey 29 room hotel in downtown Hilo is across from Kalakaua Park and opposite the post office. The rooms are spacious with simple furnishings and are very clean. TV is available in Deluxe rooms and Suites only. The suites in the newer addition are immaculate with full kitchens. Complimentary continental breakfast for hotel guests is served every morning from 7-10 AM in hotel restaurant (Restaurant Fuji). The hotel is located two blocks from Hilo Bayfront and makes it easy to explore old downtown Hilo shops. This is an excellent choice for budget travelers. *Standard $40, Deluxe $45, Suite (max 4) $115*

HILO BAY HOTEL (W)
87 Banyan Drive, Hilo, HI 96720; 1-800-367-5102, (808) 935-0861, FAX (808) 935-7903. This is a 145 unit standard hotel located right on Hilo Bay. The rooms are all air-conditioned with TV. Uncle Billy's Restaurant, cocktail lounge, gift shops, and lovely tropical gardens are on grounds. There is no beach as the

shoreline is rugged lavarock. It is located across from the Naniloa Country Club golf course; walking distance to Coconut Island, Liliuokalani Park, and Suisan Fish Auction.
Standard $59/69, Superior g.v. $64-74, Deluxe g.v. $69-79, Oceanview $79-89, Studio/kitchen $69-79, extra person $10

HILO HAWAIIAN HOTEL ★ (W)
71 Banyan Drive, Hilo, HI 96720; 1-800-367-5004, (808) 935-9361, FAX (808) 533-0472, toll free FAX 1-800-477-2329. Agent: Hawaiian Pacific Resorts 1-800-272-5275, FAX (808) 961-9642. This beautiful 285 room hotel fronts directly on Hilo Bay just behind Coconut Island. There is no sand beach as the shoreline is rugged lavarock. The spacious comfortable rooms are air-conditioned with TV. The Queen's Court Restaurant, cocktail lounge, meeting room, and shops are on grounds. It is located across from the Naniloa Country Club golf course; walking distance to Coconut Island, Liliuokalani Park, and Suisan Fish Auction. Extra person $15 each. *Standard $99, Deluxe $120, Suite $240*

HILO SEASIDE HOTEL
126 Banyan Drive, Hilo, HI 96720. (808) 935-0821. Agent: Sands, Seaside, and Hukilau Hotels 1-800-367-7000, Canada 1-800-654-7020. This 145 room hotel is located just opposite Reeds Bay small boat harbor and the Ice Pond swimming hole but there is no good beach here. The rooms are standard but clean and feature ceiling fans and TV. The Hukilau Restaurant, cocktail lounge, and meeting rooms are on premises. It is adjacent to the Naniloa Country Club golf course; walking distance to Suisan Fish Auction, Liliuokalani Park, and Coconut Island. *Standard $47, Deluxe $52, extra person $10 each*

WAIAKEA VILLAS HOTEL (W)
400 Hualani Street, Hilo, HI 96720. 1-800-367-7042, (808) 961-2841, FAX (808) 544-1868. There are 141 units available as rentals in this apartment hotel. The rooms are comfortable and spacious with air-conditioning and TV; room phones are $5 extra. John-Michael's Restaurant, Miyo's Restaurant, a cocktail lounge, meeting rooms, tennis court, and shops are on grounds. The hotel has a tropical garden setting with its location on Waiakea Pond and Wailoa River State Park. *Standard $60-80, Deluxe $80-90, 1BR $100-110, extra person $10*

BANYAN TREES   J. BAYOT

NORTH HILO - HAMAKUA DISTRICTS

INTRODUCTION

Just north, outside the town of Hilo, and running the length of the Big Island's east side some 40 miles to Honoka'a and another 10 miles beyond to Waipio Valley is the Hamakua Coast. The Hamakua Coast overlaps the districts of North Hilo and Hamakua. This area is marked by vast rolling sugar plantations producing thousands of tons of raw cane to feed the sugar mills located along the coast. Interspersed here and there are recently planted macadamia nut orchards which are gradually taking over old sugar cane lands.

Along the Hamakua Coast are numerous gulches and ravines filled with gushing streams and waterfalls, verdant tropical rain forest vegetation, and scattered stands of forest. Weathered old sugar plantation villages appear amidst the fields of cane presenting a vestige of Hawai'i's past. Fifty years ago, most of the Big Island's population lived in such plantation camps.

Driving the length of the Hamakua Coast can be a most enjoyable experience with beautiful scenic vistas of ocean, sugar cane fields, and tropical rain forest. Be cautious of large slow cane trucks hauling tons of sugar cane to the mills. The route passes through a number of small towns and settlements along the way, each with a melodious Hawaiian name: Papa'ikou, Pepe'ekeo, Honomu, Hakalau, Laupahoehoe, O'okala, Pa'auilo, and Pa'auhau.

As is the immediate Hilo area, the Hamakua Coast is generally quite wet receiving well over 100 inches of rainfall annually. This accounts for the rain forest and lush fields of sugar cane. However, rainfall varies by elevation and you will notice changes in vegetation and terrain as you travel north towards Honoka'a. It does become somewhat drier.

Most of the coastline on this eastern side of the island is quite rugged, marked by high cliffs sometimes several hundred feet high which drop straight to the pounding ocean surf. There are very few safe beach areas along this entire coast due to the rugged rocky nature of the coastline. However, the parks and overlooks along the way provide wonderful scenic vistas, often with cascading streams and waterfalls dropping into the ocean. Compared to the island's west side, the east is indeed a Paradise and a Garden of Eden, it is so lush and green.

WHAT TO DO AND SEE / WHERE TO SHOP

The Hamakua Coast doesn't offer a whole lot in the way of activities or shopping. Being a predominately rural agricultural area, it is marked by several small villages and settlements and a fair number of scenic sites. Some of the small villages have one or two unique shops, maybe an antique shop or two, and usually a Mom n' Pop general store.

Five miles north of Hilo is the old Highway 19 scenic route, **Mamalahoa Highway** ★, that winds along the coast for four miles. It is a short but very scenic drive along the twisting old coastal highway which was the only route around the island in the pre-World War II days. Also on this old scenic route is the *Hawai'i Tropical Botanical Garden* ★. See the section on HILO in the WHAT TO DO AND SEE chapter for other details.

About 11 miles north of Hilo is the village of *Honomu*, a typical old plantation town. Stop at *Ishigo's Store & Bakery*, an old family run operation, for a glimpse of a Hawai'i of long ago. Also check *Akaka Falls General Store, The Crystal Grotto and Akaka Falls Flea Market* for browsing.

From Honomu, take Route 22 on out from town. The paved road rises sharply through the hilly cane fields above town on its 3.6 mile route to *Akaka Falls State Park* ★. Here under a rainforest canopy, the ocean tradewinds are cool and delightful. The 66 acre park is a refreshing stop after the climb through the canefields. Restrooms and picnic tables are available. The main attraction is the fascinating walk down into the ravines where mountain streams are gushing and waterfalls are splashing. Beautiful stands of bamboo, ginger, and many flowering trees and plants delight walkers. It's a gorgeous tropical greenhouse. The walk is highlighted by inspiring views of the 420 ft. cascades of Akaka Falls and nearby Kahuna Falls tumbling into deep gorges. If you like tropical splendor, don't miss this attraction.

Continuing on Highway 19 out of Honomu, it is about 12 miles to *Laupahoehoe Point*. There is a scenic overlook alongside the highway before you get to the gulch leading down to the point. The point itself is a lava peninsula extending into the ocean. There is a grassy park area with picnic tables, restrooms, and shelters. Small boat launching facilities are available and from the point there are scenic views of the Hamakua Coast. A monument stands on the point in memory of the 24 teachers and school children who were swept to sea in a 1946 tidal wave that devastated a school which occupied the site.

It's another 10 miles or so to *Pa'auilo*, another decrepit sugar plantation village. Be sure to stop just south of the village at *Donna's Cookies* for the best home-made cookies on the Big Island. Next door is *Sandra's Store*, a typical Big Island country general store featuring cold juice, sodas, and local goodies.

From Pa'auilo, it is only six miles to *Honoka'a*, the largest country town on the Hamakua Coast. Honoka'a has an old west look about it with weathered store-fronts and wooden walks and even an occasional Hawaiian paniolo (cowboy) strolling about town. Visit the *Hawaiian Macadamia Nut Plantation Factory* located just below town at the end of the main street, watch for the signs. There are numerous macadamia nut and chocolate creations on display, as well as many other products in the gift shop, and free factory tours. For more gift ideas, check out *Kama'aina Woods*, located on Lehua Street. Hand turned bowls of koa, milo, and other native Hawaiian woods are crafted in the factory here.

There are clothing shops, a general store or two, the usual small town hardware store, a second hand shop, and even a soda fountain along Honoka'a's main street. Back on Highway 19 above town, don't miss a Honoka'a institution, *Tex's Drive-In*, famous for fresh hot malasadas (deep-fried Portuguese doughnuts, a sheer delight anytime), and other local fast-food items as well.

Out of Honoka'a, take Route 240 north nine miles to the tiny village of ***Kukui-haele***. Stop at ***Waipio Wood Works Art Gallery*** which features hand crafted Hawaiian wood products, paintings, prints, photos, glasswork, pottery, jewelry, baskets, batik art, and general Hawaiiana created by island artists. Also, in this shop you can book a tour with ***Waipio Valley Shuttle*** (775-7121), to take a narrated one and a half hour 4x4 drive down into the magnificent ***Waipio Valley*** ★, just a half mile further on.

The tour details the history and culture of the valley from past to present, and includes information on taro growing, the main economic activity at present. The shuttle tour is $20 per person, children under 12 are $10. A similar tour is offered by ***Waipio Valley Wagon Tours*** (775-9518) using horse or mule drawn open wagons for a two hour tour. The wagon tour is $25 per person with children half price. ***Hawaii Resorts Transportation*** (885-7484) offers a two-and-a-half hour horseback ride tour on the floor of Waipio Valley.

The steep winding road into the valley begins at ***Waipio Valley State Park*** ★. *CAUTION NOTE*: Under no circumstances should you attempt to drive your rental car down the dangerously steep valley road. Only 4x4 vehicles are allowed. In addition to the steep road, there are numerous streams which must be crossed on the valley floor and regular rental cars will not make it.

Waipio Valley Park provides a covered picnic pavilion and restrooms at the top of the valley and spectacular views from an overlook of the six mile long valley interior with its almost vertical 2000 ft. walls, and also of the northern coastline of the Big Island. The valley fronts the ocean with a wide black sand beach and heavy pounding surf. This beach is not safe for swimming due to hazardous undercurrents.

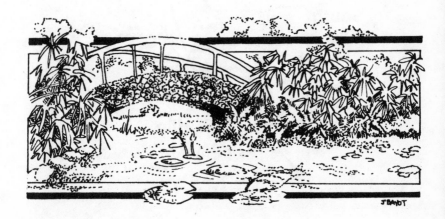

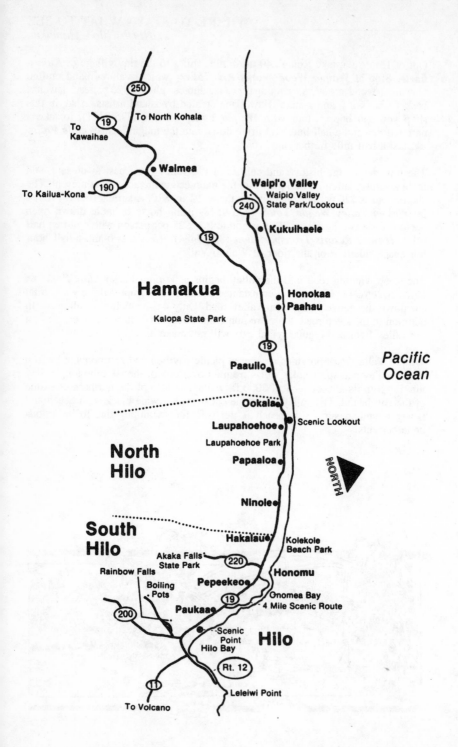

ACCOMMODATIONS - NORTH HILO AND HAMAKUA

Visitors will not find any world class accommodations in this area of the island. In fact, there are only a handful of lodgings available. Probably the best reason to even consider staying along the Hamakua Coast is to thoroughly relax, enjoy, and soak up the country ambiance of this predominately rural area. For those seeking an escape from the usual beach resorts and hustle and bustle of tourist centers, this area of the island provides lots of appeal. For those looking for strictly budget accommodations, this area will also fill the bill nicely. The North Hilo and Hamakua areas can actually provide some wonderfully quiet and peaceful vacation experiences and memories in one of the Big Island's most beautiful areas. Also check the Bed & Breakfast listings for this area.

BEST BETS: *Hamakua Hideaway* - This is a comfortable country cottage near the beautiful Waipio Valley State Park and valley overlook.
Hotel Honoka'a Club - This small country town hotel is dated but provides cheap basic accommodation where there's not much other choice in the immediate area.

NORTH HILO AND HAMAKUA ACCOMMODATIONS

Hamakua Hideaway
Hotel Honoka'a Club
Waipio Tree House
Waipio Valley Hotel

HAMAKUA HIDEAWAY ★
P.O. Box 5104, Kukuihaele, Hamakua Coast, HI 96727. (808) 775-7425. Located in the small country village near Waipio Valley lookout. Accommodations are one self-contained cottage, **The Cliffhouse,** and a separate room, **The Treehouse Suite.** Cliffhouse sleeps up to four people, Treehouse sleeps two. Cliffhouse has a full kitchen, bathroom, and fireplace and sits on a pali (cliff) with wonderful views of Hamakua Coast up past Waipio Valley and to the southern coast. Treehouse has bath and kitchen. Hikes or guided jeep trips into Waipio Valley available nearby. *$75 nightly, or $60 for two or more nights, $10 extra person*

HOTEL HONOKA'A CLUB
P.O. Box 185, Mamane Street, Honoka'a, HI 96727; (808) 775-0533/775-0678. This rambling old wooden building has been a Honoka'a landmark for years. It is centrally located on the main street of town off Highway 19. The hotel has just 14 rental rooms available with TV, full bathroom, 2 queen size beds, and each features a distant ocean view. Restaurant and parking on grounds. There is nothing fancy about this hotel but it provides basic accommodation in an area where there is little else. The back-packing no-frills adventurous traveler will find it accommodating. *Standard $35, Deluxe $42-44*

WAIPIO TREE HOUSE
P.O.Box 5086, Honoka'a, HI 96727; (808) 775-7160. This is a fantasy lodging for an adventurous few and one of the most unusual lodgings on the Big Island. **The Tree House** is for real, located in a huge monkeypod tree in Waipio Valley. The facility has a double and single bed, refrige, hot plates, electricity and running water. There is a Japanese ofuro hot tub, hikes on jungled valley trails, swimming

in quiet pools and splashing waterfalls or horseback and mule-drawn wagon rides. The Tree House can accommodate 3 adults or 2 adults and 2 children. There is a separate private cottage, **The Hale**, available which sleeps up to six people. The Hale has full kitchen, livingroom and loft. Guests supply their own food at both units. **Note:** There can be a few days each year (about 10) when these units are inaccessible because of high river water. Should guests be unable to leave, food and lodging during their delay are complimentary. For the adventure-minded only! *Tree House - $150 nightly, The Hale - $125 nightly, both units have two-day minimum, $25 extra person, under age-12 kids free.*

WAIPIO VALLEY HOTEL

25 Malama Place, Hilo, HI 96720. (808) 775-0368 in Waipio, 935-7466 in Hilo. This too is one of the Big Island's most unusual accommodations. Located on the floor of Waipio Valley it is a very simple rustic inn providing only the bare essentials: a bed, toilet, and a cold shower. Guests bring their own food and other essentials and share cooking facilities. Five guest rooms with twin beds are available at a rate of $15 per person per night. Reservations should be made at least 3-4 weeks in advance. The hotel is run by taro farmer, Tetsuo Araki, who spends lots of time tending his taro patches in the valley. He also lives in Hilo and drives back and forth. Contact him at the hotel at (808) 775-0368 in Waipio or in Hilo at (808) 935-7466. If you don't have the necessary 4-wheel drive transport to get down the hazardous valley road, you can either hike (2 miles from top of valley to the hotel) or get a ride with the Waipio Valley Shuttle tours mentioned above. This is a great place to hike and explore the wonders of a tropical rain forest valley. Don't forget the mosquito repellant!

NORTH KOHALA DISTRICT

INTRODUCTION

The North Kohala District occupies the northern two-thirds of the Kohala Mountains peninsula, the Big Island's top end. This is one of the smallest districts on the island. To get there, take the Akoni Pule Highway 270 which follows the west coast from Kawaihae (and from the South Kohala resorts) and the intersection of the cross island Highway 19. North Kohala can also be reached from Kamuela via the Kohala Mountain Road, Highway 250.

The Akoni Pule coastal highway passes through some of Hawaii's driest country where rainfall is less than ten inches annually. Kohala's hot dry winds blow across fields of dry grass and acres of hardy keawe trees. The road also passes through Kohala Ranch country and the North Kohala towns of Hawi and Kapa'au.

Of the two, the Kohala Mountain Road, Highway 250, is perhaps the more scenic drive. Running from the town of Kamuela on the South Kohala plateau, the road immediately ascends the Kohala Mountains. Scenic views of the plateau ranging across to the base of Mauna Kea and sweeping vistas of the slope down to the South Kohala coast are at every angle as the highway climbs to over 3000 ft. elevation. There is a scenic overlook with a panoramic view of South Kohala about five miles from Kamuela town. The road passes through beautiful rolling Kahua Ranch and Kohala Ranch lands where herds of cattle graze and numerous sheep frolic in the lush green meadows. This is the heart of Kohala's "paniolo" (cowboy) country. And because the Kohala winds blow with such regularity up here, the highway is lined with evergreens that serve as a windbreaker. This adds to the real "country lane" atmosphere of the Kohala Mountain Road which is emphasized by the panoramic views of green hills and mountains, grazing cattle and sheep, and the sweeping views of the Kohala-Kona Coasts.

As the road nears the town of Hawi, it descends rapidly and another road branches off to Kapa'au town. In Hawi, the Kohala Mountain Road joins the Akoni Pule Highway allowing a complete circle drive around the North Kohala District. Route 270 continues on through the towns of Hawi and Kapa'au and angles south along the eastern coast of the peninsula. It passes through a few old sugar plantation settlements and past the old Kohala Mill, which went out of business in 1970. The road terminates at Pololu Valley Lookout about eight miles from Hawi.

The small settlements, villages and abandoned old mill in this area of North Kohala are all that's left of a once viable sugar plantation industry. The cane fields have long since lain fallow but some are being replanted to macadamia nuts, flowers, ornamental plants, etc. The closing of the sugar mill created an economic wasteland here as sugar was its only business for almost a century.

The last ten years has seen these North Kohala communities rebound from disaster to the point where development, growth, and improvement is happening again. Much of it is attributed to the rise of the plush resorts in neighboring South Kohala which provide jobs and a sense of security for North Kohala residents.

WHAT TO DO AND SEE / WHERE TO SHOP

North Kohala is a predominately rural area, with lots to see but little to shop for in the towns. This is Kamehameha Country and, as mentioned in the A HISTORY OF HAWAI'I section earlier, is the birthplace of King Kamehameha the Great who united the islands of Hawai'i under one rule in 1795. Because of this, North Kohala is filled with the lore of Kamehameha.

In front of the county courthouse in Kapa'au is a statue of *King Kamehameha* ★ which has an interesting history. The statue was originally commissioned as a monument for Honolulu. It was cast in bronze in the 1880's in Paris and, after a rather turbulent history, including being sunk in the South Atlantic Ocean near Cape Horn at Port Stanley in the Falkland Islands, ended up here at the Kapa'au Courthouse in 1912. Before this statue was salvaged from the icy waters of the Atlantic, a duplicate model was cast and that one now stands in front of the Judiciary Building, Aliiolani Hale, across from Iolani Palace in Honolulu. Since the original statue was no longer needed in Honolulu, it was placed in North Kohala. This final resting place for the original Kamehameha statue in quiet lonely North Kohala seems fitting. The meaning of the name Kamehameha is "the lonely one." Each June 11, Kamehameha Day, local residents drape the statue with beautiful flowing flower leis.

Across from King Kamehameha's statue in Kapa'au, the *Ackerman Gallery* features fine arts and island crafts plus antiques and unique gifts. In the same building *Don's Family Deli* has ice cream treats, sandwiches, and light lunches.

Highway 270 continues east of Kapaʻu to Pololu Valley, a distance of nine miles. Before reaching the end of the road at the valley however, there is a turnoff for **Keokea Beach Park**. This is a secluded little beach park reached by a two mile winding road through an old sugar village. The beach is very rocky and not recommended for swimming. There are picnic pavilions and restrooms here. The bay of this beach is framed by interesting picturesque cliffs 75-100 feet high. If you brought a picnic lunch this is a good place for a restful stop.

The road continues on to its termination and turnaround at **Pololu Valley** ★. The Pololu Valley is second only to the famed Waipio Valley just a short distance down the east Kohala Coast. From the parking area and overlook there is a majestic view of the valley walls and floor as it reaches back toward the Kohala Mountains. Perhaps most eye-catching are the two or three rock islets that stand just off the mouth and beach of the valley. These islets are actually chunks of the Big Island that were separated at some time in the far past probably by some volcanic activity. They present interesting subjects for photography buffs. The beach of Pololu Valley is composed of fine black lava sand. However, the surf here is quite dangerous as the undertow is very strong and swimming is not advised. The trail leading down to the valley floor and the beach is a nice hike but can be hazardous in or just after rain and caution is advised.

Back in Hawi town, check out **Takata Store** and **Nakahara Store** for a look at more examples of old country general stores. Also check out **Vea Polynesian Gifts** for interesting handmade collectibles. Just two miles west of Hawi on Route 270, is the turnoff for the **Upolu Airport Road** which leads down two miles to the coast and the tiny airstrip at Upolu Point, the northernmost point on the Big Island. The airport road is paved but very narrow.

At the airstrip, signs point the direction west along the coast to the ancient settlement that is **King Kamehameha's Birthplace** ★ and the adjacent **Moʻokini Luakini Heiau** ★. The 1 1/2 mile bumpy, rutted, and very dusty road from the airstrip along the coast to the restored birthplace site is unimproved dirt and driving it can be hazardous. While restoration work on these two sites is ongoing, both are beautiful and impressive. Kamehameha's birthplace is a large square shaped rock wall enclosure about 75 yards per side, and encloses various other foundations and structures. It sits about 50 yards from the beach in an open sloping area. The wind and sun are both strong here.

Moʻokini Luakini Heiau is located just off the same road as the birthplace site. It occupies the summit of a hill and as such dominates the immediate area. The temple is where the aliʻi nui, the kings and ruling chiefs, fasted, prayed, and offered human sacrifices to their gods. The temple was built about 480 A.D. and is one of the largest on the Big Island, measuring 267 ft. by 250 ft. on the west and east walls, and 135 ft. and 112 ft. on the north and south walls. The walls are 30 ft. high and 15 ft. wide. The structure is in the shape of an irregular parallelogram. The stones used in constructing the temple are of smooth water worn basalt. Legend has it that the stones come from Pololu Valley on the east side of the Kohala peninsula, a distance of some 10-14 miles. It is said that each stone was passed by hand from man to man the entire distance, a feat requiring from 15,000 to 18,000 men. By this method, so says the legend, the temple was built in a single night, from sunset to sunrise.

Moʻokini Luakini was constructed under the direction of High Priest Kuamoʻo Moʻokini and was dedicated to the battle god, Ku. The priestly order of Ku, through the Kahuna Nui, provides the guidance and direction of the temple. Throughout its 1500 year history, members of the Moʻokini family have served as Kahu (guardian) of the Moʻokini Luakini. The latest member of the family to inherit the title of Kahuna Nui (high priestess and councilor to a high chief) is Leimomi Moʻokini Lum, a direct descendant of High Priest Kuamoʻo Moʻokini.

Today, the heiau and adjoining Kamehameha Birthplace are open to visitors to stroll the grounds and learn about the history and culture of old Hawaiʻi. Various celebrations and cultural days are held here on special occasions such as King Kamehameha Day (June 11).

About eight miles from Hawi and twelve miles from Kawaihae on Route 270 is the turnoff for *Lapakahi State Historical Park* ★. Located right on the Kohala Coast, Lapakahi Park is the site of a restored ancient Hawaiian fishing village. It is a chance to stretch your legs and walk through a once inhabited, living village and get a sense of what life in old Hawaiʻi was like. It's well worth your time.

The park provides a self-guided walking tour and follows well laid out trail of wood chips and mulching that make for easy walking. You'll notice a number of stone wall foundations for houses which served the Hawaiians as protection against the almost constant Kohala winds. Within the walls, the people built their "hales" (houses), canoe sheds, and other structures. The sites are all clearly marked and can be identified with the trail guide brochure picked up at the entrance to the park. Following the trails and learning from the displays and sites, you'll come to appreciate how the old Hawaiians lived in harmony with the land and sea. The park has remnants of a family heiau, a fish shrine, lamp stand, salt pans (depressions carved in rocks) where sea water was left to crystallize into salt, old fire pits, a water well, and plantings of sugar cane, sweet potatoes, bananas, and gourds, all important to Hawaiian life.

ACCOMMODATIONS - NORTH KOHALA DISTRICT

There are no hotel accommodations in the remote North Kohala District. Readers wishing to stay in the area are advised to check the **Bed and Breakfast Lodging** section of this book for B&B reservation services as to what may be available in the North Kohala area. The closest other accommodations would be in Waimea about 20 miles south, or the Kohala Coast resorts, see **Accommodations - South Kohala,** for details. There is only one B&B operation currently in North Kohala and it is cross-listed here for convenience.

ISLAND'S END B&B
P.O. Box 1234, Kapaʻau, HI 96755; (808) 889-5265. This older plantation era home has two shared-bath rooms and a separate studio unit available. Breakfast included. Under age-12 children free. *$45-50 nightly.*

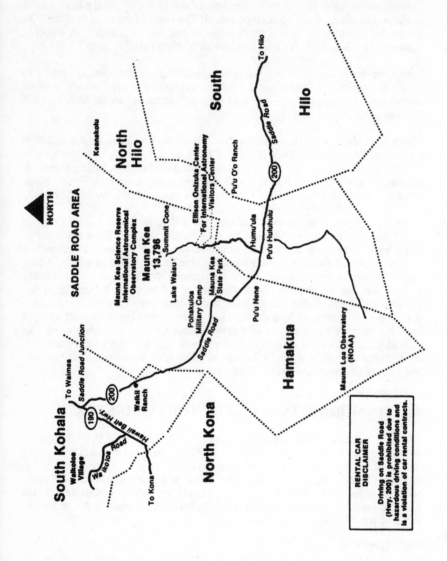

NORTH

SADDLE ROAD AREA

South
Hilo

North
Hilo

Hilo

Keanakolu

To Hilo

Saddle Road

200

Pu'u O'o Ranch

Ellison Onizuka Center
For International Astronomy
-Visitors Center

Mauna Kea Science Reserve
International Astronomical
Observatory Complex

Mauna Kea
13,796

Summit Cone

Humu'ula

Pu'u Huluhulu

Lake Waiau

Pohakuloa
Military Camp

Mauna Kea
State Park

Pu'u Nene

Saddle Road

Hamakua

Mauna Loa Observatory
(NOAA)

To Waimea

Saddle Road Junction

200

190

Hawaii Belt Hwy.

Waiki'i
Ranch

Waikoloa Road

North Kona

South Kohala

Waikoloa Village

To Kona

RENTAL CAR
DISCLAIMER

Driving on Saddle Road
(Hwy. 200) is prohibited due to
hazardous driving conditions and
is a violation of car rental contracts.

142

THE SADDLE ROAD AREA

This section is added for informational purposes even though there are no towns or villages, no stores or services of any kind other than a state park, and for the most part no permanent inhabitants through the entire area. It is included because it passes through some incredibly surreal country of stark lava flows, cinder cones, ranch lands and towering volcanic peaks and is the route used to its primary attractions: the world renowned telescope observatories at the summit of Mauna Kea mountain and the weather observatory on Mauna Loa.

Caution!: Driving on Saddle Road, Highway 200, is prohibited in regular rental cars due to hazardous driving conditions and an unstable roadway and is in violation of car rental contracts. Only 4x4 vehicles are recommended for driving on the Saddle Road. While the Saddle Road is paved its entire length it is very narrow and winding in some areas.

The Saddle Road is so-called because it passes through the plateau adjoining the massive Mauna Kea and Mauna Loa. From Waimea/Kamuela to Hilo via the Saddle Road is a distance of 60 miles and from Kailua-Kona to Hilo it is 87 miles. However because of the narrow winding road conditions (especially near the Hilo side) and the extreme caution needed when driving it, this route often takes longer to drive than other routes around the island.

The drive does present some different scenery however. The towering peaks of Mauna Kea and Mauna Loa are seen from a closer perspective on the drive over the plateau separating them. This of course is possible assuming clouds don't obscure one's vision from the Saddle Road elevation. The early morning hours are generally clear while from mid-day on into the afternoon, clouds roll upslope from the eastern Hilo and Hamakua districts and tend to fill up the plateau area between the mountains. From the Waimea and Kona side, the road passes through vast tracts of ranch grazing lands extending down from Mauna Kea's lower slopes. This is generally dry, windy and wide-open countryside. On the Hilo side, the road passes through several miles of heavy rainforest vegetation above the town which gives way to extensive fern and ohia lehua forest of the mountain's mid-elevation slopes. Interspersed here and there are rough and rugged lava flows until at the 3000 ft. level on the central plateau it appears to be one huge lava flow. On the lower slopes of Mauna Kea, ranch grazing lands stand out as large green patches against the upper level brown barrenness of the mountain and the lower level grey and mottled green of the fern and ohia lehua forest and lava flows.

Midway on the Saddle Road from either the Kona/Waimea (28 miles) or the Hilo side (27 miles) is the turnoff for the Mauna Kea Summit Road. This road leads to the summit of the 13,796 ft. mountain. At the 9200 ft. elevation level (6.5 miles up the summit road) is the *Ellison Onizuka Center for International Astronomy* ★. A visitors center has displays and programs of interest on Mauna Kea and astronomy. The visitors center is open Friday from 1 - 5PM and Saturday-Sunday from 8AM - 5PM. Every Friday and Saturday night a public information presentation is held from 7 - 9PM and includes a "star gazing" tour using an 11-inch telescope. Official Mauna Kea summit day tours through the University of Hawai'i 88-inch observatory are given on Saturday and Sundays only at

2:30PM. All programs are free and open to the public. For more information, call the center at (808/961-2180) for a recorded message.

The Onizuka Center also serves as the base camp housing the many scientists and astronomers engaged in research projects utilizing the telescopes at the summit. This center is at the 9200 ft. elevation level and is more conducive to a comfortable existence for those working long hours in the extremely thin air at the nearly 14,000 ft. summit. The center is named in honor of Astronaut Ellison Onizuka, a native son of the Big Island, who died in the 1986 Challenger spaceshuttle tragedy.

Above the Onizuka Center, the "John A. Burns Way" extends another 6.6 miles to the final cinder cones at the summit. A paving project on the hazardous gravel road has been underway over the last couple of years and due to extreme conditions on the mountain, progress has been slow. The road is cut into the side of the steep mountain slopes and winds around giant cinder cones. This part of the drive is an eerie yet spectacular journey across a moonscape panorama. There is nothing but fine volcanic dust, pumice, and jagged rocks and lava flows. There is little in the way of vegetation above 10,000 ft. on Mauna Kea. The extreme dryness of the entire summit area is precisely why the observatories were built here. Mauna Kea offers some of the finest and most consistent conditions for optical and infrared astronomy of any site in the world. Here at the summit, the observatories are above 40% of the earth's atmosphere, water vapor in the air is at a minimum and the number of cloud-free nights for viewing through the telescopes is higher than anywhere else in the world.

It is no wonder then that Mauna Kea has become known as the premier site for optical and infrared astronomy in the entire world. The major observatories currently in operation are the University of Hawai'i 88" optical-infrared instrument, the NASA 3 meter infrared instrument, the Canada-France-Hawai'i 3.6 meter optical-infrared telescope, the United Kingdom 3.8 meter infrared telescope, the Caltech 10.4 meter submillimeter observatory, and the James Clerk Maxwell 15 meter submillimeter facility. The W.M. Keck Observatory is a 10 meter optical-infrared new technology multiple-mirror instrument that is the largest telescope of its kind in the world.

But more facilities are planned and expected to be constructed by the end of the century. The W.M.Keck Foundation will build a twin 10 meter telescope, Keck II, next to the recently completed Keck I. The Smithsonian Institute will build a high tech multi-dish radiotelescope with an array of six 6 meter dishes. Astronomy research groups from Japan will build the Japanese National Large Telescope, a 7.5 meter optical-infrared facility. Also planned are the U.S. New National Observatory and an Italian facility which will fill up the available space in the Mauna Kea Science Complex. With these high-tech state-of-the-art astronomy facilities, Mauna Kea Observatory has more viewing surface and power than any other site on earth. Little wonder it is so well known in the astronomy world. For information on visiting Mauna Kea Observatory or visitor center tours, call *Mauna Kea Support Services* in Hilo (808/935-3371). Visitors must provide their own 4x4 (4-wheel drive) transport to the Onizuka Center and to the summit. For those wishing to visit the summit but not wanting to drive themselves, there are two tour operators with Mauna Kea summit tours.

Both *Waipio Valley Shuttle/Mauna Kea Summit Tours* (808/775-7121) and *Paradise Safaris* (808/322-2366) offer full day summit tours with lunch included. See RECREATION AND TOURS for details.

Caution Note: Youngsters under 12, pregnant women and anyone with respiratory or cardiac problems are advised *not* to go to Mauna Kea's summit. The very thin air (60% of normal oxygen) can cause altitude sickness and nausea. Even scientists working at this elevation experience difficulties. Also be advised that Mauna Kea's weather can change suddenly and dramatically, especially in winter months. From November to March, it can snow anytime and blizzard conditions are possible. Even the summer months can bring below freezing temperatures at the summit.

The Mauna Loa Access Road leads off the Saddle Road in the opposite direction of the Mauna Kea Summit Road. This drive of just over 17 miles to the 11,000 ft. level of Mauna Loa passes through nothing but stark barren lava flow country. There are sweeping views back across the Saddle Road plateau and to Mauna Kea on cloudless days. But other than that, the 34 mile round trip on this road is a drive across a moonscape rock desert. At the end of the Mauna Loa Access Road is the National Oceanic and Atmospheric Administration (NOAA) Mauna Loa Weather Observatory which keeps track of developing weather over Hawai'i using sophisticated instruments and satellite communications.

A hiking trail from the end of the road here continues on up to Mauna Loa's summit and to a hiker's cabin. Hikers can connect there to a trail system leading downslope on the other side to Hawai'i Volcanoes National Park headquarters. But it is not a hike for novices or unprepared casual hikers. It is a very strenuous hike over very rugged terrain. Only experienced backpackers with full supplies should attempt the route. Check the section on "Camping - National Park" for details.

Along the Saddle Road is Pohakuloa Military Camp, a large reserve used by the army for live firing exercises and military maneuvers. Be on the alert for large slow military trucks on the Saddle Road and even an occasional convoy of military vehicles.

Mauna Kea State Park is perhaps the island's best maintained park and is also located on the Saddle Road. Indeed, it has some of the nicest rental cabins of any state park. This is due in part to its remoteness and isolation and thus it is not overused by the camping public. See the "Camping - State Parks" section for details. There are no other accommodations in the Saddle Road area. The park is on the plateau at the foot of Mauna Kea and the area abounds in introduced wild game birds like pheasant, quail and partridge as well as many species of native Hawaiian bird life. Visitors can enjoy the peace and solitude of this remote area and stroll through the trails and backroads of the park area to gain a perspective of this most unusual part of Hawai'i.

PUNA DISTRICT

INTRODUCTION

The Puna District comprises the area immediately south and southeast of Hilo town. It is a wide open area of lava lands, rugged coasts, and rain-forest slopes leading up to Hawai'i Volcanoes National Park which straddles the Puna-Ka'u border. Within Puna are the country towns of Kea'au, Kurtistown, Mountain View, Pahoa, Volcano, and a few other small settlements. In addition, there are a number of heavily populated country residential subdivisions. Puna is bisected by the main Hilo to Volcano Highway 11 and by Highway 130 which branches off from Highway 11 to Pahoa town.

Puna is noted for orchid, anthurium, papaya, banana, macadamia nut, and other tropical products. Numerous farms and orchards are found throughout the district. The combination of adequate rainfall and warm sunny conditions make it ideal for cultivating tropical fruits and flowers.

About the eastern one-third of Hawai'i Volcanoes National Park is located within the Puna District. And since January, 1983, this east rift zone, as it is called, has been the site of a series of ongoing volcanic eruptions and spectacular lava flows from Kilauea Volcano's vents of Pu'u O'o and Kupaianaha. The first three years of Kilauea's eruption were episodic outbreaks of dramatic lava fountaining and bursts from Pu'u O'o vent which gradually formed a cinder cone several hundred feet high. The eruptive activity of the last few years has come from the large lava pond and vent called Kupaianaha, located at the 2200 foot elevation level. Both of these vents are in remote inaccessible areas. Viewing of eruption activity is best done by plane or helicopter. See "Air Tours" for information.

This almost continuous volcanic eruption is unprecedented in recent history. For some nine years the volcano has steadily erupted and sent lava flows rolling downslope in search of the sea and in the process, causing considerable damage to man-made structures as well as destroying thousands of acres of Hawaiian forests. The entire village and residential areas of Kalapana have been almost totally destroyed by the various lava flows. Area residents have been forced to evacuate their homes and relocate elsewhere. Altogether, almost 200 homes have been destroyed since 1983.

Some 25 square miles of land have been covered by lava up to 50-70 feet deep. Damage estimates run into the millions with some 2 1/2 miles of roads, 2 miles of waterlines and 2 miles of utility lines wiped out by the lava flows. The lava courses its way downslope some seven miles to the sea at Kalapana through an extensive underground system of lavatubes. Over 100 acres of new land have been added to the Big Island's coastline since this eruption activity began in 1983.

Highway 130, which passed through Kalapana, has been cut off at various points and it is no longer possible to drive through Kalapana and on out the coast to the south entrance of Hawai'i Volcanoes National Park. Even the famed Kaimu and Kalapana Black Sand Beaches have been covered with lava and are no longer accessible. Visitors can travel Highway 130, the Chain of Craters Road, from

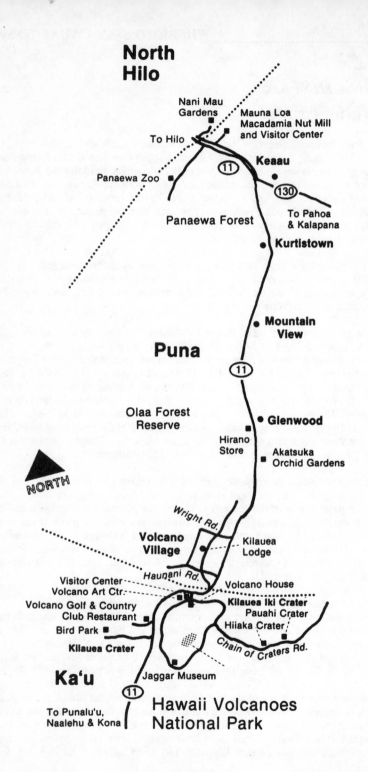

inside Volcanoes National Park, but it deadends now just west of the Kalapana area due to the lava cutoff. Visitors must return to the national park via the Chain of Craters Road.

WHAT TO DO AND SEE / WHERE TO SHOP

For most visitors, the biggest attraction is the volcanic activity. During the current eruption phase (late 1992) it was possible to drive to Volcanoes National Park south entrance on the Chain of Craters Road, Highway 130, to near the location of the former *Waha'ula Visitors Center*. The visitors center was destroyed by lava flows in summer, 1989. National Park rangers now operate a mobile visitors center van at the end of the road here. The rangers provide maps and information on hiking trails to the current eruption site and lava flows. You should check first to see if conditions are safe for hiking the area.

From this point, a trail along the coast for one-quarter of a mile afforded a dramatic view of the lava flow entering the sea. Great steam clouds were visible and at night the sky glowed from the fiery lava as it entered the water. It was also possible to view the recent flows at various other places on both the Waha'ula side and the Kalapana side of the road closure. If the eruption activity is still ongoing in 1993 or later, as you use this guidebook, you can possibly see the lava flows enter the sea. However, no one can predict or guarantee eruption activity, not even the scientists at the national park observatory.

As noted earlier, *Kaimu Black Sands Beach Park* and *Kalapana Black Sand Beach* were both destroyed and made inaccessible by 1990 lava flows. These famous beaches, long popular with photographers and visitors, are no more. Just west along the coast from the former Kalapana area, beyond where the lava flows have cut across the highway, there is a newly formed black sand beach at *Kamoamoa Park and Campground*.

To reach this area, you have to backtrack through Pahoa and go through the main entrance of Hawai'i Volcanoes National Park and follow Highway 130, the Chain of Craters Road to Kamoamoa (minimum 2 hour drive from Kalapana). The Kamoamoa beach has been formed by the ongoing lava flows that enter the sea just down the coast near Kalapana. As the molten lava enters the sea it explodes and shatters into fine pumice and cinders which are carried by the surf along the coast. At Kamoamoa this volcanic residue has accumulated in such great quantities that it has entirely covered a once rocky coast with a heavy layer of fine black sand. Swimming at this beach is not advised due to heavy surf and dangerous currents. Sharp and penetrating fragments and slivers of volcanic ash and pumice can cause severe problems for bare feet as well.

Another of Kalapana's more famous attractions, the historic *Star of the Sea Painted Church* ★, was rescued from lava flow destruction in 1990 and moved to a temporary location; permanent relocation is pending. This wooden frame structure dates from the early 1900's and was built by an early Belgian Catholic missionary priest who also did the intricate paintings of religious scenes on the walls and ceiling.

Other sights in the Puna District that are easily accessible include the Opihikao and Kapoho areas. These areas are off the main Highway 130 and form a loop using Highway 132 (Kapoho Road) and Highway 137 (Opihikao Road) leading from Pahoa town to the coast down to Kalapana and back to the main Hwy. 130.

Highway 132 (Kapoho Road) passes through papaya and orchid fields to the site of the former *Kapoho Village*, which was completely covered by a fiery lava flow in 1960. A historic plaque marks the site. At the end of the Kapoho Road you can drive right up to the *Cape Kumukahi Lighthouse* which, according to local lore, was spared by Madame Pele to protect Hawaiian fishermen at sea. The lava flowed around and past the lighthouse grounds but did not touch the lighthouse itself. Also on the Kapoho Road is *Lava Tree State Park* where hollow lava impressions of tree stumps are visible. The lava flowed around the living trees and baked them, leaving a hollow lava shell.

The end of Kapoho Road near the Cape Kumukahi Lighthouse intersects with Highway 137, known as the Opihikao Road. Highway 137 follows the coast south toward Kalapana. While driving on this road, be aware that it is very narrow and winding in places. There are large orchards of papaya and macadamia nut trees in the area as well as some magnificent views of rugged coastline. Along this stretch are *Issac Hale Park* which has a natural geothermal pool for bathing heated by underground steam vents and *Mackenzie State Park* which features a restored section of the old *"King's Highway,"* the former around-the-island trail used long ago. *Kahena Beach* is a lovely black sand beach at the base of a cliff but swimming is considered dangerous due again to heavy surf and currents. The beaches and parks in this area have suffered from severe overuse and overcrowding from area residents after the recent loss of the Kalapana and Kaimu black sand beach areas and parks to the lava flows. Also on the Opihikao Road there is an area called *"Pu'u Lapu,"* a haunted hill where your car will appear to coast uphill without power.

And speaking of going uphill, the 32 mile drive from Hilo to Volcano Village near Hawai'i Volcanoes National Park is all uphill. The drive on Highway 11 goes from sea level in Hilo to 4000 ft. at Volcano. Along the way, the route passes through the abandoned cane fields of the former Puna Sugar Company and its old mill near Kea'au. Further on upslope, the cane fields give way to groves of eucalyptus trees and vegetation of the tropical rainforest. Fields of wild ginger, orchids, and other exotic plants fill the roadsides and meadows of the scattered country homesites and small ranches of the area. Finally, stands of the rugged and hearty ohia lehua tree with its deep red blossoms become apparent nearer the Volcano area.

For tropical flower aficionados, there are numerous orchid and anthurium farms and nurseries throughout the Puna District and many welcome visitors. On the main Highway 11 at the 22 1/2 mile marker in the Glenwood area, is *Akatsuka Orchid Gardens* (967-7660), the largest cymbidium orchid farm in Hawai'i. Many varieties of orchids are on display and for sale. *Yamamoto Dendrobiums Hawai'i* (968-6955), *Hawaiian Flower Exports* (968-6174), and *Hawaiian Heart Inc.* (968-6322) are but a few of the orchid and anthurium farms in Mountain View just off the highway that welcome visitors. In Pahoa, try *Hawaiian Greenhouse Inc.* (965-8351), *Puna Flowers & Foliage* (965-8444), or *Anthuriums of Pahoa*

(965-8247), and in Kurtistown stop at *Hata Farm* (966-9240) for all types of tropical flowers and plants. In addition, as you drive along be on the lookout for farm and nursery signs welcoming visitors to stroll the gardens.

The small towns and villages of the Puna District don't offer much in the way of shopping opportunities. The towns of Kea'au and Pahoa, the largest of the district, have more shops and stores than the rest but most cater to the needs of residents rather than visitors. Each town and village has a Mom and Pop general store which can always provide sodas, snacks, and local favorites. For something quite different, stop in Mountain View at *Mountain View Bakery* (968-6353) for some of their famous "Stone Cookies." These cookies were made for dunking in coffee! When you bite into one, you'll understand their name. Good! At the Glenwood area at the 20-mile marker is *Hirano Store* (968-6522) where you can buy cold drinks, sandwiches, snacks, gas and general store supplies.

Along the old Volcano Highway in Volcano Village, which is just a mile from the national park entrance, there is the *Volcano Store and Diner* (967-7210) where picnic supplies or snacks, sandwiches and plate lunches can be bought. They have gas pumps if you're in need. *Volcano Vineyards and Winery* (967-7772) is also located nearby and you can sample the Symphony wine and tropical fruit wines produced here. In the same area is *Kilauea General Store* (967-7555) which provides deli snacks, sandwiches, groceries and gas too.

ACCOMMODATIONS - PUNA DISTRICT

BEST BETS: Kilauea Lodge - This is such a lovely place in the delightfully cool and crisp (especially in winter!) climate at Volcano Village; rooms have charming graceful decor, and some have a fireplace to take the nip from the mountain air. The restaurant also has a good reputation.

PUNA ACCOMMODATIONS

Hale Ohia Cottage   (For other Puna area accommodations, see the
Kilauea Lodge   "Bed & Breakfast" listing earlier in this chapter)
Volcano Vacations

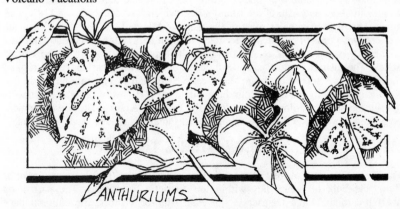

ANTHURIUMS

HALE OHIA COTTAGE

P.O. Box 599, Volcano, HI 96785. (808) 967-7986. This lovely cottage offers 3 bedrooms and sleeps up to 5 people. Cottage has well equipped kitchen, large living room and one tub-shower bath. Bedrooms have 1 double, 2 singles and a sleeping punee (sofa) in living room. There is a large covered deck with table, chairs and hibachi barbeque for cookouts. Located one mile from Hawai'i Volcanoes National Park in Volcano Village. Near hiking trails, picnic areas, national park facilities, golf course, volcano observatory, etc. Cottage is 26 miles from Hilo. *Rates up to 5 people, $50 nightly, $300 weekly, 2 day minimum*

KILAUEA LODGE ★

P.O. Box 116, Volcano Village, HI 96785. (808) 967-7366. A rustic old YWCA camping lodge and dormitory built in 1938 has been renovated and reopened in 1988 as a lodge and general restaurant. Set amidst the quiet cool country air of Volcano Village near Hawai'i Volcanoes National Park headquarters and visitors center. There are 4 guest rooms with private bathrooms and fireplaces and one private cottage. The restaurant offers full American-Continental lunch and dinner menu Tues.-Sun, closed Mondays. *Rates: Standard $75 Deluxe $95*

VOLCANO VACATIONS

P.O. Box 608, Kailua-Kona, HI 96745. (808) 325-7708. This operation offers a luxury 2 bedroom, 1 bath cottage in the cool and quiet Volcano area. The cottage has sauna room, fireplace, fully equipped kitchen, washer-dryer and a 1/2 acre yard. Guests can play golf at nearby Volcano golf course, hike Volcanoes National Park trails and take in all the scenic splendor of the area plus enjoy the cool crisp climate. The cottage is about 26 miles from Hilo. *Rates for up to 4 persons, daily $70, weekly $430, monthly $1290. One day's rate required for deposit within 10 days to confirm.*

KA'U DISTRICT

INTRODUCTION

The Ka'u District comprises one of the largest geographic districts on the Big Island and at the same time one of the more remote and least populated as well. It takes in about one-fifth of the island's land which represents some 800+ square miles. The district includes most of the massive Mauna Loa (13, 680 ft.) and the western two-thirds of Hawai'i Volcanoes National Park. Along this southern coast of the Big Island is *Ka Lae*, South Point, the southernmost point in the United States. The district is mostly dry lava desert, windblown grasslands, and rugged rocky coastline. Inland there are sugar cane fields and macadamia nut orchards. Ka'u is serviced by the main around the island road, Highway 11, which connects the remote area to Volcano and Hilo to the east and Kona to the west. Sparsely populated, Ka'u has only three small towns: Pahala, Na'alehu, and Waiohinu.

WHAT TO DO AND SEE / WHERE TO SHOP

The Ka'u District's biggest attraction is no doubt *Hawai'i Volcanoes National Park*, the bulk of which lies within the district's boundaries. The park does overlap into the Puna District to the east. But for visitors, the national park headquarters, visitor center, volcano observatory, campgrounds, Volcano House Inn, and related sites are centrally located at Kilauea Caldera in Ka'u near Volcano Village. Visitors from Hilo will drive to the park via Highway 11, a distance of 35 miles, through the Puna District described in the previous section. Visitors from the Kailua-Kona area will have to travel a distance of 96 miles via Highway 11 around the South Point area. This is a rather long drive through some pretty desolate stretches of open lava lands, dry scrub land, and the Ka'u desert. The road is paved but has some short stretches in the South Kona area where it is winding and narrow. Otherwise the road is excellent and if you have your own rental car you should plan at least a day trip to Volcano. If you have time, plan on an overnight or longer visit which will allow you to explore the area in more depth. Allow a minimum of two and a half hours for the drive from Kailua-Kona to the national park. It's best to get an early start.

The drive up to the park passes through South Kona's coffee farm, fruit orchard, and flower farm country gradually turning away from the coast and heading further inland as it turns around Mauna Loa's southernmost slopes. The land here, some 8-10 miles inland from the coast and at 2000 ft. elevation, is damp and cool, a contrast to the drier resort areas of Kona and the lands traversed along the way. The terrain is marked by lush vegetation and stands of tropical forest. Ranch grazing lands appear intermittently along with macadamia nut orchards in an otherwise sparsely populated area.

Along this route is *Manuka State Park*, a lovely and well-maintained arboretum with a variety of plants and trees. Picnic tables and restrooms are provided. *Ka Lae*, South Point, is reached via South Point Road which branches off from Highway 11 at the extreme southern tip of the Ka'u District. The narrow road courses its way some twelve miles to the South Point Peninsula where it terminates. It passes by the *Kamao'a Wind Farm*, a wind powered electricity generation facility utilizing huge wind turbines. This stark, windswept, hot, dry and grassy area is the southernmost point geographically in the United States. The first Hawaiians are believed to have landed here and settled the area around 400 A.D. There are old canoe mooring holes and the ruins of a fishermen's heiau (temple). Fishermen still use South Point to moor their boats but they must hoist them up and down the high cliffs to the relatively calm waters below. The foundations of an old World War II military camp are also found in the area.

Green Sand Beach, composed of green olivine crystals giving it a marked green hue, is located five miles east of South Point but is accessible only by hiking or with a 4x4 vehicle as the coastal road is extremely rough and rugged over rocky terrain. The beach is at the bottom of a steep cliff, reached by a hazardous trail, and is not safe for swimming due to rough surf and strong currents.

The small town of *Na'alehu*, proclaims itself to be "the southernmost town in the USA" and has a large sign stating the claim alongside the town shopping center. At the shopping center, located right on the highway in mid-town, there is a coffee shop, grocery store, and snack shop for refreshments. Across the road from the shopping center is the *Punalu'u Sweetbread Visitor Center*. This is a bakery and snack shop that produces some 4,000 loaves weekly of its popular "Portuguese Sweetbread." The snack shop has fresh Kona coffee, sweetbread, pastries and other refreshments.

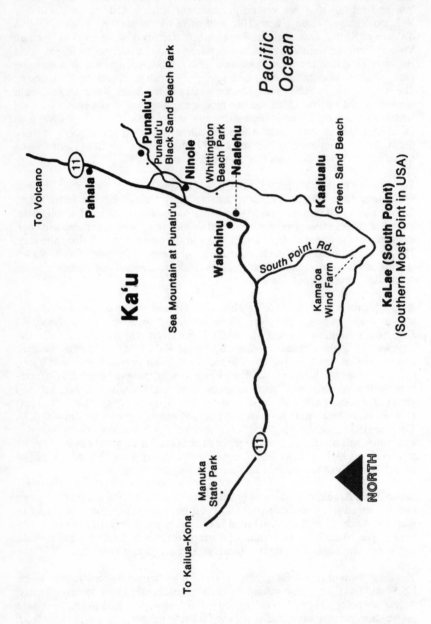

The neighboring town of *Waiohinu* boasts the *Mark Twain Monkeypod Tree* planted by the famous author during his 1866 visit. The original tree toppled in a storm several years ago but the roots have sprouted new saplings and the tree lives. Just down the road is *Kauahaao Church*, a century old New England colonial styled church. Passing through these very small Hawaiian country towns will give you a sense of having stepped back into an earlier time where the fast-paced modern world hasn't quite made any inroads yet. It's all a very pleasant and refreshing experience to know that places like these tiny quiet villages still exist. They are indeed havens of refuge in an all too busy world.

At *Punalu'u*, eight miles further on toward the national park, there is *Punalu'u Beach Park, Seamountain Golf Course*, and *Punalu'u Black Sands Restaurant*. At *Punalu'u Black Sand Beach Park*, spend a few minutes to watch the shoreline for sea turtles which are often seen feeding on sea weed on the rocks and coral. The turtles are quite common in this area. Five miles from here is the very small sugar town of *Pahala*. If you are looking for a grocery store or gas station turn off the highway at the sign for the town; the Ka'u Hospital is right at this intersection also. You can also drive by the Ka'u Sugar Mill just off the main center of the town to see the unloading of cane and general mill operations. The lovely green cane fields of Pahala form a beautiful background vista as you travel along Highway 11 in this area. The fields lie several miles off the road at the base of the foothill slopes of Mauna Loa. From Pahala it is 25 miles on to the national park through generally dry desert and lava rock country.

Hawai'i Volcanoes National Park ★ is one of the island's most popular visitor attractions and a must for visitors. On any given day, there can be several hundred or a few thousand visitors passing through the park. The marvels of the park should not be missed by anyone. The park *Visitor Center* is located a mile west of Volcano Village just inside the main entrance. Here visitors will find a natural history museum detailing information on the national park, a free eruption movie shown several times daily, and park rangers on duty to provide information. Entry fees into the national park are: $5 per car with the pass good for 7 days; $15 for a yearly pass; $2 for walk-in visitors or on bicycle, moped, etc. The *Volcano Art Center* (967-7179) is located adjacent to the visitors center and provides historic information on the park as well as beautiful arts and crafts produced by local artisans. Artwork can be purchased here.

The Art Center also stages and conducts art shows, performances and art and photography workshops the year around. Some of the programs allow visitors and residents a chance to interact with artists who receive their inspiration from working within Hawai'i Volcanoes National Park. Occasionally, a resource artist will lead a walk through some spectacular area of the park to describe and demonstrate the use of natural materials and/or atmosphere of the park environment in creating artwork. The walks focus on protecting and enhancing the fragile national park environment. Call the center for information.

The gigantic, and still steaming fire pit, *Halemaumau*, a 3000 ft. diameter 1300 ft. deep lava vent lies on the floor of *Kilauea Caldera*. *Kilauea Iki*, is a huge cinder cone vent that last erupted in 1959. Both of these vents are easily viewed from *Crater Rim Drive* and can be reached on foot by easy hiking trails. At the *Jaggar Volcano Observatory*, volcanologists study the latest seismograph readings that would foretell of an impending eruption. Here visitors can view the crater and see the steam vents hissing and sulfur banks smoking and marvel at what the forces of nature have created. Educational displays explain the natural history of volcanoes and related geology. There are vast fields of lava, once molten rivers of liquid rock, spewed out from the earth's center. Two types of lava emerge from Hawai'i's volcanoes: pahoehoe with its black and relatively smooth surface (much like cake batter) and 'a'a, which solidifies in a jumble of small clinker like rocks with sharp edges and rough surfaces.

Kilauea Volcano is the legendary home of the Hawaiian fire goddess, **Madame Pele**. Native Hawaiians have long had a healthy respect for her and even today, ceremonial offerings are cast into Halemaumau fire pit while chants, songs, and dances are performed in her honor. It is said that Madame Pele has a fondness for gin.

One of the outstanding features of Hawai'i Volcanoes National Park is its fine system of hiking trails. The trails begin at various points along the Crater Rim Drive and Chain of Craters Road. Hikers can choose from trails that offer outstanding closeup views of volcanic craters, steaming lava vents and colorful sulfur banks, to sweeping vistas of Kilauea's lava flows and sloping flanks, to a cool pastoral trail leading through a rare bird sanctuary.

Along other trails of the park, hikers may see some rare and endangered flora and fauna. Among these are the sacred ohelo berry, held in high regard as an offering of appeasement to Madame Pele, or the pukiawe used in making leis and the rare sandalwood tree. Birds likely to be seen are the Hawaiian honeycreeper and the wren-like 'elepaio that inhabit the **Bird Park Sanctuary**. Visible along some trails are petroglyphs, ancient Hawaiian rock carvings.

Devastation Trail, a raised boardwalk path, located behind the cinder cone of Kilauea Iki, winds through the vast fields of lava cinders and pumice that buried and burned off most of the living vegetation. All that is left is a myriad of picturesque tree stumps and stark cinder landscape.

Thurston Lava Tube Trail is located just off the Crater Rim Drive two miles from the visitors center. Here one can walk through a giant lava tube much like a cave. The short trail leading to it passes through a pleasantly cool fern forest.

At the park's south entrance, accessible only via the Chain of Crater's Road, is **Waha'ula Heiau**, an ancient Hawaiian sacrificial temple. Built about 1250 A.D., this temple was the site of the last known human sacrifices in the early 1800's. The heiau was surrounded but not destroyed by the recent lava flows from Kilauea's volcanic eruptions. The park visitors center at this site was however totally destroyed in summer, 1989.

In addition to traditional campgrounds, the national park's premier place to stay is the venerable and historic **Volcano House Inn**. The Volcano House is located across from the visitors center at the main entrance. The Volcano House was first built in the 1860's as an overnight station for visitors who rode on horseback all the way from Hilo to see the splendors of the volcano. It's had a number of distinguished visitors down through the years including Mark Twain who visited here in 1866. Twain described the hotel as "a neat little cottage with four bedrooms, a large parlor and dining room." The hotel has been rebuilt several times since 1866 and now features 37 comfortable rooms with private bath and even heat, an unusual feature for hotels in Hawai'i. The Volcano Art Center noted earlier is, in fact, part of the old Volcano House Hotel from 1877. The hotel today features a lobby fireplace that has burned continuously for more years than anyone can remember. It's sort of a Volcano House tradition and the fire burns day and night to help keep guests comfortable. The wood paneling and cozy decor create a rustic country lodge atmosphere that gives the Volcano House its special charm. The *Ka Ohelo Dining Room* is the inn's restaurant. It is about the only lodging in the world that perches on the edge of an active volcano.

ACCOMMODATIONS - KA'U DISTRICT

BEST BETS: Volcano House Inn - simply because it is one of Hawai'i's better known landmark accommodations and the only place in the world where you can sleep comfortably next to an active volcano. *Shirakawa Motel* - a simple yet comfortable motel-type accommodation in a very quiet, rural area especially nice for those seeking solitude.

SHIRAKAWA MOTEL ★ (W)
P.O. Box 467, Na'alehu, HI 96772. (808) 929-7462. Advertised as "The Southernmost Motel in the U.S.", this 13 unit country motel offers simple accommodations for relaxation, peace and quiet. It is nestled amidst the cool climate of a coffee tree grove and lush vegetation. The Shirakawa family combine the warmth of true old-fashioned Hawaiian hospitality with simple yet modern conveniences. No TV. This is a no frills, simple getaway for those wanting the solitude of the countryside. *Standard $27-33, Standard w/kitchenette $36-40, extra person $8-10*

VOLCANO HOUSE INN (W)
P.O. Box 53, Hawai'i Volcanoes National Park, Hawai'i 96718. (808) 967-7321, FAX (808) 967-8429. This 42 room hotel has a rustic country lodge atmosphere with generally spacious well-kept rooms. The quiet cool volcano climate is invigorating and a pleasant change from Hawai'i's standard beach and tourist center accommodations. The Ka Ohelo Dining Room features American-Continental cuisine, and cocktail lounge, gift shop, and meeting room are available. The national park headquarters and the visitors center are directly opposite. *Cabins $34, standard $79, non-crater view $105, crater view $131, extra person $10*

SEAMOUNTAIN AT PUNALU'U COLONY I (W)
P.O. Box 70, Pahala, HI 96777. (808) 928-8301/928-6200, 1-800-488-8301, FAX (808) 928-8008. Agent: Casa De Emdeko Commercial Space, 1-800-344-7675, FAX (808) 326-2445. This condominium/hotel has 62 rental units available. Located in the fairly remote Punalu'u area of Ka'u, the development is situated at the Seamountain Golf Course and near the ocean front and Punalu'u Black Sand Beach and Ninole Cove. The beach is hazardous due to heavy surf and strong currents and swimming can be dangerous. The nearest town is Pahala, five miles away. All units have kitchen facilities, TV and fans. Punalu'u Black Sand Restaurant, cocktail lounge, swimming pool, tennis courts, golf course, meeting rooms are on grounds or nearby. Extra person $8, 2 day minimum stay. *Studio KF $63-83, 1 BR KF $91-114, 2 BR (max 4) KF $125-151*

BOOKING AGENTS

**ASTON HOTELS
& RESORTS**
2255 Kuhio Avenue
Honolulu, HI 96815
1-800-367-5124
Canada 1-800-423-8733 ext.250
Hawai'i 1-800-342-1551

Aston Royal Sea Cliff Resort
Aston The Shores at Waikoloa
Kona By The Sea
Kona Islander Inn

BRADLEY PROPERTIES LTD.
P.O. Box 3408
Waikoloa Village Station
Kamuela, HI 96743
(808) 883-9000

Waikoloa Villas

**CASA DE EMDEKO
COMMERCIAL SPACE**
75-6082 Alii Drive, Suite 10A
Kailua-Kona, HI 96745
1-800-344-7675
FAX (808) 326-2445

Sea Mountain Resort
  Colony One

CENTURY 21
75-5689 Alii Drive
Kailua-Kona, HI 96740
1-800-255-8052
(808) 329-9566

Keauhou Punahele
Kona Plaza

CLASSIC RESORTS
50 Nohea Kai Drive
Lahaina, HI 96761
1-800-642-6284
(808) 667-1400 collect
from Hawai'i and Canada

Mauna Lani Point

**COLONY HOTELS
& RESORTS**
841 Bishop St.
Honolulu, HI 96813
1-800-367-6046

Holua at Mauna Loa
Kanaloa at Kona
Kona Bali Kai

**GOLDEN TRIANGLE
REAL ESTATE**
P.O. Box 1926
Kailua-Kona, HI 96740
(808) 329-1667

Alii Villas
Casa De Emdeko
Keauhou Akahi
Keauhou Kona Surf
Keauhou Palena
Kona Makai

**HAWAI'I APARTMENT
LEASING ENTERPRISES**
1-800-854-8843
California 1-800-472-8449
Canada 1-800-824-8968

Country Club Villas
Hale Kai O Kona
Kona Alii
Kona Makai
Kona Mansions
Mauna Lani Point
Shores at Waikoloa
White Sands Village

HAWAI'I RESORT MNGMT.
75-5782 Kuakini Hwy, Suite C-1
Kailua-Kona, HI 96740
1-800-553-5035, (808) 329-9393

Hale Kona Kai
Kona Alii
Kona Billfisher
Kona Isle Condo
Kona White Sands Apt-Hotel

**HAWAIIAN ISLANDS
RESORTS INC.**
606 Coral St.
Honolulu, HI 96813
1-800-367-7042, (808) 531-7595

Waikoloa Villas

**HAWAIIAN PACIFIC
RESORTS**
1150 S. King St.
Honolulu, HI 96814
1-800-272-5275

Hilo Hawaiian Hotel

HAWAIIANA RESORTS
1100 Ward Avenue, Suite 1100
Honolulu, HI 96814
1-800-367-7040

Kona Reef

**KEAUHOU-KONA
REALTY, INC.**
P.O. Box 390282
Kailua-Kona, HI 96739
1-800-367-8047 ext.246
Hawai'i (808) 322-3101

Country Club Villas
Kanaloa at Kona
Keauhou Kona Surf
Keauhou Palena
Keauhou Punahele

KNUTSON & ASSOCIATES
75-6082 Alii Drive
Kailua-Kona, HI 96740
(808) 326-9393
FAX: (808) 329-2178

Casa De Emdeko
Kona Isle
Kona Reef
Sea Village

KONA VACATION RESORTS
77-6435 Kuakini Highway
Kailua-Kona, HI 96740
1-800-367-5168, (808) 329-6488

Alii Villas
Casa de Emdeko
Country Club Villas
Hale Pohaku
Keauhou Akahi
Keauhou Palena
Keauhou Punahele
Keauhou Surf & Racquet
Kona Bali Kai
Kona Islander Inn
Kona Luana
Kona Magic Sands
Kona Makai
Kona Nalu
Kona Onenalo
Kona Palms
Kona Reef
Kona West
Sea Village
White Sands Village

PARADISE MANAGEMENT
50 S. Beretania St.
Kukui Plaza, Suite C207
Honolulu, HI 96813
1-800-272-5252

Kalanikai
Kona Alii
Kona Makai
Sea Village

RON BURLA & ASSOCIATES
75-5864 Walua Rd, Suite 202
Kailua-Kona, HI 96740
(808) 329-2421

Country Club Villas
Hale Kai O Kona
Keauhou Kona Surf
Kona Isle

**SANDS, SEASIDE
AND HUKILAU HOTELS**
2222 Kalakaua Ave., Suite 714
Honolulu, HI 96815
1-800-367-7000
Canada 1-800-654-7020

Hilo Seaside Hotel
Kona Seaside Hotel

SOUTH KOHALA MGMT.
P.O. Box 3301
Waikoloa, HI 96743
1-800-822-4252, (808) 883-8500

Mauna Lani Terrace
Shores at Waikoloa
Vista Waikoloa

TRIAD MANAGEMENT
North Kona Shopping Center
75-5629-P Kuakini Highway
Kailua-Kona, HI 96740
(808) 329-6402

Hale Kona Kai
Keauhou Akahi
Kona Mansions
Malia Kai
Royal Kahili
White Sands Village

VILLAGE REALTY
75-5742-J Hualalai Rd 104
Kailua-Kona, HI 96740
(808) 329-1577
Casa De Emdeko
Keauhou Akahi

Keauhou Kona Surf
Keauhou Palena
Keauhou Punahele
Kona Makai

**VACATIONLAND
SALES & RENTALS**
75-5995 Kuakini Hwy., Suite 123
Kailua-Kona, HI 96740
(808) 329-5680

Kalanikai

**WEST HAWAI'I PROPERTY
SERVICES, INC.**
Keauhou Shopping Village
78-6831 Alii Drive, #237
Kailua-Kona, HI 96740
(808) 322-6696

Kalanikai
Kailua Village
Keauhou Kona Surf
Keauhou Palena
Kona Alii
Kona Makai
Kona Nalu
Kona Plaza

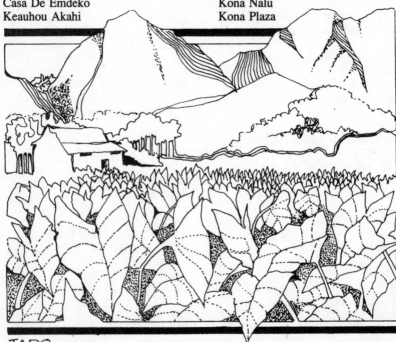

TARO

RESTAURANTS

INTRODUCTION

Like so many other things, the Big Island is blessed with a wide variety of restaurants, cafes, coffee shops, drive-ins and island-style eateries. And like most things in life, there are disputes and friendly disagreements as to what and where is the best. For Hawai'i is no different from anywhere else when it comes to eating: everybody has his/her own personal favorite.

The Big Island has restaurants of all types serving a wide variety of food from local ethnic to mainland continental, from fresh to frozen, from fast food to superb gourmet. It's doubtful that anyone can attest to having dined in every restaurant on the Big Island. This writer certainly does not. However, this section profiles a good number of Big Island dining spots that have actually been tried and proven. In addition, a great effort has been made to gather the opinions and experiences of many other people in order to get as wide an input as possible. Your comments and opinions are also welcome. See the READER RESPONSE.

On the following pages, you will find the restaurants first indexed alphabetically and then also by food type. The restaurants are then divided by geographical area, separated by price range, and listed alphabetically in those price ranges. These are: "INEXPENSIVE," under $10 per person, "MODERATE," $10 to $25 per person, and "EXPENSIVE," $25 and up per person. The price ranges were decided by comparing an average dinner meal, exclusive of tax, alcoholic beverages and desserts. Due to changes in menus, management, supplies or other factors, restaurant prices are obviously subject to change at any time. If you are a senior citizen, be sure to ask about a "Senior Citizen Discount" as more restaurants are extending such a courtesy.

For simplicity, the following lists do not include McDonalds, Burger King, Jack in the Box, Kentucky Fried Chicken, Dairy Queen or similar fast-food outlets or 7-Eleven Food Stores and other convenience stores located around the Big Island. Most folks are aware of the type of food to be had in such fast food operations and they do not merit a separate listing in this book.

In the following listings, those restaurants marked with a ★ indicate an exceptional value in quality of food and service, decor and ambiance, or unique and unusual cuisine and dining experience or a combination of these factors and not just cost alone. Great effort has been given to ensure that those restaurants so marked as an exceptional value have in fact earned the accolade. This has been done through personal visit and evaluation of a meal or by close and careful consultation with reliable patrons, sometimes both. In spite of this, restaurants, like everything else, can and do change over time. What may have been an enjoyable dining experience last week or last month, may well be a complete disaster the next time around. The consistency factor of good food and service for the level of dining carries much weight in the evaluation and consideration. Those restaurants marked as an exceptional value have proven themselves consistent on these last points noted.

BEST BETS

TOP RESTAURANTS
The criteria for being listed as a top restaurant is the excellence and quality of food preparation and presentation, a pleasant relaxing dining atmosphere, and gracious courteous service where the guest is everything. Only a choice few Big Island restaurants make this category and those that do are really excellent overall. Almost without exception, any meal will be superb. Of course, any restaurant can have an "off" night but that is certainly a rare occurance at these restaurants. As with fine dining anywhere, you can expect to pay dearly for it. Meals at the following restaurants can run anywhere from $50-100 or more per person depending upon entree selected, appetizer, soup and salad, wine or alcoholic beverages, dessert, and of course, gratuity. But generally a gourmet meal at any of these fine restaurants will be a memorable part of your Big Island experience. Dinner jackets for gentlemen may be required dress for some of these restaurants.

Batik Room	-	Mauna Kea Beach Hotel
Bay Terrace	-	Mauna Lani Bay Hotel
Hale Samoa	-	Kona Village Resort
Le Soleil	-	Mauna Lani Bay Hotel
The Dining Room	-	Ritz-Carlton Mauna Lani
The Gallery	-	Mauna Lani Resort
The Garden	-	Mauna Kea Beach Hotel
The Grill	-	Ritz-Carlton Mauna Lani
The Pavilion	-	Mauna Kea Beach Hotel
Tiare Room	-	Royal Waikoloan Hotel

TOP RESTAURANTS IN A MORE CASUAL ATMOSPHERE
The following restaurants are less expensive, but a dinner meal can still cost $25 or more per person depending on what is ordered. The dining experience is superior in a less formal atmosphere.

Canoe House	-	Mauna Lani Bay Hotel
Donatoni's	-	Hyatt Regency Waikoloa
Edelweiss	-	Waimea
Hale Moana	-	Kona Village Resort
Imari	-	Hyatt Regency Waikoloa
Kilauea Lodge	-	in Volcano Village
Knickers	-	Mauna Lani Resort
La Bourgogne	-	Kailua-Kona
Merriman's	-	Waimea
Roussel's	-	in Hilo
The Cafe	-	Ritz-Carlton Mauna Lani

BEST BUFFETS

Buffets are a great way to enjoy a wonderful meal at a generally more moderate price compared to an a la carte menu. In addition, buffets often include a wide selection of various Hawaiian ethnic and international foods than can be a delightful experience in cross-cultural dining. You may not otherwise get to sample some of these diverse delicacies and dishes. The following are the best buffets on the Big Island.

Bay Terrace	-	Mauna Lani Bay Hotel	(Sunday brunch)
Cascades	-	Hyatt Regency Waikoloa	(breakfast,lunch,dinner)
Hele Mai Dining Room	-	Kona Hilton	(Sunday brunch)
Island Clam Bake at the Hau Tree	-	Mauna Kea Beach Hotel	(Saturday dinner)
Kona Beach Restaurant	-	King Kamehameha Kona Beach Hotel	(Sunday brunch)
Kuakini Terrace	-	Keauhou Beach Hotel	(dinner)
Queen's Court	-	Hilo Hawaiian Hotel	(Fri-Sat dinner)
Royal Terrace	-	Royal Waikoloan Hotel	(dinner)
The Terrace	-	Mauna Kea Beach Hotel	(lunch daily)

TOP "LOCAL STYLE" RESTAURANTS

The Big Island abounds in inexpensive local-style restaurants where you can sample and enjoy the diverse range of Hawaiian-ethnic cuisine. Most of the establishments are not fancy in decor or looks, but often the service is even better than at the big expensive restaurants. This is true of the family-operated restaurants where courtesy and friendliness are just the way they do business. So if you enjoy inexpensive food that is colorful, plentiful and just plain good, and you don't mind simple decor and surroundings while you eat, you'll have a fun time exploring the world of Big Island local-style restaurants. Some of the best are listed below.

Don's Grill	Hilo	(varied local)
Hukilau Restaurant	Hilo	(seafood)
Jimmy's Drive Inn	Hilo	(Japanese)
Kay's Lunch Center	Hilo	(Korean)
Kimo's Ono Hawaiian Food	Hilo	(Hawaiian)
Kow's Restaurant	Hilo	(Chinese)
Leung's Chop Suey	Hilo	(Chinese)
Nori's Saimin	Hilo	(Japanese noodles)
Sachi's Gourmet	Hilo	(Japanese)
Sophie's Place	Hilo	(Filipino)
T's Saimin Shop	Hilo	(Japanese)
Ting Hao	Hilo	(Mandarin Chinese)
Don's Pake Kitchen	Waimea	(Chinese)
Great Wall Chop Suey	Waimea	(Chinese)
Paniolo Country Inn	Waimea	(BBQ-Mexican)
Yong's Kal-Bi	Waimea	(Korean)

RESTAURANTS
Best Bets

Cynthia's Hawaiian Kitchen	Kailua-Kona	(Hawaiian)
King Yee Lau	Kailua-Kona	(Chinese)
Manago Hotel	Captain Cook	(Oriental)
Ocean View Inn	Kailua-Kona	(Oriental)
Peacock House	Kealakekua	(Chinese)
Rosies Kitchen	Kailua-Kona	(varied local)
Royal Jade Garden	Kailua-Kona	(Chinese)
Sibu Cafe	Kailua-Kona	(Indonesian)
Teshima's	Honalo, Kona	(Japanese)
Thai Rin Restaurant	Kailua-Kona	(Thai)
Akaka Noodle Shop	Honomu	(Oriental)
Hotel Honoka'a Club	Honoka'a	(American-Oriental)
Naalehu Coffee Shop	Naalehu	(American-Oriental)

NIGHTCLUBS AND ENTERTAINMENT

Consult the local visitor publications and newspapers to see what entertainers or groups are currently playing what clubs. The following are some of the more popular nightclubs and lounges which have nightly entertainment in the form of contemporary rock or disco music or more relaxed easy listening Hawaiian music. My personal favorite watering hole is the Billfish Bar at the King Kamehameha Kona Beach Hotel. The bar sits poolside and has nice views of Kailua Pier, Kamakahonu Beach fronting the hotel and glorious sunsets over Kailua Bay.

Kona

Banana Bay Cafe	-	Kona Bay Hotel
Billfish Bar	-	King Kamehameha Kona Beach Hotel
Eclipse Restaurant	-	Kuakini Highway
Fisherman's Landing	-	Kona Shopping Village
Huggo's	-	on Alii Drive next to Kona Hilton
Makai Bar	-	Keauhou Beach Hotel
Nalu Terrace	-	Kona Surf Resort
Windjammer Lounge	-	Kona Hilton

Kohala

Batik Lounge	-	Mauna Kea Beach Hotel
Canoe House Lounge	-	Mauna Lani Bay Hotel
Spats Disco	-	Hyatt Regency Waikoloa
Vanda Lounge	-	Royal Waikoloan Hotel

Hilo

Crown Room	-	Hawai'i Naniloa Hotel
Roussel's	-	60 Keawe Street, Hilo
Uncle Billy's	-	Hilo Bay Hotel
Lehua's Bay City Bar & Grill	-	11 Waianuenue Ave., Hilo

ALPHABETICAL INDEX

AC's Chinese Restaurant 175
Ah Dunno Bar & Restaurant .. 175
Akaka Noodle Shop 211
Aloha Cafe 175
Aloha Luigi 189
Auntie Alice's Pie & Coffee .. 189
Banana Bay Cafe 182
Batik Room 194
Bay Terrace 194
Beach Club Restaurant 183
Bear's Coffee 198
Betty's Chinese Kitchen 175
Blane's Drive In 171
Blue Dolphin Restaurant 171
Bob's Drive In 171
Boomer's Fountain 198
Buns In The Sun Deli 175
Cafe Calypso 183
Cafe 100 171
Cafe Pesto 189
Canaan Deli & Restaurant ... 175
Canoe House 194
Cap's Drive In 171
Capt. Beans' Cruises 174
Cascades 191
Cattleman's Steakhouse 191
CC Jon's Snack In Shoppe ... 211
Chapman's Land & Cattle Co. . 207
Cheng's Chop Suey House ... 199
Chili by Max 176
Clyde's Okazuya 172
Coffee Pub 176
Country Kitchen 199
Cynthia's Hawaiian Kitchen .. 176
d'Angoras Restaurant 172
Dick's Coffee House 199
Donatoni's 194
Don Drysdale's Club 53 176
Don's Family Deli 212
Don's Grill 199
Don's Pake Kitchen 189
Dotty's Coffee Shop 199
Drysdale's Two Restaurant ... 176
Earl's Drive In 211
Edelweiss 191
Eclipse Restaurant 183
Fast Stop Foods 172
Fez's Pizza 176

Fiasco's 207
Firehouse Coffee Shop 206
Fisherman's Landing 183
Francesca's Deli 199
Freddy's Manono Mini-Mart .. 200
Garden Cafe 191
Giuseppe's Italian Cafe 176
Golden Chopstix Restaurant .. 176
Great Wall Chop Suey 190
Green Door 200
Hale Moana 188
Hale Samoa 188
Harrington's 192,209
Harbor House 177
Hartwell's Hale Kea 194
Hele Mai Dining Room 188
Henri's on Kapiolani 207
Herb's Place 211
Highlands Bar & Grill 195
Hilo Coffee Co. 200
Hilo Lunch Shop 172
Hiro's Place 200
Honey's Country Kitchen 212
Honoka'a Pizza & Subs 211
Hong Kong Chop Suey 177
Hotel Honoka'a Club 211
Huggo's 183
Hukilau Restaurant 200
Hyatt Regency Waikoloa Luau 173
Imari 195
Ishigo's Store & Bakery 212
Jameson's By the Sea 183
Jasper's Espresso Cafe 200
Jennifer's Korean Barbecue ... 177
Jesters Tavern 184
Jimmy's Drive In 200
Jinho's 190
John-Michael's 201
Jolly Roger 184
JP's Restaurant 207
K's Drive In 171
K K Tei 202
Kaminari Japanese Restaurant . 178
Kamuela Bread Depot 190
Kamuela Deli 171
Kanazawa Tei 184
Kandi's Snack Shop 171
Ka Ohelo Room 216

RESTAURANTS
Alphabetical Index

Karen's Lunch Shop 172
Karrots 201
Kawamoto Lunch Shop 172
Kawili Cafe 201
Kay's Lunch Center 201
Keawe Diner 201
Ken's House of Pancakes ... 201
Kilauea Lodge 214
Kimo's Ono Hawaiian Food 172,201
King Kamehameha
    Kona Beach Hotel Luau ... 173
King Yee Lau 178
Knickers 195
Koji's Bento Korner 172
Kona Amigos 185
Kona Beach Restaurant 185
Kona Broiler 185
Kona Chuckwagon 178
Kona Hilton Beach
    & Tennis Resort Luau 173
Kona Inn Restaurant 185
Kona Mixed Plate 172
Kona Provision Company 192
Kona Ranch House 185
Kona Village Luau 174
Koreana Restaurant 202
Kow's Restaurant 202
Kuakini Cafe 172
Kuakini Terrace 186
La Bourgogne
    French Restaurant 188
La Cella 214
Lanai Coffee Shop 178
Lanky's Pastries & Deli 202
Lehua's Bay City Bar & Grill . 208
Leung's Chop Suey House ... 202
Le Soleil 196
Lequin's Mexican Restaurant . 213
Lida's Pasta & Salad Buffet .. 178
Lisa's Kitchen 172
Low International Food 202
Mama Lani's Mexican 213
Manago Hotel 178
Marty's Steaks & Seafood ... 186
Masayo's Restaurant 190
Matthew's Place 212
Mauna Kea Beach Hotel Luau . 174
McGurk's Fish & Chips 178
Merriman's 196
Mit's Drive In 171
Miu's 213

Miyo's 203
Mizoguchi Sushi Store 172
Mrs. Shirley's 179
Mun Cheong Lau 203
Na'alehu Coffee Shop 215
Na'alehu Fruit Stand 215
Nani Mau Garden Restaurant . 203
New China Restaurant 203
Nihon Restaurant 208
Nihon Saryo Restaurant 210
Nori's Saimin & Snacks 204
Ocean Bar & Grill 192
Ocean Grill 192
Ocean View Inn 179
Orchid Cafe 192
Our Place 172
Pahoa Chop Suey House 213
Pahoa Inn Coffee Shop 213
Palm Cafe 188
Paniolo Country Inn 190
Papagayos Mexican Grill 186
Paradise West Cafe 213
Paramount Grill 204
Parker Ranch Broiler 193
Parker Square Cafe 190
Parkside Restaurant 204
Peacock House Restaurant ... 179
Pele's Court 186
Pescatore 208
Phillip Paolo's Italian Restaurant 188
Pickle Barrel 204
Pizza Hut 204
Players Restaurant 186
Pot Belli Deli 179
Punalu'u Black Sand Restaurant 216
Puna Sands Restaurant 214
Queen's Court 208
Quinn's Almost-by-the-Sea ... 179
Real Mexican Food 179
Reuben's Mexican Food 205
Reuben's Mexican Restaurant . 179
Restaurant Fuji 208
Restaurant Miwa 208
Restaurant Osaka 204
Restaurant Satsuki 205
Rib House 214
Rocky's Pizza & Deli 179
Rosal's Bakery & Deli 214
Rosies Kitchen 180
Roussel's 210
Royal Jade Garden 180

Royal Siam 205
Royal Terrace 193
Royal Waikoloan Hotel Luau . 174
Sachi's Gourmet 205
Sam Choy's Diner 180
Sam Choy's Restaurant 180
Sandalwood Room 210
Sandra's Store 212
Sandy's Drive-In 171
Sato Lunch Shop 172
Seaside 205
Shibata Lunch Shop 172
Shokoen 209
Short Stop Drive-In 171
Sibu Cafe 180
Sizzler 180
Snappy's Pizza 205,214
Soontaree's 209
Sophie's Place 205
South Point Restaurant 216
Spinnaker's 181
Stan's Restaurant 181
Stratton's 209
Stumble Inn 172
Sum Leung Chinese Kitchen . . 206
Sun Sun Lau Chop Sui House . 206
Su's Thai Kitchen 181
T's Saimin Shop 206
T/C Lunch Shoppe 172
Teru's Restaurant 181
Teshima's Restaurant 181
Tex Drive In 171
Thai Rin Restaurant 181
The Baron 193
The Cafe 196
The Chart House 186

The Dining Room 196
The Gallery 181
The Gallery Cafe 196
The Garden 197
The Grill 197
The Hideout 181
The Makee Restaurant 187
The 19th. Hole 193
The Pavilion 197
The Rusty Harpoon 187
The Teppan Yaki 197
The Terrace (Kona Condos) . . 187
The Terrace (Mauna Kea Hotel) 197
Tiare Room 197
Ting Hao
    Mandarin Restaurant 206
Tom Bombadil's 187
Tonya's Cafe 214
Tres Compadre's 182
Uncle Billy's 209
Veranda Restaurant 182
Verna's Drive In 171
Vista Restaurant 187
Volcano Country
    Club Restaurant 215
Volcano Store Diner 171
Waikoloa Beach Grill 193
Waikoloa Village Restaurant . . 190
Waimea Coffee & Co. 190
Wakefield Gardens 182
Woolworth's Restaurant 207
Yae-Dake Sushi Ya 182
Y's Lunch Shop 172
Yong's Kal Bi 191
Yuni Korean Restaurant 182
Yu Sushi 182

FOOD TYPE INDEX

AMERICAN
Beach Club Restaurant 183
Harbor House 177
Harrington's 192,209
Hele Mai Dining Room 188
Jesters Tavern 184
Ken's House of Pancakes . . . 201
Naalehu Coffee Shop 215
Nani Mau Garden Restaurant . 203
Ocean Bar & Grill 192
Rib House 214

Roussel's 210
Spinnaker's 181
Tom Bombadil's 187
Veranda Restaurant 182
Waikoloa Village Restaurant . . 190

BUFFET
Cascades 191
Kona Chuckwagon 178
Kuakini Terrace 186
The Terrace 197

CHINESE
AC's Chinese Restaurant 175
Betty's Chinese Kitchen 175
Cheng's Chop Suey House . . . 199
Don's Pake Kitchen 189
Francesca's Deli 199
Golden Chopstix Restaurant . . 176
Great Wall Chop Suey 190
Hong Kong Chop Suey 177
King Yee Lau 178
Kow's Restaurant 202
Leung's Chop Suey House . . . 202
Miu's 213
Mun Cheong Lau 203
New China Restaurant 203
Ocean View Inn 179
Peacock House Restaurant . . . 179
Royal Jade Garden 180
Shokoen 209
Sum Leung Chinese Kitchen . . 206
Sun Sun Lau Chop Sui House . 206
Ting Hao Mandarin Restaurant 206

CONTINENTAL - INTERNATIONAL
Batik Room 194
Bay Terrace 194
Cafe Calypso 183
Canoe House 194
Eclipse Restaurant 183
Edelweiss 191
Garden Cafe 191
Hale Moana 188
Hale Samoa 188
Hartwell's Hale Kea 194
Highlands Bar & Grill 195
Jesters Tavern 184
Jolly Roger 184
Ka Ohelo Room 216
Kilauea Lodge 214
Knickers 195
Kona Beach Restaurant 185
Kona Provision Company 192
Lehua's Bay City Bar & Grill . 208
Low International Food 202
Merriman's 196
Ocean Grill 192
Pele's Court 186
Players Restaurant 186
Punalu'u Black
    Sand Restaurant 216

Queen's Court 208
Royal Terrace 193
Sam Choy's Restaurant 180
Sandalwood Room 210
South Point Restaurant 216
Stratton's 209
The Baron 193
The Cafe 196
The Dining Room 196
The Gallery 181
The Grill 197
The Makee Restaurant 187
The Pavilion 197
The Rusty Harpoon 197
The Terrace 187
Waikoloa Beach Grill 193

DRIVE INS
Blane's Drive In 171
Bob's Drive In 171
Cafe 100 171
Cap's Drive In 171
Earl's Drive In 211
K's Drive In 171
Kamuela Deli 171
Kandi's Snack Shop 171
Sandy's Drive In 171
Short Stop Drive Inn 171
Tex Drive Inn 171
Verna's Drive In 171
Volcano Store Diner 171

FAMILY DINING
Auntie Alice's Pie & Coffee . . 189
Boomer's Fountain 198
Country Kitchen 199
Dick's Coffee House 199
Don's Family Deli 212
Don's Grill 199
Fiasco's 207
Herb's Place 211
Hotel Honoka'a Club 211
Ishigo's Store & Bakery 212
John-Michael's 201
Kawili Cafe 201
Kona Broiler 185
Kona Ranch House 185
Lanai Coffee Shop 202
Lanky's Pastries & Deli 178
Manago Hotel 178
Mrs. Shirley's 179

FAMILY DINING (con't)

Orchid Cafe 192
Pahoa Coffee Shop 213
Rosies Kitchen 180
Sam Choy's Diner 180
Stan's Restaurant 181
The Firehouse Coffee Shop . . . 206
Volcano Country
    Club Restaurant 215
Wakefield Gardens 182
Woolworth's Restaurant 207

FILIPINO (Philippines)

Dotty's Coffee Shop 199
Sophie's Place 205

FRENCH

La Bourgogne
    French Restaurant 188
La Cella 214
Le Soleil 196
Tiare Room 197

HAWAIIAN / POLYNESIAN

Banana Bay Cafe 182
Cynthia's Hawaiian Kitchen . . 176
Jimmy's Drive Inn 200
Kimo's Ono Hawaiian Food 172,201
The Garden 197

INDONESIAN

Sibu Cafe 180

ITALIAN

Aloha Luigi 189
Cafe Pesto 189
Canaan Deli & Restaurant . . . 175
d'Angoras Restaurant 207
Donatoni's 194
Fez's Pizza 176
Giuseppe's Italian Cafe 176
Honoka'a Pizza and Subs 211
Lida's Pasta & Salad Buffet . . 178
Paniolo Country Inn 190
Pescatore 208
Phillip Paolo's
    Italian Restaurant 188
Pizza Hut 204
Rocky's Pizza & Deli 179
Snappy's Pizza 205,214
The Gallery Cafe 196

JAPANESE

Akaka Noodle Shop 211
Hiro's Place 200
Imari 195
K K Tei 202
Kaminari Japanese Restaurant . 178
Kanazawa Tei 184
Keawe Diner 201
Masayo's Restaurant 190
Miyo's Restaurant 203
Nihon Restaurant 208
Nihon Saryo Restaurant 210
Nori's Saimin & Snacks 204
Parkside Restaurant 204
Restaurant Fuji 208
Restaurant Miwa 208
Restaurant Osaka 204
Restaurant Satsuki 205
Sachi's Gourmet 205
T's Saimin Shop 206
Teru's Restaurant 181
Teshima's Restaurant 181
The Teppan Yaki 197
Yae-Dake Sushi Ya 182
Yu Sushi 182

KOREAN

Jennifer's Korean Barbecue . . . 177
Kay's Lunch Center 201
Koreana Restaurant 202
Yuni Korean Restaurant 182

LUAUS
HAWAIIAN DINNER SHOWS
DINNER CRUISES

Capt. Bean's Cruises 174
Hotel King Kamehameha 173
Hyatt Regency Waikoloa 173
Kona Hilton
    Beach & Tennis Resort . . . 173
Kona Village 174
Royal Waikoloan Hotel 174
Mauna Kea Beach Hotel 174

MEXICAN

Kona Amigos 185
Lequin's Mexican Restaurant . 213
Mama Lani's
    Mexican Restaurant 213
Papagayos Mexican Grill 186
Real Mexican Food 179

MEXICAN (con't)
Reuben's Mexican Food 205
Reuben's Mexican Restaurant . 179
Tonya's Cafe 214
Tres Compadre's 182

PLATE LUNCH SHOPS
Blue Dolphin Restaurant 171
Clyde's Okazuya 172
Fast Stop Foods 172
Hilo Lunch Shop 172
Karen's Lunch Shop 172
Kawamoto Lunch Shop 172
Koji's Bento Korner 172
Kona Mixed Plate 172
Kuakini Cafe 172
Lisa's Kitchen 172
Mizoguchi Sushi Store 172
Our Place 172
Sato Lunch Shop 172
Shibata Lunch Shop 172
Stumble Inn 172
T/C Lunch Shoppe 172
Y's Lunch Shop 172

SANDWICHES & BURGERS
Ah Dunno Bar & Grill 175
Aloha Cafe 175
Bear's Coffee 198
CC Jon's Snack In Shoppe . . . 211
Chili by Max 176
Don Drysdale's Club 53 176
Freddy's Manono Mini-Mart . . 200
Green Door 200
Hilo Coffee Co 200
Jasper's Espresso Cafe 200
Jinho's 190
Kamuela Bread Depot 190
Matthew's Place 212
Na'alehu Fruit Stand 215

Paramount Grill 190
Parker Square Cafe 204
Pickle Barrel 204
Puna Sands Restaurant 214
Rosal's Bakery & Deli 214
Sandra's Store 212
The Hideout 181
The 19th. Hole 193
Waimea Coffee & Co. 190

SEAFOOD
Fisherman's Landing 183
Hukilau Restaurant 200
Jameson's By the Sea 183
Kona Inn Restaurant 185
McGurk's Fish & Chips 178
Palm Cafe 188
Quinn's Almost-by-the-Sea . . . 179
Seaside 205
Uncle Billy's 209
Vista Restaurant 187

STEAKS
Cattleman's Steakhouse 191
Chapman's Land & Cattle Co. . 207
Drysdale's Two Restaurant . . . 176
Henri's on Kapiolani 207
Huggo's 183
JP's Restaurant 207
Marty's Steaks & Seafood . . . 186
Parker Ranch Broiler 193
Sizzler 180
The Chart House 186

THAILAND
Karrots 201
Royal Siam 205
Soontaree's 209
Su's Thai Kitchen 181
Thai Rin Restaurant 181

DRIVE-INS

To economize on space, drive-ins, fast food operations and plate lunch shops on the Big Island, of which there are several, are listed separately in this section rather than detailed and listed with regular restaurants in each area of the island. Big Island drive-ins generally offer similar fare for breakfast, lunch, and dinner. Food ranges from egg-pancake items for breakfast, to sandwiches, burgers, saimin, and a variety of local style beef, pork, chicken, fish dishes, etc. for lunch-dinner.

The emphasis is on quantity and fast service. Quality varies from mediocre to magnificent, and from day to day, at many of the drive-ins. But generally you can count on a good meal for a reasonable price, most of the time for less than $5. One local Big Island favorite is "loco moco" which is essentially a bowl of rice with a hamburger patty and egg on top. Since it originated at Cafe 100 in Hilo a few years ago, "loco moco" has become a hot fast food item with many imitations and variations around the island. As for judging which drive-in has the best food, well you'll just have to try them all and decide for yourself.

BLUE DOLPHIN RESTAURANT (882-7771) Kawaihae Harbor on Hwy. 270, 2 miles north of the Mauna Kea Beach Hotel, Kawaihae.

BOB'S DRIVE IN (935-8848)
217 Waianuenue Ave, Hilo, 1/2 block above the downtown post office

CAFE 100 (935-8683) 969 Kilauea Ave, Hilo, across from Kapiolani School

CAP'S DRIVE IN (323-3229) On Highway 11, Captain Cook, Kona

BLANE'S DRIVE IN (935-8326) 150 Wiwoole St., Hilo, just off Kanoelehua Ave. (Volcano Hwy) in the industrial area

K'S DRIVE IN (935-5573) 194 Hualalai St., Hilo, 1/2 block below St. Joseph's School

KAMUELA DELI (885-4147) On Hwy 19 in Waimea, next to the Parker Ranch Shopping Center and across from the Waimea Center

KANDI'S SNACK SHOP (959-8461) 56 W. Kawailani St., Hilo, near the intersection of Kilauea Ave. and Kawailani Streets

MIT'S DRIVE IN (889-6474) Hwy. 270, across the street intersection from the post office in Kapa'au, Kohala

SANDY'S DRIVE IN (322-2161)
On Hwy 11, at Kainaliu, Kona, about 5 miles south of Kailua-Kona

SHORT STOP DRIVE INN (929-7103) In Naalehu, Ka'u

TEX DRIVE INN (775-0598) Just off Hwy 19 above Honoka'a, a must stop to try their fresh hot Portuguese malasadas (doughnuts)

VERNA'S DRIVE IN (966-9288)
Just off Hwy 130, Kea'au, across from Kea'au School

VOLCANO STORE DINER (967-7707) Located one block off Highway 11 in Volcano village, next door to the post office; part of the Volcano Store.

PLATE LUNCH SHOPS

Throughout the islands of Hawai'i, the plate lunch has become sort of a revered institution and an established regional cuisine. Everywhere you go, you're probably not far from a plate lunch shop or a lunch wagon. These generally offer a number of selections ranging from teriyaki beef, to fried fish, to noodles, potato salad, and the usual two scoops of rice plus a whole lot more. Plate lunch shops were the original Hawaiian fast food outlets. Many folks pop into one, get a plate and take it back to the office, or to the park, corner bench, or under the nearest shade tree to enjoy. And like comparing restaurants, no two are the same. Everybody has his/her own personal favorite. You may see or hear the term "bento" being used for lunch also, and that is exactly what the Japanese term means. It generally refers to a box or picnic lunch to be taken out from an "okazu-ya" lunch shop. As with drive-ins, the quality of plate lunch shops varies from place to place and even day to day. Depending on where you are on the Big Island, you might want to drop into one of the following, pick up a plate lunch and judge for yourself.

CLYDE'S OKAZUYA - 74-5490 Kaiwi, Kailua-Kona (329-6476)

FAST STOP FOODS - 74-5484 Kaiwi St., Kailua-Kona (329-7226)

HILO LUNCH SHOP - 421 Kalanikoa, Hilo (935-8273)

KAREN'S LUNCH SHOP - 31 Haili Street, Hilo (935-0323)

KAWAMOTO LUNCH SHOP - 784 Kilauea Avenue, Hilo (935-8209)

KIMO'S ONO HAWAIIAN FOOD - 806 Kilauea Avenue, Hilo (935-3111)

KOJI'S BENTO KORNER - 52 Ponahawai St., Hilo (935-1417)

KONA MIXED PLATE - Kopiko Plaza, below Lanihau Center, Palani Road, Kailua-Kona (329-8104)

KUAKINI CAFE - 75-5629 Kuakini Highway, North Kona Shopping Center, Kailua-Kona (329-1166)

LISA'S KITCHEN - 333 Keawe St., Hilo (961-5656)

MIZOGUCHI SUSHI STORE - 856 Kilauea Avenue, Hilo (935-2051)

OUR PLACE - 270 Kamehameha Avenue, Hilo (935-5399)

SATO LUNCH SHOP - 750 Kinoole St., Hilo (961-3000)

SHIBATA LUNCH SHOP - 264 Keawe St., Hilo (961-2434)

STUMBLE INN - 74-5596Q Pawai Place, Kailua-Kona (329-0109)

T/C LUNCH SHOPPE - 1348 Kilauea Avenue, Hilo (961-5188)

Y'S LUNCH SHOP - 263 Keawe St., Hilo (935-3119)

LUAUS / HAWAIIAN DINNER SHOWS

There are several hotel luau-Hawaiian dinner show operations along with one dinner cruise boat in the Kona-Kohala areas. Most of the luau and Hawaiian dinner shows feature authentic Hawaiian luau food like roast pig cooked in an imu (underground oven), island fish, poi, and tropical fruits. Some of these allow for wide variations and adaptations of local-regional luau foods. Most of them also include performances of Hawaiian and Polynesian music and dance as part of the program. The following is a listing of luaus and dinner shows.

HYATT REGENCY WAIKOLOA
Kohala Coast, Waikoloa (885-1234). The "Legends of Polynesia" dinner show takes place at Kamehameha Court each Tuesday and Friday at 6PM and includes a lavish and authentic Hawaiian luau complete with roast pork and all the traditional foods like poi, lomi salmon, chicken laulau, fish, crab, and fresh tropical fruits. Following dinner is a captivating show of Polynesian song and dance which is one of the most exciting and colorful productions on the Kohala Coast. Reservations required. Adults $49, children 5-12 years, $29, 4 and under free.

KING KAMEHAMEHA KONA BEACH HOTEL ★
75-5660 Palani Road, Kailua-Kona (329-2911). This authentic luau is put on each Tue., Thurs., and Sun. evening at 6PM with showtime at 7:45PM. (You can watch the pig being placed in the underground oven, imu, at 10:15AM on Luau days.) The luau begins with the arrival of torch bearers via canoe from Ahu'ea Heiau, King Kamehameha's temple fronting Kamakahonu Beach and the hotel grounds. Conch shells are sounded as the torch bearers land and light the pathway to the luau grounds. Visitors can then watch the ceremonial removal of the roast pig from the imu (underground oven). The luau that follows is a feast of authentic Hawaiian foods and specialties from Oceania. A Polynesian performance of song and dance follows the luau. It's all very colorful and touristy. Adults $42 children 6-10, $15. Reservations required and Aloha attire preferred.

KONA HILTON BEACH AND TENNIS RESORT ★
75-5852 Alii Drive, Kailua-Kona (329-3111). This hotel luau is put on each Mon., Wed., and Fri. evening at 6PM. The luau includes an Aloha shell lei greeting and

continuous island entertainment. Prior to the luau beginning, there is the traditional opening of the imu (underground oven) and removal of the roast pig. The lavish buffet with authentic Hawaiian foods includes an open bar. A Polynesian Review performance of song and dance follows. Adults are $44, children under 12, free when each accompanied by one full-rate adult. Reservations are suggested and Aloha attire preferred.

KONA VILLAGE RESORT ★

Kaupulehu-Kona (325-5555). This luau held at the South Seas-style Kona Village Resort has an element of authenticity which the other hotels don't quite match. It has something to do with the beachside environment. This luau is held each Friday evening at 6:15PM and begins with the traditional removal of the roast pig from the imu (underground oven). Following this are cocktails and the luau feast with an incredible buffet of Hawaiian and Polynesian foods, probably the grandest luau spread on the Big Island. A Polynesian performance of music and dance provides a stirring end to a memorable evening. Adults are $46, children under 2 are $23. Get there a little early to take part in the walking tour of this wonderful beach resort given by the general manager himself.

MAUNA KEA BEACH HOTEL ★

Kohala Coast (882-7222). This authentic "Old Hawai'i Aha'aina" (luau) is held each Tuesday evening at 6PM. The famed Mauna Kea Beach Hotel, noted for its outstanding cuisine and award-winning dining rooms, produces an equally extravagant luau buffet. Guests gather on the luau grounds under the stars at water's edge to sample authentic Hawaiian foods such as laulau (fish and pork wrapped in taro leaves) lomilomi salmon, hulihuli pig, poi, baked bananas and taro, poi palau made with sweet potatoes and haupia (coconut pudding). In addition to the lavish feast, guests enjoy authentic Hawaiian music and dance as interpreted by members of the Lim family of Kohala. Adults $49.50 and children 5-12, $29.

ROYAL WAIKOLOAN HOTEL ★

Waikoloa (885-6789). The Royal Luau is held each Sunday evening at 6PM and begins with the traditional torch lighting ceremony and removal of the roast pig from the imu (underground oven). The music, dance, food, products and costumes are reflections of Hawai'i's history. The feast and entertainment are produced, prepared, and performed by the area's fastidious practitioners of authentic Hawaiiana. On Wednesdays, there is a traditional Hukilau feast where guests join in an help haul in the hukilau nets from the fish ponds. Then all enjoy a feast of fish, salads and barbecue steaks while enjoying Hawaiian entertainment. For either the Royal Luau or Hukilau Feast, adults are $40, children 4-12, $20.

DINNER CRUISES

CAPT. BEANS' DINNER CRUISE

P.O. Box 5199, Kailua-Kona, Hawai'i 96745-5199, (808) 329-2955. This sunset dinner cruise onboard Capt. Beans' Polynesian-style sailing canoe departs Kailua Pier daily at 5:15PM. The cruise along the famous Kona Coast includes island entertainment, an open bar and all you can eat for $45 per person; adults 21 and over only, no children. Call for reservations and transportation pick-up at area hotels and condos. Aloha attire is preferred.

SOUTH AND NORTH KONA

INTRODUCTION

There is a real variety of cuisine available in Kailua-Kona. The fare ranges from the local plate lunch and drive-in to exotic Chinese and Thai dishes, to fine gourmet French and Continental-International food. In addition, there is lots of excellent fresh island seafood to choose from as many restaurants feature it on their daily menus. Dining out in Kailua-Kona can be a real adventure.

INEXPENSIVE

AC'S CHINESE RESTAURANT   *Chinese - Inexpensive*
74-5596 Pawai Place, Kailua-Kona (326-2466). Cantonese cuisine is the mainstay of this Chinese restaurant. A variety of plate lunches and Chinese-style meals as well as take outs are available. It is located in the industrial park area of Kailua-Kona and caters to the working people. Open Mon-Thurs 9AM - 8PM, Fri 9AM - 9PM, and Sat 9AM - 8PM.

AH DUNNO BAR & RESTAURANT   *Inexpensive*
74-5552A Kaiwi St., Kailua-Kona (329-7113). The menu features all you can eat spaghetti or BBQ ribs plus broasted chicken, seafood platters, pasta, and some German dishes plus daily specials. Located on one of the main streets of the Kailua-Kona industrial area and are easily accessible. Open for lunch and dinner, Mon-Sat 11:30AM - 9PM.

ALOHA CAFE   *Sandwiches & Burgers - Inexpensive*
Kainaliu, Kona (322-3383) in the old Aloha Theater Building on Highway 11. The specialties here are fresh baked pastries and cookies, sandwiches, and char-broiled burgers. Meals are enjoyed on the open-air veranda along with fresh juices, Kona Espresso, beer & wine. Open Mon-Sat 8 - 8PM, Sun 9AM - 1PM.

BETTY'S CHINESE KITCHEN   *Chinese - Inexpensive*
Palani Rd, Kailua-Kona (329-3770) in the Kona Coast Shopping Center. Specializes in a full range of Chinese dishes as well as manapua (steamed meat rolls). A good variety of food served in ample quantities. Take outs available. This is a popular spot with shopping center crowds. Open Mon-Sat 10AM to 9PM.

BUNS IN THE SUN BAKERY-DELI-COFFEE SHOP ★   *Pastries/snacks*
75-5595 Palani Road, Kailua-Kona (326-2774) in the Lanihau Shopping Center. This small shop is bright, clean, and very popular with residents and visitors alike. They serve up a full range of fresh baked pastries, breads, rolls, desserts, and gourmet sandwiches. Open Mon-Sat 5:30AM - 8PM, Sun to 7PM.

CANAAN DELI & RESTAURANT   *Deli Snacks - Inexpensive*
Kealakekua, Kona (323-2577) on the main street, Hwy 11. Specializing in fresh New York-style deli sandwiches, soups, and salads in addition to Italian pasta and pizza. Inside dining is limited but pleasant, and they do have an outside lanai table. Open for breakfast, lunch and dinner, Mon-Fri 7AM-8PM, Sat 7-2PM.

CHILI BY MAX   *Chili & Snacks - Inexpensive*
Located in the upper level of the Kona Marketplace Shopping Center on Alii
Drive. This small lunch-counter serves up oven-baked chili, chili dogs, sandwiches
and more. Open Mon-Sat 10AM - 8PM and Sunday 11AM - 8PM.

COFFEE PUB   *Sandwiches & Snacks - Inexpensive*
Waterfront Row, 75-5770 Alii Drive, Kailua-Kona, across from St. Michael's
Church. This small coffee bar features a variety of snacks, sandwiches and
pastries along with freshly brewed Kona coffee. Open daily, 8AM - 5PM.

CYNTHIA'S HAWAIIAN KITCHEN ★   *Hawaiian cuisine - Inexpensive*
Located in the Kopiko Plaza (326-9402) below the Lanihau Center on Palani
Road. They specialize in authentic Hawaiian food including lau lau, kalua pork,
lomi salmon, squid luau, chicken long rice, pipikaula, poke and more. Regular
plate lunch varieties and daily specials. Open for lunch daily 10AM - 2PM, dinner
5 - 10PM. Take outs.

DON DRYSDALE'S CLUB 53 ★   *Sandwhiches & Burgers - Inexpensive*
Kailua-Kona (329-6651) in the Kona Inn Shopping Village. This pleasant open-air
veranda dining room claims the "Best Hamburgers in Town." They are good,
along with sandwiches and other specialty items. Baseball memorabilia of Don
Drysdale, of Los Angeles Dodgers fame, decorates the walls. Cocktail lounge
features TV sports events. This is a popular late night spot with residents and
visitors alike. Lunch and dinner daily, 11AM till closing. Credit cards.

DRYSDALE'S TWO ★   *Steaks & Burgers - Inexpensive*
78-6831 Alii Drive, Kailua-Kona (322-0070) in the Keauhou Shopping Village.
This is an instant replay of Drysdale's Club 53 with large screen TV featuring
cable sports. The menu features heavier fare however with prime rib, steaks, and
fresh island fish leading off. Cocktail lounge. Lunch and dinner daily, 11AM till
closing. Credit cards.

FEZ'S PIZZA   *Inexpensive*
Alii Drive, Kailua-Kona (329-7199) in the Kona Marketplace, near the Kailua
Pier. The specialties here are gourmet deep dish pizza, spaghetti, pasta, sand-
wiches, and Italian salads. Open daily for lunch and dinner, 11AM - 9PM.

GIUSEPPE'S ITALIAN CAFE ★   *Italian - Inexpensive*
75-5699F Alii Drive, Kailua-Kona (329-7888) in the Kailua Bay Shopping Plaza.
Fine Italian dining is the feature of this smallish courtyard cafe. The menu offers
a full line of pasta items like spaghetti, ravioli, lasagna, plus chicken, seafood
and more. Open daily for lunch and dinner, 11AM - 9PM.

GOLDEN CHOPSTIX CHINESE RESTAURANT   *Chinese - Inexpensive*
74-5467 Kaiwi St., Kaahumanu Plaza, Kailua-Kona (329-4527). This Chinese
eatery specializes in Mandarin, Szechwan, and Hunan cuisine. Many varied and
interesting dishes using beef, pork, chicken, duck, and seafood, plus vegetarian
staples. This is a bright, clean and well-kept restaurant in a shopping plaza
adjacent to the industrial area. Open daily for lunch 11AM - 2:30PM, dinner
4:30PM - 9:00PM. Take out orders. Reservations accepted.

HARBOR HOUSE   *American - Inexpensive*
74-425 Kealakehe Parkway, located in Gentry Marina, Honokohau Harbor, Kailua-Kona, 326-4166. This open airy cafe offers harborside views great for watching gamefish weigh-ins and harbor traffic. The menu offers a variety of hot and cold sandwiches, burgers, seafood specials, and local favorites. Open daily for breakfast, lunch and dinner, 6AM - 8PM.

HONG KONG CHOP SUEY ★   *Chinese - Inexpensive*
Kealakekua, Kona (323-3373). On Highway 11 in the Kealakekua Ranch Center. This simple but clean Chinese kitchen serves up some delicious Cantonese food. Many daily plate lunch-dinner specials include chicken, pork, beef, and vegetarian dishes plus noodles. You'll find good Chinese food at reasonable prices here. Take outs are available. Open daily except Sun., 10AM - 8:30PM.

JENNIFER'S KOREAN BARBECUE   *Korean - Inexpensive*
75-5605 Luhia St., in Kailua-Kona's industrial area upstairs in Luhia Center next to Cablevision shop, 326-1155. This local style eatery features Korean and Yakiniku barbecue specials and lots of local favorites. Open daily for lunch and dinner continuously 10:30AM - 10:30PM.

KAMINARI JAPANESE RESTAURANT ★   *Japanese - Inexpensive*
Located in the Kopiko Plaza below the Lanihau Center, Palani Road, Kailua-Kona (326-7799). This new dining spot features grilled Japanese cuisine specializing in chicken, yakitori, seafood and varied Japanese delicacies. Authentic Japanese atmosphere and cuisine. Open Mon-Sat for dinner only, 5 - 9PM.

KING YEE LAU ★   *Chinese - Inexpensive*
In Ali'i Sunset Plaza, Alii Drive, Kailua-Kona (329-7100). Their extensive menu lists 100 varied items including soups, chicken and duck, beef and pork, seafood, egg-veggie-tofu, noodles and rice dishes, Catonese cuisine, served family-style. Their specialty is a "Peking Duck Dinner." They also feature an all-you-can-eat buffet lunch Mon-Sat, 11 - 2 PM. Open Mon-Sat 11AM - 9PM, Sun. 4 - 9PM.

KONA CHUCKWAGON ★   *Buffet - Inexpensive*
On Kaiwi Street, Kaiwi Square Shopping Center, in Kailua-Kona's industrial area (329-2818). This is a reasonable all-you-can-eat buffet. Breakfast features bacon, sausage, eggs, pancakes, waffles, hash browns, rice, gravy and biscuits. Lunch and dinner menus include chicken, ribs, soup, chili and a well-stocked salad bar along with numerous other hot table items; sundaes for dessert. Breakfast 7 - 11AM, lunch 11 - 5PM, dinner 5 - 9PM daily. Popular with the local folks. Credit cards.

LANAI COFFEE SHOP   *Family Dining - Inexpensive*
75-5852 Alii Dr. (329-3111) in the Kona Hilton Hotel. There are lovely views of Kailua Bay and the village from this edge-of-the-water location. The menu is light fare of sandwiches and burgers, varied seafood salads (a specialty), omelettes, and local favorites like saimin noodles, fish & chips, stir-fried beef and chicken, chow mein, fried noodles and more. Breakfast is served ala carte or buffet style. Open for breakfast 6:30 - 11AM, lunch and dinner 11AM - 9:30PM. Credit cards.

LIDA'S PASTA & SALAD BUFFET   *Pasta - Inexpensive*
Located in the Kopiko Plaza below the Lanihau Center, Palani Road, Kailua-Kona (326-7700). This small buffet counter operation features spaghetti, lasagne, ravioli, etc. and a few local specials like pork adobo, pork guisantes and chicken papaya. Open Mon-Sat for lunch 11AM - 1:30PM, diner 5 - 8PM, closed Sunday.

MANAGO HOTEL ★   *Family Dining - Inexpensive*
Highway 11, Kona (323-2642) ten miles south of Kailua-Kona at Captain Cook. The home cooking and Japanese-American specialties are popular with the local folks. Standard selections include teriyaki, tempura, noodle dishes, fried fish, and more. There's no menu, the day's selections are on a board on the wall. Good food in simple surroundings. Open Tuesday-Sunday for breakfast 7 - 9AM, lunch 11AM - 2PM, and dinner 5 - 7:30PM; closed Monday. Call ahead for box picnic lunches to pick up on the way to the Volcanoes National Park. Credit cards.

McGURK'S FISH & CHIPS   *Seafood - Inexpensive*
Two locations, 75-5699 Alii Drive, (329-8956) just opposite Hulihee Palace in the Kailua Bay Shopping Plaza; also at Lanihau Shopping Center, 75-5595 Palani Road, Kailua-Kona (329-4226). The menu features fast food items specializing in fish and chips, sandwiches, and light meals. The Alii Drive location features open-air dining with tables outside overlooking Kailua Bay. The Lanihau Center location features inside dining. Open daily, 10AM - 8PM.

MRS. SHIRLEY'S   *Family - Inexpensive*
Located on Highway 11 in Captain Cook, (323-2080). This is a family style operation featuring local specials and favorites including plate lunches, bentos, sandwiches and burgers, salads, seafood plates, Korean-style chicken by the bucket and more. They have drive-thru service, take outs or dine in service. Open daily for breakfast, lunch and dinner, 7AM - 8PM.

OCEAN VIEW INN ★   *Family - Inexpensive*
Located in the heart of Kailua-Kona on Alii Drive just down from Kailua Pier, (329-9998). This is a very popular family restaurant with local folks. The menu is extensive with varied Chinese, American, and Hawaiian food. The decor and ambience are simple and nothing fancy but the food is good and plentiful. Go early for dinner as it gets crowded rapidly. Breakfast 6:30 - 10AM, lunch 11AM - 2:45PM, dinner 5:15 - 9PM. Also bar and take out food. Closed Mondays.

PEACOCK HOUSE RESTAURANT ★   *Chinese - Inexpensive*
81-6587 Mamalahoa Highway #11 in Kealakekua, Kona, across from Kamigaki Market, (323-2366). The menu is Cantonese and Mandarin Chinese cuisine with dim sum, manapua, Chinese pastries, rice cake and a large selection of varied dishes featured. Lunch and dinner served Monday-Saturday, 10AM till closing. Dim sum served 10AM - 5 PM daily; lunch buffet 10AM - 5 PM daily.

POT BELLI DELI   *Plate lunches, varied - Inexpensive*
74-5543 Kaiwi Road, Kailua-Kona (329-9454). This full line deli serves sandwiches, salads, plate lunches, and other deli items. The booths and tables are jammed in tightly making for crowded conditions. It is located in the industrial area and caters to the working people there and is very busy during lunch. Take outs available. Open daily, 5AM - 4PM.

QUINN'S, ALMOST BY THE SEA   *Seafood - Inexpensive*
75-5655A Palani Road, Kailua-Kona (329-3822). This restaurant features a full menu of sandwiches and burgers, steaks, fresh island fish and seafood. They offer casual late night dining on the lanai, one of the few Kona dining spots serving late night dinner. Daily for lunch 11:30 - 5:30PM, dinner 5:30 - 1AM.

REAL MEXICAN FOOD ★   *Mexican - Inexpensive*
Highway 11, Kealakekua, Kona (323-3036) in the Kealakekua Ranch Center. Featured in this small cafe is excellent and varied Mexican food including tacos, burritos, cantitas, and more. Open daily except Sunday, 11AM - 7PM.

REUBEN'S MEXICAN RESTAURANT   *Mexican - Inexpensive*
Kona Plaza Arcade, 75-5719 Alii Drive, Kailua-Kona (329-7031). The menu is all Mexican offering everything from enchiladas, to tacos and burritos. Lunch and dinner, Mon-Fri 11AM - 10:30PM, Sat 12 - 10:30PM, and Sun 4 - 10PM.

ROCKY'S PIZZA & DELI   *Italian - Inexpensive*
78-6831 Alii Dr, Kailua-Kona (322-3223) in the Keauhou Shopping Village, and 75-5595 Palani Rd, Kailua-Kona (326-2734) in the Lanihau Shopping Center. The menu features excellent pizza (whole or by the slice), sandwiches, and salads. Open daily, lunch and dinner, 10:30AM - 10PM.

ROSIES KITCHEN ★   *Local-style, varied - Inexpensive*
Located in the Kamehameha Square Shopping Center on Kuakini Highway behind the King Kam Hotel (326-7433). This is a clean, bright, pleasant place with pretty pink checkered curtains on the windows. The menu is local-style plate lunches with everything from curry stew to beef stew and chopped steak, teri beef and chicken, chili, sandwiches and more. Open Mon-Thurs 7AM - 3PM, Fri 7AM - 8PM, Sat 7AM - 2PM, closed Sunday.

ROYAL JADE GARDEN ★   *Chinese - Inexpensive*
75-5595 Palani Road, Kailua-Kona (326-7288) in the Lanihau Shopping Center. This neat family-run restaurant offers a full line of delicious Chinese food. The varied cuisine features some regional hot and spicy dishes. The food is generally good quality and of ample quantity. The surroundings are quite new and also clean, bright, and comfortable. Open daily, 10:30AM - 10PM.

SAM CHOY'S DINER ★   *Family Dining - Inexpensive*
75-5586 Ololi Road, just above the Lanihau Shopping Center off Palani Road in the Frame Ten Bowling Center, Kailua-Kona (329-0101). This clean well-kept diner serves the bowling crowd but attracts a loyal following with local celebrity Sam Choy's special local-style cuisine. The menu has plate lunches, burgers, sandwiches and local fast food favorites. Eat at a booth or table or take your plate in and watch the bowling action live. Open daily from 9AM - 10PM.

SAM CHOY'S RESTAURANT ★   *International - Inexpensive*
73-5576 Kauhola Bay 1, in the Kaloko Industrial Park near the airport, Kailua-Kona (326-1545). This long anticipated eatery opened in late fall, 1991. Sam, formerly chef at the Kona Hilton, is something of a local media celebrity and also has "Sam Choy's Diner" listed above. As at the Diner, Sam turns out excellent varied local-style cuisine with an international accent. The menu features such things as tomato beef, teriyaki steak, chicken stir fry, fried fish, lau lau and lomi salmon and lots more. This dining spot is a little hard to locate but turn into the Kaloko Industrial Area just north of Kailua-Kona and south of the airport. Look for the Kauhola Street sign to locate the building. Well worth the search. Open daily, except Sunday, from 5AM - 2PM for breakfast and lunch only.

SIBU CAFE ★   *Indonesian - Inexpensive*
75-5695E Alii Drive, Kailua-Kona (329-1112) in the Kona Banyan Court Shopping Arcade. Exotic, tasty Indonesian dishes such as chicken and beef sate', curry, and other special dishes of Bali. A variety of imported beers is featured. Inside and lanai-courtyard dining. This is one of those delightful surprise discoveries, especially if you like exotic hot spicy Southeast Asian cuisine. Open daily, 11:30AM - 9PM. No reservations, no credit cards.

SIZZLER ★   *Steaks - Inexpensive*
Palani Road, Kailua-Kona (329-3374) in the Kona Coast Shopping Center. This is the Big Island's only outlet for this national steakhouse chain and is popular with residents and visitors alike. The menu features reasonably priced steak, seafood, and combination dinners. Good salad bar. Breakfast, lunch, dinner daily, Sun-Thurs 6AM - 10PM, Fri-Sat 6AM - 12 midnight. Credit cards.

SPINNAKER'S *American - Inexpensive*
75-5770 Alii Drive, Waterfront Row Complex, across from St. Michael's Church (326-6000). This is a small shop in the food arcade and features a soup and salad bar, special desserts, ice cream and snacks. Open Mon-Sat, 10AM - 8PM.

STAN'S RESTAURANT *Family Dining - Inexpensive*
On Alii Drive, back of Kona Seaside Hotel (329-2455). The restaurant has a beautiful open-air view of Kailua Bay right across the street. The menu features steak, seafood, chicken, scampi, lots of local favorites and many daily specials. Open daily for breakfast 7 - 9:30AM and dinner 5 - 8PM. Credit cards.

SU'S THAI KITCHEN *Thai - Inexpensive*
74-5588A Pawai Place, Kailua-Kona (326-1222). The menu features many exotic offerings such as crab claw in pot, spicy ginger beef, garlic pork, Thai barbeque chicken, sweet-sour fish, seafood platter, Thai red curry, Mussamar yellow curry, green curry, noodle dishes and varied soups and appetizers. Hot chili pepper is used liberally! The restaurant is located in the middle of Kailua-Kona's industrial area which detracts somewhat from the exotic atmosphere. Open for lunch Monday-Friday 11:30AM - 2:30PM, dinner nightly 5 - 9PM.

TERU'S BAR AND RESTAURANT *Japanese/American - Inexpensive*
74-5583 Pawai Place, Kailua-Kona (329-5288). The menu at this local eatery features Japanese and American cuisine including teriyaki, fresh fish, shrimp tempura, noodles, and more. Located in the middle of the Kailua-Kona industrial area, this is a popular place for lunch and dinner with local folks. Open Mon-Sat, breakfast 6 - 11AM, lunch 11AM - 2:30PM, dinner 5 - 9:30PM.

TESHIMA'S RESTAURANT ★ *Japanese/American - Inexpensive*
On Highway 11, Honalo, Kona (322-9140) seven miles south of Kailua-Kona. This neat and very clean family restaurant is popular and features very friendly old-fashioned service by the Teshima family. Specialties are Japanese-American cuisine and local favorites and the menu has something for everyone. Open daily for breakfast and lunch 6:30AM - 2PM, dinner 5 - 10PM.

THAI RIN RESTAURANT ★ *Thai cuisine - Inexpensive*
Located in Alii Sunset Plaza, Alii Drive, Kailua-Kona (329-2929). This new restaurant turns out great versions of trendy hot and spicy Thai cuisine. The menu features over two dozen items including crispy and fried noodles, chicken satay, three kinds of curry, spicy soups, Thai garlic shrimp or squid and much more. Open Mon-Sat for lunch 11 - 2:30PM, dinner 5 - 9:30PM, Sun. for dinner only.

THE GALLERY CAFE *Pasta-sandwiches - Inexpensive*
Located in the Kealakekua Art Center, Highway 11, Kealakekua, Kona (323-3306). This eatery is located on the upper level of the artisans complex and the menu offers a small selection of soups, sandwiches, salads and pasta dishes. They also prepare picnic baskets to take out. Open Monday - Friday 10AM - 7PM, Saturday 11AM - 7PM, closed Sundays.

THE HIDEOUT *Sandwiches & Burgers - Inexpensive*
75-5629T Kuakini Highway, in the North Kona Shopping Center, around back next to Hele Mai Laundromat, 326-1911. This is a very small eatery with a

counter inside and a couple of tables on outside walkway. The simple menu features turkey, ham, pastrami, corned beef, steak, reuben sandwiches and something called "Killer Tuna," also burgers; eggs and things for breakfast. Open Monday-Friday 8AM - 5PM, Saturday 10AM - 4PM, closed Sunday.

TRES COMPADRE'S   *Mexican - Inexpensive*
74-5596Q Pawai Place, in the Kona industrial area (326-7422). This rather unpretentious place provides very informal dining featuring homemade Mexican and Spanish food at reasonable prices. If you're an aficionado of Mexican food, you might want to check this place out. Open Mon-Sat for dinner only, 5 - 10PM.

VERANDA RESTAURANT   *American - Inexpensive*
75-5660 Palani Rd., Kailua-Kona (329-2911) in the Hotel King Kamehameha. This hotel coffee shop menu features beef, chicken, and fresh island fish as well as sandwiches and lighter fare for lunch. Bright, cheerful atmosphere, generally pleasant service. Open daily for breakfast and lunch only, 5:30AM - 1:30PM. Credit cards.

WAKEFIELD GARDENS   *Family Dining - Inexpensive*
On the road to Honaunau Bay, Kona (328-9930). This is an interesting little country house set amidst a macadamia nut orchard and botanical garden. They serve lunch daily from 11AM - 3PM and have a simple menu of salads, varied sandwiches, other light fare, and delicious homemade fresh fruit pies. After lunch or a snack, stroll the grounds and take in their self-guided botanical tour.

YAE-DAKE SUSHI YA   *Japanese - Inexpensive*
75-5629 Kuakini Hwy, North Kona Shopping Center, 326-7222. This local Japanese-style eatery offers varied plate lunches, plus bento, sushi, chicken cutlet, fish tempura, fish platter, and other local favorites. Open Monday-Friday, 5AM - 2PM.

YUNI KOREAN RESTAURANT ★   *Korean - Inexpensive*
Located 75-5595 Palani Road, in the Lanihau Center, Kailua-Kona (329-3167). This new restaurant serves up a wide range of Korean specialties including kal-bi beef ribs, mun doo, spicy Korean chicken, noodles, mixed plates and more. Open Mon-Sat 10:30AM - 9PM, Sun 10:30AM - 7PM.

YU SUSHI ★   *Japanese - Inexpensive*
75-5770 Alii Drive, Kailua-Kona, in the Waterfront Row shopping-dining complex across from St. Michael's Church (326-5653). This small eatery offers the best of authentic Japanese sushi, those artistically created rice rolls using fresh fish and seafood. For an unusual and intriguing experience in relaxing surroundings, give it a try. Open daily for lunch 11AM - 2:30PM, dinner 4:30 - 9:30PM.

MODERATE

BANANA BAY CAFE ★   *Hawaiian/Polynesian - Moderate*
75-5739 Alii Dr. (329-1393) in the Kona Bay Hotel. A South Seas dining atmosphere with a menu heavy in Polynesian-Hawaiian cuisine. Sample selections are fresh island fish with tropical fruit sauces, prawns Tahitian, shrimp curry Javanese, sweet-sour chicken Samoa, brandied breast of chicken, coconut shrimp, and many others. All meals are complimented with South Seas flavors of fresh banana,

sweet potato, Hawaiian taro, pineapple, and coconut. Nightly hula show featured. Breakfast and dinner buffet and special Sunday brunch also. Open daily for breakfast 7 - 11AM, dinner 5 - 9PM. Dinner reservations suggested. Credit cards.

BEACH CLUB ★ *American - Moderate*
75-6106 Alii Drive (329-0290) in the Kona by the Sea Condos. The feature here is southwest cuisine in a Hawaiian scene. The menu offers such things as quesadilla, blue corn chips, spicy Thai beef and chicken salads, black calamari pasta, fish, game hen, steak, and more. Open daily for dinner, 6 - 9:30PM. Reservations suggested. Credit cards.

CAFE CALYPSO ★ *Steaks/Seafood - Moderate*
Across from King Kam Hotel and Kailua Pier on Alii Drive, upstairs (329-5550). Features open air harbor views of Kailua Bay and lovely sunsets from its upstairs location. Menu offers a Continental-International selection of seafood, steaks, chicken and local favorites. Good food attractively presented with friendly service. Bright clean decor with tropical paintings on the walls. Open daily for lunch 11AM - 5PM, and dinner 5 - 9:30PM. Reservations suggested. Credit cards.

ECLIPSE RESTAURANT *Continental/International - Moderate*
75-5711 Kuakini Highway, Kailua-Kona (329-4686). This casually elegant restaurant is centrally located in Kailua-Kona town. Menu features fresh fish, seafood specials, steaks, veal, and special international coffees and desserts. Open for lunch, Mon-Fri 11AM - 2PM, and dinner every day 5 - 9PM. Dance music is provided evenings, 10PM - 1:30AM with special big band music on Sundays. Reservations suggested. Credit cards.

FISHERMAN'S LANDING ★ *Seafood - Moderate*
75-5744 Alii Drive, Kailua-Kona (326-2555) in the Kona Inn Shopping Village. This ocean front restaurant features the best in fresh island seafood. Located directly on Kailua Bay, the restaurant has five separate Hawaiian dining huts with nautical theme decor. Fresh island fish such as ono, opakapaka, ahi, etc. are mainstays along with lobster, shrimp, and a number of daily specials. Beef, veal, and chicken as well as local style specialties round out the menu. This is an especially nice location right on the water's edge, great for sunsets. Lunch 11:30AM - 2:30PM, dinner 5:30 - 10PM daily. Reservations suggested.

HUGGO'S *Steaks - Moderate*
75-5828 Kahakai Road, Kailua-Kona (329-1493). This oceanside restaurant is just next door to the Kona Hilton Hotel and sits over the water's edge. There are beautiful views of Kailua Bay and romantic sunsets. The menu features steaks and prime rib. Cocktail piano bar and special free pupus daily 2:30 - 5:30 PM. Open for lunch Mon-Fri 11:30AM - 2:30PM, dinner 5:30 - 10PM, Sat-Sun, dinner only 5:30 - 10PM. Credit cards.

JAMESON'S BY THE SEA *Seafood - Moderate*
77-6452 Alii Drive (329-3195) next to Magic Sands Beach. The beachside location lends a nice atmosphere with a menu featuring varied American-Continental selections such as pasta, beef, veal, lamb, chicken, and fresh island fish. Specialties include veal Marsala, veal piccata, filet mignon, lobster, calamari, and rack of lamb. Special silver platters include beef, seafood, and combo dinners.

Pleasant Hawaiian background music, white table cloths, and cheerful bright surroundings add a nice touch. Beautiful sunsets complimentary with dinner. Open for lunch Mon-Fri 11:30AM - 2:30PM, dinner nightly from 6PM.

JESTERS TAVERN   *Moderate*
75-5995A Kuakini Highway, Kailua-Kona (326-7633). This is the latest of "theme" restaurants in Kona and is promoted as a "medieval-theme" bar-b-que restaurant featuring bbq beef, fresh fish, chicken, salads, sandwiches and more. The "Quaffery Bar" offers a variety of international beers. Jesters promotes an atmosphere recalling a bygone era of lords and ladies, knights and maidens, wenches and pranksters, royalty and, of course, jesters. Open Mon.- Sat. for lunch and dinner from 11 AM, Sunday brunch 11AM - 3 PM.

JOLLY ROGER ★   *Continental/International - Moderate*
75-5776 Alii Drive, Kailua-Kona (329-1344). The menu at this beachside restaurant features steak, teriyaki beef or chicken, ribs, seafood, chicken Polynesian, pasta, sandwiches, salads, and more. It's next door to the new Waterfront Row shopping complex and across from St. Michael's Catholic Church. Open daily for breakfast 6:30 - 12 noon, lunch 11AM - 4PM, and dinner 4 - 10PM. Happy hour is 11AM-7PM. Credit cards.

KANAZAWA TEI   *Japanese - Moderate*
75-5845 Alii Drive (326-1881) across from the Kona Hilton. There is authentic Japanese food here plus a sushi bar specializing in those delightful and surprising little rice roll appetizers stuffed with fish, shrimp, vegetables, pickles, etc. Dinner entrees include Japanese style steak, beef, chicken, and a variety of seafood. In addition to a complete lunch and dinner menu, the house special is a bento (box lunch) served with miso (soybean) soup. Open for lunch Mon-Fri 11:30AM -2PM, dinner nightly 6 - 9:30PM. This is a pleasant Japanese-style restaurant and the only drawback is dinner prices that lean toward expensive even though it's moderate overall. Credit cards.

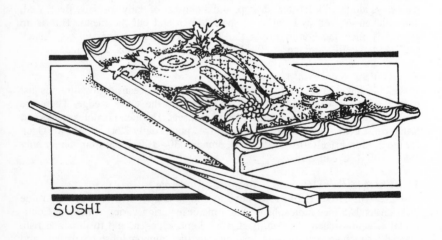

SUSHI

KONA AMIGOS RESTAURANT   *Mexican - Moderate*
75-5669 Alii Drive, upstairs, across from Kailua Pier (326-2840). The menu here is obviously Mexican and features a variety of bontanos (appetizers), ensaladas (salads), soups and entradas (entrees). Dinner menu bontanos include nachos, calamari, and quesadilla; ensaladas include guacamole, taco, sea scallops/fish; soups-daily specials; entrees include burritos, fajitas fiesta, pescado Yucatan, crab enchiladas, chimichanga, pollo verde and pollo adoba, beef tenderloin and pork loin. There is a similar lunch menu with additional egg and sandwich items listed. Lovely open-air views of Kailua Bay. Open daily for lunch 11AM - 4PM, dinner 4-10PM, bar serves up fresh fruit margaritas and more till midnight.

KONA BEACH RESTAURANT ★   *Continental/International - Moderate*
75-5660 Palani Road (329-2911) in the Kona Beach King Kamehameha Hotel. Formerly Moby Dick's, this room has an attractive nautical-whaling decor theme. There are big picture window views of Kailua Wharf and Bay, Ahuena Heiau directly in front of the hotel and Kamakahonu Beach. The menu features specialties such as Pacific Broiled Salmon, Kiawe-smoked Prime Rib, Herbal Breast of Chicken, Cajun Prawns with pasta and more. Delightful setting with live piano music, attractive wood paneling and fish tanks to amuse the kids. Good service and they take good care of youngsters, providing extra goodies. Open daily with breakfast buffet 6:30 - 10:30AM, lunch 11AM - 2PM and dinner 5:30 - 9PM. The Sunday Brunch is excellent. Reservations suggested. Credit cards.

KONA BROILER ★   *Steaks/seafood - Family dining - Moderate*
Located upstairs in the Kona Marketplace Shopping Center on Alii Drive, Kailua-Kona (329-7728). This new restaurant features Kona's only "broil your own" service. The menu features sirloin and New York steak, shrimp kabob, mahi-mahi and fresh island fish, chicken and burgers. Place your order and then you "broil your own" on the large grills. Tables in an old trolly bus out front and old-fashioned ad signs decorate the walls. Good for family dining. Open daily for lunch and dinner, 10:30AM - 10:30PM.

KONA INN RESTAURANT   *Seafood - Moderate*
75-5744 Alii Drive (329-4455) in the heart of Kailua-Kona in the Kona Inn Shopping Village. There is a pleasant casualness in this open-air veranda restaurant which is the original dining room of the old Kona Inn Hotel. The ceiling fans add to the tropical ambiance and informality. There are lovely views of Kailua Bay and the waterfront. The menu features fresh island fish, seafood, prime rib, steaks, and local favorites. Open daily for lunch from 11AM with dinner served 5:30 - 10PM. Dinner reservations suggested. Credit cards.

KONA RANCH HOUSE ★   *Family Dining - Moderate*
(329-7061) Near intersection of Kuakini Highway and Palani Road, just above the Shell Station. The restaurant has an attractive old ranch house decor with a casual, turn-of-the-century Hawaiian atmosphere. The menu features ranch fare including paniolo BBQ platters, roast beef, roast turkey, ribs, and chicken. Good food and friendly service in a very pleasant atmosphere. This is a good place for families. Open daily for breakfast and lunch 7AM - 2PM, dinner 5 - 9PM. Closed between 2 - 5 PM. Reservations for dinner suggested. Credit cards.

KUAKINI TERRACE ★ *Buffet - Moderate*
78-6778 Alii Drive, Keauhou-Kona (322-3441) in the Keauhou Beach Hotel. Open daily from 6:30AM - 9PM serving breakfast, lunch and dinner. The dining room features a nightly buffet, 5 - 9PM. Monday through Thursday it's a Chinese Buffet with roast duck, dim sum, mandarin salad, and an array of Cantonese and Szechwan selections. Friday through Sunday it's a fabulous seafood buffet with Alaskan Crab, island fish, shrimp, Pacific clams, oysters, and even prime rib of beef. On Sunday, there is a Champagne Sunday Brunch from 9AM - 1:30PM featuring prime rib, special eggs, island fish, shrimp tempura, a variety of salads and tropical fruits and desserts. Reservations suggested. Credit cards.

MARTY'S STEAKS & SEAFOOD ★ *Steak/Seafood - Moderate*
75-5699 Alii Drive (329-1571) in the Kailua Bay Shopping Plaza opposite Hulihee Palace. There are nice views of Kailua Bay and tropical sunsets from this casual upstairs setting. The menu offers steaks, ribs, seafood, and salad bar. Open daily for lunch 11AM - 3PM, dinner 5 - 10PM, Sun dinner only 5 - 10PM. Reservations suggested. Credit cards.

PAPAGAYOS MEXICAN GRILL *Mexican - Moderate*
Kamehameha Center, Kuakini Highway, Kailua-Kona (326-5660). The menu features everything from tacos to enchiladas, fajitas to chimichangas and a few Continental dishes for good measure. Open daily for lunch and dinner continuously, 11AM - 9PM. Live music offered Thur-Fri-Sat, 10PM - 2AM, Sunday on the patio for dining 4 - 8PM.

PELE'S COURT *Continental/International - Moderate*
78-128 Ehukai (322-3411) in the Kona Surf Resort Hotel. This is a lovely open-air dining room on the hotel's lower level with relaxing garden views. The lunch menu offers a variety of sandwiches, seafood, chicken and pasta dishes plus pizza. Dinner entrees featured include seafood, beef prime ribs, teriyaki steak, chicken, pasta, burritos, plus salad bar and sandwiches. A varied breakfast menu is also available. Open daily for breakfast 6:30-11AM, lunch 11-2PM, dinner 5-9PM.

PLAYERS RESTAURANT *Continental-Regional - Moderate*
78-7190 Kaleopapa Road, Keauhou-Kona area (322-2727) in the Holua at Mauna Loa Village Condominium complex just above the Kona Surf Resort. This restaurant is in the Holua Tennis Center with neat views of the surrounding courts. The menu selections include mixed grills, pasta, fresh island fish and seafood specialties and regional-Continental specials. Open daily except Monday for lunch 11:30AM - 1:30PM, dinner 6:30 - 9:30PM.

THE CHART HOUSE ★ *Steaks - Moderate*
75-5770 Alii Drive, Kailua-Kona, in the Waterfront Row shopping-dining complex, across from St. Michael's Church (329-2451). This open-air verandah-style restaurant offers excellent steaks, prime rib and fresh fish and other seafood selections as well as an interesting appetizer and salad bar. Most dinner entrees are in the moderate range with some getting into the expensive bracket. Casual relaxing atmosphere overlooking the ocean shoreline. Reservations suggested. Credit cards.

THE MAKEE RESTAURANT   *Continental/International - Moderate*
78-128 Ehukai (322-3411) in the Kona Surf Resort Hotel. This elegant dining room offers Continental/Pacific dining with menu selections such as fresh island fish, Big Island Parker Ranch beefsteak, veal chops, tiger prawns, Pacific lobster and other Hawaiian seafood specials. Open daily for dinner only, 6 - 9:30PM. Reservations suggested. Credit cards.

THE RUSTY HARPOON ★   *Continental/International - Moderate*
Alii Drive across from Kona Inn Shopping Village in the Kona Plaza Condos (329-8881). The menu features lots of pupus (appetizers), salads, and soups while entrees cover a wide range including seafood, scampi, fresh island fish, chicken, prime rib (house specialty), Korean ribs, and local favorites. Open daily for breakfast 7 - 11AM, lunch 12 - 4PM, dinner 5 - 10PM. Upstairs location in the heart of the village overlooks Kailua Bay and Alii Drive. Credit cards.

THE TERRACE   *Continental/International - Moderate*
78-261 Manukai (322-9625) in Kanaloa at the Kona Condominiums. There is a casual poolside-garden setting, in addition to being on the ocean's edge. The mixed menu includes sandwiches, salads, steaks, ribs, prawns, chicken, pasta, and fresh island fish. Open daily for breakfast 8 - 11:30AM, lunch 11:30AM - 2:30PM, and dinner 5:30 - 9:30PM. Credit cards.

TOM BOMBADIL'S FOOD AND DRINK   *American - Moderate*
75-5864 Walua Road, at the intersection of Alii Drive and Walua Road, Kailua-Kona, across from the Kona Hilton (329-1292). The menu features pizza, pasta, broasted chicken, and sandwiches like French dip, sausage and Reuben Burger plus some local specialties. Dinner specials include steak, chicken teriyaki, fresh island fish, soups and salads. Cocktail lounge. Open daily for lunch and dinner, 11AM - 10PM. Credit cards.

VISTA RESTAURANT   *Seafood - Moderate*
78-7000 Alii Drive, Keauhou-Kona (322-3700) at the Kona Country Club. Open for breakfast and lunch only and features fresh island fish, burgers, sandwiches and many local favorites. Early morning golfers keep the place busy. Open daily, 6:30AM - 2:30PM.

EXPENSIVE

HALE MOANA ★ *Continental/International - Expensive*
Kaupulehu-Kona (325-5555) at the Kona Village Resort. This pleasant and airy dining room is the main restaurant for this South Seas style resort. It has a beach location with adjacent garden terrace for open-air dining. The cuisine includes American, European, and Hawaiian specialties. Reservations required. Open daily for breakfast, lunch, and dinner, 6:30AM - 10PM. Credit cards.

HALE SAMOA ★ *Continental/International - Expensive*
Kaupulehu-Kona (325-5555) at the Kona Village Resort. This small intimate dining room features gourmet cuisine South Seas-style. The room features a Samoan motif complete with an outrigger canoe hanging from the ceiling. The menu is heavy in seafood Polynesian-style but also features lamb, beef, veal, and duck. Attentive service in a romantic South Seas atmosphere is the tradition here. The sunsets are gorgeous. Reservations are a must. Dinner only, daily 6 - 9PM. Credit cards.

HELE MAI DINING ROOM *American - Expensive*
75-5852 Alii Drive (329-3111) in the Kona Hilton Hotel. This is a pleasant place for that special evening out in Kona. It's location on the water's edge creates a nice atmosphere to enjoy the lights of Kailua Bay and the usually good food for which Hilton is noted. The menu ranges from Polynesian/Pacific entrees like ono (fish) with crabmeat stuffing, sauteed mahimahi, Kona Hilton's famous seafood pasta, prawns, lobster and Chinese roast duck to Continental-American selections like prime rib, steaks and chicken, to house specialties like combination platters. Open daily for dinner 6 - 9:30PM. Special buffet nights are Friday (pasta), Saturday (prime rib) and Sunday (international). There is also a lavish Sunday buffet served 9AM - 1:30PM. Reservations suggested. Credit cards.

LA BOURGOGNE FRENCH RESTAURANT *French - Expensive*
Kuakini Highway #11, 4 miles south of Kailua-Kona, in the Kuakini Plaza South Center (329-6711). Specializing in fresh fish, shrimp, scallops, roast duck, chicken, pork tenderloin, lamb, steak, and veal all with a French accent. Luscious desserts like chocolate mousse, caramel creme, and cherries jubilee finish the menu. Dinner only, Mon-Sat 6 - 10PM. Reservations suggested. Credit cards.

PALM CAFE *Steaks/seafood - Expensive*
Located in the Coconut Grove Marketplace on Alii Drive, adjacent from the Kona Hilton Hotel and across from the waterfront (329-7765). The Cafe is an elegant open-air dining room with ceiling fans and nice views of Kailua Bay and boat traffic. Great for sunsets! The menu features a few beefsteak selections and the emphasis is on seafood and fresh island fish. Open daily for dinner only, 5:30 - 10PM. Reservations suggested.

PHILLIP PAOLO'S ITALIAN RESTAURANT ★ *Italian - Expensive*
Waterfront Row, 75-5770 Alii Drive, across from St. Michael's Church, (329-4436). Located on the upper level of the complex, this room has a lovely open veranda view of the ocean. The decor attempts to imitate an Italian villa with decorative accents, marble columns, etc. The tables and booths are placed close together and don't allow for much intimacy in dining. The food, however, is

excellent. The menu features varied pasta, seafood, veal, chicken and steaks. A nice selection of fresh salads, soups and appetizers is also available. The servings are skillfully prepared and very generous. Good food and good service. Open daily for lunch, 11Am - 2:30PM; dinner 4:30 - 11PM. Early bird specials; dinner reservations suggested; credit cards.

SOUTH KOHALA

INTRODUCTION

The accent in Kamuela is ranch country and that's what the restaurants offer, a country atmosphere and generally good hearty food. The fare ranges from local-style Oriental to Continental-International at several inexpensive and moderate category restaurants. Down on the fashionable Kohala Coast where the world-class luxury resorts are, the accent is definitely upscale. Here dining is an indulgence in fine gourmet cuisine. With the large number of award-winning dining rooms from which to choose, the Kohala Coast is an epicurean's delight.

INEXPENSIVE

ALOHA LUIGI ★   *Italian - Inexpensive*
Located on Kawaihae Road in the heart of Waimea next door to Paniolo Country Inn (885-7277). Recent renovation work on this place resulted in a pleasant dining spot featuring great Italian food. The menu offers appetizers like minestrone soup and artichoke parmesan dip; Caesar Luigi salad; a variety of Italian sandwiches; pasta including homemade meatballs and spaghetti, five cheese lasagna, and eggplant Luigi; a variety of pizza. Open Monday-Thursday 10AM -8PM, Friday and Saturday till 9PM, closed Sunday.

AUNTY ALICE'S PIE & COFFEE SHOP ★   *Family Dining - Inexpensive*
Parker Ranch Shopping Center, Kamuela (885-6880). The menu features home-made daily specials, pastries, sandwiches, meat rolls and pies, soups, and light meals plus their famous homemade pies. Open daily 6AM - 4PM.

CAFE PESTO ★   *Italian - Inexpensive*
Kawaihae Center, Kawaihae (882-1071). This small pizzeria offers a wide variety of excellent pizza, pasta, sandwiches, and specialties including fresh baked pastries. They even deliver to Kohala Coast resort area and Kamuela for an extra charge. Open daily 11AM - 10PM, Fri-Sat till 11PM.

DON'S PAKE KITCHEN   *Chinese - Inexpensive*
Highway 19 just east (Honoka'a side) of Waimea in the old Fukushima Store building (885-2025). This smallish Chinese kitchen serves up a varied menu of freshly prepared Cantonese and Szechwan specialties. House specials are char siu (pork) and roast duck. Look for the old-fashioned gas pump in front. Open daily 10AM - 9PM.

GREAT WALL CHOP SUEY ★   *Chinese - Inexpensive*
This Chinese eatery is located in the Waimea Center Shopping Mall in the heart of Kamuela (885-7252). The variety of Cantonese food offered is excellent in quality and quantity. There is a full selection of beef, pork, chicken, seafood, and noodle dishes. Open daily for lunch and dinner except Monday, 11AM - 8PM.

JINHO'S   *Sandwiches - Inexpensive*
Across from the Kawaihae Wharf on Hwy. 270 in Kawaihae (882-7922). A small local-style fast food spot offering a menu of sandwiches, teribeef, chicken, chili, saimin and plate lunches. Open Mon.-Fri. 6AM-5PM; Sat. 7-5PM; closed Sunday.

KAMUELA BREAD DEPOT ★   *Sandwiches - Inexpensive*
Kawaihae Road, Kamuela (885-6354) in the Opelu Plaza Shopping Center. This bakery-deli serves up wonderful French bread, fresh pastries, and delicious sandwiches, soups, and salads. Dine in or take out. Open daily except Sunday, 6:30AM - 5:30PM.

MASAYO'S RESTAURANT   *Japanese - Inexpensive*
Kawaihae Road, Kamuela (885-4295). This very small country cafe specializes in Japanese-American cuisine. Menu specials include teriyaki, tonkatsu, saimin, and several other local favorites. You can eat at the counter or take out. It's not a fancy place but they serve a satisfying inexpensive meal if you're on a budget.

PANIOLO COUNTRY INN ★   *Family Dining - Inexpensive*
Kawaihae Road in the heart of Kamuela (885-4377) next door to Parker Ranch Lodge. This family cafe has a real country ambience and ranch-style decor. The menu features a variety of burgers and sandwiches, BBQ ribs, chicken, pasta, Mexican food, and pizza. The food is excellent quality and service is courteous. There is an interesting collection of branding irons from Big Island ranches decorating the walls and a beautiful aquarium with Hawaiian reef fish that will interest youngsters. Open daily for breakfast, lunch, and dinner continuously from 6AM - 9PM, weekends till 10PM.

PARKER SQUARE CAFE   *Sandwiches - Inexpensive*
Located in the Parker Square shopping complex, Hwy. 19, in Kamuela town (885-3455). This small eatery features breakfast, lunch and snack specialties. For breakfast, choose croissants, pastries, crepes or baked papaya. Lunch specials include crepes, quiche, pasta salad, stuffed croissants, soups and sandwiches. A variety of coffees, espressos and desserts are also featured. Open daily 8AM-4PM.

WAIKOLOA VILLAGE RESTAURANT   *American - Inexpensive*
Waikoloa Village Golf Course, Waikoloa Village (883-9644). The menu features steaks, fresh island fish, chicken, local favorites, burgers, and special sandwiches. The dining room is bright, open, and airy with pretty golf course views. Open daily for breakfast 7 - 10:30AM, lunch 10:30AM - 5PM, and dinner 5 -9PM. Credit cards.

WAIMEA COFFEE & CO.   *Sandwiches - Inexpensive*
Located on Highway 19 across from Edelweiss Restaurant on the Kawaihae Road in Kamuela (885-4472). This small coffee shop offers light fare such as pastries, croissants, bagels, fruit and ice cream as well as hot and cold beverages. They

specialize in over 20 varieties of arabica coffee from around the world. Daily beverages include a coffee of the day, espresso, cappuccino, chocolate drinks, fresh juices and more. Open Monday-Saturday 9AM til closing.

YONG'S KAL-BI ★   *Korean - Inexpensive*
Located in the Waimea Center, Highway 19, Waimea (885-8440). This small family restaurant features local and Oriental foods with an emphasis on Korean cuisine. The menu lists kal-bi ribs, barbeque beef, Korean chicken, chicken katsu, mandoo (Korean won ton), fish and more. The food is very good with ample portions served plate-lunch style. Clean attractive location, simple decor; eat here or take out. Open daily for breakfast, lunch and dinner, 9:30AM - 9PM.

MODERATE

CASCADES ★   *Buffet - Moderate*
Hyatt Regency Waikoloa Hotel, Kohala Coast (885-1234). This dining room offers buffet dining only for breakfast, lunch, and dinner. It is a lovely pastel peach-pink colored room with lots of greenery and lovely pool and waterfalls with swans floating about. Serving lines can move slow when it's busy due to the congested area around the serving counters. The varied buffet menus change daily and the food is generally excellent. There is an emphasis on Polynesian dishes. Open daily for breakfast 6 - 11AM, lunch 11AM - 3PM, and dinner 5 - 12PM. Credit cards.

CATTLEMAN'S STEAKHOUSE   *Steaks - Moderate*
Highway 19 near the center of Kamuela (885-4077). This rustic country restaurant features a Hawaiian paniolo "cowboy" decor. Mounted trophy heads of wild boar, goat, sheep, deer, etc. and brands of Hawaiian ranches decorate the walls. The menu features steaks, prime rib, lamb chops, game hen, chicken, and seafood selections. The steaks and prime rib are excellent. Open nightly for dinner 5:30 - 9PM. Credit cards.

EDELWEISS ★   *Continental/International - Moderate*
Highway 19, Kawaihae Road, Kamuela (885-6800). This delightful chalet-like village inn fits in with the cool upcountry ranch climate of Kamuela and features varied continental-international cuisine. Specialties include veal, rack of lamb, fresh island seafood and other creative dishes. Master Chef Hans-Peter Hager ensures a pleasant dining experience. Open daily except Monday for lunch 11:30AM - 2PM, and dinner from 5PM. No reservations. Credit cards.

GARDEN CAFE ★   *Continental/International - Moderate*
Royal Waikoloan Hotel, Kohala Coast (885-6789). Quiet comfortable surroundings with greenery and garden view and koi swimming in a lagoon provide a pleasant atmosphere. The menu features a varied fare of fresh island fish, seafood selections, steak and prime rib, chicken and pork loin. Interesting appetizers include local style Portuguese bean soup, won ton mein, and sashimi (raw fish). Salads are led by a seafood pasta, oriental chicken salad, and a tropical fruit platter. A nice selection of sandwiches rounds out the menu. Open daily for breakfast 6 - 10 AM, Continental 10 - 11AM, and lunch-dinner continuously 11AM - 10PM. Credit cards.

HARRINGTON'S   *American - Moderate*
Kawaihae Center, Kawaihae (882-7997). The menu features lobster, prawns, scallops, calamari, and other seafood specialties plus Slavic steak, New York steak, prime rib, and chicken. Open dinner only, Sun-Thurs 5 - 9PM, Fri-Sat 5:30 - 10PM. Credit cards.

KONA PROVISION COMPANY ★   *Continental/International - Moderate*
Hyatt Regency Waikoloa Hotel, Kohala Coast (885-1234). This is a beautiful open air restaurant situated on a bluff overlooking the Kohala Coast surf and shoreline. The decor is provincial Thailand-Malaysian influenced with greenery, artwork, and multi-leveled rooms much like a Thai-Malaysian house. Ceiling fans add a touch of relaxing ambiance. The menu is very creative featuring Oriental stir-fried chicken and shrimp, seafood mixed grill, beef sate, steaks and excellent fresh island fish. Desserts are marvelous including Moloka'i Lime Pie and papaya pie with cinnamon ice cream as standouts. Open daily for lunch 11:30AM - 2:30PM and dinner 5:30 - 10:30 PM. Credit cards.

OCEAN BAR & GRILL   *American - Moderate*
Located poolside at the Ritz-Carlton Mauna Lani Hotel (885-2000) at Mauna Lani Resort on the Kohala Coast. This open-air cafe offers daily breakfast, lunch and snacks from early morning until late afternoon. The menu features grilled American favorites, sandwiches, pasta, pizza, salads and a special childrens' menu. The daily breakfast buffet is especially pleasant if its not too windy.

OCEAN GRILL   *Continental/International - Moderate*
Mauna Lani Bay Hotel, Kohala Coast (885-6622). This oceanside cafe provides a bright breezy location between the hotel pool and the beach. The menu offers snacks and light fare of sandwiches, seafood specials, salads and more. Open daily 10AM - 6PM.

ORCHID CAFE ★   *Family Dining - Moderate*
Hyatt Regency Waikoloa Hotel, Kohala Coast (885-1234). This hotel coffee shop has a pleasant poolside setting surrounded by coconut trees. Colorful parrots squawk and talk while you enjoy a meal or snack under parasol-covered tables or under roof. The breakfast menu is quite traditional while lunch features specials

KOI

like rib eye beef, chicken breast, charred fresh ahi (tuna), bouillabaisse, sandwiches, salads, and even pizza. Dinner is a nice combination of turf and surf specials including lamb, beef tenderloin, chicken, and seafood like red snapper and sea scallops rounded out by burgers, sandwiches, and pizza. Open daily continuously from 6AM - 11PM. Credit cards.

PARKER RANCH BROILER   *Steaks - Moderate*
Parker Ranch Shopping Center, Kamuela (885-7366). The menu features steaks and seafood grilled on a kiawe wood broiler, which adds to the distinct flavor of the food. Other entrees include prime rib, pulehu ribs, Kohala catfish, steamed fish with shoyu (soy sauce) and ginger, sandwiches, salads, and desserts. Open daily for lunch 11 - 2PM, from 2 - 3PM for soup and salads, and for dinner 5 - 10PM; on Fridays an island lunch buffet and special Hawaiian fare is featured. Credit cards.

ROYAL TERRACE ★   *Continental/International - Moderate*
Royal Waikoloan Hotel, Waikoloa (885-6789). This room has lovely views overlooking gardens, ancient fishponds and lagoons and glorious evening sunsets over Anaehoomalu Bay. Recent renovations have turned the room into a buffet-only dining room. Dinner buffets are served Thurs-Sat nights and each evening menu is different but features Pacific regional cuisine with an Oriental flair. There are a wide variety of appetizers, salads, soups and special entrees as well as a tempting dessert bar. Live Hawaiian music adds a relaxing romantic touch to an enjoyable dining experience. The daily morning buffet features a wide selection of breakfast entrees as well. Open for breakfast daily 6:30 -11AM, dinner Thurs-Sat only 6-9PM.

THE BARON   *Continental/International - Moderate*
Located on Kinohou Street just off Highway 19 on the Honoka'a side of Waimea town (885-5888). This attractive contemporary decor dining room opened in early 1992 (in the former Bree Garden location) and offers a wide selection of continental/international dishes prepared under the direction of Chef Heinz D.K. Hennig von Traunstein. The menu features fresh island fish and seafood, veal, lamb, chicken, beef, pork and pasta with a variety of international accents. The bar features German Warsteiner beer on tap. Open daily for lunch 11AM - 2PM and dinner 5PM till closing.

THE 19TH. HOLE   *Sandwiches/light fare - Moderate*
Located at the Mauna Kea Beach Golf Course Clubhouse, Mauna Kea Beach Hotel, Kohala Coast (882-7222). This restaurant provides relaxing country club privacy and a menu of light luncheon specials including sandwiches, salads, sushi, saimin and more. Open daily 11AM - 4:30PM.

WAIKOLOA BEACH GRILL   *Continental/regional - Moderate*
Located in the Waikoloa Beach Golf Course Clubhouse at Waikoloa Resort on the Kohala Coast (885-6131). The menu features a variety of appetizers, salads and sandwiches for lunch and steaks, chicken and seafood for dinner entrees. The menu also has a nice selection of wines. There is attractive contemporary decor and fairway views lend a nice accent. Golfers enjoy a continental breakfast from 7AM with lunch served daily 9:30AM - 4:30PM and dinner 5:30 - 10PM.

EXPENSIVE

BATIK ROOM ★   *Continental/International - Expensive*
Mauna Kea Beach Hotel, Kohala Coast (882-7222). This hotel's fine dining room
is perhaps the best known of Mauna Kea's award-winning restaurants. The menu
features specialties of the Pacific and Far East including fresh Kohala fish,
Ceylon-inspired curries, delicate steaks, Chateaubriand, lobster, and many other
classic dishes. A full range of appetizers, soups, and salads is available as well as
an extensive wine list. The ambiance, service, and dining experience are superb.
Dinner jackets for gentlemen required. Daily for dinner, 7-10PM. Credit cards.

BAY TERRACE ★   *Continental/International - Expensive*
Mauna Lani Bay Hotel, Kohala Coast (885-6622). This open-air garden terrace
restaurant provides a delightful dining atmosphere. The a la carte dinner menu
ranges from Continental to International selections of beef, fresh island fish,
seafood, chicken, lamb, and many specialties. The daily lunch buffet is a lavish
affair with a wide selection of salads, appetizers, hot and cold entrees, and
desserts. The Sunday buffet is especially nice, and even more sumptuous, and
includes many Japanese and Oriental specialties. A different dinner menu is
presented each evening. A recent addition is an excellent Fri. and Sat. night
seafood buffet with superb entrees, salads and dessert bar. Daily for breakfast 6 -
11AM, lunch 11-2PM, dinner 6-9:30PM. Reservations recommended. Credit cards.

CANOE HOUSE ★   *Continental/International - Expensive*
Mauna Lani Bay Hotel, Kohala Coast, (885-6622). This pleasant dining room
specializes in regional Pacific Rim cuisine in a beachside open air setting. The
food is wonderfully diverse, the service is superb and the Hawaiian-contemporary
music is relaxing. The dinner menu features exotic pupus (appetizers) such as
sesame shrimp, Thai beef, lobster dumplings and curried chicken lumpia; entree
selections include seafood hot pot, seared peppered ahi, bamboo steamed mahimahi, Kohala Coast snapper, five spice duck and many other specials. Daily for
lunch 11AM - 5PM; dinner nightly, 5 - 9PM. Reservations suggested; credit cards.

DONATONI'S ★   *Italian - Expensive*
Hyatt Regency Waikoloa Hotel, Kohala Coast (885-1234). This original Italian
restaurant has been relocated to the former Water's Edge dining room but still
features fine northern Italian cuisine including pastas, veal dishes, seafood, pizza
and more. plus Italian desserts, cappuccino and espresso. Open nightly for dinner
only, 6 - 10PM with live music. Reservations suggested; credit cards.

HARTWELL'S   *Continental/International - Expensive*
Located at Hale Kea (White House) ranch estate on Highway 19 just west of
Kamuela on the Kawaihae road (885-6094). This rustic old Hawaiian ranch
manager's home features dining in various rooms of the rambling structure
including the parlor, library, sitting room, veranda and main dining room. The
menu features special sandwiches, salads, soups and specials for lunch. Dinner
includes such entrees as Waimea rainbow duckling, fresh island fish, seafood,
chicken, lamb, veal, prime rib and ranch ribs. Sunday offers a special brunch with
eggs, pancakes, crepes, seafood pasta and other specials. Pleasant atmosphere and
lovely lobby with fireplace. Reservations suggested; credit cards.

HIGHLANDS BAR & GRILL ★ *Continental/International - Expensive*
Located in the Waikoloa Highlands Shopping Center in Waikoloa Village above
the resort area (883-8770). This attractive room is arranged semi-circle fashion
with an open kitchen grill and dining area on one side and a bar/lounge and dance
floor on the other. The bar features TV sports and live music for dancers. The
menu features interesting selections such as New Zealand venison, fresh island
fish, steaks, roast duck and much more. During the day, there are nice golf course
views. Open for lunch Wednesday-Saturday only, 11:30AM - 2:30PM, dinner
nightly 6 - 9:30PM, closed Tuesday.

IMARI ★ *Japanese - Expensive*
Hyatt Regency Waikoloa Hotel, Kohala Coast (885-1234). A visit to this distinctive Japanese restaurant allows you to step into the quiet serenity of old Japan.
Reflecting ponds with koi carp swimming along, splashing waterfalls, and an
accent of gentle Japanese music put you into a relaxing mood. The menu is
traditional Japanese with sushi (rice rolls) and sashimi (raw fish) served as
appetizers followed by varied specials of tempura, roast duck, fish shabushabu,
teriyaki, and more in addition to interesting Japanese pickled vegetables. For those
wanting a little more flair, try the teppanyaki tables where gourmet chefs prepare
your meal on cooking tables right in front of you. They do wonders with chicken,
steak, shrimp, and all manner of traditional Japanese cuisine. Open daily for
dinner only 5 - 10PM. Reservations suggested, casual dress. Credit cards.

KNICKERS ★ *Continental/International - Expensive*
Located at the Mauna Lani Golf Course clubhouse, Mauna Lani Resort (885-
6699). This elegant room has plush upholstered chairs and booths with golf course
fairway views. Art work and pictures of early golfers in "knickers" line the walls
with bookshelves adding to an "old clubhouse" atmosphere. Menu features lamb,
steaks, chicken and fresh island fish and seafood specials. Soups, salads, appetizers and an attractive dessert cart round out the offerings. Meals are expertly
prepared and attractively presented and portions are more than ample. Daily for
lunch 11AM - 3PM, dinner 5:30 - 9:30PM. Reservations recommended for dinner.
Credit cards.

LE SOLEIL ★ *French - Expensive*
Mauna Lani Bay Hotel, Kohala Coast (885-6622). This elegant fine dining restaurant is the hotel's signature gourmet room. It features American and International cuisine including several dishes from the Pacific area. In addition, it has an extensive wine inventory with an unusual depth in California varietals as well as rare vintages from Europe. Dinner is an exquisite experience in this room. Some menu highlights are sauteed New Zealand scallops, escargots, smoked lilikoi (passion fruit) chicken for appetizers. Entree selections include blackened ahi (tuna), rack of lamb, Hawaiian snapper, roast duckling and more. The service, attention and cuisine are superb. Reservations are required as are dinner jackets for gentlemen. Open for dinner only, 6 - 9:30PM. Credit cards.

MERRIMAN'S ★ *Continental/International - Expensive*
Opelo Plaza, Route 19, Kamuela, 885-6822. Since its opening three years ago, this restaurant has won wide acclaim for fine dining specializing in fresh Big Island products expertly prepared. Chef Peter Merriman has esablished a reputation for excellence. The menu features Parker Ranch prime rib (house special), fresh island fish, cioppino, steaks, veal, Kahua Ranch lamb, chicken and daily specials. An interesting selection of appetizers, soups, salads and fancy desserts rounds out a fine menu. Open for lunch Mon.- Fri., 11:30AM - 1:30PM; dinner nightly 5:30 - 9PM; Sunday brunch 10:30AM - 1:30PM. Reservations suggested; credit cards.

THE CAFE *Continental - Expensive*
Located at the Ritz-Carlton Mauna Lani Hotel (885-2000) at Mauna Lani Resort on the Kohala Coast. This is a casual open-air terrace dining room offering indoor or outdoor seating. The menu features Pacific Rim specialities and American favorites including special fitness cuisine and childrens' selections. Open from early morning until late.

THE DINING ROOM ★ *French/Continental - Expensive*
Located at the Ritz-Carlton Mauna Lani Hotel (885-2000) at Mauna Lani Resort on the Kohala Coast. This is the hotel's signature fine dining room and has lovely classical Continental decor. Menu selections are contemporary offerings with inspirations from Provence. Selections include fresh island fish, Maine lobster, lamb loin, veal, beef tenderloin, duck and chicken. Service and presentation are superb and food generally excellent. There is an extensive fine wine list. A private function room seats up to 14 for the ultimate in elegant private dinner parties. Open nightly for dinner, 6 - 10PM. Jackets for gentlemen and reservations required; credit cards.

THE GALLERY ★ *Continental/International - Expensive*
Located at Racquet Club tennis court complex, Mauna Lani Resort (885-7777). This Travel/Holiday Fine Dining Award restaurant features a varied American-Hawaiian Regional menu with a few Asian-Pacific specials in elegant contemporary classic decor. The menu features appetizers such as fresh fish poke, sesame chicken, cajun pasta, Thai beef and sashimi. Soups include a daily special and Portuguese Bean while a classic tomato-onion vinaigrette and mixed greens salads are offered. Entrees reflect the Pacific region, including Hawaiian shrimp, filet steak Kiana, lilikoi (passionfruit) scallops, Kung Pao chicken, lamb chops, wok charred ahi (tuna), steak and lobster, and lobster Americana. Fresh catch of the day is usually two or three offerings prepared in a variety of wonderful ways. The

food is superb and service attentive. Open daily for dinner only 6 - 9PM. Reservations recommended; credit cards.

THE GARDEN ★ *Hawaiian/Polynesian - Expensive*
Mauna Kea Beach Hotel, Kohala (882-7222). This dining room is unique in that it celebrates the regional culinary specialties of the Big Island. Menu selections include fresh island fish, seafood, beef, lamb and other local favorites done with a gourmet flair. Open daily for dinner only, 6:30 - 9:00PM. Dinner jackets for gentlemen are required. Credit cards.

THE GRILL ★ *Continental/Hawaiian Regional - Expensive*
Located at the Ritz-Carlton Mauna Lani Hotel (885-2000) at Mauna Lani Resort on the Kohala Coast. This room has the atmosphere of a plush manor house club room and offers varied Continental/Hawaiian regional cuisine. Menu selections include fresh pastas and appetizers, fresh island fish, steak, lamb, veal, Maine lobster, Hawaiian Fisherman's Stew and more. Service, presentation and quality are superb. Live dinner music featured. Open nightly for dinner 6 - 9PM. Reservations suggested. Credit cards.

THE PAVILION ★ *Continental/International - Expensive*
Mauna Kea Beach Hotel, Kohala (882-7222). This award-winning hotel dining room offers a splendid varied menu each evening featuring an international array of gourmet food. Menu selections range from steaks, fresh Kohala fish, seafood specialties, venison, and lamb, to other creative dishes. A complete wine selection compliments the gourmet fare. Pleasant live dinner music with dancing lends a sophisticated yet relaxed manner to an evening's entertainment. Open daily for breakfast, 6:30 - 11AM, dinner 6:30 - 9:00PM. Dinner jackets for gentlemen required. Credit cards.

THE TEPPAN YAKI ★ *Japanese - Expensive*
Mauna Kea Beach Hotel, Kohala Coast (882-7222). The Terrace takes on a new personality in the evening when it changes to feature the best of grilled-at-your-table teppan yaki Japanese cuisine. Grilled steak, fresh island fish, shrimp, chicken, vegetables and more are freshly prepared with the creative flair of Mauna Kea's skilled chefs. Open daily except Tuesday for dinner only, 6:30 - 8:30PM. Tasteful casual attire required. Credit cards.

THE TERRACE ★ *Continental/International - Expensive*
Mauna Kea Beach Hotel, Kohala Coast (882-7222). This is the home of the Mauna Kea's popular daily buffet luncheon, widely acclaimed as the finest throughout Hawai'i. It has a variety of salads, soups, fruits, hot and cold entrees, and a wide selection of incredible desserts. A la carte lunch sandwiches and other specialties are also available. It also has a very pleasant daily buffet breakfast. Open daily for breakfast 7 - 10AM, lunch 12 - 2:30PM. In the evening, the restaurant changes over to The Teppan Yaki for dinner. Credit cards.

TIARE ROOM ★ *French - Expensive*
Royal Waikoloan Hotel, Waikoloa (885-6789). The attraction of this gourmet room is the traditional French cuisine. The setting and room decor are very lavish and lovely. The menu features a full offering of appetizers including beefsteak tartar, shrimp & scallops, calamari, escargot, smoked salmon and charred ahi tuna.

Soups include peas and shrimp chowder, red snapper consomme and a daily special. Salads include a salad Tiare, sliced tomatoes, spinach and a Plantation salad. Entrees are diverse and include chicken breast boursin, opakapaka (snapper) Chinese style, stuffed shrimp Macadamia, fresh island fish, lamb, beef, fillet royale, veal, roast duck, and a special Plantation Platter which includes lobster, filet mignon, fresh fish and shrimp. The wine list is quite extensive. Jackets required for gentlemen. Open daily for dinner only, 6:30 - 10PM. Reservations suggested. Credit cards.

HILO

INTRODUCTION

Dining out in Hilo has always been something of an adventure. For a long time, dining out meant choosing from a limited number of neighborhood ethnic restaurants such as a chop suey house, saimin noodle shop or two, a coffee shop, a plate lunch shop or a simple drive-in. Luckily, for both Hilo residents and visitors alike, the dining out options have diversified and improved over the last few years. The Hilo area now offers a wide selection of ethnic cuisines in a variety of local-style and trendy contemporary-style cafes and restaurants for every budget. There is something of a renaissance going on in downtown Hilo what with old buildings being renovated and restored and many of the new businesses relocating in the once decrepit spaces are, fortunately, restaurants. Its all part of the new image being created in downtown Hilo. While there is much variety in quality, price and service, the genuinely good restaurants are marked with a ★ indicating good value, good food and good service.

While Hilo may not yet be quite ready to proclaim itself the gourmet cuisine capital of the Pacific, it has made some strides in providing residents and visitors some enjoyable dining experiences.

INEXPENSIVE

BEAR'S COFFEE   *Sandwiches - Inexpensive*
106 Keawe St., old downtown Hilo (935-0708). This small deli shop and espresso cafe features a variety of salads, sandwiches, individual pizza, and other light lunch specials. A full range of international coffees, espresso and pastries are also mainstays. Sidewalk tables are nice, however, a real negative is the restroom which is accessible only by walking through the middle of the kitchen where food is prepared. A recent visit revealed that patrons and others will stop in mid-kitchen and "chat" with cooks preparing food while leaning against counters and over food-preparation areas. Because of this, the place has lost its star ranking. In spite of these undesirable characteristics, it remains a popular place with locals. You be the judge. Open Mon-Fri 7AM - 5PM, Sat 8AM - 5PM. Closed Sunday.

BOOMER'S FOUNTAIN   *Family Dining - Inexpensive*
Prince Kuhio Plaza Shopping Center, 111 E. Puainako (959-3339). This is an old-fashioned soda fountain with a 1950's theme decor. They have all the favorite soda fountain treats along with daily luncheon specials, sandwiches and local favorites. Open Sat. through Wed. 10AM - 5PM, Thurs.-Fri. till 9PM.

CHENG'S CHOP SUEY HOUSE ★ *Chinese - Inexpensive*
777 Kilauea Ave. in the Kaiko'o Mall (935-3404). An extensive Cantonese menu with a full selection of soups, chop suey, noodles, seafood, pork, beef, chicken, duck, and egg dishes. Specialties include egg flower soup, cake noodles, abalone, lup chong sausage, chicken with ginger, pineapple duck, and combination plates. The won ton min (noodle soup) is excellent. There are only 10 tables and it can get busy at peak lunch and dinner hours. Decor is simple with generally clean surroundings. They provide good food at very reasonable cost. Open daily 10AM - 12PM, Fri. 10AM - 2AM, Sun. 10AM - 3PM.

COUNTRY KITCHEN ★ *Family Dining - Inexpensive*
Prince Kuhio Plaza Shopping Center, Hilo (959-4422). This national chain family dining outlet features a standard menu of sandwiches, hot plate specials, full dinners, soups, salads and desserts. Clean, bright and generally good food and service. Open daily for breakfast, lunch and dinner, 7AM - 10PM.

DICK'S COFFEE HOUSE ★ *Family Dining - Inexpensive*
Corner of Kekuanaoa and Kilauea Avenues (935-2769), in the Hilo Shopping Center. Breakfast, lunch, and dinner. A family restaurant featuring beef, chicken, and fish in a variety of complete coffee shop meals. Soup and sandwich items, light meals also. Popular with local folks. Open Mon-Sat 7AM -10:30PM, Sunday for breakfast only 7 - 10:30AM.

DON'S GRILL ★ *Family Dining - Inexpensive*
485 Hinano Street, Hilo (935-9099). Since its opening about four years ago, this pleasant family restaurant has proven to be one of Hilo's consistently best inexpensive dining out options. The menu features beef, chicken, pork chops, fish, sandwiches, burgers, soups and salads, daily specials and many local favorites. The house specialty is an excellent rotisseried chicken. The clean facilities, fast courteous service, generally reat food and very reasonable prices have earned this restaurant a spot in this book's **BEST OF THE BIG ISLAND** ratings for family dining. And should you have to wait in line awhile, its well worth it. Open daily for lunch and dinner Tues-Thurs 10:30AM - 9PM, Fri-Sun 10AM - 10PM, closed Mon. Credit cards.

DOTTY'S COFFEE SHOP ★ *Filipino - Inexpensive*
2100 Kanoelehua Avenue, in the Puainako Town Center (959-6477). The daily dinner menu offers several specials including one or two Filipino dishes. Home-made cornbread, banana muffins and fruit cream pies are delicious! Generally good food at reasonable prices. The dining room expanded into an empty space and there is now more room for smoking/non-smoking areas. Open Mon-Sat for breakfast-lunch 7AM - 2PM, dinner 5 - 8PM, Sun 7AM - 1:30PM and 5 - 9PM. Credit cards.

FRANCESCA'S DELI *Oriental/Local - Inexpensive*
Located in the Prince Kuhio Shopping Plaza (959-9977). This lunch and snack shop has a selection of Chinese noodles and varied beef, pork, chicken and seafood dishes. Open daily 11AM - 5PM, Thursday and Friday shopping nights till 9PM.

FREDDY'S MANONO MINI MART   *Sandwiches - Inexpensive*
Corner of Manono and Piilani Streets, opposite the Civic Auditorium in Hilo, (935-0611). Freddy's occupies a rather large two-story metal building at the rear of the large corner lot. They have lots of parking for a small general store-deli which offers a variety of fresh made (huge!) corned beef, pastrami, turkey, etc. sandwiches and local style fast food items. Open daily 8AM - 10:30PM.

GREEN DOOR   *Sandwiches - Inexpensive*
777 Kilauea Avenue, in the Kaiko'o Mall (928-6288). Lunch and cocktails only. This is a small, dark and dank tavern with a luncheon sandwich menu. Nothing fancy in either decor or menu. The main features are pastrami, turkey, corned beef, French dip beef, etc. with choice of salad. Open daily 6AM - 8:30PM.

HILO COFFEE CO.   *Sandwiches/snacks - Inexpensive*
99 Keawe Street (935-3333) is at the corner of Keawe and Waianuenue in downtown across from the Keawe Collection of Shops. This is a coffee shop operation with some outside/sidewalk tables. They bake their own bagels, croissants, pastries and bread and make other snack goodies. The shop features Kona estate-grown coffees. Open daily except Sunday, 9AM - 5PM.

HIRO'S PLACE   *Japanese - Inexpensive*
50 E. Puainako (959-6665) in the KTA Supermarket Center. This is a local fast-food operation serving up Oriental-American specialties including teriyaki beef, chicken, fish, plate lunches, sandwiches, sushi rice, noodles, bentos and more. Tables on walkway; eat here or take out. Daily for breakfast, lunch 6AM - 5PM.

HUKILAU RESTAURANT ★   *Seafood - Inexpensive*
136 Banyan Way, in the Hilo Seaside Hotel off Banyan Drive (935-4222). This local style family restaurant specializes in a complete line of seafood entrees for lunch and dinner. They usually have three or four fresh island fish entrees, along with crab, lobster, scallops, abalone and more. It's also about the only restaurant on the island which offers frog legs on its menu. They also have traditionals like prime rib, steak, fried chicken, roast pork and more. The place is especially popular at lunchtime with local folks. A renovation in mid-1990 gave the dining room a needed brightening up with new floor and wall tiles, booths and tables; good food, friendly service and reasonable cost. Open daily for breakfast, lunch, and dinner 7AM - 9PM, weekends till 10PM.

JASPER'S ESPRESSO CAFE   *Sandwiches/Snacks - Inexpensive*
110 Kalakaua St. (969-6686). This is a new addition to downtown Hilo's growing list of eateries. Opened in spring, 1992, this nicely renovated old shop is located across from the East Hawai'i Cultural Center and next to Kalakaua Park. They feature an espresso coffee bar and a simple menu of breakfast items, sandwiches, light fare and more. Open Tues-Wed 6:30AM - 8PM, Thurs-Fri-Sat 6:30AM - 10PM, Sun 9AM - 2PM, closed Mon.

JIMMY'S DRIVE INN ★   *Hawaiian/Polynesian - Inexpensive*
362 Kinoole St. (935-5571). Despite its name, this popular restaurant features sit-down dining service and does not have traditional drive-in service. Specializing in Hawaiian cuisine but also offering Japanese, Korean, and American dishes as well. Open breakfast, lunch, dinner Mon-Sat 8 AM - 9:30 PM.

JOHN-MICHAEL'S *Family Dining - Inexpensive*
400 Hualani St., Waiakea Villas Hotel (961-6624). The menu features local style Japanese-Korean-American specials such as tonkatsu, beef or chicken curry, oxtail and pig's feet soup, roast pork, Korean chicken, nishime and more. The quiet setting along fishponds is pleasant. Open daily for breakfast, 7 - 10:30AM, lunch 10:30AM - 1:30PM and dinner Fri-Sat-Sun only, 5 - 9PM.

KARROTS *Family Dining - Inexpensive*
197 Keawe St, Spencer Health & Fitness Center, downtown Hilo (935-6191). This is a strictly health-food store and cafe operation with a menu featuring items like tofu burgers and dishes, egg dishes, pizza and Italian pasta, Mexican fare like quesadilla, burritos and tacos, vegetarian fare, etc. They also promote vitamins, herbal supplements, health products for body enhancement as well as other health food related products. The decor is clean, bright and attractive. Open for breakfast, lunch and snacks Mon-Fri. 6:30AM-7:30PM, Sat. from 6:30AM-3:30PM.

KAWILI CAFE *Family Dining - Inexpensive*
399 E. Kawili St. (935-6565). This is a local family-style restaurant featuring Korean and local dishes. The menu has a wide selection of local style lunches and dinners plus Korean specials like hot spicy beef sop, hot fried squid and more. Special children's menu available. Take out orders also. Breakfast, lunch, and dinner, open daily from 6:45AM till late.

KEAWE DINER *Japanese - Inexpensive*
332 Keawe St., Hilo (935-8855). This is a very small cafe in old downtown Hilo that serves up inexpensive local-style food. Specials include Japanese-American dishes such as teriyaki, chicken tonkatsu, and saimin in addition to plate lunch specials. No fancy decor here; just inexpensive local cuisine for the no-frills diner. Eat here or take out. Open daily for lunch only 10AM - 1PM.

KAY'S LUNCH CENTER ★ *Korean - Inexpensive*
684 Kilauea Avenue, across from Kaiko'o Mall (968-1776). This sit-down dining spot also provides plate/box lunches to take out. This is a real local-style restaurant featuring Korean cuisine including BBQ beef, short ribs, and the original crispy Korean chicken. Homemade cream cheese pies for dessert are wonderful. The decor and ambiance here are simple, nothing fancy, nothing glitzy. The focus is generous servings of well-prepared food and equally reasonable prices which have earned this restaurant a spot in this book's **BEST OF THE BIG ISLAND** ratings. Open for breakfast, lunch, and dinner Tues-Sun 5 AM - 2PM and 5 PM - 9 PM. Closed Mon.

KEN'S HOUSE OF PANCAKES ★ *American - Inexpensive*
1730 Kamehameha Avenue (935-8711) at the intersection of Kam Avenue and Banyan Drives near Hilo's hotel row. The menu features all types of pancakes and breakfast items in addition to a full range of American foods, sandwiches, and some local-style dishes. Popular with visitors as well as locals because it is open 24 hours a day, every day of the year, the only 24-hour restaurant in Hilo.

KIMO'S ONO HAWAIIAN FOOD ★ *Hawaiian/Polynesian - Inexpensive*
806 Kilauea Avenue, across from Kaiko'o Mall (935-3111). This tiny shop features, just as their name says, "ono" (Hawaiian for delicious!) authentic

Hawaiian food. The menu features fresh made daily specials and a regular menu of plate lunches with laulau, kalua pig, lomi salmon, chicken luau, haupia (coconut) pudding and more. You could spend the usual $45-50 or so per person for a fancy hotel luau and not get anywhere near the quality of this Hawaiian food. It's without a doubt the best Hawaiian food anywhere on the island of Hawai'i. The shop is so small inside there are no tables only a couple of counters with stools. They will provide everything for your own take out luau. Excellent! Open Mon.-Sat. for lunch 10-2PM, dinner 5-8PM, Sund. lunch only 11-3PM.

KK TEI RESTAURANT *Japanese - Inexpensive*
1150 Kamehameha Avenue (961-3791) across from Naniloa Golf Course. This is a Japanese-American theme restaurant with private dining rooms for Japanese style dining, low tables and cushions on the floor rather than chairs. General dining room also. The menu features steaks, shrimp tempura, ahi (tuna), and oxtail soup plus many Japanese specialties. The restaurant has a Karaoke sing-along bar now. Reservations recommended. Open Mon-Sat for lunch 11AM - 2PM and dinner 5 - 9PM. Credit cards.

KOREANA RESTAURANT *Korean - Inexpensive*
200 Kanoelehua Avenue (961-4983) in the Waiakea Square Shopping Center. This small restaurant offers a full menu of Korean cuisine including kal-bi ribs, Korean spicy chicken, BBQ beef, and more. Korean food tends toward the hot spicy side and those with that preference will enjoy trying these dishes. Open daily for lunch 10:30AM - 2:30PM, dinner 5 - 10PM. Credit cards.

KOW'S DELI & CHINESE RESTAURANT ★ *Chinese - Inexpensive*
87 W. Kawailani St. (959-3766) open Mon.-Sat. 10AM - 10PM, Sunday 10AM - 9PM, credit cards. Also in the Kaiko'o Mall (969-4944). Featuring Cantonese style food, Kow's serves up a wide range of delectable items such as beef broccoli, chicken and Chinese peas, sweet and sour shrimp, won ton, cake noodles, and more. Everything is good. Order from the menu board or select from the buffet counter.

LANKY'S PASTRIES & DELI ★ *Family Dining - Inexpensive*
At Kekuanaoa and Kilauea Avenues (969-9133) in the Hilo Shopping Center. This small bakery-cafe serves up local style oriental-American meals, daily specials, sandwiches, and snacks. Also featured are their fresh pastries and doughnuts in the morning. Open daily 6AM - 4PM.

LEUNG'S CHOP SUEY HOUSE ★ *Chinese - Inexpensive*
530 E. Lanikaula St. (935-4066) at the intersection of Kanoelehua Avenue. This small eat-in/take out Chinese kitchen is popular with folks working in the nearby industrial area of Hilo. A range of Cantonese a la carte dishes and a buffet counter to select your own plate lunch-dinner are available. Cake noodles are a must! Good quality food at good prices in a not too fancy place. Open daily except Tuesday, 9AM - 8:30PM.

LOW INTERNATIONAL FOOD *Continental/International - Inexpensive*
Corner of Kilauea and Ponohawai St.'s (969-6652). This place is operated by the Low family which runs Sun Sun Lau Chop Sui House, one of Hilo's better known Chinese restaurants. This is basically a fast-food counter operation with a varied

menu of Chinese, Korean, and local-style favorite plate lunches, sandwiches, and specials. Chicken tonkatsu, teriyaki beef, and burgers are popular items here. You can eat here - several tables are available on the lanai area - or take out. They also bake a line of unusual breads such as sweet potato, taro, guava and more. Open daily except Wednesday, 9AM - 8PM.

MIYO'S ★ *Japanese - Inexpensive*
400 Hualani Street (935-2273) in the Waiakea Villas Hotel shops. This inexpensive family-style restaurant features excellent Japanese cuisine. Sample selections include sesame chicken, tonkatsu, tempura, teriyaki beef, fish, noodles, and donburi soups. The upstairs location (makes for nice views) overlooks lovely Waiakea Fish Pond and Wailoa Park. Open daily except Sunday, lunch 11AM - 2PM, dinner 5:30 - 8:30PM. No credit cards.

MUN CHEONG LAU *Chinese - Inexpensive*
172 Kilauea Street (935-3040) in old downtown Hilo. This Chinese eatery provides good basic Cantonese-style food in something less than sparkling surroundings. But if less than elegant decor is no problem, you'll find good reasonably priced food here. The menu offers a variety of beef, chicken, duck, pork, and seafood dishes or one can order combination plates. Open daily 11AM - 2:30AM, but Friday and Saturday they stay open till 4:30AM.

NANI MAU GARDEN RESTAURANT ★ *American - Inexpensive*
421 Makalika Street (959-9591) just south of town off Volcano Highway #11. This dining room is part of the Nani Mau Gardens operation and is located upstairs of the gift shop in the main complex. Lunch is served buffet style and includes four or five entrees highlighted with Hawaiian regional specialties such as teriyaki, oriental chicken and fish. Open daily for lunch only, 10:30AM - 3PM.

NEW CHINA RESTAURANT ★ *Chinese - Inexpensive*
510 Kilauea Avenue (961-5677) next to Hawai'i Hardware Company. The menu features Cantonese and Hong Kong-style cuisine with a wide selection of beef, pork, chicken, duck, seafood, and noodle dishes. They feature some interesting special platters like oyster with ginger and onion, pork chop Hong Kong style, stuffed clams, fresh scallop and chicken along with unusuals like abalone soup,

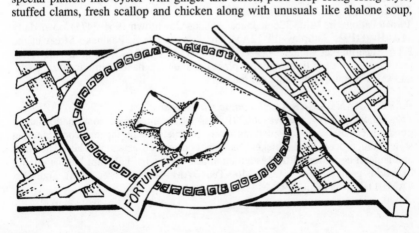

lemon chicken, squid with green pepper and black beans, and lots more to tempt your exotic palate. Try the pot stickers (small appetizer-like fried cakes stuffed with meat filling). You'll find good food at reasonable prices here. This is a very clean, bright restaurant with simple pleasant decor. Open daily 10AM - 10PM.

NORI'S SAIMIN ★   *Japanese - Inexpensive*
688 Kinoole St. (935-9133) across from the Hilo Lanes bowling alley. This Japanese-American noodle shop promotes itself as having "the best saimin in town." Granted they do have great saimin noodle dishes and other oriental specialties, but *the* best?, you'll have to decide for yourself. They also have Bento box lunches as well as rare chocolate mochi, a rice cake dessert. The varied hours are a little confusing however: Sun 5 - 12PM, Mon-Thu 10:30AM - 2PM and 4 - 12PM, Fri 10:30AM - 2PM and 4PM - 1AM, Sat 5PM - 1AM.

PARKSIDE RESTAURANT   *Japanese/American - Inexpensive*
413 Kilauea Avenue (969-1454). This local style eatery serves up Hilo's own dry saimin along with a wide selection of American, Japanese and local specials. There is sit down dining or take-outs available. Hours are varied: Monday 7:30AM - 3PM, Tuesday-Thursday 7:30AM - 6PM, Friday-Saturday 7:30AM - 8:30PM, closed Sunday.

PARAMOUNT GRILL   *Sandwiches - Inexpensive*
37 Haili St. (935-8017) in old downtown Hilo. This small cafe has a few booths and a soda-fountain counter reminiscent of the 1950's. A limited lunch-dinner menu of Oriental-American local dishes, sandwiches, and snacks, but generally good food at reasonable prices. Open daily 5AM-2PM, Sunday 5-10:30AM only.

PICKLE BARREL   *Sandwiches - Inexpensive*
Located in the Hilo Shopping Center, corner of Kekuanaoa and Kilauea Avenues, Hilo (935-1077). This small island-style eatery features sandwiches and lots of local specials like saimin, Japanese bento (box) lunches, chili and rice and more. They also have a nice selection of that famous local favorite, "cracked seed." Open Mon-Thurs. 9AM-5PM, Fri. 9AM-7PM, Sat. 9AM-4PM. Closed Sunday.

PIZZA HUT   *Italian - Inexpensive*
Two locations in Hilo. 326 Kilauea Avenue downtown (961-3471) open daily 11AM - 11PM, Saturday till 12AM, credit cards. 50 E. Puainako Street in the KTA Supermarket Center (959-9119) open 11AM - 12AM, Saturday till 1AM, credit cards. Both of these national pizza chain outlets have a similar pizza, pasta, and salad menu as the mainland outlets.

RESTAURANT OSAKA   *Japanese - Inexpensive*
762 Kanoelehua Avenue (961-6699). This restaurant-lounge combination has a good variety of Japanese-American food. Complete meals Japanese or American style include beef, pork, chicken, and seafood as well as sandwiches. The floor and general condition of the restaurant appear somewhat unkempt but the quality of food is generally good. Open Mon-Tues 7AM - 9PM, (closed Wed), Thurs-Fri 7AM -11PM, Sat-Sun 6:30AM - 11PM. Credit cards.

RESTAURANT SATSUKI ★ *Japanese - Inexpensive*
168 Keawe St. (935-7880) in old downtown Hilo. This small restaurant features Japanese style lunches and dinners. Menu items include tempura, yakitori, beef teriyaki, butterfish, tonkatsu, donburi, sukiyaki, noodles, tofu dishes, a unique local style salad bar, and more. This is a generally neat, clean, and well-kept restaurant with simple decor. Open daily for lunch 10:30 - 2PM, dinner 4:30 - 9PM. Credit cards.

REUBEN'S MEXICAN FOOD *Mexican - Inexpensive*
336 Kamehameha Avenue (961-2552) on the bayfront in old downtown Hilo. Featuring crab enchiladas, chicken flautas, La Canasta, chile rellenos. Mexican food lovers will appreciate this fare which is good in quality, variety, and quantity. Margaritas too. Open Mon-Sat 11AM - 9PM. Take outs available.

ROYAL SIAM ★ *Thai Cuisine - Inexpensive*
68 Mamo St., old downtown Hilo (961-6100). Formerly Tomi Zushi Japanese restaurant this eatery now serves up some wonderful spicy hot Thai food. Small and unprententious but clean, the restaurant has a dozen tables or so. The menu features over 50 items including chicken, seafood, beef, pork and veggie dishes. There are also wonderful Thai curries, appetizers and daily specials. Food can be ordered either mild, medium or spicy hot. Take-outs available. Open Monday through Saturday for lunch 11AM - 2:30PM, dinner 5 - 9PM; closed Sunday.

SACHI'S GOURMET ★ *Japanese - Inexpensive*
250 Keawe St. (935-6255) in old downtown Hilo. This small Japanese-style eatery, recently re-decorated and re-furbished, continues to provide good quality Tokyo-style Japanese food. Take outs and bentos available. Good selection and variety of beef, pork, chicken, and fish dishes on the menu. Open for breakfast, lunch, and dinner daily except Sunday, 8AM -2PM, evenings 5 - 9 PM.

SEASIDE *Seafood - Inexpensive*
1790 Kalanianaole St. (935-8825) Keaukaha area of Hilo. This small local family run restaurant is located in the middle of Keaukaha's fish ponds area where seafood for the table can't get any fresher. Local mullet, trout, and other fresh fish selections make up the menu. Reservations accepted for groups of four or more only. Open daily except Monday 11AM - 2PM, 5 - 8PM. Credit cards.

SNAPPY'S PIZZA *Italian - Inexpensive*
421 Kalanikoa St. (961-5864). In addition to the pizza, the menu features chicken, ribs, submarine sandwiches, and other special items. There is also an all you can eat buffet. They deliver pizzas within Hilo town limits. Open daily 11AM - 10:30PM, Friday till 11PM.

SOPHIE'S PLACE *Filipino - Inexpensive*
207 Kilauea Avenue (935-7300) in old downtown Hilo. This is one of the Big Island's few Filipino restaurants. Features Filipino dishes like pork adobo, chicken papaya, and dinadaraan as well as some American selections. It's located in a row of ramshackle old shops and is a place for adventurous diners. Take out orders also. Open daily except Sunday 7:30AM - 3PM.

SUM LEUNG CHINESE KITCHEN   *Chinese - Inexpensive*
50 E. Puainako St. (959-6025) in the KTA Supermarket Center. Offers a full range of Chinese plate lunches, noodles, and varied Chinese specialties. Take outs available. Open daily except Sun. 8:30AM - 6:45PM, Fri. till 7:45PM.

SUN SUN LAU CHOP SUI HOUSE ★   *Chinese - Inexpensive*
1055 Kinoole St. (935-2808). This large and attractive dining room is one of Hilo's oldest Chinese restaurants. They have an extensive menu of Cantonese dishes in beef, pork, chicken, duck, and seafood. Cocktail lounge and banquet room available. Good food in a bright clean dining room cooled by ceiling fans. Open daily except Wed 10:30AM - 8PM, weekends till 9PM. Credit cards.

T's SAIMIN SHOP ★   *Japanese - Inexpensive*
88 Kanoelehua Avenue (961-2611) in the Waiakea Kai Shopping Plaza. This Japanese-American restaurant's advertising slogan is "Hilo's finest noodles." They do have good saimin and other noodle dishes including teriyaki, chicken, sandwiches, and other favorite local snacks, but *the* finest?, you'll have to decide. They feature homemade pies and bentos and take outs as well. Open Mon-Fri 5AM - 11PM, Sat 8AM - 12AM, Sun 9AM - 10PM.

TING HAO MANDARIN RESTAURANT ★   *Chinese - Inexpensive*
Kanoelehua Ave. (959-6288) in the Puainako Town Center. This Chinese restaurant offers the only Mandarin cuisine in town. It features exotic spicy meals from Szechwan and Hunan, delicious non-spicy gourmet dishes from Taiwan, Beijing, and other parts of China, as well as healthy vegetarian delights. Cocktails too. Excellent food at reasonable prices. A real dining adventure. Open daily for lunch 10:30AM - 2:30PM, dinner 4 - 9PM, Sunday 4:30 - 9PM only.

THE FIREHOUSE RESTAURANT   *Family Dining - Inexpensive*
Kilauea Avenue, in the Kaiko'o Mall (935-1016). This is a very small place with dining booths jammed into a long narrow space. If you don't mind cramped quarters and aren't subject to claustrophobia, you can enjoy a meal from their selection of Filipino and Oriental local favorites, American dishes, sandwiches, etc. They serve an unusual fried rice omelette at breakfast. Open Mon.-Sat. for breakfast and lunch, 6AM - 2PM, Sunday for breakfast only 6-11AM.

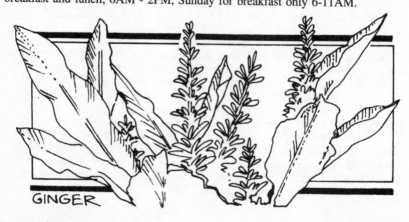

GINGER

WOOLWORTH'S RESTAURANT ★   *Family Dining - Inexpensive*
Kanoelehua Ave. (959-3591) in the Prince Kuhio Plaza. This bright colorful
coffee shop is popular with the shopping center crowds. The menu provides
typical American coffee shop meals as well as a few local style dishes. Very
popular with local folks who spend time strolling the center after dinner. Open
Mon-Wed-Sat 7:30-5PM, Tues-Thurs-Fri 7:30-8:30PM, closed Sun. Credit cards.

MODERATE

CHAPMAN'S LAND & CATTLE CO.   *Steaks - Moderate*
760 Pi'ilani St. (935-7552) across from the Hilo Civic Stadium complex. This
newest of Hilo's dining spots features an upscale paniolo (cowboy) theme with
the recreation of old ranch house dining. The menu accents are Pacific Rim
cuisine with local favorites including crab and kal-bi rib combo, teriyaki chicken,
steak and lobster, fresh island fish and sandwiches. Homemake soups are specials
like clam chowder and bean soup, along with salads. Open daily for lunch 11AM
- 2:30PM, dinner 5:30 - 10PM, Friday and Saturday till 10:30PM.

d'ANGORAS   *Italian - Moderate*
101 Aupuni St. (935-8501) in the Hilo Lagoon Center building across from
Kaiko'o Mall. The menu is Continental-American with an Italian accent. Traditional entrees include steak, island fish, chicken and seafood. Special sandwiches
highlight lunch. Soups, salads and appetizers round out the offerings. Lunch
served Mon-Fri 11AM - 2:30PM and dinner served daily from 5:30PM. Credit
cards.

FIASCO'S ★   *Family Dining - Moderate*
200 Kanoelehua Avenue (935-7666) in the Waiakea Kai Shopping Plaza. This
popular eatery offers American and some local-style selections of beef, chicken,
and seafood. Also Mexican, pasta, and sandwich plate selections from a varied
menu. Salad bar and cocktail lounge. Individual booths decorated with old
photographs and posters of early Hawai'i. Good food served in a festive atmosphere. Daily for breakfast 6:30 - 9AM, lunch and dinner, 11:30AM -10PM, Sat.
till 11PM. Credit cards.

HENRI'S ON KAPIOLANI   *Steaks - Moderate*
139 Kapiolani St. (961-9272) in residential building of Urawatandai Hawaii
College, a Japanese-English language training school. This small restaurant
features prime rib on its dinner menu as well as other beef selections. Lunch is
mainly sandwiches but with a varied selection including pastrami, turkey, corned
beef, French dip, etc. The decor and atmosphere are simple. Daily except Mon,
lunch 11AM - 2PM, dinner 6 - 9PM. Credit cards.

JP'S RESTAURANT & LOUNGE   *Continental-American - Moderate*
111 Banyan Drive, along Hilo's Hotel row (961-5802). Features charbroiled
slections including beef, chicken and fresh island fish. Extensive salad bar and
cocktail lounge. Open nightly for dinner only, 5:30 - 10PM, Sunday 5:30 - 9PM.
Credit cards.

LEHUA'S BAY CITY BAR & GRILL ★ *Continental/International - Mod.*
11 Waianuenue Avenue at Kamehameha (935-8055) is one of old downtown Hilo's trendy dining spots. The menu features varied sandwiches, salads and light entrees for lunch while dinner features fresh island fish, seafood, steaks and specials. Try the fruit juice iced tea-delightful! There is an "old Hilo" atmosphere created with old shop signs, ornaments, etc. Good food and generally good service. Open daily except Sunday, lunch 11AM - 5PM, dinner 5 - 9:30PM.

NIHON RESTAURANT ★ *Japanese - Moderate*
123 Lihiwai St., just opposite the Liliuokalani Gardens and Banyan Drive hotels, on Hilo Bayfront. The building is Japanese style with private dining rooms, lots of Japanese art and decor, and Japanese music as a background. Waitresses are dressed in kimonos. The menu offers a full range of Japanese cuisine including beef, pork, chicken, and seafood, plus noodle dishes and a sushi bar serving a wide variety of excellent sushi. Good Japanese food in authentic surroundings. Open daily except Sunday, lunch 11AM - 2PM, dinner 5 - 8:30PM. Credit cards.

PESCATORE ★ *Italian - Moderate*
Corner of Keawe and Haili Streets in old downtown Hilo (969-9090). This is one of the newer additions to the Hilo dining scene, and what a delight! The restaurant features genuine Italian cuisine. Tasty soups, salads and appetizers compliment a wonderful variety of creative seafood, chicken, veal, vegetarian and pasta dishes. Melt-in-your-mouth bread and scrumptious desserts begin and end a filling lunch or dinner. Warm woodwork decor, great food and pleasant service make this small eatery a real dining-out discovery. Open for lunch Monday-Saturday 11AM - 2PM, dinner Sunday-Thursday 5:30 - 9PM and Friday-Saturday 5:30 - 10PM. Reservations suggested; credit cards.

QUEEN'S COURT ★ *Continental/International - Moderate*
71 Banyan Drive (935-9361) in the Hilo Hawaiian Hotel. This is one of Hilo's nicest dining rooms with lovely views of Hilo Bay and Coconut Island. The menu features varied Continental, American, and local-style items. Try the fresh Big Island rainbow trout, raised right in Hilo. Weekend buffets Fri-Sat feature seafood and Hawaiian cuisine and are very popular with local folks and visitors. Live relaxing dinner music. Reservations suggested. Open daily, lunch 11AM - 1:15PM, dinner 6 - 8PM. Credit cards.

RESTAURANT FUJI ★ *Japanese - Moderate*
142 Kinoole St. (961-3733) in the Hilo Hotel downtown. This well-kept and attractive restaurant has the Big Island's best Japanese cuisine without exception. Casual Japanese inn atmosphere where the food is ample, well-prepared, and nicely presented, yet not overly sophisticated. Best menu items are butterfish, wafu steak, teriyaki, tonkatsu, tempura, and noodle dishes. Waitresses are dressed in kimonos to add to Japanese atmosphere. Excellent food with generally good service. Lunch daily, except Monday, 11AM - 2PM, and dinner 5 - 9PM. Reservations suggested. Credit cards.

RESTAURANT MIWA ★ *Japanese - Moderate*
At Kekuanaoa and Kilauea Avenues (961-4454) in the Hilo Shopping Center. This recently opened dining spot offers high quality Japanese cuisine in an exceptionally clean well-kept environment, right down to the white tablecloths. The menu

listings are extensive and varied featuring beef teriyaki, tonkatsu, seafood selections, and noodle dishes; the combination plates are excellent. The sushi bar turns out a full range of interesting and delightful varieties for those who like that form of rice. Service is attentive. This is a fine choice for Japanese food and should delight and excite anyone from first-timers to veterans. Lunch and dinner, Mon-Thurs 11AM - 11PM, Fri-Sat 11AM - 12PM, Sun 4 - 9PM. Reservations suggested. Credit cards.

SHOKOEN   *Chinese - Moderate*
Hawai'i Naniloa Hotel, Banyan Drive (969-3333). This Chinese restaurant features a full range of Cantonese cuisine with many varied specialties and delicacies from an ala carte menu. Pleasant atmosphere with contemporary decor. Open Wednesday to Sunday for dinner only, 5:30 - 9:30PM.

SOONTAREE'S THAI RESTAURANT ★   *Thai Cuisine - Moderate*
1261 Kilauea Avenue in the Hilo Shopping Center (934-SIAM/934-7426). This is the former Keaau Steakhouse which has been redone with bright new contemporary decor. The menu features hot spicy Thai cuisine. Typical offerings are Kareng Khiaw Wan Gai (green chicken curry), Bhi Gai Yat Sai (stuffed chicken wings), Yam gung (spicy shrimp salad), beef or chicken satay sticks and several more selections. Take-outs available. Open for lunch Monday-Friday 11AM - 2PM and dinner Monday-Saturday 6 - 9PM. Closed Sunday.

STRATTON'S   *Continental/International - Moderate*
121 Banyan Drive in the Country Club Hotel (961-6815). This dining room has a contemporary art decor theme providing a pleasant atmosphere. The menu features continental cuisine such as rack of lamb, New York steak, prawns, honey chicken, fresh island fish, Korean Kal Bi ribs and prime rib (Fri-Sat only). Lunch offers a variety of sandwiches, soups, salads and daily chef's specials. Dessert features homemade ice cream and pies, with macadamia blueberry cream cheese being their best. Children's menu available; seniors discount; credit cards. Open daily for breakfast 6 - 10AM, lunch 11AM - 2PM and dinner Tuesday to Saturday only 5:30 - 9PM.

UNCLE BILLY'S   *Seafood - Moderate*
87 Banyan Dr. (935-0861) in the Hilo Bay Hotel. The attraction here is casual dining in a Polynesian atmosphere with island decor. An extensive menu features steak and fresh island seafood. Nightly Hawaiian hula show from 6PM and Hawaiian dinner music 7:30 - 9PM. Breakfast, lunch, dinner daily. Credit cards.

EXPENSIVE

HARRINGTON'S ★   *American - Moderate*
135 Kalanianaole Avenue, Hilo (961-4966) right on the Ice Pond, Reed's Bay, opposite Banyan Drive. Their other location is in the Kawaihae Center on Highway 270 in Kawaihae, South Kohala (882-7997). The Hilo location features dining overlooking the pond and bay. Menu highlights include fresh island fish and seafood, slavic steak, filet mignon, prime rib, and calamari. Dessert selections are simply rich and wonderful! Dinner only from 5:30 PM nightly. Reservations suggested. Credit cards.

NIHON SARYO RESTAURANT   *Japanese - Expensive*

Hawai'i Naniloa Hotel, Banyan Drive (969-3333). This is an authentic Japanese-style restaurant with a varied menu of shabu-shabu, tempura, sukiyaki, teriyaki steak, fish, and lobster. Specialties include teppan grill cooking, fresh sashimi (raw fish) and sushi (rice rolls). The service is average and the decor is bland. Open Fri-Tues. only, lunch 11:30-1:30PM, dinner 5:30-9:30PM. Credit cards.

ROUSSEL'S ★   *American - Expensive*

60 Keawe St., old downtown Hilo (935-5111). Roussel's introduced Louisiana-inspired cuisine to the Big Island a few years ago. The restaurant is one of Hilo's most popular dining out options and is noted for quiet casual dining and good Continental-American food. The menu is heavily Louisiana Cajun/Creole, with specialties like blackened fish, shrimp creole, and other fresh seafood selections, even oyster and crab sandwiches. Dinner only, nightly 5 - 10PM. Reservations recommended. Credit cards.

SANDALWOOD ROOM   *Continental/International - Moderate*

93 Banyan Drive (969-3333) in the Hawai'i Naniloa Hotel. The menu features Continental selections, specialties include seafood, steaks, local favorites and a Hawaiian plate. Dining is in a tropical garden setting overlooking Hilo Bay. Breakfast 6:30 - 11AM, lunch 11AM - 2PM, dinner 5:30 - 9PM daily. Reservations recommended for dinner. Credit cards.

GINGER &
ANTHURIUMS

SOUTH HILO AND
THE HAMAKUA DISTRICT

INTRODUCTION

The South Hilo and Hamakua Districts are basically rural small village and small town areas with few restaurant options. The available fare tends to be local-style Oriental and pretty ordinary otherwise. Some of the eateries are interesting since they are located in old buildings or facilities that reflect Hawai'i's old sugar plantation days when these small coastal towns were booming places. History can be quaint.

INEXPENSIVE

AKAKA NOODLE SHOP ★ *Japanese - Inexpensive*
Main Street, Honomu Village (963-6701). What you'll find here is a country town cafe in a very quiet village. It's on the main road through the village on the way to Akaka Falls State Park. There's nothing fancy about the place but it features a variety of noodle dishes, oriental local-style food, sandwiches and short order items. Open daily except Wednesday, 9AM - 5PM.

CC JON'S SNACK IN SHOPPE *Sandwiches - Inexpensive*
Honoka'a, Hamakua Coast (775-0414). There is a wide range of local and international foods, short order items, and snacks available in this small deli-cafe. Open Mon-Sat 6:30AM - 5PM.

EARL'S DRIVE IN *Drive In - Inexpensive*
Paauilo Store on Highway 19 in the small village of Paauilo, on the Hamakua Coast. The menu features local-style fast foods and snacks including sandwiches, teribeef and chicken plates, saimin, chili and rice, and more. There are a couple of tables on the veranda of this old plantation store where you can relax and enjoy the genuine country atmosphere of the place. Open Monday-Friday 8:30AM - 7PM, Saturday 8:30AM - 6PM, Sunday 8:30AM - 12:30PM.

HERB'S PLACE *Family Dining - Inexpensive*
Main Street, Honoka'a, Hamakua Coast (775-7236). The menu features prime rib, chicken, and other local favorites with a salad bar. Located in heart of Honoka'a town in a non-descript building on the main street. Open daily except Sunday, 5AM - 9PM. Credit cards.

HONOKA'A PIZZA & SUBS *Italian - Inexpensive*
Main Street, Honoka'a, Hamakua Coast (775-9966). This pizzeria serves up a good variety of pizza, submarine sandwiches, salads, Italian favorites, and features fresh baked pastries, cheesecake, eclairs, and heavenly cream puffs. Lunch and dinner, Mon-Sat 11AM - 9PM. Take outs available.

HOTEL HONOKA'A CLUB ★ *Family Dining - Inexpensive*
Main Street, Honoka'a, Hamakua Coast (775-0533/775-0678). The dining room in Honoka'a's only hotel is a popular local spot for lunch and dinner. The room

is wide and rambling with plenty of tables and chairs and a 1940's era plantation house decor, very plain, very simple. The menu features steaks, chicken, and some local-style dishes served up in an old fashioned country atmosphere. The cocktail lounge adjacent gets lively on the weekends with local folks partying. Open daily for breakfast 6 - 11AM, lunch 11AM - 2PM, dinner 5:30 - 8PM. Credit cards.

ISHIGO'S STORE ★　*Family Dining - Inexpensive*
Main Street, Honomu Village (963-6128). This is a country general store and bakery featuring fresh rolls, pastries and Kona coffee. Other snacks and light meal selections are available. A pleasant stop right on the main road through Honomu Village on the way to Akaka Falls State Park. Open Mon-Fri 7AM - 6PM, Sat-Sun 7AM - 5:30PM.

SANDRA'S STORE　*Sandwiches - Inexpensive*
Just south of Paauilo on Highway 19, Hamakua Coast, and next door to Donna's Cookies bakery. This is a typically Hawaiian country store offering a selection of snacks, sandwiches, local fast food items like manapua, musubi (rice balls) and more. This is a popular truck-stop of sorts for the truckers hauling freight around the island. Open Mon.-Fri. 6AM - 8PM, Sat. 7AM - 8PM, Sunday 9AM - 8PM.

NORTH KOHALA DISTRICT

INTRODUCTION

The top end of the Big Island, the North Kohala District, is rural, quiet, and sparsely populated. Even with its handful of historic attractions, most visitors don't linger too long here. There are only three eateries worth noting here.

INEXPENSIVE

DON'S FAMILY DELI　*Family Dining - Inexpensive*
Main street, Highway 270, Kapa'au (889-5822) right across from the King Kamehameha Statue and the courthouse. This is an ice cream parlor-cafe featuring sandwiches, salads, international foods, and desserts. Open daily 10AM - 6PM.

HONEY'S COUNTRY KITCHEN　*Family Dining - Inexpensive/Moderate*
Junction of Highways 250 and 270 in the heart of Hawi town (889-0294). This is a newly refurbished country cafe with contemporary Hawaiian decor. The menu features burgers, sandwiches, local favorites, plus seafood, chicken and steaks. Open daily for breakfast and lunch 7AM - 2PM, and dinner 5PM - 10PM.

MATTHEW'S PLACE　*Sandwiches - Inexpensive*
1 block west of the intersection of Highways 250 and 270 in the heart of Hawi town (889-5500) next door to K. Takata Store. This tiny hole-in-the-wall place features Italian food, pizza, sandwiches and fast food. Varied hours of service. Strictly for the budget conscious traveler.

PUNA DISTRICT

INTRODUCTION

Puna's population is spread among several country subdivisions in the sprawling district southeast of Hilo. While it has a handful of small towns and villages, it doesn't have any real district center unless Pahoa qualifies, since it has a high school, police and fire station, and a main street. The restaurants are located in or near the village shopping centers and offer fairly ordinary food with a little Mexican and Italian for spice. The one exception is the Kilauea Lodge Restaurant near Hawai'i Volcanoes National Park, which is surprising many folks with its Continental-International menu in a relaxing country lodge atmosphere.

INEXPENSIVE

LEQUIN'S MEXICAN RESTAURANT   *Mexican - Inexpensive*
On the main street in Pahoa, Hwy 130 (965-9990). The dinner only menu features a variety of Mexican dishes like tacos, burritos, enchiladas, and other specialties. The decor and building it is located in are somewhat rough but the place may appeal to the adventurous diner who likes Mexican food. Open daily, 3:30 - 9PM.

MAMA LANI'S MEXICAN RESTAURANT ★   *Mexican - Inexpensive*
Keaau Town Center, Keaau (966-7525). This attractive restaurant features Mexican decor along with a wide menu of South-of-the-Border selections like tacos, burritos, tostadas, chimichanga, quesadilla, and sandwiches. Open daily, lunch 11AM - 4PM, dinner 4 - 9PM, Sunday dinner only 4 - 9PM. Credit cards.

MIU'S   *Chinese - Inexpensive*
Keaau Town Center, Keaau (966-6911). This small Chinese eatery specializes in a variety of excellent Cantonese specials served up plate lunch style. Take outs available. Open daily 8:30AM - 5:30PM.

PAHOA CHOP SUEY HOUSE   *Chinese - Inexpensive*
Just off the main highway in Pahoa town, across from the 7/11 Store (965-9533). This Chinese eatery offers a full menu of Cantonese-style cuisine. The menu features seafood, pork, beef, chicken and duck dishes, a variety of chop sueys and noodles. Set dinners for 2-4 people are also available. Open daily except Monday, 10:30AM - 8PM.

PAHOA INN COFFEE SHOP   *Family Dining - Inexpensive*
On the main street in Pahoa, Highway 130 (965-9733). This small country town cafe features a typical coffee shop menu of breakfast and lunch selections. Features are eggs, pancakes, breakfast meats and sandwiches, soups, salads, and some local-style favorites for lunch. Open daily 7AM - 2PM.

PARADISE WEST CAFE   *Family Dining - Inexpensive*
On the highway in the middle of Pahoa town (965-8334). This local-style cafe offers a varied menu featuring eggs Benedict, fresh catch, homemade buttermilk biscuits with sausage gravy, whole grain pancakes, burgers, homemade soups, vegetarian specials, steaks and fine desserts. Dinner menu of international entrees changes nightly. Open daily, 7AM - 9PM.

PUNA SANDS RESTAURANT   *Sandwiches - Inexpensive*
Next to Akebono Theatre in Pahoa just off the highway through town (965-8988). This local style hole-in-the-wall eatery features spaghetti, croissant sandwiches, daily local favorites, seafood salads, soups and more. Open Monday through Saturday for lunch and dinner, 11AM - 9PM.

RIB HOUSE   *American - Inexpensive*
Pahoa Village Center, Pahoa (965-7427). This is a fairly new restaurant featuring a variety of rib cuts such as bar-b-que ribs, Korean ribs and baby back ribs, chicken, steaks, fish, pizza, and pasta, along with some local specialties. Open daily except Thursday, breakfast 6:30 - 11AM, dinner 5 - 9PM. No lunch served. Credit cards.

ROSAL'S BAKERY & DELI   *Sandwiches-Burgers - Inexpensive*
On old Keaau Road in Keaau town (966-8069). This is a former bakery shop turned lunch-snack shop. They still bake fresh bread, cakes, pies and pastries but also feature pizza, local style plate lunches and more. Open Monday-Saturday, 6AM - 6PM.

SNAPPY'S PIZZA   *Italian - Inexpensive*
In the Keaau Town Center (966-7557). This local style pizzeria serves up a variety of pizza, chicken, ribs, and submarine sandwiches similar to its Hilo outlet. Open Mon-Sat 11AM - 10PM, Sun 4 - 9PM.

TONYA'S CAFE   *Mexican - Inexpensive*
In Keaau town across from the post office and the Keaau Town Center. This small natural food cafe features Mexican foods like tostadas, nachos, burritos, and more, plus special sandwiches, soups and stews, desserts, smoothies and drinks. Located in an old plantation-era building but neat and clean. Open Monday through Friday only, 11AM - 7PM.

MODERATE

KILAUEA LODGE RESTAURANT ★   *Continental/International - Moderate*
On Highway 11 in Volcano Village (967-7366). This cozy dining room is part of the Kilauea Lodge Bed & Breakfast operation (see "Bed & Breakfast" in the ACCOMMODATIONS section). It offers a mixed Continental-International cuisine menu featuring fine seafood, beef, veal, and chicken selections for dinner, along with a variety of appetizers and salads. Fine service in an attractive setting with dining room fireplace and relaxed country lodge atmosphere. Open for dinner 5 - 9:30PM. Credit cards.

LA CELLA   *Italian-French - Moderate*
In the Keaau Shopping Plaza, Keaau (966-8066), formerly Papa Aldo's, is right across from Keaau School. The new menu features distinctive Italian and French cuisine such as coq au vin (chicken in wine sauce), steak au poivre (steak with black pepper/butter/brandy sauce), escalopes de veau moutarde (deal in Dijon-cream sauce) and coquilles St. Jacques (scallops in cream sauce/Gratinee). Homemade French onion soup is a menu specialty. Open daily for dinner, 4 - 8:30PM.

KA'U DISTRICT

INTRODUCTION

Like the top end at North Kohala, the lower end of the Big Island is rural, quiet, and sparsely populated. Its few small villages are remote and far from the district's main attraction of Hawai'i Volcanoes National Park. There are few restaurants, but those that follow do serve some interesting, local-style and Continental-International cuisine.

INEXPENSIVE

NA'ALEHU FRUIT STAND   *Sandwiches - Inexpensive*
Main street, Highway 11, in Naalehu, the self-proclaimed "Southernmost Community in the USA." This snack shop features a variety of sandwiches, pizza, fresh baked pastries, macadamia nut treats, and fresh squeezed juices. Open Mon-Thurs 9AM - 6:30PM, Fri-Sat 9AM - 7PM, and Sunday 9AM - 5PM.

VOLCANO COUNTRY CLUB RESTAURANT ★ *Family Dining - Inexpensive*
Hawai'i Volcanoes National Park, just off Highway 11 at the 30 mile marker from Hilo, across from Kilauea Military Camp (967-7721). This rustic dining room is located in the golf course clubhouse and features a variety of sandwiches, beef, chicken, fish, and local style favorites. Open daily for breakfast 7AM - 11AM, lunch 11AM - 3PM, cocktails only 11AM till closing.

MODERATE

NA'ALEHU COFFEE SHOP ★   *American - Moderate*
Across the street from the Naalehu Shopping Center in the middle of the "Southernmost Community in the USA" (929-7238). This delightful country coffee shop serves up American-style food including steaks, seafood, fresh island fish, chicken and salads. Sandwiches are featured for lunch. Open Mon. through Sat. for breakfast, lunch and dinner continuously 8AM - 8PM; closed Sunday. Some days they may close for short periods in mid-afternoon but re-open for dinner hour.

JANORA BAYOT

KA OHELO ROOM   *Continental/International - Moderate*
Volcano House Hotel, Hawai'i Volcanoes National Park (967-7321). The menu features prime rib, steaks, chicken, lamb, pork, island fish, and local favorites. The daily buffet lunch is popular with visitors. The dining room overlooks majestic Kilauea Caldera and it's steaming vents. While the charming rustic lodge atmosphere is nice it's not enough to make up for mediocre food and service. A few years ago this was a great dining room but it has declined significantly and lost its star rating. If you can overlook the less than exciting cuisine perhaps the experience of dining on the edge of the volcano will make up for it. Daily for breakfast 6:30 - 10AM, lunch 10:30 - 2PM, dinner 5:30 - 8:30PM. Credit cards.

PUNALU'U BLACK SANDS RESTAURANT   *Continental - Moderate*
Off Highway 11 on the black sand beach next to Punalu'u Beach Park, Ninole, near the Seamountain Golf Course (928-8528). The breezy location on the black sand beach makes for a casual tropical lunch. The menu features a tropical lunch buffet with many local style favorites like fish, chicken, pork as well as a full a la carte menu for dinner. Lunch 10:30AM - 2PM, dinner 5:30 - 8:30PM, daily. Credit cards.

SOUTH POINT RESTAURANT   *Continental - Moderate*
This isolated eatery is located in the desolate lavalands of the Ka'u district in the Hawaiian Oceanview Estates subdivision area (929-9343). It's located right on Highway 11 between South Point and Milolii right out in the middle of nowhere. The menu features sandwiches and burgers for lunch. For dinner, entrees include honey and lemon chicken, teriyaki chicken, kalua pig, veal, New York steak, calamari steak, prime rib, ahi, shrimp, several pastas, plus soups and salads. They also have a cocktail lounge. Open Monday-Saturday for lunch and dinner, 11AM - 9PM, dinner only on Sunday, 5 - 9PM.

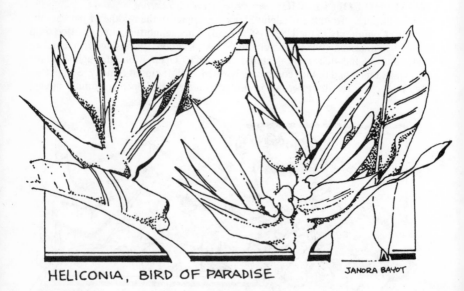

HELICONIA, BIRD OF PARADISE   JANORA BAYOT

RECREATION
AND TOURS

INTRODUCTION

The Big Island's diversity in climate, terrain, and geophysical features, not to mention its sheer size in comparison to the other islands of Hawai'i, provides a wide range and scope of activities. There is something to please everyone from the sedentary toes-in-the-water set to the adventure-seeking backpacker bent on exploring the island's most remote areas. This chapter details the more popular activities available to visitors.

BEST BETS:

A glassbottom boat cruise along the famed Kona Coast and over its famous coral reefs.

A submarine cruise through Kona's fabulous underwater world.

A golf outing at either the Mauna Kea Beach Hotel Golf Course or the Mauna Lani Resort Golf Course, both named among "America's Top 12 Resort Courses."

An airtour over Hawai'i Volcanoes National Park and/or current/recent eruption sites or along the scenic Hamakua Coast.

A snorkeling adventure at Kahalu'u Bay at Keauhou-Kona, Kealakekua Bay Underwater Marine Preserve in Kona, Anaeho'omalu Bay on the Kohala Coast, or Leleiwi Beach Park in Hilo.

If conditions permit, a ski run down Mauna Kea's fabulous snow-covered slopes.

A 4-wheel drive tour to the summit of 13, 796 ft. Mauna Kea or into the lush Waipio Valley.

For adventurous anglers, a fishing boat charter to pursue the mighty marlin in the fabled waters of the Kona Coast.

A hike through any of Hawai'i Volcanoes National Park trails to take in the awesome natural beauty and wonders of the volcanoes.

OCEAN ACTIVITIES

BEACHES - SNORKELING

Contrary to popular belief among many visitors, the Big Island of Hawai'i does have many beaches. In fact, it has more than 100 of them. Some are black sand, some white sand, some golden and some even have green sand. At the same time, many are very rugged rocky shorelines that have not yet fully eroded to a fine sand consistency. This is due to the geologic fact that the Big Island is still young and has not fully developed its beaches like Hawai'i's other islands. It is still a growing island and its volcanic eruptions still create new beaches while transforming old coastline.

The problem is that many of these beaches are not easily accessible for the average visitor or resident. This is due to poor or non-existant access roads, access via private roads and lands only, access through difficult and remote country, or access only from the ocean and often through treacherous waters. And even if a remote isolated beach is accessible via a road, it is usually via four-wheel drive off-road vehicle due to the difficult terrain. For these reasons, this section contains a listing only of those beaches, parks, and recreation areas that are easily accessible to the average visitor or resident. Most of the beaches listed in this section are directly accessible from main roads or well-marked and designated trails. Others are available via marked public beach access over private lands. The listings note the location of the beach area and any facilities and activities available at that site. For more detailed information on the Big Island's beaches, readers are referred to *Beaches of the Big Island*, by John R. K. Clark, published by the University of Hawai'i Press (1985).

Snorkelers will find lots of good areas to explore near some of the more popular beaches around the island. However, much of the better snorkeling is done over lava rock outcroppings and rocky coves and small bays where the water is usually fairly calm. There are lots of good coral patches and beds growing around these

areas which attracts varied marine life. However, because the Big Island is so young geologically, there are no extensive fringing coral reefs that encircle the island or extend out from the shoreline. The best snorkeling is at Napo'opo'o Beach Park and the adjacent Kealakekua Bay State Marine & Historic Underwater Preserve with its teeming marine life, Kahalu'u Beach Park in Keauhou-Kona with myriad schools of colorful reef fish, Anaeho'omalu Beach at Waikoloa, Kohala Coast, Leleiwi Beach Park in Hilo with its tide pools and rock formations, and Kapoho Bay in Kapoho with its calm tide pools, clear water, and abundant marine life. As in all ocean areas, snorkelers need to be aware of their direction, distance from the shore, and keep alert to currents, surges and surf action especially near rock outcroppings.

WATER SAFETY

Whether you are experienced or inexperienced with the ocean, it is advisable to use caution and think safety when you are going into it. There are a few rules to follow:

1. An old Hawaiian saying states: "Never turn your back to the sea." Don't be caught off guard, waves come in sets with spells of calm in between.
2. Use the buddy system, never swim or snorkel alone.
3. If you are unsure of your abilities, use flotation devices attached to your body, such as a life vest or inflatable vest. Never rely on an air mattress or similar device from which you may become separated.
4. Study the ocean before you enter; look for rocky areas and breakers or currents.
5. Duck or dive beneath breaking waves before they reach you.
6. Never swim against a strong current which will tire you rapidly. Swim across it.
7. Know your limits.
8. Small children should be allowed to play near or in the surf ONLY with close supervision and should wear flotation devices.
9. When exploring tidal pools or reefs, always wear protective footwear and keep an eye on the ocean for high surf. Also, protect your hands from sharp rocks and coral. When swimming or snorkeling around coral, be careful where you put your hands and feet. Sea urchin stings can be painful and coral cuts can be dangerous.

BEST BETS:

Most Beautiful Beaches
Anaeho'omalu Beach - Waikoloa, Kohala Coast
Hapuna Beach State Park - Kohala Coast
Kauna'oa Beach (Mauna Kea Beach) - Kohala Coast

Safest Playing - Swimming Beaches for Youngsters
Spencer Beach Park - Kawaihae Bay, Kohala Coast
Onekahakaha Beach Park - Keaukaha area, Hilo
Kamakahonu Beach - next to the pier, Kailua-Kona
Kahalu'u Beach Park - Keauhou-Kona

RECREATION AND TOURS
Beaches - Snorkeling

Snorkeling Beaches
Napoʻopoʻo Beach Park - Kealakekua Bay, Kona
Puʻuhonua O Honaunau National Historic Park - Honaunau, Kona
Kahaluʻu Beach Park - Keauhou-Kona
Anaehoʻomalu Beach - Waikoloa, Kohala Coast
Spencer Beach Park - Kawaihae Bay, Kohala Coast
James Kealoha Park - Keaukaha area, Hilo
Leleiwi Beach Park - Keaukaha area, Hilo
Kapoho Bay - Kapoho area, Puna District

Shelling-Tidepooling Beaches
Onekahakaha Beach Park - Keaukaha area, Hilo
Holoholokai Beach Park - South Kohala at Mauna Lani Resort

Sunbathing Beaches
White Sands Beach Park - Kailua-Kona
Anaehoʻomalu Beach - Waikoloa, Kohala Coast
Hapuna Beach State Park - Kohala Coast
Kaunaʻoa Beach (Mauna Kea Beach) - Kohala Coast

BEACH INDEX

SOUTH KONA AREA
Hoʻokena Beach Park 221
Puʻuhonua O Honaunau
   Natl. Historic Park 221
Napoʻopoʻo Beach Park 221

NORTH KONA AREA
Kahaluʻu Beach Park 222
White Sands Beach Park 222
Kamakahonu Beach 222
Old Kona Airport
   St. Recreation Area 222
ʻAlula Beach 222
Kaʻupulehu Beach 223
Kona Coast State Park 223

SOUTH KOHALA AREA
Anaehoʻomalu Beach 223
Kalahuipuaʻa Beach 224
Puako Beach 224
Hapuna Beach State Park 224
Holoholokai Beach Park 224
Kaunaʻoa Beach 224
Spencer Beach Park 225
Kawaihae Beach 2254

NORTH KOHALA AREA
Lapakahi State
   Historical Park 225

Mahukona Beach Park 225
Pololu Valley Beach 225

HAMAKUA AREA
Waipio Valley Beach 226

NORTH HILO AREA
Laupahoehoe Point Park 226

SOUTH HILO AREA
Kolekole Beach Park 227
Honolii Beach Park 227
Reed's Bay Boat
   Harbor and Ice Pond 227
Onekahakaha Beach Park 227
James Kealoha Park 227
Leleiwi Beach Park 227

PUNA AREA
Kapoho Bay 228
Isaac Hale Beach Park 228
Kamoamoa Beach Park 228
Kehena Beach 228

KAʻU AREA
Punaluʻu Beach Park 229
Green Sand Beach 229

SOUTH KONA AREA

The beaches of South Kona are mostly used by local residents. None of these listed are near any resorts. The Pu'uhonua O Honaunau Park and marine reserve at Kealakekua Bay-Napo'opo'o Park do get some visitor use due to other attractions of the sites. These beaches are fairly isolated and not near any major town or commercial areas.

HO'OKENA BEACH PARK
Three miles south of Pu'uhonua O Honaunau National Historic Park at the end of a narrow, winding and bumpy paved spur road off Highway 11. Ho'okena has a small coconut grove, a handful of old Hawaiian homes and beach houses, restrooms and picnic tables, and some shade trees. The beach is a combination of black and white sand and mixed lava debris giving the sand a gray cast. The bay is generally calm and swimming, snorkeling, and diving are generally good but caution is advised during high surf times.

PU'UHONUA O HONAUNAU NATIONAL HISTORIC PARK ★
Honaunau Bay is one of the Big Island's most popular attractions. In addition to the visitor's center displays and the old Hawaiian heiau (temple) structures, the park has restrooms, a picnic area, and some of the best near shore snorkeling and scuba diving on the island. The generally rocky shoreline has pockets of sandy beach here and there and the shoreline waters teem with marine life.

NAPO'OPO'O BEACH PARK ★
Adjoins the village of Napo'opo'o at Kealakekua Bay. The beach consists of pebbles, cobblestones, and boulders with only a very narrow strip of sand at the water's edge. The beach attracts many sunbathers and swimmers and the limited wave action attracts some surfers and boogie boarders. The adjacent Napo'opo'o Beach Park has very limited parking, restrooms, and a couple of picnic tables. Also next to the park are the ruins of Hikiau Heiau, an old Hawaiian temple. Snorkelers will revel in the offshore Kealakekua Bay State Historical & Underwater Parks Marine Preserve. The area teems with fascinating and colorful marine life and offers excellent snorkeling and scuba diving. Many of the commercial

KIHIKIHI   JBayot boat tours from Kailua-Kona include Kealakekua Bay as part of their route. At the north end of the bay beyond the towering cliffs and on a flat point of land jutting into the bay is the Captain James Cook Monument which marks the spot where the famous explorer met his fate.

NORTH KONA AREA

The beaches listed for North Kona will have a considerable number of visitors as well as local residents using the facilities. These beaches are generally quite nice and popular for all sorts of outings and activities. Their proximity to the hotels and resorts of Kailua-Kona make them busy places on most good beach days.

KAHALU'U BEACH PARK ★
This one of the most popular swimming and snorkeling sites in the Kona area. Located next to the Keauhou Beach Hotel at Keauhou-Kona, just south of Kailua-Kona. The beach is composed of white sand speckled with black lava pebbles, cobblestones, and fragments. The bay waters provide excellent snorkeling and near shore scuba diving in waters protected by a fringing reef and the area is generally free of strong currents. Outside the reef, surfers can find good waves to ride but the rip currents along the reef edge are extremely strong. Caution is advised. Park facilities include picnic pavilions, restrooms, showers, water, lifeguard, parking, and concession stands.

WHITE SANDS BEACH PARK ★
Located on Alii Drive four miles south of Kailua-Kona town. Facilities include restrooms, showers, lifeguard, and small parking lot. A grove of coconut trees provides some shade and lends a touch of beauty to this small beach park. The lovely white sand and small wave action make this a popular swimming and boogie boarding beach for both residents and visitors. Winter storms often wash the white sand into deeper water only to carry it back later, hence the park's other names of "Disappearing Sands" and "Magic Sands."

KAMAKAHONU BEACH ★
This is a small cove of sandy beach immediately next to the Kailua Pier and fronting the King Kamehameha Kona Beach Hotel. Extending onto a peninsula in front of the beach is Ahuena Heiau, the temple of King Kamehameha the Great. Kamehameha resided here at Kamakahonu during the last years of his life. The beach is very protected and is excellent for sunbathing and swimming. The beach is especially good for young children. No public facilities exist on the beach itself but there are public restrooms on the adjacent pier.

OLD KONA AIRPORT STATE RECREATION AREA
The area consists of a long beach composed of storm and reef debris, pebbles, and rocks with a few pockets of white sand with safe sand channels for entering the water. However the coast here tends to be rocky overall. The swimming and snorkeling are generally fair to good here, but best on calmer days. Facilities include picnic pavilions, restrooms, showers, water, and plenty of parking.

'ALULA BEACH
The beach is located in a small protected cove just to the south of Honokohau Harbor near Kailua-Kona, and is a lovely crescent of white sand speckled with

lack lava fragments. It is a secluded spot for sunbathing, swimming, snorkeling, and near shore scuba diving. The boat traffic of Honokohau Harbor can be viewed easily from the beach. The shallow sandy bottom makes this a pleasant calm beach especially for youngsters. Public facilities at adjacent boat harbor.

KA'UPULEHU BEACH
Fronts the Kona Village Resort north of Kailua-Kona. The white sand beach is speckled with black lava fragments and pebbles. The waters of Kahuwai Bay here are good for swimming and snorkeling. There is convenient public access and some parking is provided by the privately-operated Kona Village Resort. There are no public facilities at the beach.

KONA COAST STATE PARK ★
This new beach park is located just a couple of miles north of Kona's Keahole Airport. It is reached off Highway 19 by a narrow somewhat bumpy road that winds across the lava fields for 1.5 miles. A regular car can make it but drive slowly. The beach is a high sand dune beach with good tidal pools for snorkeling and swimming but don't go out too far. This is a new park just being developed and as of mid-1992 there were only temporary restoom facilities and a few picnic tables plus a parking lot area. Bring your own water.

SOUTH KOHALA AREA

South Kohala probably has the best sandy beaches on the island. Some like Hapuna and Spencer Parks are used by both local residents and visitors alike. Others like 'Anaeho'omalu and Kauna'oa Beaches front major hotels, and while public access is provided, the majority of beach goers are hotel guests. Still, the public has access and full use of the beaches.

'ANAEHO'OMALU BEACH ★
This is a long curving white sand beach speckled with grains of black lava. It is a lovely crescent accented with graceful coconut palms and backed by two old fishponds, Ku'uali'i and Kahapapa, which were reserved for Hawaiian royalty in the old days. The beach park fronts the Royal Waikoloan Hotel. Swimming, snorkeling, scuba diving, windsurfing, and board surfing are enjoyed in the bay.

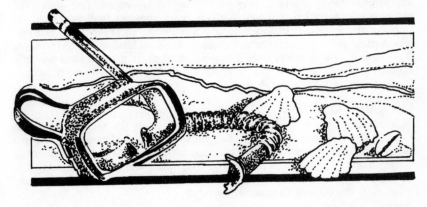

A water sports-activities concession on the beach provides equipment rentals and instruction for hotel guests and other visitors. The beach park facilities include restrooms, showers, and picnic tables plus parking.

KALAHUIPUA'A BEACH
Located at the Mauna Lani Resort. The beach is adjacent to a series of well maintained old Hawaiian fishponds which are still used for aquaculture purposes. The beach access is through a historic preserve and public park maintained by the Mauna Lani Resort. The best swimming area of the beach is Nanuku Inlet, a wide, shallow, sandy-bottomed cove enclosed by natural lava rock barriers. This part of the lovely white and black sand speckled beach immediately fronts the Mauna Lani Bay Hotel.

HOLOHOLOKAI BEACH PARK ★
This is a new public access beach park located just north of the Ritz Carlton Mauna Lani Hotel. The park was developed by the Mauna Lani Resort Company and provides restrooms and showers, parking stalls for over 30 cars and barbeque grills on the beach. The beach is not sandy but composed of white coral rocks and some black lava and debris. There are small pockets of sand here and there. It's a good beach for sunning, tidepool exploring, shelling and snorkeling in the larger tidal pools. Great views of the Kohala Coast. A trail from the parking lot leads to the *Puako Petroglyph Fields* which provide an interesting view of old Hawaiian rock carvings and drawings. The trail is a 1.4 mile round trip (about 40 minutes) through kiawe and haole koa trees and brushland. Wear good hiking shoes and take sunscreen and water as it can be a warm dry hike.

PUAKO BEACH
The beach extends the entire length of shoreline along Puako Road in North Kohala below Hapuna Beach State Park. The beach is mostly rocks and pebbles indented by inlets, coves, and tidal pools but sunbathers, swimmers, and snorkelers can find some white sand beach stretches to enter the water. Public access is via the boat ramp at Puako Bay or any of several points along Puako Road which follows the shoreline homes.

HAPUNA BEACH STATE PARK ★
This is undoubtedly one of the Big Island's largest expanses of fine white sand beach. It stretches for over a half mile. The beach provides shallow waters that slope gently to deeper offshore waters. Swimming, snorkeling, bodysurfing, windsurfing, and near shore scuba diving are excellent. Shallow, protected coves at the beach's north end provide sandy-bottomed pools that are ideal for little children to splash and play. Beach facilities include picnic pavilions, restrooms, showers, and parking.

KAUNA'OA BEACH ★
This is better known as Mauna Kea Beach and fronts the Mauna Kea Beach Hotel. It is a long, wide crescent of fine white sand which slopes gently into the deeper offshore waters and offers excellent swimming, snorkeling, and windsurfing. Surf conditions often permit good bodysurfing and boardsurfing also. The hotel provides some public parking and maintains a public access right-of-way and there are restrooms and showers on the beach.

SPENCER BEACH PARK ★
The park is located near the port village of Kawaihae and immediately below Pu'ukohola Heiau National Historic Park, a famous temple built by Kamehameha the Great. The beach here is a fine white sand expanse with a very gentle slope to deeper water. The conditions are excellent for swimming, snorkeling, and near shore scuba diving. The protected nature of the bay affords very calm waters with usually gentle surf. It is an excellent swimming beach for little children.

KAWAIHAE BEACH
This is a coral rubble and landfill beach next to the boat harbor which resulted when the harbor was dredged years ago. Many local folks use the area for varied activities such as fishing, canoe paddling, sailing, windsurfing, swimming, and picnicking. From the south end of the landfill area is a great view of the nearby Pu'ukohola Heiau.

NORTH KOHALA AREA

The beaches of North Kohala tend to be of a more rugged variety, often composed of small pockets of coral pebbles and small rocks with an isolated pocket of sand. Often the beach area is rugged lava rock outcropping.

LAPAKAHI STATE HISTORICAL PARK ★
The park is north of Kawaihae Harbor and has no good sandy beaches. There are small pockets of coral pebbles and rocky beaches where swimmers and snorkelers can enter the water. At the point where the park trail follows the shoreline and meets a small peninsula of land, there is a small cove with remarkably clear water which slopes gradually before dropping off sharply. Swimmers and snorkelers should not venture out more than fifty yards into the cove however due to strong alongshore currents in the area. There are no facilities right on the shore but restrooms are located near the parking lot area and entrance.

MAHUKONA BEACH PARK
Between Kawaihae and Hawi on Highway 270 is the site of an old port of the Hawai'i Consolidated Railway Company, which transported sugar from the Kohala Mill to boats for trans-ocean shipment. Remnants of the old railway port still exist and old train wheels, parts, and related rubble attract snorkelers and divers in the bay's clear waters. There is no real sand beach here, only coral rubble and pebbles. Facilities include picnic tables, a pavilion, restrooms, showers, camping area, and parking lot but all facilities are rough and in need of some maintenance work.

POLOLU VALLEY BEACH
At the end of Highway 270, past the village of Kapa'au, the beach is reached by a difficult trail down to the valley at the end of the highway. The trail is often treacherous if wet and caution is advised. The beach is a wide expanse of fine black sand with high dunes at the back shore. While swimmers, bodysurfers, and surfers use the beach, there are dangerous rip currents that are real hazards. This is a remote, isolated beach, and extreme caution is advised. The flatlands of the valley were once extensively planted in taro farms but are now abandoned. There are no facilities of any kind on the beach.

HAMAKUA AREA

The eastern side of the Big Island, the Hamakua Coast, is marked by a high pali (cliff) which is often a sheer verticle drop of more than 200 feet. The coastline here is very rough and rugged with very few places where sandy beaches have had a chance to form. The fact that there is no coral reef extending outwards from the coast accounts for the lack of coral sand here. Waipio Valley Beach, the one exception listed, is composed of black sand eroded from the surrounding lava.

WAIPIO VALLEY BEACH
At the end of Highway 240, at the Waipio Valley State Park lookout, the beach fronting the valley is reached via a hazardous and very steep single lane road carved along the valley wall. A four-wheel drive vehicle is required to gain access to the beach. The beach is a long black sand crescent bisected in the middle by the Waipio River. There are many large smooth boulders and rubble at the south end. While some swimmers, bodysurfers, and surfers ride the often good waves here, the presence of strong rip currents make the beach extremely dangerous to even advanced swimmers. Caution is advised. There are no facilities of any kind on the beach.

NORTH HILO AREA

Like the Hamakua Coast, the North Hilo area has formed few sandy beaches. There are small pockets of black lava rock sand in some areas, but coral sand beaches are non-existant. The generally high coastline pali (cliff) also accounts for a lack of good beaches in the area. But the area has a special rugged beauty that is captured in places like Laupahoehoe Park listed here.

LAUPAHOEHOE POINT PARK ★
The park is a lava rock peninsula jutting into the ocean at Laupahoehoe. The area is typical of the Hamakua Coast in that there are steep rugged cliffs throughout the area and hardly any safe sandy beaches. The beach on this sea-level peninsula is mostly coral pebbles and rocks. Strong surf and rip currents prevent most water activities although some do swim and surf. The rocky shoreline requires extreme caution. Park facilities include picnic pavilions, restrooms, showers, water,

parking, and camping sites. A new small boat launching facility was recently completed. It is a pleasant park to picnic and enjoy the scenic beauty of the Hamakua Coast. On a warm day, lots of ironwood trees provide cool shade to enjoy the pastoral Hawaiian scenery.

SOUTH HILO AREA

The South Hilo area is marked by a few lovely beach parks. Most of these facilities are frequented by local residents enjoying a pleasant day at the beach usually with youngsters. The Keaukaha area beaches in Hilo have generally calm tide pools that are good for children. Onekahakaha Park has a protected pool with a sandy bottom which is especially good for youngsters.

KOLEKOLE BEACH PARK ★
Despite not having a sandy beach this is one of the Big Island's loveliest parks. It is fronted by a shoreline of smooth waterworn lava rocks with an adjacent coldwater stream and waterfall. The park grounds and surrounding valley walls are lush and full of tropical vegetation. The stream flows from the beautiful Akaka Falls Park located upstream some four miles. While water activities are somewhat limited, the park is an excellent place for a day outing to picnic, explore, and enjoy Hawaii's tropical outdoors. Park facilities include restrooms, pavilions, water, showers, and camping areas.

HONOLII BEACH PARK
Located just north of Hilo off Hwy. 19, on the old scenic route, Mamalahoa Hwy. This is a favorite with local teenagers as it is one of the best surfing beaches in the Hilo area. Restrooms and very limited parking along the roadside are available. It's a good spot for just watching local kids catch the waves on a nice day.

REED'S BAY BOAT HARBOR AND ICE POND
These are just off Kalanianaole Avenue on Banyan Drive and across from the Hilo Seaside Hotel. Though not exactly a beach area, the Ice Pond is a spring-fed stream which flows into Hilo Bay via Reed's Bay small boat harbor. It's a popular swimming hole for local kids.

Spread out along Kalanianaole Avenue in the Keaukaha area of Hilo town and past the airport and harbor piers are Hilo's beach parks.

ONEKAHAKAHA BEACH PARK ★
The park features a protected sandy bottom swimming area for youngsters, pavilions, picnic tables, camp sites and restrooms.

JAMES KEALOHA PARK
The park has a smooth lava rock beach and picnic areas and restrooms. Good swimming, surfing and snorkeling are available here.

LELEIWI BEACH PARK
This park also has smooth lava rock beach and pavilions, picnic areas, and restrooms. Swimming, snorkeling and surfing are good here. This is the site of the Richardson Ocean Center, a marine education and aquatic display center open to the public. There is no charge. See page 33 for details.

PUNA AREA

The Puna beaches tend to be in fairly isolated areas several miles from the nearest town or commercial areas. The most popular are the Kalapana area black sand beaches. The black sand beaches have long been among the Big Island's more notable features and attractions for their contrasting beauty.

CAUTION!: The beaches of the Puna area have had extremely heavy use by area residents since the lava flows of 1990 destroyed the Kalapana area and its famed black sand beaches. Area residents who used to frequent the Kalapana beaches have now moved on to the other beaches in the area, causing serious problems of overcrowding, heavy facilities use, etc. These beaches for the most part were undeveloped and had virtually no restroom, water-showers, parking and other park facilities. The local government has yet to provide any new beach park recreational facilities in this area. Visitors should keep in mind that the following beaches may be very crowded and facilities non-existant or seriously overloaded.

KAPOHO BAY

The bay is the back shore area fronting Kapoho Beach Lots and Vacationland Estates subdivisions in the Kapoho area. While there is not a sandy beach here, it is a beautiful tidal pond and pool area which is great for snorkeling and swimming. The tidal pools have a variety of marine life and small fish to view. There are no facilities.

ISAAC HALE BEACH PARK

The park is on Cape Kumikahi, along the Puna Coast, and is the site of a busy boat launching ramp used by commerical fishermen. Other activities of the bay include surfing, bodyboarding, and swimming. The beach here is mostly smooth pebbles and cobblestones and not fine sand. There are restrooms and showers available. Behind the beach area in a natural lava rock pool are the Pohoiki Warm Springs, a natural warm water bath heated by underground geothermal action that are used for bathing and soaking.

KEHENA BEACH

Located on Pohoiki Road between Cape Kumikahi and Kaimu-Kalapana. The beach is a broad expanse of fine black sand below the Kehena Lookout and parking area. Access is via a steep trail down the cliff face. Kehena Beach is popular with swimmers and bodysurfers. No facilities available.

KAMOAMOA BEACH

The beach fronting the Kamoamoa Campground inside Hawai'i Volcanoes National Park bondary is a newly created beach. Previously this stretch of coastline was rugged lava rock. The recent volcanic eruptions and lava flows into the Kalapana area have created this new beach. As the lava flows entered the ocean just to the east of Kamoamoa, the sand, cinders and pumice created was deposited on this section of the coast. However, due to the usual heavy surf and currents in this area, the beach is not considered safe and suitable for swimming. Restroom facilities and picnic tables are available.

KA'U AREA

The Ka'u area is most famous for its Green Sand Beach which is quite remote, but accessible with some effort and a 4-wheel drive vehicle, or a long hot hike. Ka'u is very dry and warm with long stretches of empty countryside. The South Point area from which Green Sand Beach can be reached is an interesting historical site with old Hawaiian canoe landings and ruins in place.

PUNALU'U BEACH PARK
Located near Pahala. This is a moderately long black sand beach backed by low dunes. The bay has a small boat launching ramp. Swimmers and snorkelers will find conditions here only fair and should be cautious about venturing beyond the boat ramp due to a powerful rip current which constantly runs out to the boat channel. The current converges with an even stronger shore current outside the bay which makes it even more hazardous for swimmers. Hawaiian green sea turtles are quite numerous in this bay and easily spotted as they surface and feed close in to shore where they graze sea weed on the rocks and coral. Showers, restrooms and picnic pavilion are available.

GREEN SAND BEACH
The beach is reached via the end of South Point Road and a very rough four mile (round trip) coastal road, negotiable only by 4-wheel drive vehicle. The really adventurous can opt to hike the four miles. If you hike, just be sure you take enough water and other necessities. The beach is accessed by a steep and hazardous trail down the cliff side which has loose rocks and cinders making for slippery footing. Caution is advised. The tinted sand is loaded with green olivine crystals, a component of Hawai'i's lava. Big grains of olivine give the sand a distinctly green color and glassy luster. The beach, at the base of a huge eroding volcanic cinder cone, is exposed to the sea directly and heavy surf and storms create dangerous surf conditions. Swimming and snorkeling are advised on only the calmest of days and extreme caution is in order.

BOOKING AGENCIES
AND REPRESENTATIVES

Check with your hotel or resort activity desk, or any of the following agencies to make reservations and arrangements for a full range of ocean or water sports activities on the Kona and Kohala Coasts. They can help you arrange everything from whale watching cruises, to diving and snorkeling cruises, fishing charters, sailboat rentals, surfboard and windsurfing rentals, etc. They represent many of the individual cruise, snorkel, and dive operators and fishing charters that are listed in the following sections. Reservations can be made directly with the operators or charter boats or through any of these agencies. You will notice that the bulk of the listings in this and other ocean activities sections are in the Kona-Kohala area of the island. The Hilo area does have a couple of charter fishing boats listed but most visitor activities take place along the Kona and Kohala Coasts.

The following are sample prices for some of the various cruises and sailings available. Check the individual listings for details and call the tour operators for the most current rates. As in the rest of this book regarding costs, prices shown are the latest at publication time and are subject to change without notice.

One hour glassbottom boat cruise	- $15 per person
One hour submarine dive	- $74 per person
2 tank scuba dive cruise	- $60 and up per person
1/2 day snorkeling cruise	- $35 and up per person
1/2 day raft trip	- $50 per person
Sunset dinner boat cruise	- $45 per person
Sunset cocktail cruise	- $18 per person
Charter yacht sunset sail	- $150 for the boat
One week comprehensive scuba diving cruise aboard an exclusive yacht	- $1,895 per person.

Aloha Kai Sailing - 33 Puako Beach Drive, Kamuela, HI 96743; (808) 882-7575. This booking service can arrange customized sailing adventures on several different sailing vessels in the Kona and Kohala areas. Customized sailing adventures range from 2 hours to 2 weeks, from around the Big Island to inter-island cruises in Hawai'i. Sailings are recreational and educational focusing on oceanography, marine science, sailing, fishing and more.

Kona Charter Skippers Association, Inc. - 75-5663 Palani Road, Kailua-Kona, HI 96740; 1-800-367-8047 ext. 360, Hawai'i (808) 329-3600. This operation provides complete booking service for Kona's charter fishing fleet, recreational, snorkle-diving cruises and related water sports and activities.

Kona Coast Activities - located in the Kona Inn Shopping Village, P.O. Box 5397, Kailua-Kona, HI 96745; 1-800-367-5105, Hawai'i (808) 329-2971. Specializing in deep-sea fishing charters, snorkel and dive cruises, pleasure cruises, dinner cruises, jet-skiing, parasailing, etc.

Kona Marlin Center - 74-381 Kealakehe Parkway, Honokohau Harbor, Kailua-Kona, HI 96740; 1-800-648-7529, Hawai'i (808) 326-1177. This booking service offers charter deep-sea fishing from a fleet of over 35 boats. Watch the daily fish weigh-ins at 11:30AM and 3:30PM on the Honokohau Harbor docks from free public viewing area. Deli, gas station and general store also available.

Kona Marina Sports Activities - Kealakehe Parkway, Honokohau Harbor, Kailua-Kona, HI 96740; (808) 329-1115, FAX (808) 329-9104. This service can arrange a variety of ocean sports activities and specialize in deep-sea fishing and dive charters. They can arrange full or half day as well as share-parties.

Kona Water Sports Inc. - 75-5695G Alii Drive, Kailua-Kona, HI 96740; (808) 329-1593. This agent provides bookings for jet boats and jet skis as well as parasailing reservations. They also carry a complete line of rental and sales water sports equipment including snorkel gear, boogie boards, underwater cameras, air mattresses, inflatable kayaks and boats, and glass bottom boats.

Ocean Sports-Waikoloa - located on Anaehoomalu Beach in front of the Royal Waikoloan Hotel, P.O. Box 3291, Kohala Coast, HI 96743; U.S. 1-800-367-8088, Hawai'i (808) 885-5555. Specializing in champagne sunset sails, whale watching, scuba dives, deep-sea fishing charters, and glass bottom boat cruises. Water sports equipment rentals.

Red Sail Sports - One Waikoloa Beach, Hyatt Regency Waikoloa, Kohala Coast, HI 96743; (808) 885-2876. This general booking agency handles everything from catamaran cruises for lunch snorkel sails, sunset cocktail sails and scuba dives, to bicycle adventures and a complete line of water sports equipment and lagoon toys.

The Charter Locker - Kealakehe Parkway, Honokohau Harbor, Kailua-Kona, HI 96740; 1-800-247-1484, Hawai'i (808) 326-2553. This service specializes in fishing and boat charters, private or shared basis, full or half day.

SEA EXCURSIONS AND
GLASSBOTTOM BOAT CRUISES

The following cruises generally sail along the Kona Coast taking in historic sites, fascinating reefs for glassbottom viewing or snorkeling, historic Kealakekua Bay marine reserve and Captain Cook Monument, and the Pu'uhonua O Honaunau National Historic Park at Honaunau, the best preserved ancient Hawaiian heiau (temple) site in the islands. The cruises generally last from 2 hours to half-day and vary in cost depending on length and what is included. Check the following listings for details.

BEST BETS:

Atlantis Submarine - underwater dive/cruise
Hawaiian Cruises - half-day swim-snorkel cruise to Kealakekua Bay marine reserve

Atlantis Submarine ★ - (329-6626, FAX 808 329-3177) 75-5660 Palani Rd. Hotel King Kamehameha, Kailua-Kona, HI 96740. These unique underwater cruises operate with a $2.5 million submarine designed to take guests through Kona's fabulous underwater world of colorful reefs where you get a fish's-eye view of marine life, down to depths of 150 ft. Daily morning and afternoon hourly departures are from Kailua Pier. There are also special twice weekly evening cruises in peak season periods. Adults $74, children under 12, $45.

Captain Bob's Kona Reef Tours - (322-3102) P.O. Box 2016, Kailua-Kona, HI 96745. This service offers glassbottom boat cruises over two miles of Kona Coast reefs. This is Kona's original glassbottom cruise since 1968. Departures are daily from Kailua Pier at 9:30 and 11AM, 1 and 2:30PM. Adults $15, children $7.50.

Captain Zodiac - (329-3199, FAX 329-7590) P.O.Box 5612, Honokohau Harbor, Kealakehe Parkway, Kailua-Kona, HI 96740. Daily expeditions in motorized inflatable rubber white-water rafts along the Kona Coast which take in sea caves, old Hawaiian village sites, and snorkeling in Kealakekua Bay marine reserve on a 4 hour cruise. Snorkel equipment and tropical lunch included. Departures at 8AM and 1PM. Adults $57, children under-12 $47.

Nautilus II - (1-800-821-2210, 808/326-2003 or 329-3390) c/o Kona Coast Activities, P.O. Box 5397, Kailua-Kona, HI 96745. This is Hawai'i's newest undersea adventure cruise using a 58-foot 34-passenger semi-submersible craft which cruises Kona's coral reefs. The spacious air-conditioned cabin has large windows for underwater reef and fish viewing as well as topside platform viewing. One-hour tour cruises depart from Kailua Pier. Tour rates are $30 for adults, $20 for children under 12.

Royal Hawaiian Cruises ★ - (329-6411/326-2999) 74-5606 Pawai Place #101, Kailua-Kona, HI 96740. Captain Cook VIII glassbottom boat cruise has twice daily departures from Kailua Pier, 8:30AM - 1PM, 1:30 - 5:30PM. Half-day cruise along the Kona Coast includes swimming and snorkeling at the Kealakekua Bay marine reserve, glassbottom viewing of reefs and fish, live Hawaiian entertainment, and continental breakfast/lunch or afternoon snack/dinner. Adults $49, children under 12 $24.50.

HUMUHUMUNUKUNUKUAPUA'A

Whale Watch - (322-0028) P.O.Box 139, Holualoa, HI 96725. Operated by long-time Kona marine biologist and whale researcher, Captain Dan McSweeney, Whale Watch guarantees a whale sighting. The cruises use 36' and 32' U.S. Coast Guard approved vessels, fully equipped with underwater window for viewing the whales. Three hour cruises depart daily at 9AM and 1PM from Honokohau Harbor just north of Kailua-Kona. Adults $39.50, children under 12 $29.50.

SNORKELING AND DIVING CRUISES

Several of the cruise operators listed in the previous section are briefly cross-listed here as they also offer snorkeling and/or diving cruises often combined with their general sight-seeing pleasure cruises. Specific information is listed in the previous section for each operator and further information and reservations can be obtained by calling the numbers listed. Other cruise operators cater to snorkelers or scuba divers exclusively and these are detailed here.

BEST BETS: **Fair Wind** - daily scuba and snorkeling cruises depart from Keauhou Bay pier, **Jack's Diving Locker** - operates special scuba charters, **Dive Makai Charters** - scuba dives at the Kona Coast's best dive locations.

Body Glove Cruises - (326-7122) P.O.Box 4523, Kailua-Kona, HI 96745. This 55' trimaran offers a 4 1/2 hour daily morning sail and snorkel, snuba, scuba cruise along the Kona Coast departing from Kailua Pier at 9AM. Continental breakfast and deli lunch included. Snorkel-diving adventure includes rich marine life, caves, arches and dolphins, manta rays and turtles. Adults $49, children $24.

Charisma Hawai'i - (325-6676) P.O.Box 3101, Kailua-Kona, HI 96745. Offers a full range of diving and snorkeling cruises and equipment rentals.

Discovery Charters - (325-7400) 73-1241 Melomelo St., Kailua-Kona, HI 96740. This is a luxury 50-yacht offering private, personal, upscale snorkeling and sailing adventures. Towels, snorkel gear, flotation equipment and kayak provided. Light snacks, beer, soft drinks included; full meals catered separately. Private boat charter rates: Half-day, $375; Full-day, $575; Two-hour sunset cruise, $275; overnight cruise, $1,250.

Dive Makai Charters - (329-2025) 74-5590I Alapa, Kailua-Kona, HI 96740. This charter shop offers a full range of dive tours and charters.

Diver One - (329-8802) 75-5614 Palani Rd., Kailua-Kona, HI 96740. This charter offers complete diving services and a full line of tours and dive charters.

Fair Wind ★ - (322-2788 or 329-2971) 78-7128 Kaleopapa Rd., Keauhou Bay, Kona, HI 96740. This sailing catamaran offers two daily snorkel and scuba diving cruises with all snorkeling gear included. The morning luncheon sail departs at 8:30AM and returns at 1PM. Adults $40, children under 12 $25, includes BBQ lunch. The afternoon cruise departs at 1PM and returns at 4:30PM, includes all gear and beverage/snack. Adults $29, children under 12 $17. Both cruises charge extra for scuba diving tanks and gear. They also offer a special Sunset Cocktail Cruise on Thursdays only departing at 6PM for an hour's cruise to enjoy cocktails and Hawaiian music for $18 per person. Cruises depart from Keauhou Bay pier.

Hapuna Beach Services - (882-1095) located at Hapuna Beach State Park, Kohala Coast. This beach concession has water sports and beach equipment rentals and also rents A-frame cabins nearby the beach (reservations required).

Jack's Diving Locker ★ - (329-7585 or 1-800-345-4807) 75-5819 Alii Drive, Coconut Grove Marketplace, Kailua-Kona, HI 96740. This dive operator offers special scuba diving charters, night dives, instruction and certification, and complete diving equipment sales and rentals. Dive rates begin at $45 per person.

Kamanu - (329-2021) 74-5588 Pawai Place, Kailua-Kona, HI 96740. This is a 36 ft. catamaran offering daily snorkeling cruises along the Kona Coast. Each 3 1/4 hour cruise includes 1 1/2 hours of snorkeling time plus all gear, instruction, drinks and tropical lunch. Good for beginning snorkelers, novices or experts. Hand feed colorful fish at Pawai Bay. Cruises depart daily from Honokohau Harbor at 9AM and 1:30PM. Adults $35, children under 12, $19.

Kona Aggressor - (329-8182) P.O. Box 2097, Kailua-Kona, HI 96740. This dive operation features one week trips with unlimited diving. Guests live aboard a 110 ft. luxurious full service diving yacht. There are private staterooms with bath, a 24-hour open galley, an onboard photo processing lab, and a sundeck with large jacuzzi. This is the ultimate in diving luxury. The boat can accommodate up to 20 people. The cost is $1895 per person for 6 1/2 days of cruising and diving, including all meals and bar beverages. Cruises depart Kailua Pier each Saturday.

Kona Dolphin - (329-2177) This sailing catamaran offers a daily 5 1/2 hour snorkel and scubair adventure to Kealakekua Bay on the Kona Coast. Includes all snorkel gear, continental breakfast, lunch, beverages, etc. Departs Kailua Pier at 8AM, returns 1:30PM. Adults $44, children under 12, $20.

Kona Water Sports Inc. - (329-1593) 75-5695G Alii Dr., Kailua-Kona, HI 96740. A complete line of water sports equipment rentals-sales, including snorkeling gear, boogie boards, underwater cameras, kayaks and boats, and glass bottom boats.

Miller's Snorkeling & Beach Rentals - Kahalu'u Beach Park, Keauhou-Kona. This shop is 5 miles south of Kailua-Kona on Alii Drive next to the Keauhou Beach Hotel. Kahalu'u Bay is the best snorkeling spot on the Kona Coast. The tropical fish are so plentiful and friendly you can actually feed them by hand. All beach and snorkeling equipment is available for rental.

Party Boat - (329-2177) 75-5699 Alii Dr., Kailua-Kona, HI 96740. This 46'sailing catamaran offers snorkeling cruises along the Kona Coast; includes narration of Kona Coast, continental breakfast, full BBQ lunch, full bar service, snorkeling gear and instruction, snorkeling at Kealakekua Bay Marine Reserve. Daily cruises depart 8AM from Kailua Peir, returns 1:30PM; adults $44, children (4-12) $20.

Sea Breeze Cruises - (325-6608) P.O.Box 37, Kailua-Kona, HI 96745 Is a 42 ft. catamaran offering daily cruises departing the Kailua Pier at 9 and 11:30AM and 2PM. This cruise features snorkeling along the Kona Coast and is fully equipped even for non-swimming beginners. Each cruise includes 1 1/2 hours of snorkeling, complete with instruction, guides, and equipment. Just bring a towel and sunscreen. Complimentary drinks and snacks. Adults $18, children under 12 $10.

Sea Quest - (322-3669) P.O.Box 390292, Kailua-Kona, HI 96739. This operator offers snorkeling cruises with inflatable boats taking in the remote areas between Keauhou Bay and Honaunau. The cruises take in sea caves, lava tubes, Captain Cook's Mounument at Kealakekua Bay and the Pu'uhonua O Honaunau National Historic Park at Honaunau with diving time allowed. $49 per person for a four hour adventure includes snacks, beverages and snorkel gear.

Snuba - (326-7446) 76-5828 Alii Drive, Kailua-Kona, HI 96740. This operator offers various snuba diving adventures and can book snorkel dives with other cruise boats in Kona. Snuba dives begin at $49 per person.

DIVE SHOPS

AAA Dive-Kona - (329-8802) 75-5614 Palani Road, Kailua-Kona, HI 96740. This shop offers a full range of dive cruises, charters and equipment rentals; emphasizes affordable aquatic activity.

Big Island Divers - (329-6068) Kealakehe Parkway, Gentry's Kona Marina, Honokohau Harbor, Kailua-Kona, HI 96740. Complete charter packages, introductory lessons, sales and rentals of equipment and certifications available. Open daily 8AM - 6PM.

Dive Makai Charters - (329-2025) 74-5590 I Alapa Road, Kailua-Kona, HI 96740. Personalized diving cruises and personal service are the emphasis of this dive shop. Complete dive packages and equipment rentals are available.

Ecoscapes - (329-7116) 75-5626 Kuakini Highway, Kamehameha Square Center, Kailua-Kona, HI 96740. This operator offers a variety of private charters for custom snorkeling and diving cruises. Rates range from snorkel dives at $50 per person and two-tank scuba dives at $100 per person. Open Mon-Thurs 8AM - 6PM, Fri-Sat 8AM - 7PM and Sunday 9AM - 5PM.

Gold Coast Divers ★ - (329-1328) 75-5744 Alii Dr., Kona Inn Shopping Village, Kailua-Kona, HI 96740. This shop offers a full line of professional equipment sales-service-rentals plus personalized dive tours, boat and beach dives, and snorkeling trips. Instruction and certification available. Open daily 9AM - 9PM.

SCUBA DIVING

Jack's Diving Locker - (1-800-345-4807, 329-7585), 75-5819 Alii Drive, Coconut Grove Marketplace, Kailua-Kona, HI 96740. This operator offers a variety of scuba charters and cruise dives, certification lessons, introductory dives and equipment sales and rentals.

King Kamehameha Divers - (329-5662) 75-5660 Palani Drive, King Kamehameha Kona Beach Hotel, Kailua-Kona, HI 96740. This shop offers scuba and snorkel charters, instruction, sales and rentals of equipment, underwater video and camera services, etc. Open Monday - Saturday 7AM - 7PM, Sunday 7AM - 5PM.

Kohala Divers Ltd. ★ - (882-7774) Kawaihae Shopping Center, Kawaihae, Kohala Coast, HI 96743. Offers a full range of professional diving services, equipment sales-rentals, and dive charters along the Kohala Coast. Open daily 8AM - 5PM.

Kona Coast Divers ★ - (329-8802) 75-5614 Palani Road, Kailua-Kona, HI 96740. They offer diving charters and a full range of sales-service-rentals on professional diving equipment. Open daily 7AM - 6PM.

Kona Kai Diving - (329-0695) P.O.Box 4178, Kailua-Kona, HI 96745. This dive operator caters to small groups with full day cruise-dives 9AM - 2:30PM on the Kona Coast. Tanks and gear available for rent.

Live Dive Hawai'i Inc. - (329-8182) P.O.Box 2097, Kailua-Kona, HI 96745. This operator offers varied diving/snorkeling cruises along the Kona Coast.

Mauna Kea Divers - (882-7730) Mauna Kea Beach Hotel, One Mauna Kea Beach Drive, Kohala Coast, HI 96743. Complete diving packages, charters and equipment rentals are available.

Nautilus Dive Center Inc. - (935-6939) 382 Kamehameha Ave., Hilo, HI 96720. This shop features complete sales-service-rentals of professional diving equipment. They also provide instruction and have a five day certification program. Scuba charters along the East Hawai'i coast are available. Open daily 9AM - 4PM.

Ocean Sports Hawai'i - (885-5555) Royal Waikoloan Hotel, Waikoloa Resort, HI 96743. Located at Anaeho'omalu Beach in front of the Royal Waikoloan Hotel, Kohala Coast. This outfitter can arrange scuba and snorkeling dives and a whole range of water sports activities.

Sandwich Isle Divers - (329-9188) 75-5729 I Alii Drive, Kailua-Kona, HI 96740, in the Kona Marketplace. This shop provides small charters with a personal touch offering daily trips along the Kona Coast. Open daily 8AM - 8PM.

Scubair of Hawai'i - (322-6665) 79-7360 Mamalahoa Highway, #4, Kailua-Kona, HI 96740. This scuba diving service offers daily four hour swimming and diving outings departing at 10AM for the Big Island's best sandy beaches. Uses "Scubair" devices and equipment rather than traditional tanks. Great for novice divers and easier than snorkeling. $45 per person for four hour outing.

Sea Dreams Hawai'i - (329-8744) P.O. Box 4886, Kailua-Kona, HI 96740. This shop can arrange complete scuba dive charters for the Kona Coast area.

Sea Paradise Scuba - (1-800-322-5662, in Hawai'i 322-2500) 78-7128 Kaleopapa Road, Kailua-Kona, HI 96740. This shop offers a full range of morning, afternoon and night dives as well as beginner "Try Scuba" dives and snorkeling outings on dive cruises. A complete line of equipment rentals is available. Cruises depart from Keauhou Bay dock.

Snorkel Bob's - (329-0770) Alii Drive, Kailua-Kona, HI 96740. This shop, adjacent to the Hilton Hotel and Huggo's Restaurant, will rent a complete snorkel set for $15 a week or by the day. Complete snorkeling equipment available, including mask, fins, sterilized snorkel, underwater cameras and boogie boards.

The Ocean Scene - (329-3666) 75-5853C Alii Drive, Kailua-Kona, HI 96740. This is not a dive shop but they do rent all manner of snorkeling gear and water sports equipment plus boogie boards.

DEEP SEA FISHING

There are few places in the world that can match the renown or reputation of the Kona Coast for the thrill and excitement of big game fishing. Kona is the site for the annual Hawaiian International Billfish Tournament which for the past 30 years or so has attracted participants from around the world. In addition, there are numerous other fishing tournaments held throughout the year. Kona and its harbors homeport a large fleet of charter fishing boats that offer a complete range of full and half-day arrangements. Prices vary depending upon the size of the boat and how it is equipped (showers, beds, fully-stocked galley, etc.). Full day charters can range from $240-450 and half-day charters can range from $175-225. These prices are for the entire boat, not a per person rate. You can private charter the entire boat or share charter with other anglers. Most boats take no more than 6 anglers at a time and provide all fishing equipment. No license is required in Hawai'i. Generally you must bring your own food and beverages as these are not included in charter rates.

Because of Hawai'i's generally low charter boat rates in comparison to other areas, the general policy among charter boat associations is that any fish caught belong to the boat rather than the fisherman. Boat captains and owners use fish caught to sell on the market to augment their low charter fares. This is the reason for the policy. However, if a fisherman really wants his catch, or part of it, he must request it from the captain. In the case of good table fish such as mahimahi or ahi tuna, most captains will be more than happy to share the catch with the fishing party to enjoy a fresh fish dinner. However, it is always best to inquire beforehand and put in a request to keep some of the catch.

And so what can you expect to catch, with a little traditional fishing luck? Kona's waters teem with a variety of Hawaiian game fish. Perhaps most popular is the Pacific Blue Marlin with an average size of 300-400 lbs., but with fish up to 1000 lbs. entirely possible. Striped marlin average 50-100 lbs. and black marlin average 200 lbs. Sailfish are also common in Kona's waters and average 50 lbs. or less. Swordfish are generally more difficult to catch but average 250 lbs. when they are landed. The popular yellowfin tuna ranges up to 300 lbs. while the dolphin (mahimahi) averages 25 lbs.

CHARTERING A BOAT: If you're familiar with deep sea fishing and boat chartering, you may contact any of the following boats directly. However, if you are unsure of just what chartering a boat entails, you would be best advised to contact one of the Booking Agencies/Representatives listed earlier in this section. Some of these agencies represent several boats and can give you complete information on booking a charter. These agencies include:

Fishing Island - (326-1491) 76-6262 Koko Olua Place, Kailua-Kona, HI 96740. This charter operator provides guests a unique fishing experience, taking them out 3 miles to their fishing platform which attracts fish. With fish congregating below the platform, guests have a good chance of hooking up with ono, mahimahi, ahi, aku and even marlin. A 5 hour fishing excursion with lunch and bar beverages and one set of tackle is $49.95 per person.

Kona Activities Center - (1-800-367-5288 or 808/329-3171, 329-3173) P.O.Box 1035, Kailua-Kona, HI 96745

Kona Marlin Center - (1-800-648-7529 or 808/326/7529, 329-7529) 74-381 Kealakehe Parkway, Honokohau Harbor, Kailua-Kona, HI 96740

Kona Charter Skippers Association - (329-3600) 75-5663 Palani Road, Kailua-Kona, HI 96740

Kona Coast Activities - (329-2971) 75-5744 Alii Drive, Kona Inn Shopping Village, Kailua-Kona, HI 96740

Kona Marina Sports Activities - (329-1115) Kealakehe Parkway, Honokohau Harbor, Kailua-Kona, HI 96740

The Charter Locker Activities - (326-2553) Kealakehe Parkway, Honokohau Harbor, Kailua-Kona, HI 96740

All charter fishing boats are completely certified and licensed. In addition to being licensing as commercial fishing boats, the captain(s) and boat must be fully certified and licensed by the United States Coast Guard.

A Black Bart - 42' Merritt, Capt. Bart Miller, Holualoa, Kona, HI 96725
(808) 329-3000

Adobie - 29' Topaz, Ron Platt, P.O. Box Y, Kailua-Kona, HI 96745
(808) 329-5669

Aerial - 38' Bertram, Capt. Rick Rose, P.O. Box 4059, Kailua-Kona, HI 96745,
(808) 329-5603

Alibi - 35' Bertram, Capt. Butch Kelley, 73-1251 Lihau, Kailua-Kona, HI 96740,
(808) 325-7755

Anxious - 31' Bertram, Capt. Ed Issacs, P.O.Box 2765, Kailua-Kona, HI 96745,
(808) 326-1229.

Bill Buster - 36' Trojan Sportfisher, Capt. Butch Lo Sasso, P.O.Box 4235, Kailua-Kona, HI 96745; (808) 329-2657, 326-8272 or FAX (808) 322-3394.

Billfisher II - 45' Sportfisher, Capt. Gary Testa, P.O. Box 5533, Kailua-Kona, HI 96745, (808) 329-1973, 326-1716

Blue Hawai'i - 53' Hatteras, Capt. Del Cannon, 78-6645 Alii Drive, Kailua-Kona, HI 96740, (808) 322-3210

Cheers - 30' Glas-Ply, Capt. Lowell Tepper, 75-6509 Sea View Circle, Kailua-Kona, HI 96740, (808) 329-6484

Cherry Pit - 30' Custom, Capt. Jim Cherry, P.O.Box 278, Kailua-Kona, HI 96745, (808) 326-7781

Chiripa - 36' Hatteras, Capt. Forrest Dowty, 73-4338 Koikoi Street, Kailua-Kona, HI 96740, (808) 325-5182

Da Warrior - 31' Bertram, Capt. Jimmy Berzanskis, 75-5744 Alii Drive, Kailua-Kona, HI 96740, (808) 326-1414

Finesse - 25' Cabo, Capt. John Tanaka, 73-4202 Eluna Street, Kailua-Kona, HI 96740, (808) 325-6406

Foxy Lady - 42' Uniflite, Capt. Bobby Erickson, P.O. Box 762 Kalaoa, Kailua-Kona, HI 96745, (808) 325-5552

Grand Slam - 46' Hatteras, Capt. Terry Dahl, P.O.Box 2089, Kailua-Kona, HI 96745, (808) 329-5536

Hanamana - 38' Custom, Capt. Chip Fischer, P.O.Box 4239, Kailua-Kona, HI 96745, (808) 326-2398

Happy Times - 41' Concorde, Capt. Tom Armstrong, P.O. Box P, Kailua-Kona, HI 96745, (808) 325-6171 or boat (808) 936-4177

HILO FISHING FLEET

High Flier - 31' Bertram, Capt. Tioni Judd, P.O.Box 566, Kailua-Kona, HI 96745, (808) 329-3453

Holiday - 44' Custom, Capt. Doug Pattengill, P.O. Box 1964, Kailua-Kona, HI 96745, (808) 325-5230 or boat (808) 329-3050

Howdy-Do - 28' Tollycraft, Capt. Mike Stanford, P.O. Box 4532, Kailua-Kona, HI 96745, (808) 325-6616

Hua Pala - 35' Uniflite, Capt. Larry Pries, 73-1089 Ahulani Street, Kailua-Kona, HI 96740, (808) 325-3277 or 325-7595

Humdinger - 37' Rybovich, Capt. Jeff Fay, P.O.Box 1995, Kailua-Kona, HI 96745 (808) 329-3823

Hustler - 32' Blackfin, Capt. Glen Hodson, P.O. Box 4976, Kailua-Kona, HI 96745, (808) 329-6303

Ihu Nui - 35' Bertram, Capt. Freddy Rice, P.O. Box 98, Kamuela, HI 96743, (808) 885-4686

Illusion - 39' Topaz, Capt. Juan Waroquiers, P.O. Box 1816, Kamuela, HI 96743 1-800-482-FISH or (808) 880-1080, boat (808) 327-8157, FAX (808) 880-1019

Island Girl - 33' Bertram, Capt. John Llanes, P.O. Box 732, Kailua-Kona, HI 96745, (808) 322-6605

Janet B - 35' Luger, Capt. Mitch Stauffer, P.O.Box 5432, Kailua-Kona, HI 96745, 1-800-658-8624, or (808) 325-6374, FAX (602) 894-2993

Kona Lure - 40' Egg Harbor, Capt. Jimmy Berzanskis, 73-5563 Olowalu Bay 18, Kailua-Kona, HI 96740, (808) 329-5646

Kona Rainbow - 35' Bertram, Capt. Mickey Ventrella, 78-6800 Alii Drive, Kailua-Kona, HI 96740, (808) 322-0084

Lady Dee - 47' Bertram, 78-6626 Alii Drive, Kailua-Kona, HI 96740 (808) 322-8026

Layla- 31' Innovator, Capt. Bruce Evans, 75-411 Hoene St., Kailua-Kona, HI 96740 (808) 329-6899/329-3398

Lil' Hooker - Capt. Jeff Parish, 75-327 Aloha Kona Drive, Kailua-Kona, HI 96740, (808) 326-1666

Maka Iwa - 40' Uniflite, Capt. Jimmy Berzanskis, 75-5744 Alii Drive, Kailua-Kona, HI 96740, (808) 326-1414

Marlin Magic - 43' Custom, Capt. Marlin Parker, Kaloko, Kona, HI, (808) 325-7138

Medusa - 38' Ocean Yacht, Capt. Steve Kaiser, 75-5660 Palani Road, SUite P-1, Kailua-Kona, HI 96740, 1-800-367-8047 ext. 458 or (808) 329-1328

Nauti Gal - 28' Tollycraft, Capt. Leonard Jose, P.O. Box 175, Holualoa, HI 96725, (808) 324-1117

No Problem - 54' Bertram, Capt. Bobby Brown, Kailua-Kona, HI, (808) 329-4004

Northern Lights - 37' Merritt, Capt. Kelley Everette, P.O. Box 2098, Kailua-Kona, HI 96745, (808) 325-6522

Omega - 28' Omega, Capt. Klaus Kropp, P.O. Box 5323, Kailua-Kona, HI 96745, (808) 325-7859 or 325-7593

Pacific Blue - 41' Hatteras, Capt. Bill Casey, 74-5071 Kumakani, Hailua-Kona, HI 96740, (808) 329-9468

Pajack - 38' Uniflite, Capt. Jeff Metzler, P.O. Box 5567, Kailua-Kona, HI 96745, (808) 329-3861

Pamela - 38' Bertram, Capt. Peter Hoogs, P.O. Box 345, Kailua-Kona, HI 96745, (808) 329-1525

Prime Time - 40' Uniflite, Capt. Chris Armstrong, P.O. Box P, Kailua-Kona, HI 96745, (808) 325-6171 or boat (808) 936-4177

Puka Kai - 35' Concorde, Capt. Dick Rogers, 73-1295 Kaiminani Drive, Kailua-Kona, HI 96740, (808) 325-7655

Red Wave - 28' Tollycraft, Capt. Keith Matuse, P.O. Box 4736, Kailua-Kona, HI 96745, (808) 329-4056

Reel Affair - 35' Bertram, Capt. John Jordan, P.O. Box 2728, Kailua-Kona, HI 96745, (808) 325-3282

Renegade - 38' Hatteras, Capt. Bobby Brown, P.O. Box 422, Kailua-Kona, HI 96745, (808) 329-4004

Sea Baby III - 35' Sportfisher, Capt. W. Kobayashi, 76-6265 Alii Drive, Kailua-Kona, HI 96745, (808) 329-5396

Sea Genie - 36' Harris, Capt. Gene Vander Hoek P.O.Box 4126, Kailua-Kona, HI 96745, (808) 329-7287 or 322-0052, FAX (808) 322-8163

Sea Wife - 42' Sportfisher, Capt. Tim Cox, P.O. Box 2645, Kailua-Kona, HI 96745, (808) 329-1806

Shaka - 40' Trojan Sportfisher, Capt. Rick Rose, P.O.Box 4059, Kailua-Kona, HI 96745, (808) 329-5603

Sheer Pleasure - 38' Custom, Capt. Robert Hudson, 73-4185 Holu, Kailua-Kona, HI 96740, (808) 325-6421, boat (808) 987-8170

Show Time - 44' Ocean Yacht, Capt. K.Y. Rogers, P.O. Box 5382, Kailua-Kona, HI 96745, (808) 326-7469 or FAX (808) 326-2561.

Stars & Strikes - 33' Bayliner, Capt. Dan Harrigan, 73-1260 Kukuna Street, Kailua-Kona, HI 96740, (808) 325-6357 or 325-3277

Summer Rain - 34' Aluminum Sportfisher, Capt. Jack Prettyman, Kealakehe Parkway, Honokohau Boat Harbor, Kailua-Kona, HI 96740, (808) 325-7558.

Sundowner - 31' Bertram, Capt. Norm Isaacs, P.O. Box 5198, Kailua-Kona, HI 96745, (808) 329-7253

Ten J's - 33' Egg Harbor, Capt. Jimmy Berzanskis, 75-5744 Alii Drive, Kailua-Kona, HI 96740, (808) 326-1414

Tightlines - 25' Aquasport, Capt. Del Dykes, P.O.Box 5619, Kailua-Kona, HI 96745, (808) 326-1122

Tropical Sun - 36' Topaz, Capt. John Kuhn, 75-378 Aloha Kona Drive, Kailua-Kona, HI 96745, (808) 326-4703 or 322-7115

Vision's - 28' Blue Fin, Capt. George Dreger, P.O.Box 2984, Kailua-Kona, HI 96745, (808) 322-2863 or boat (808) 936-4264

Wild West - 44' Pacifica, Capt. Robert West, 74-381A Kealakehe Parkway, Honokohau Harbor, Kailua-Kona, HI 96745, (808) 329-4700 or 322-4700

Won on One - 36' Pacifica Sportfisher, Capt. Rutledge "Ruddy" Bray P.O.Box 908, Kailua-Kona, HI 96745, (808) 326-2055 or 327-8155

WINDSURFING

WINDSURFING / JETSKIIS
PARASAILING / KAYAKS-HOBIE CATS

WINDSURFING

Windsurfing conditions and locations are best on the west side of the Big Island. The Kona and Kohala beaches generally have the most favorable wind and surf conditions for windsurfing over other areas of the Big Island.

BEST BETS: **Anaeho'omalu Beach** - Waikoloa, Kohala Coast
Hapuna Beach - Kohala Coast
Kauna'oa Beach - Kohala Coast

Activity Information Center - (329-7700) 76-5828 Alii Drive, Kailua-Kona, HI 96740

Ka'u Wind - (929-9517) Located in Naalehu, Ka'u District. Full line of windsurfing equipment, sales, rentals, service and high wind wave gear, plus a 24 hour wind line.

Kona Coast Activities - (329-2971) 75-5744 Alii Drive, Kona Inn Shopping Village, Kailua-Kona, HI 96740

Kona Water Sports Inc. - (329-1593) 75-5695G Alii Drive, Banyan Court Mall, Kailua-Kona, HI 96740.

Ocean Sports - (885-5555) Royal Waikoloan Hotel, Waikoloa Resort, Kohala Coast, HI 96743. Full line of windsurfing equipment plus instruction available.

JET SKIING

Jet skiing is centered in Kona on Kailua Bay and up and down nearby areas of the Kona Coast. Rates average $25 per half hour/$50 per full hour. Restrictions apply; consult booking agencies below.

Activity Information Center - (329-7700) 76-5828 Alii Drive, Kailua-Kona, HI 96740

Kawaihae Water Sports - (329-9445) In Kona Square Shopping Center, Alii Drive, across from Kailua Pier, Kailua-Kona

Kona Coast Activities - (329-2971) 75-5744 Alii Drive, Kona Inn Shopping Village, Kailua-Kona, HI 96740

Kona Water Sports Inc. - (329-1593) 75-5695G Alii Drive, Banyan Court Mall, Kailua-Kona, HI 96740

PARASAILING

Parasailing is done on the relatively calm waters of Kailua Bay and along nearby areas of the Kona Coast.

Activity Information Center - (329-7700) 76-5828 Alii Drive, Kailua-Kona, HI 96740

Kona Skyrider - (329-1007) 75-5669K Alii Drive, Kailua-Kona, HI 96740 Parasail adventures are $35-40 per person.

Kona Coast Activities - (329-2971) 75-5744 Alii Drive, Kona Inn Shopping Village, Kailua-Kona, HI 96740

Kona Water Sports Inc. - (329-1593) 76-5695G Alii Drive, Banyan Court Mall, Kailua-Kona. HI 96740

KAYAKING - HOBIE CATS

Kayaking and Hobie Cat sailing are popular resort activities. The best places are the Kohala Coast resorts and beaches. The hotel activity desks and beach concessions can help make arrangements. Individual raft-floats with glass viewing panels can also be used to float over areas where fish and marine life can be observed.

Activity Information Center - (329-7700) 76-5828 Alii Drive, Kailua-Kona, HI 96740

Kona Coast Activities - (329-2971) 75-5744 Alii Drive, Kona Inn Shopping Village, Kailua-Kona, HI 96740

Kona Water Sports Inc. - (329-1593) 76-5695G Alii Drive, Banyan Court Mall, Kailua-Kona, HI 96740

Ocean Sports - (885-5555) Royal Waikoloan Hotel, Waikoloa Resort, Kohala Coast, HI 96743. A full line of kayaks, hobie cats for sailing, and other water sports equipment are available for rental.

SEA KAYAKING

LAND ACTIVITIES

LAND TOURS

The tour operators in this section offer a range of tours through some of the Big Island's most spectacular, historic and culturally unique attractions. The itineraries vary as do the costs. If you are considering a circle island tour such as that offered by Polynesian Adventure Tours, you should compare the cost of $50-60 per person with the cost of renting your own car which would be considerably less. Having your own car would mean greater mobility and independence and perhaps even more comfort in addition to the savings realized. A circle island tour can be somewhat tiring since it is a distance of about 260 miles and would require a full-day (8-10 hours) allowing time for scenic stops and lunch along the way. A mini-van or bus coach tour is a comfortable way to see the Big Island since you "leave the driving to us." Generally, such tours include narration on the scenic and historic attractions taken in on the tour. A rental car on the other hand can be equally comfortable since you don't have others around and you are on your own. And with a good tour map of the major attractions, you can get by without the narration and find your own way around. My personal recommendation is to rent a car and experience the Big Island at your own pace. You can't get lost as there is essentially only one road all the way around the island. And there is lots to explore and experience at your leisure.

In addition to regular land tours, this section lists some unique tours to places like Waipio Valley and the summit of Mauna Kea. You'll find that these operators provide special insight on their respective attractions and areas of the Big Island.

Gray Line Hawai'i - (935-2835) 34 Wiwoole Street, Hilo, HI 96720 or (329-9337) Kona. They offer a variety of Hilo area, Kona-Kohala area, and around-the-island bus-coach tours.

Hawai'i Resorts Transportation Company - (885-7484) P.O.Box 183, Honoka'a, HI 96727. They run a variety of tours around the Big Island including Waipi'o Valley on horseback, Waipi'o Valley Van tours, and Mauna Kea Summit tours.

Jack's Tours ★ - (961-6666) 226 Kanoelehua, Hilo, HI 96720 and (329-2555) 73-4770 Kanalani, Kailua-Kona, HI 96740. They provide a variety of Hilo, Kona, Kohala and circle-island bus-coach tours.

Paradise Safaris - (322-2366) P.O.Box A-D, Kailua-Kona, HI 96745. This operator specializes in evening-sunset 4-wheel drive vehicle tours to the summit of 13,796 ft. Mauna Kea and the telescope observatory complex. Hotel pick-ups in Kona and Kohala are provided for the daily tour departure at 3PM, returning about 10:30PM. Tour rates are $95-100 per person.

Polynesian Adventure Tours - (329-8008) 74-5596 Pawai Place, Kailua-Kona, HI 96740. This operator specializes in deluxe "Grand Circle Island Tour", a complete 260 mile ten hour drive around the island. All the major sites and attractions are included. Daily departures in spacious, deluxe "big window" mini-coaches are 8-8:30AM from Kona with return at 6-6:30PM. Tour price from Kailua-Kona area, adults $52.50, children under 12, $46; from Waikoloa Resort area, adults $55, children under 12, $48; from Mauna Lani and Mauna Kea Resorts, adults $60, children under 12, $53.

Robert's Hawai'i Inc. ★ - (935-2858) Hilo International Airport, Hilo, HI 96720 and (329-1688) Keahole Airport, Kailua-Kona, HI 96740. They offer a variety of Hilo and Kona-Kohala area and circle-island bus-coach tours.

Russ Apple Tour Tapes - (967-7375) P.O. Box 47, Hawai'i Volcanoes National Park, Volcano, HI 96718. This is not a tour company as such but rather a service providing narrated cassette tapes for touring some of the Big Island's more noted areas and attractions. Russ Apple, Ph.D., is a retired national park service employee and noted historian, lecturer, and columnist for the local newspaper. The excellent set of tapes he has produced add greatly to understanding and experiencing Hawai'i's unique natural history, flora and fauna, geology, geography, culture and color, in addition to being an excellent self-drive narration to highlight one's own tour. The three tapes on the Hilo to Volcano route, the national park Crater Rim Drive, and the drive to Waha'ula Visitors Center and Heiau in the national park are available individually or as a set. The tapes are available in Hilo at the Lyman House Museum, the Hawai'i Naniloa Hotel, or the Hilo Hawaiian Hotel; in the national park at the Volcano Art Center and Kilauea Military Camp; and in Kona through Kona Charter Skippers Association on a rental or sale basis. Tape players are available for rent at $7, tapes are rented at $3 each. Tapes can also be purchased for $10 each or $25 per set. Mail orders are accepted.

SpeediShuttle - (329-5433) Kailua-Kona, HI 96740. This operator offers airport shuttle service as well as tours to Kona area attractions. Daily tours include sightseeing through Kona coffee country to Kealakekua Bay and National Marine Sanctuary and time to enjoy the beach or driving the Kohala Coast to enjoy beautiful whitesand Hapuna Beach. Tours range from $25-35 per person depending on location pickup and dropoff.

Waipi'o Valley Shuttle - (775-7121) P.O.Box 5128, Kukuihaele, HI 96727. They specialize in comprehensive 4-wheel drive tours of the lush Waipi'o Valley and its history, culture, and use, adults $25, children under 12, $12.50. Also a tour to the summit of Mauna Kea and the telescope complex, flat rate of $75 per person.

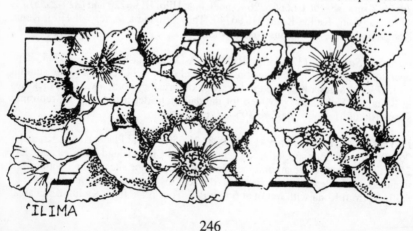

'ILIMA

Waipio'o Valley Wagon Tours - (775-9518) P.O.Box 1340, Honoka'a, HI 96727. This operator offers one and a half hour historic Waipi'o Valley tours with mule drawn open-carriage wagons. Cross streams and get close-up looks at Hawai'i's lush tropical rainforest and taro fields. This is an excellent chance for photographers to capture some of Hawai'i's lush tropical beauty on film. Adults $38, children under 12, $22.

BOOKING AGENTS/REPRESENTATIVES
The following agents and representatives can book various land tours and activities as well as ocean-related activities, cruises, and the like. They would be a good source of additional information on tours or activities in a given area of the Big Island.

Activity Information Center - 76-5828 Alii Drive, Kailua-Kona, HI 96740
 (808) 329-7700
Island Resort Activity Desk - 75-5663A Palani Road, Kailua-Kona, HI 96740
 (808) 329-1187
Kohala Coast Activities & Tours Center - Waikoloa Resort, Kohala Coast, HI
 96743, (808) 885-5532
Kona Coast Activities - 75-5744 Alii Drive, Kona Inn Shopping Center, Kailua-
 Kona, HI 96740, (808) 329-2971

BICYCLE TOURS

The Big Island offers some of the most varied scenery anywhere in the Hawaiian Islands. It also has some of the largest expanses and stretches of wide-open uninhabited country in the islands. The geography ranges from desert beaches, to tropical rain forests, to lush sugar fields and dry lava deserts. An excellent way to see and experience the changing scenes is by bicycle touring.

Many visitors to the Big Island bring their own bicycles and camping equipment with them and make up their own itinerary. The Big Island's highway system is generally good to excellent in most areas but often the shoulders are unimproved. Bikers need to exercise caution on the open road especially in narrow winding sections of highway. If you are an adventurous bicyclist, you may want to plan your own tour of the island. Just keep in mind the long distances between towns in some areas like the Ka'u, South Kona, and Kohala Coast areas and plan accordingly for water, food, lodging, etc. If you want to opt for an organized commercial bicycle tour you might try the following operator.

Island Bicycle Adventures - P.O.Box 458, Volcano, HI 96785, 1-800-233-2226, (808) 967-8603. This operator offers unique one-of-a-kind six day bicycle tours of the Big Island. The "Hawai'i Highlights" tour begins in Hilo, takes in the stunning vistas of Hawai'i Volcanoes National Park, continues on through the Ka'u District to South Point, and finishes up in the Kailua-Kona resort area town. The comprehensive tours include all accommodations, meals, support vehicle, guides, maps and related equipment. Tour price is $860 plus $95 bicycle rental charge. Several tour dates are offered throughout the year. They also have bicycle tours on Maui and Kaua'i.

Hawaiian Pedals Bicycle Rentals - 75-5744 Alii Drive, Kona Inn Shopping Village, Kailua-Kona, HI 96740 (808) 329-2294 or 325-6416. This operation offers a full range of bike rentals. Standard bikes rent for $20 per day, discounts for longer periods. Performance bikes are $25 per day. Tandem bikes go for $35 per day. Free pickup and delivery in the Kailua-Keauhou area.

Teo's Mt. Bike Safaris - Star Route 11051, Keaau, HI 96749, (808) 966-6115, offers a full range of guided bicycle tours on the Big Island. An Olaa Rainforest tour is only $10 per person and includes bicycle, helmet and expert instruction. Other adventures include Mauna Loa or Mauna Kea down-hill rides, tropical forest rides with waterfalls and pools, ruggest coast and remote exotic beach rides and moonlight rides for both beginners and experts. All rides are off-road with no traffic or crowds, just fresh air, beautiful scenery and rewarding challenging trails. Bicycle rentals also available to independent riders. Top quality 21 speed mountain bikes and equipment are used. Free delivery to Hilo.

BICYCLES CAN ALSO BE RENTED AT:
B & L Bike & Sports - (329-3309) 74-5576B Pawai Place, Kailua-Kona, HI 96740
Ciao Activities (326-4177) 75-5663A Palani Road, Kailua-Kona, HI 96740
Dave's Bike & Triathlon Shop (329-4522) 75-5626 Kuakini Hwy., Kamehameha Square Center, Kailua-Kona, HI 96740
Teo's Mt. Bike Safaris - (966-6115) Star Route 11051, Keaau, HI 96749

GOLF

Golfers will find some extremely challenging, exciting and incredibly beautiful golf courses on the Big Island. Courses range from Hilo's fine, though somewhat damp Municipal course, to the lovely Volcano Country Club near Volcanoes National Park, and the stunning Kohala Coast resort courses, the Francis H. I'i Brown and Mauna Kea Beach links both of which are widely acclaimed and recognized.

Discovery Harbour Golf and Country Club - Located in the small town of Waiohinu, Ka'u District (929-7353). This is a very nice 18-hole course in the middle of a country residential sub-division in a remote southern coast area of the Big Island. Greens fee is $6 and cart fee $12.

Fore Golf Hawai'i - 73-1150 Oluolu Street, Kailua-Kona, HI 96740, U.S. 1-800-729-1490, Hawai'i (808) 325-6755. This golf tour operator specializes in both group and custom individual golf tour packages using several of the Big Island's best courses. Complete packages are available including inter-island airfare, hotel or condo accommodations, rental car, special luau and cocktail parties, and prearranged tee times on championship courses.

Hamakua Country Club - P.O.Box 751, Honoka'a, HI 96727, no phone, is located on Highway 19 in Honoka'a on the Hamakua Coast about 40 miles north of Hilo. It's a nine hole course laid out on very sloping terrain. Lovely views of Honoka'a and the ocean. Greens fee are $10 for all day. Entrance is easy to miss, just off the highway and next to the Union 76 gas station.

Hapuna Golf Course - at the new Hapuna Beach Prince Hotel (hotel opens in 1994), Mauna Kea Resort, contact Mauna Kea Beach Hotel Golf Course (882-7222). This new 18-hole championship Arnold Palmer designed course opened in 1992. It is nestled on the natural contours of the hilly coastlands about 700 ft. above sealevel. There are stunning views of coastline, ocean and surrounding volcanic mountains. Greens fee include carts: $50 for Mauna Kea Beach Hotel guests, $75 for non-guests.

Hilo Municipal Golf Course - 340 Haihai Street, Hilo (959-7711). This is a very nicely maintained 18-hole course operated by the County of Hawai'i. It gets a lot of use from local golfing cadres especially on weekends. During Hilo's rainy periods the fairways can get pretty water-logged. Inexpensive green fees make it a popular place. Greens fee weekdays $6, weekends $8, $12.50 per cart. A new driving range lighted for night use was completed in 1992.

Kona Country Club - 78-7000 Alii Drive, 6 miles south of Kailua-Kona in the Keauhou resort area (322-2595). Open daily, starting times required. This is actually two golf courses in one. The 18-hole Ocean Front championship course runs oceanside and in the heart of the Keauhou resort condo area. The new Alii Country Club 18-hole layout runs upslope providing spectacular ocean and coastline views. Complete pro shop with rental clubs, carts, and instruction available. The Vista Restaurant & Lounge are on premises. Greens fee for Kona Surf and Keauhou Beach Hotel guests are $67, others $97.

Mauna Kea Beach Hotel Golf Course - located at the Mauna Kea Beach Hotel, Kohala Coast (882-7222). This championship golf course has won wide acclaim for its consistent golfing excitement and challenge. *Golf Magazine* ranks it as one of "America's Top 12 Resort Courses" while *Golf Digest* ranks it among "America's 100 Greatest," "Hawai'i's Finest," and as one of "America's Top 10 in Aesthetics." Director of Golf is John "JD" Ebersberger. Call one day in advance for tee time. Greens fee for hotel guests is $75, for off property guests is $125, including shared cart.

Mauna Lani Resort Golf Course - Located at the Mauna Lani Resort, Kohala Coast (885-6655). This is a gorgeous and challenging 36-hole layout with two

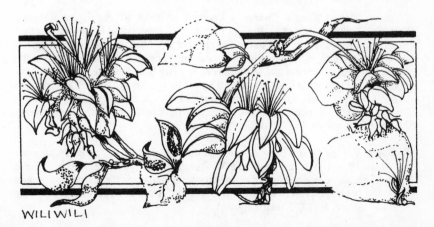

WILIWILI

separate North and South championship courses. There are several breath-taking holes and fairways carved out of raw lava rock and next to the pounding ocean surf. The links surround the Mauna Lani Bay Hotel, Ritz-Carlton Mauna Lani and condo complexes. It's the home of the PGA Senior Skins Tournament held each January and provides an incredibly beautiful golfing experience. *Golf Magazine* ranks it as one of "America's Top 12 Resort Courses." Director of Golf is Jerry Johnston. Call for tee time. Greens fee for resort guests is $65, for off property guests is $130, including cart.

Naniloa Country Club - 120 Banyan Drive, Hilo, on hotel row along Hilo Bay, (935-3000). This is a short 9-hole, par 36 course. There is a pro shop with club and cart rentals available. For the quality of the facilities and the course itself, they charge visitors an exorbitant $35 weekends and $25 weekdays to play a round. However, if you can produce a Hawai'i driver's license, you can play for $6 weekends and $5 weekdays. Otherwise, it's really not worth playing golf here. If you really want to play, you'd be better off at one of the Volcano, Kona, or Kohala courses. Even the Hilo Municipal course is a much better deal.

Sea Mountain Golf Course - At Punalu'u, in the Ka'u Dist. (928-6222). A superb 18-hole championship course in the peaceful southern coast area of the Big Island. Daily greens fee, cart included, $36 per person. New resort development plans may cause alteration of the existing course layout over the next couple of years.

Volcano Golf and Country Club - Located in Hawai'i Volcanoes National Park (967-7331). This is a lovely and lush 18-hole course set amidst the grandeur of the national park country. There is a pro shop with club and cart rental available and the Volcano Country Club Restaurant is on premises. Call for tee time. Greens fee are $18.75 weekdays, $22 weekends, including cart.

Waikoloa Beach Resort Golf Club - Located next to the Royal Waikoloan and Hyatt Regency Waikoloa Hotels at Waikoloa Resort, Kohala Coast (885-6060). An 18-hole course designed by Robert Trent Jones Jr. set amidst the dramatic contrast of black lava flows and the blue Pacific Ocean. Director of Golf is PGA pro Dennis Rose. Call for tee time. Greens fee includes cart and unlimited use of practice facilities. Off property guests $90, resort guests $55, property owners $45.

Waikoloa Resort King's Course - Located adjacent to the Hyatt Regency Waikoloa, Kohala Coast (885-4647), this par 72 championship layout was created out of barren lava desert by Tom Weiskopf and Jay Morrish and was influenced by the famous open, windswept links of Scotland. The course features some of the most intimidating bunkers and sand traps of any Big Island course. We are talking about major chasms and gorges here. The challenges to golfers are natural: the strong Waikoloa winds, lava rock formations, sand traps, bunkers and an occasional water hazard. Masochists will take special delight in this course. Greens fee are $80 for resort guests and $110 for others.

Waikoloa Village Golf Club - Located in the cool and breezy uplands between Highways 19 and 190, and above the Waikoloa resorts (883-9621). Robert Trent Jones Jr. artfully designed this fine golf course to challenge the serious golfer and please the beginner as well. Director of Golf is PGA pro Randall Carney. Call for tee time. Greens fee, $62 including cart.

TENNIS

PUBLIC COURTS

The County of Hawai'i maintains a number of tennis courts at county parks and locations around the island. Some are lighted for evening use and are basically on a first-come first-served basis. For a map detailing public tennis court locations around the island contact the Department of Parks and Recreation, County of Hawai'i, 25 Aupuni St., Hilo, HI 96720 or call (808) 935-1842. The following is a listing of tennis court facilities around the island.

Hilo: *Hoolulu Park Tennis Stadium* - (935-8213) 3 indoor lighted courts and 5 outdoor courts. Operated by County of Hawai'i. Fees for indoor courts are $2 per hour 9AM-4PM, $4 per hour 4-10PM. Reservations suggested.

South Hilo District: *Ainaola Park, Hakalau Park, Lincoln Park, Lokahi Park, Malama Park, Mohouli Park, Panaewa Park* (most of these are right in the Hilo town area)

North Hilo District: *Papaaloa Park* - in Papaaloa Village.

Hamakua District: *Honokaa Park* - in Honokaa town.

North Kohala District: *Kamehameha Park* - in Kapaau town.

South Kohala District: *Waimea Park* - in Waimea-Kamuela town.

North Kona District: *Greenwell Park* - in Captain Cook, *Higashihara Park* - in Keauhou, *Kailua Park* - at Old Kona Airport, *Kailua Playground* - on Kuakini Hwy. near town

Ka'u District: *Naalehu Park* - on the highway through Naalehu town, *Pahala School Grounds* - at the school in Pahala Village

Puna District: *Kurtistown Park* - on the hwy. in Kurtistown, *Shipman Park* - at junction of Volcano and Pahoa Highways in Keaau town

PRIVATE COURTS OPEN TO THE PUBLIC

King Kamehameha Kona Beach Resort - Kailua-Kona (329-2911), has four hard-surface courts with two lighted for night play; pro shop available. Fee is $5 per person for all day.

Holua Tennis Center - Holua at Mauna Loa Village, Keauhou-Kona (322-0091), features 14 hardsurface courts, seven lighted for night play and a stadium court; pro shop available. Fee is $8 per hour on-property guests, $10 for others.

Hyatt Regency Waikoloa Hotel - Kohala Coast (885-1234), Tennis Garden features eight hardsurface courts, two clay courts and a tournament stadium; pro shop available. Fee is $9 per hour.

Keauhou Beach Hotel - Keauhou-Kona (322-3441), has 6 hardsurface courts, 2 lighted for night play, pro shop available, $3 an hour or $5 per day per person.

Kona Hilton Beach & Tennis Resort - Kailua-Kona (329-3111), has four hardsurface courts, three lighted for night play; pro shop available. $5 per hour/$7 all day for hotel guests, $6 hour/$8 day for others.

Mauna Kea Beach Hotel - Kohala Coast (882-7222), features 13 hardsurface courts, none lighted; pro shop available. Fee is $18 per hour during hours 7-11AM, and $9 per hour during hours 11AM - 3PM.

Mauna Lani Bay Hotel & Bungalows - Kohala Coast (885-6622), features 10 hardsurface courts; pro shop available. Fee is $7 per day for resort guests.

Mauna Lani Racquet Club - Kohala Coast (885-7755), has six hardsurface courts, two grass courts and a stadium court, three courts are lighted for night play; pro shop available. Fee is $10 per day for resort guests; memberships available.

Ritz-Carlton Mauna Lani - Kohala Coast (885-2000), the Tennis Pavilion has 11 hardsurface courts, seven lighted for night play, and a stadium court; pro shop available. Fee is $6 per hour for hotel guests, $8 per hour for others.

Royal Waikoloan Hotel - Kohala Coast (885-6789), the Tennis Club has six hardsurface courts for day play only; pro shop available. No charge for court use by hotel guests; others must get a membership for which there are varied rates; call for details.

PUBLIC SWIMMING POOLS

The County of Hawai'i maintains seven free public swimming pools around the island. These facilities are generally excellent and include full programs of swimming and aquatics instruction, adult lap swimming, and open recreational swimming hours daily and weekly. For specific daily and weekly schedules of activities contact the individual pools listed.

Honokaa Swimming Pool - in Honokaa, Hamakua (775-0650)
Kawamoto Swim Stadium - in Hilo (935-8907)
Kohala Swimming Pool - in Kapaau, North Kohala (889-6933)
Kona Swimming Pool - at Konawaena High School (323-3252)
Laupahoehoe Swimming Pool - at Laupahoehoe (962-6993)
NAS Swimming Pool - which stands for Naval Air Station, is a remnant of Hilo's
    World War II military airfield, at the old Hilo Airport (935-4401).
Pahala Swimming Pool - in Pahala, Ka'u District (928-8177)

HIKING

Hawai'i Volcanoes National Park has an excellent system of hiking trails for everyone from novice casual strollers to adventurous independent backpackers. There are easy hikes of less than an hour to several hours in length to full-scale 2-3 day remote country treks. The national park is by far the best place on the island to hike and backpack over some startling, stunning and desolate country. It has the best marked and well laid-out trail system on the island.

Some of the easiest and most popular hikes in Hawai'i Volcanoes National Park are Kilauea Iki Trail and Kipuka Puaulu (Bird Park). The Kilauea Iki Trail hike is a 2 1/2 hour loop trip of 2.5 miles from Crater Rim Drive in the park down into and across the floor of the still steaming Kilauea Iki crater. One gets an incredible closeup view of Hawai'i's volcanism with lava rubble and cinder cones and the ominous steaming cracks in the crater floor.

The Kipuka Puaulu (Bird Park) hike is a 1 hour loop trip of 1.1 miles. The trail courses through a virtually unspoiled native Hawaiian forest at the cool elevation of 4100'. There are numerous examples of native Hawaiian plants and glimpses of rare and endangered Hawaiian birds. The park service maintains a nature trail with many of the plants marked and booklets available at the trailhead which explain the unique ecosystem of this plant and bird sanctuary. This is a hike well worth taking. A word of caution is in order here. When hiking the national park or anywhere on the Big Island for that matter, be sure to check first with rangers or let someone know where you are going. Some national park trails require you

RED CRESTED CARDINAL

to sign in and sign out. Also, *do not* venture out onto lava flows and fields by yourself. Old lava flows are marked by deep holes and crevasses which are extremely hazardous to hikers. The hardened crust of lava can be deceiving. What looks like a firm rigid shell can be a thin weak cover to a large hole or crevasse and there are many instances of people falling in and being lost. You could be badly injured or even lost in a remote area with little chance of rescue. Over the years, several people have died as a result of such incidents.

The Akaka Falls State Park (near Honomu Village) nature trail is a 30 minute 0.4 mile loop trip. It is a very popular and easily accessible hike. The trail winds down into the canyon where Akaka and Kahuna Falls plunge some 400+ feet. The trail meanders through lush tropical rain forest of hapu ferns, red and white ginger, banana trees, bird-of-paradise, plumeria, and giant philodendrons. Handrails aid in areas where the paved trail is quite steep and tends to be slippery when wet.

Hawaiian Walkways - P.O.Box 2193, Kamuela, HI 96743 (808) 885-7759, is the only commercial hiking tour operation on the Big Island. They offer a variety of half-day and full day hikes over the Big Island's mountains and valleys and along its shorelines. Spectacular mountain and coastline vistas, secluded beaches, upland meadows, lush tropical rain forest, hidden pools and streams, fishponds and ancient Hawaiian petroglyphs or rock carvings are some of the features of these hiking tours. Costs range from $45 for half-day to $80 for full day, per person. There are also special 3 day/2 night camping hikes at $425 per person and a heavy-duty 14-day cross-island trek with backpacking, mountain biking and sea kayaking combined on a 150 mile journey. The 14-day trek cost varies and is custom planned.

Visitors are invited to join the local *Moku Loa Group* of the *Hawai'i Sierra Club* on the Big Island for its monthly hikes on island trails. It's a great way to see some of the Big Island and meet a group of local folks who enjoy Hawai'i's great outdoors and are knowledgeable about its history and culture. You can write to the Moku Loa Group-Hawai'i Sierra Club, P.O. Box 1137, Hilo, HI 96721-1137 for information on its hiking schedule. Or you can contact the Hawai'i Sierra Club office in Honolulu for information at 1100 Ala Kea Street, Room 330, Honolulu, HI 96813, (808) 538-6166. They have a listing of all the scheduled hikes and activities on all the islands.

Another active hiking group is the *Kona Hiking Club*, an informal group which takes monthly day hikes to the Big Island's less accessible and private beaches, forests and backcountry areas. Most of these hikes are not difficult or long and require minimal gear or hiking experience. The group encourages family hiking outings. The club generally takes hikes on the first Saturday and third Thursday of each month. Membership is open to everyone. There are no dues or fees and visitors are welcome to participate. This is a good way to get to know some local folks and enjoy a Hawaiian outdoors experience. Watch the local Big Island newspapers community news files for hike announcements.

For maps and information on hiking the national park, write to: Superintendent, Hawai'i Volcanoes National Park, Volcano, HI 96718.

For information and maps relating to state forest reserve lands, write to: Division of Forestry, Department of Land and Natural Resources, Island of Hawai'i, 75 Aupuni St., Hilo, HI 96720.

For information on state parks write to: Division of State Parks, Hawai'i District Office, Dept. of Land and Natural Resources, P.O. Box 936, Hilo, HI 96720.

For information on county beach parks write to: Department of Parks and Recreation, County of Hawai'i, 25 Aupuni St., Hilo, HI 96720.

Another good source of hiking information is *Hawaiian Hiking Trails*, by Craig Chisholm, Fernglen Press (1989). Available from Paradise Publications, see ordering information in the back of this guide.

CAMPING

See the section on Camping in WHERE TO STAY - WHAT TO SEE.

SNOW SKIING

To the surprise of many, visitors can enjoy some fabulous seasonal snow skiing on the Big Island, the only place in Hawai'i where it is possible. Granted, snow skiing is a strictly seasonal activity and at best is sporadic and unpredictable given the erratic nature of snowfall on Mauna Kea the past few winters. However, from approximately November through March and sometimes into April and May, the nearly 14,000 ft. summit of Mauna Kea can be covered with snow. When conditions are just right, skiers can enjoy some incredible downhill runs on the treeless slopes. There are no ski lifts, no lodge, and no facilities whatsoever on the summit and most skiers transport themselves via a four-wheel drive vehicle rental.

However, there is one ski tour operator specializing in Mauna Kea ski tours. Contact **Ski Guides Hawai'i**, P.O. Box 2020, Kamuela, HI 96743, (808) 885-4188. They offer complete package tours to Mauna Kea on snowdays including four-wheel drive transportation, ski rental, equipment, and lunch. Contact them for the current season schedule and rates.

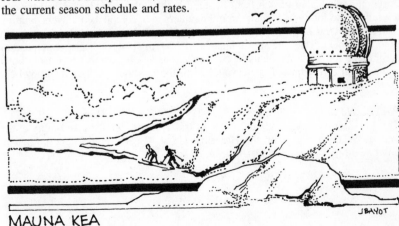

MAUNA KEA

JBAYOT

HORSEBACK RIDING AND POLO LESSONS

For the would-be "paniolos" (Hawaiian cowboys and cowgirls) there are a few stables and trail ride operators with a variety of rides and horseback outings available in different island locations. One operator also offers polo lesson packages. Check out any of the following:

E-Z Riders Trail Rides - (928-8410) Pahala, Ka'u, HI 96777. This operater is located five minutes from the small town of Pahala in the southern Ka'u District. E-Z Riders offers various trail riding tours through some of the most beautiful parts of the rolling Ka'u countryside.

Ironwood Outfitters - (885-4941) Kohala Ranch, Kamuela, HI 96743. This operator features daily morning mountain rides, picnic rides, afternoon excursions, and customized rides through the stunning mountains and meadows of the Kohala Mountains and Kohala Ranch lands.

King's Trail Rides O' Kona - (323-2388) Kealakekua, Kona, HI 96750. They offer horseback trail rides exploring the backcountry lands of 20,000 acre Kealakekua Ranch and Kona Coast trail rides to Pine Trees Beach in Kohanaiki.

Mauna Kea Beach Stables - (885-4288) P.O. Box 218, Kamuela, HI 96743. This operation primarily serves the Mauna Kea Beach Hotel guests and offers a full range of trail rides, picnic rides, and sunset rides.

Roughriders Hawai'i - (885-0057) Kamuela, HI 96743. This outfitter offers a range of trail rides, riding lessons and even a summer riding camp.

Waiki'i Ranch Polo Club - (883-8223, FAX 883-9715), P.O.Box 111333, Suite 125, Kamuela, HI 96743-0050. Waiki'i Ranch offers varied polo vacation packages in conjunction with Kohala Coast resorts the year around. The Club hosts an annual polo season from September through December. Polo packages are tailored to individual needs, from beginners to accomplished players wanting to fine-tune their hitting or riding skills. Quality ponies are provided, along with polo equipment. Rates are approximately $1,500 for six days of instruction and/or scrimmage for two hours daily, accommodations at a luxurious beach-front hotel and a rental car. Adjusted rates available for those who book their own hotel-car arrangements.

Waipi'o Na'alapa Trail Rides - (775-0419) P.O.Box 992, Honoka'a, HI 96727. This operator offers a standard 2 1/2 hour trail ride through the lush beauty of the famous Waipi'o Valley on the Hamakua Coast. Riders should be agile and in good health; no children under 8 years of age.

ART AND FUN

Aloha 'Aina Arts - P.O. Box 2066, Kamuela, HI 96743 (885-6109). This unique operation offers the opportunity of "painting in Paradise." They offer different painting sites around the Big Island including Waipio Valley, Mauna Kea, the Hamakua Coast, Waimea/Kamuela area, the Kona Coast, etc. The $125 per person fee includes everything for a day's (5-7 hours) excursion to beautiful outdoor spots. Included are all painting materials--canvas, paints, brushes, French easels, transportation to/from your hotel, picnic lunch, special instruction and personalized tours. Just bring your inspiration! You also take home your painting. This is a new and exciting way to see Hawai'i and express your creativity. The staff is headed by Robert Althouse, noted artist, who lives in Waimea and has exhibited his work throughout Hawai'i and California.

HEALTH AND FITNESS CENTERS

Many of the newer resorts and hotels, and even some of the older ones, have added on health and fitness centers, exercise rooms, and work-out equipment to meet the growing demand for such services among visitors. And with Hawai'i's emphasis on outdoor activities, it is easy to see why there is a lot of interest in keeping healthy and fit. If your hotel or condo doesn't have such a facility and you want to workout with the weights and other exercise equipment, you might try any of the following health and fitness centers. They welcome the public on a walk-in basis. They generally charge an hourly use fee for the equipment, spa, pool, etc.

Big Island Gym - 74-5605 Alapa Street, Kailua-Kona, HI 96740 (329-9432)

Keauhou Massage & Spa - 78-6740 Alii Dr., #227, Kailua-Kona, HI (322-0048)

Pacific Coast Fitness - 65-1298A Kawaihae Road, Waimea, HI 96743 (885-6270)

Pacific Raquetball Club - 74-5606 Pawai Place, Bay 19, Kailua-Kona, HI 96740 (329-7766)

Physiques - 29 Shipman, Suite 104, Hilo, HI 96720 (961-0003)

Slender You of Kona - 75-5995 Kuakini Highway, Suite 313, Kailua-Kona, HI 96740 (326-4747)

Spencer Health & Fitness Center - 197 Keawe St., Hilo, HI 96720 (969-1511)

The Club in Kona - Kona Center, Kailua-Kona, HI 96740 (326-2582)

The Program - 74-5588 Pawai Place, #N, Kailua-Kona, HI 96740 (326-3285)

HUNTING

Outdoorsmen and hunting enthusiasts would find an enjoyable and challenging outing to the fields and slopes of Mauna Kea or other island hunting grounds. Whether it would be for Hawaiian big game like wild boar, Mouflon sheep, or mountain goat or wild game birds like turkey, quail, pheasant, chukar, or franklin, hunting the Big Island will provide special thrills, action, and unique outdoor experiences. The following hunting guide services and outfitters can make all the arrangements.

Arrington Adventures - Kona Paradise, Kailua-Kona, HI 96740 (808) 328-2349. Guide Steve Arrington specializes in both hunting and fishing packages.

Ginger Flower Charters - 78-6989 Mamalahoa Highway, Holualoa, Kona, HI 96725, (808) 324-1444. Guide Kenny Llanes specializes in wild boar hunting on the Big Island's remote mountain and forest slopes. In addition, bird hunting for wild turkey, pheasant, quail, chukar, and franklin is available November through January. Archery hunts are available for sheep and goat in season.

Hawai'i Hunting Tours - P.O. Box 58, Paauilo, Hamakua, HI 96776, (808) 776-1666. Guide Eugene Ramos specializes in custom hunts for sheep, wild boar, goat, and game birds on private hunting grounds on the slopes of Mauna Kea. Scenic 4-wheel drive tours through majestic backcountry are also available.

McCandless Ranch - Kai Malino, Kona, HI 96740, (808) 328-2389. This ranch has a private hunting preserve of some 61,000 upcountry acres and guided hunts are arranged for wild boar, sheep, turkey, pheasant and other game birds.

WILD BOAR

AIR TOURS
SMALL PLANE FLIGHTSEEING

Scenic flights in a small plane are a good way to see the Big Island from a bird's-eye view. Scenic flight operators fly from Hilo or Kona airports and generally include the island's most outstanding features and attractions, volcano activity and lava flows, waterfalls and valleys, lava deserts and rainforests, and rugged coastlines, on their fixed routes and standard air tours.

Big Island Air - Kailua-Kona, 1-800-367-8047 ext.207, Hawai'i Inter-island 1-800-533-3417, Big Island (808) 329-4868. This small airline offers complete 2 hour circle-island, 4-island scenic flights, and historic Kona-Kohala Coasts flights plus custom charter flights are arranged. Aircraft include Cessna 402's and a Citation jet for VIP executive luxury. Tours begin at $125 per person; circle island tours at $150 per person.

Classic Aviation Corporation - Keahole Airport, P.O.Box 1899, Kailua-Kona, HI 96745 (in Hawai'i 1-800-695-8100, Big Island 329-8687). This flying service offers a unique experience flying in a reproduction of an open-cockpit 1935 WACO bi-plane. The plane carries two passengers and the pilot. You get the special thrill of open-air flight while enjoying the incredible aerial views only possible on the Big Island. Most tours last 1/2 hour. Prices range from $95 per person. Twice weekly airtours are also offered from Hilo International Airport, call for details.

Hawai'i AirVentures - Keahole Airport, Kailua-Kona, HI 96740 (329-0014). This small airline offers charters, scenic flightseeing tours, and photographic air tours.

Hawai'i Island Hoppers - Old Air Terminal, Hilo International Airport, Hilo, HI 96720 (969-2000). They provide personalized volcano and waterfall scenic flights in six and ten passenger twin engine aircraft. Tours begin at $65 per person.

Hawai'i Pacific Aviation - Hilo International Airport, Hilo, HI 96720 (961-5591). Charter flights and tours are offered. A 50 minute Volcano Tour in a comfortable 4-seat aircraft includes Kilauea's recently active lava flows and eruption sites and Hawai'i's famous black sand beaches ($55 per person). A narrated 35 minute Waterfall Tour follows the beautiful Hamakua Coast taking in spectacular rain forests and waterfalls, sugar cane fields, macadamia nut orchards, gulches and valleys, and rugged scenic coastline ($45 per person). A combined 1 1/2 hour Volcano and Waterfall Tour is $85 per person.

'Io Aviation - Hilo International Airport, Hilo, HI 96720 (935-3031). Charter flights and tours are offered. A basic Volcano Tour of 45-60 minutes takes in recent eruption and lava flow sites ($55 per person) and the Island Tour takes in coastal Hamakua, agricultural areas, and inland sections in a 45-60 minute flight ($55 per person). Special Waipio Valley Photo Flights are also offered.

Kainoa Aviation - Hilo International Airport, Hilo, HI 96720 (961-5591). This charter airline operates various small plane island flightseeing tours. A basic volcano air tour begins at $65 per person.

Koa Air Service Hawai'i - Keahole Airport, Kailua-Kona, HI 96740 (326-2288). This air tour operation has Cessna airplanes equipped with intercom for personalized narrated airtours of the Big Island. They specialize in air photo safaris covering volcanoes, waterfalls, rainforests, seacliffs, beaches, blue lagoons, tropical gardens and wildlife.

HELICOPTER TOURS

Helicopter tours are a thrilling way to see the island's scenery up close. They are a wonderful way to get some fantastic video or photography of your Big Island experience. The standard tours offered by most helicopter lines take in all the attractions of Hawai'i Volcanoes National Park including eruption sites, recent or current lava flows, the site where lava enters the ocean, and more. Other tours highlight the town of Hilo, the beautiful Hamakua Coast with its tropical rain forest and countless waterfalls, the grand Waipio Valley, Parker Ranch, mountain meadows, and rugged coastline vistas. The costs are generally expensive, as one might expect. One hour Volcanoes National Park tours range from about $100-150 per person. Tours along the Kohala or Hamakua Coasts are about $135 per person for a 1-1 1/2 hour tour. Some of the lines offer deluxe circle island tours from about $275 per person for a two hour tour. Most lines require a minimum number of people for their various tours. Check with the helicopter lines for specifics.

Dragonfly Helicopters Inc. - (935-9744) Hilo International Airport, Hilo, HI 96720. This operator offers a full range of helicopter tours to the volcano area and Big Island scenic attractions.

Hilo Bay Air - (969-1545/969-1547) Commuter Terminal, Hilo International Airport, Hilo, HI 96720. This operator offers a complete range of helicopter tours to the volcano area and other scenic sections of the Big Island. The standard one hour Volcano Tour is $145 per person, minimum of two. A slightly longer Hamakua Coast Waterfall Tour is one hour and fifteen minutes and is $175 per person, minimum of two.

'Io Aviation - Hilo International Airport, Hilo, HI 96720 (935-3031). They offer personalized volcano area and general island air tours in helicopters. One hour volcano and island tours are $99 per person, two person minimum.

Kainoa Aviation - Hilo International Airport, Hilo, HI 96720 (961-5591). This helicopter line offers a full range of volcano tours, aerial photography and general air sightseeing tours. Volcano tours from $99 per person.

Kenai Air Hawai'i - P.O.Box 4118, Kailua-Kona, HI 96745 (US 1-800-622-3144, Hawai'i 329-7424). They offer a full range of varied air tours to the Big Island's most spectacular coastal, mountain, volcano, and forest scenery. The Circle Island Deluxe Tour is $265 per person, three person minimum. A Hamakua Coast and Waipio Valley Tour is $149 per person, three minimum.

Lacy Helicopters - Kohala Airport, Kamuela, HI 96743 (885-7272, 775-9273 or 885-4657). They offer complete helicopter service including charters, custom tours, and aerial photography.

Mauna Kea Helicopters - Kohala Airport, Kamuela, HI 96743 (885-6400). This line provides complete island sightseeing tours, charters, aerial photography and video expertise. The Waipio Valley tour using an exclusive Waipio helipad takes in the beauty of the valley and the North Kohala Coast ($80 per person).

Papillon Helicopters Ltd. - Waikoloa Airport, P.O.Box 55, Kamuela, HI 96743 (329-0551, FAX 808/326-9431). This line offers a full range of flightseeing tours to the Big Island's scenic attractions. Tours include a Kohala Coast Adventure (45-50 mins.) at $145 per person; Pele's Spectacular volcano tour (80-90 mins.) at $245 per person; Volcano/Kohala Deluxe combines best of both (2 hrs.) at $295 per person. They have had occasional special volcano tours for $129 per person.

Volcano Heli-Tours - Volcano Golf Course Heliport, Volcano, HI 96785 (967-7578). They offer a full range of sightseeing tours into Hawai'i Volcanoes National Park and surrounding countryside.

HAWAIIANA READING FOR ADULTS

Bailey, Paul. *Those Kings and Queens of Old Hawaii*. Tucson, Arizona: Westernlore Press. 1988.

Barrow, Terence. *Incredible Hawaii*. Vermont: Charles Tuttle Co. 1974.

Boylan, Dan. *Hawaii Aloha*. Kailua, Hawaii: Press Pacifica. 1987.

Berger, Andrew J. *Hawaiian Birdlife*. Honolulu: University of Hawaii Press. 1981.

Brennan, Joseph. *The Parker Ranch of Hawaii*. New York: Harper & Row. 1974.

Brown, DeSoto. *Hawaii Recalls: Nostalgic Images of the Hawaiian Islands, 1910-1950*. New York: Methuen Inc. 1986.

Casil, Kathleen. *Hawaiian Wedding Book*. Honolulu: Bess Press. 1986.

Chisholm, Craig. *Hawaiian Hiking Trails*. Oregon: Fernglen Press. 1991.

Clark, John R. K. *Beaches of the Big Island*. Honolulu: University of Hawaii Press. 1985

Clay, Horace F. and Hubbard, James C. *The Hawaii Garden Tropical Exotics*. Honolulu: University of Hawaii Press. 1987.

Day, A.G., Editor. *Mark Twain's Letters from Hawaii*. Honolulu: University of Hawaii Press. 1975.

Day, A.G. and Stroven, Carl. *Hawaiian Reader*. Honolulu: Mutual Publishing Co. 1985.

Daws, Gavan. *Shoal of Time: A History of the Hawaiian Islands*. Honolulu: University of Hawaii Press. 1974.

Fielding, Ann and Robinson, Ed. *An Underwater Guide to Hawaii*. Honolulu: University of Hawaii Press. 1989.

Greenberg, Idaz. *Hawaiian Fishwatcher's Field Guide*. Miami: Seahawk Press. 1983.

Hobson, E. and Chave, E.H. *Hawaiian Reef Animals*. Honolulu: University of Hawaii Press. 1979.

Hoffman, Phil. *Comprehensive Guide to Scuba Diving in Hawaii*. Kailua, Hawaii: Press Pacifica. 1984.

Hosaka, Edward. *Shore Fishing in Hawaii*. Hilo, Hawaii: Petroglyph Press. 1987.

Judd, Gerrit. *Hawaii, an Informal History*. New York: Macmillan. 1961.

Martin, Lynn, Editor. *Na Paniolo O Hawaii*. Honolulu: Honolulu Academy of Arts. 1987.

Morey, Kathy. *Hawaii Trails, The Big Island*. Wilderness Press. 1992.

Pratt, H. Douglas, Bruner, P.L., and Berrett, D.G. *The Birds of Hawaii and the Tropical Pacific*. Princeton, N.J.: Princeton University Press. 1987.

Rayson, Ann. *Modern Hawaiian History*. Honolulu: The Bess Press. 1984.

Sohmer, S. H. and Gustafson, R. *Plants and Flowers of Hawaii*. Honolulu: University of Hawaii Press. 1987.

Smith, Robert. *Hawaii's Best Hiking Trails*. California: Hawaiian Outdoor Adventures. 1991.

Smith, Robert. *Hiking Wawaii: The Big Island*. California: Hawaiian Outdoor Adventures. 1990.

Tinker, Spencer Wilkie. *Fishes of Hawaii*. Honolulu: Hawaiian Service. 1982.

Westervelt, W. *Hawaiian Legends of Volcanoes*. Vermont: C.E.Tuttle. 1963.

Whitson, Skip. *Hawaii-Nei, the Kingdom of Hawaii One Hundred Years Ago*. New Mexico: Sun Publishing Co. 1976.

HAWAIIANA READING FOR CHILDREN

Adair, Dick. *The Story of Aloha Bear*. Honolulu: Island Heritage. 1986.
Adair, D. *Aloha Bear and the Meaning of Aloha*. Honolulu: Island Heritage. 1987.
Brennan, J. *Duke Kahanamoku, Hawaii's Golden Man*. Honolulu: Hogarth. 1974.
Brown, Marcia. *Backbone of the King: The Story of Paka'a and His Son Ku*. New York: Scribner. 1966.
Carpenter, Allan. *Hawaii*. Chicago: Childrens Press. 1979.
Day, A. Grove. *Kamehameha, First King of Hawaii*. Honolulu: Hogarth. 1974.
Feeney, S. *Hawaii is a Rainbow*. Honolulu: University of Hawaii Press. 1980.
Feeney, Stephanie and Fielding, Ann. *Sand to Sea: Marine Life of Hawaii*. Honolulu: University of Hawaii Press. 1989.
Fradin, Dennis. *Hawaii: In Words & Pictures*. Chicago: Childrens Press. 1980.
Hale, Bruce. *The Legend of the Laughing Gecko*. Honolulu: Geckostufs. 1989.
Hazama, Dorothy. *The Ancient Hawaiians. Who Were They? How Did They Live?* Honolulu: Hogarth. 1974.
Kahalewai, Marilyn. *Maui Mouse's Supper*. Honolulu: Bess Press. 1988.
Kahalewai, Marilyn. *Whose Slippers are Those?* Honolulu: Besss Press. 1988.
Knudsen, Eric A. Spooky Stuffs. *Aiea*. Hawaii: Island Heritage Publishing. 1989.
Laird, Donivee Martin. *The Three Little Hawaiian Pigs and the Magic Shark*. Honolulu: Barnaby Books. 1988.
Laird, Donivee. *'Ula Li'i and the Magic Shark*. Honolulu: Barnaby Books. 1985.
Laird, Donivee Martin. *Wili Wai Kula and the Three Mongooses*. Honolulu: Barnaby Books. 1983.
Laird, Donivee. *Keaka and the Lilikoi Vine*. Honolulu: Barnaby Books. 1982.
Land-Nellist, Cassandra. *A Child's First Book About Hawaii*. Hawaii: Press Pacifica. 1987.
Lyons, Barbara. *Maui, Mischievous Hero*. Hilo: Petroglyph Press. 1969.
McBarnet, Gill. *A Whale's Tale*. Hawaii: Ruwanga Trading. 1988.
McBarnet, Gill. *Fountain of Fire*. Hawaii: Ruwanga Trading. 1987.
McBarnet, Gill. *The Wonderful Journey*. Hawaii: Ruwanga Trading. 1986.
McBarnet, Gill. *The Whale Who Wanted to be Small*. Hawaii: Ruwanga Trading. 1985.
McBride, Leslie R. *About Hawaii's Volcanoes*. Hilo: Petroglyph Press. 1986.
Missler, Dux. *Hawaii Fun Activity Book*. Hilo: Petroglyph Press. 1986.
Pape, Donna L. *Hawaii Puzzle Book*. Honolulu: Bess Press. 1984.
Radlauer, Ruth. *Hawaii Volcanoes National Park*. Chicago: Childrens Press. 1979.
Thompson, Vivian. *Hawaiian Tales of Heroes and Champions*. Honolulu: University of Hawaii Press. 1986.
Titcomb, Margaret. *The Ancient Hawaiians: How They Clothed Themselves*. Honolulu: Hogarth. 1974.
Tune, Suelyn Ching. *How Maui Slowed the Sun*. Honolulu: University of Hawaii Press. 1988.
Wagenman, Mark A. *The Adventures of Aloha Bear and Maui the Whale*. Honolulu: Island Heritage. 1989.
Warren, Bonnie. *Aloha from Hawaii!* Honolulu: Warren Associates. 1987.
Williams, Julie Stewart. *And the Birds Appeared*. Honolulu: University of Hawaii Press. 1988.
Young, Margaret. *Hawaii's People from China*. Honolulu: Hogarth. 1974.

INDEX

ACCOMMODATIONS INDEX . 67
ACCOMMODATIONS LIST
  Ka'u District 157
  North Hilo-Hamakua Districts 137
  North Kohala District 141
  North-South Kona Districts . . 98
  Puna District 151
  South Hilo District 131
  South Kohala District 117
Ahuena Heiau 89
airlines 27
air tours - helicopter 260
air tours - small plane 259
airports 27
Akaka Falls State Park 134
annual events 54
antiques 52
art and fun 257
Atlantis Submarine tour 232
babysitting 31
BEACHES 218
  BEST BETS 219
  Ka'u District 229
  North Hilo-Hamakua Districts 226
  North Kohala District 225
  North-South Kona Districts . 221
  Puna Districts 228
  South Hilo District 227
  South Kohala District 223
bed & breakfast lodging 69
bicycle tours 247
BIG ISLAND'S BEST BETS
  overall 14
  accommodations (see accom. list)
  restaurants 162
  recreation and tours 217
  beaches 220
camping 83
Cape Kumikahi Lighthouse . . . 150
Coconut Island 124
Cook, Captain James . . . 16,17,90
County of Hawai'i 20
cruises-boats 231
diving 235
deep sea fishing 237
Destination Hilo 39,123
earthquakes 61
East Hawai'i Cultural Center . . 126
Ellison Onizuka
  Cntr. International Astronomy 143
  Space Museum at Kona Airport 29

emergencies 31
fish, seafood 47
Fuku-Bonsai Center 89
gifts 52
glassbottom boat cruises 231
golf 248
grocery shopping 49
Hale Kea 112
Hamakua Coast 133,137
Hawai'i Comm. College 124
Hawai'i Tropical
  Botanical Gardens 126
Hawai'i Visitors Bureau 39
Hawai'i Volcanoes
  National Park 147,152,155
  Bird Park Sanctuary 156
  Chain of Craters Drive 156
  Crater Rim Drive 155,156
  Devastation Trail 156
  Halemaumau 155,156
  Jaggar Volcano Observatory 155
  Kilauea Iki 155
  Thurston Lava Tube 156
  Volcano Art Center 155
  Waha'ula Heiau 156
Hawaiian language 20
  glossary 21
  pidgin English 23
Hawi 138-140
health & fitness centers 257
hiking 257
Hilo 121-132
Hilo Farmers' Market 128
Hilo Tropical Gardens 127
Hirose Nurseries 127
history 16
Holualoa 90
Honalo 90
Honaunau 89
Honoka'a 134
horseback riding 256
Hulihe'e Palace 89
hunting 258
jet skiing 243
Kailua-Kona 87-108
Kainaliu 90
Ka Lae (South Point) . . . 152,153
Kamehameha the Great
  history 16-19
  statue 139
Kamoamoa Park 149,228

Kamuela/Waimea 109-117
Kamuela Museum 112
Kapaʻau 138-140
kayaks-Hobie cats 244
Kealakekua 87,90,91
Keauhou 93,95,97
Keauhou Visitors Assoc. 39
Keaau 147
Kilauea Military Camp 82,83
Kona coffee 88,91
Kona's Gold Coast 88
Kohala Coast 109-111
Kohala Coast Resort Assoc. . . . 39
Kurtistown 147
Lapakahi State Historical Park . 141
laundries, self-service 53
Laupahoehoe Point 134
Lava Tree State Park 150
Liliuokalani Park 123
Little Grass
    Shack at Kealakekua 91
luaus/dinner show 172
Lyman House Museum 125
macadamia nut factories
    Mauna Loa 126
    Mrs. Fields 90
    Hawaiian Macadamia
    Nut Plantation 134
Mauna Kea 143-145
Mauna Kea summit tours . 144,145
Mauna Kea Observatory 144
Mauna Loa 145
Moʻokini Luakini Heiau 140
Mountain View 147,150,151
Naalehu . . . : 153
Nani Mau Gardens 127
Pahala 155
painted churches
    St. Benedict's 91
    Star of the Sea 149
Panaewa Rainforest Zoo 126
parasailing 244
Paradise Orchid Gardens 127
Parker Ranch Visitors Center . 111
Parker Ranch, Puʻuopelu 111
PARKS
    County of Hawaiʻi 83
    State of Hawaiʻi 85
    Hawaiʻi Volcanoes
    National Park 86
photography, tropical 61
physicially impaired
    travel tips 34
polo, lessons 256

Pololu Valley 140
private residences 81
products, Big Island 50
Puna 147-152
Puʻukohola National
    Historical Park 18,112
Puʻuhonua O Honaunau
    National Historical Park 89
Rainbow Falls Park 124
Rainbow Tropicals 127
rental agents 158
rental cars 42
RESTAURANTS 161
    BEST BETS 161
    drive ins/plate lunch shops . 170
    INDEX - ALPHABETICAL   165
    INDEX - FOOD-TYPE 167
    luaus/dinner shows 172
    dinner cruises 173
    top restaurants 162
    top local-style restaurants . . 163
    South and North Kona 174
    South Kohala 198
    Hilo 198
    South Hilo/Hamakua 211
    North Kohala 212
    Puna 213
    Kaʻu 215
Royal Kona Coffee Mill 91
Saddle Road 143
sailing 244
senior citizens, travel tips 35
snorkeling 218,233
snow skiing 255
St. Benedict's, Honaunau, Kona   91
Star of the Sea(painted church)   149
Suisan Fish Auction 124
swimming pools (public) . 252,253
tennis 251,252
transportation 40
    bus - limousine 41,42
    motorbikes, bicycles, etc 44
    rental cars, vans, etc 42
    taxi 40,41
tsunamis (tidal waves) 61
University of
    Hawaiʻi at Hilo 124,125
Waikoloa Village 109,113
Wailoa State Park 126
Waimea/Kamuela 109-117
Waipio Valley 135
weather 59
weddings - honeymoons 36
windsurfing 243

Finally, Hawaiian guides for every budget and for every member of the family. Designed for travelers who want to set their own pace with complete vacation control. These are *THE* guides to have. Complimented by quarterly newsletters which update the changes in the islands between guidebook revisions. Plenty of "insider" information from authors who really know the islands! These and other Hawaiian titles and videos may be ordered direct from **Paradise Publications, 8110 SW Wareham #202, Portland, OR 97223. Phone or FAX (503) 246-1555.**

READER RESPONSE
ORDERING INFORMATION

Dear Reader:

I hope you have had a wonderful visit to Hawai'i The Big Island. Since this book expresses primarily my own opinions on accommodations, restaurants, and recreation, I would sincerely appreciate hearing of your experiences. Any updates or changes would also be welcomed. Please address all correspondence to Paradise Publications.

FREE! A complimentary copy of Paradise Publication's quarterly newsletter, *HAWAI'I, THE THE BIG ISLAND UPDATE*, is available (at no charge) by writing Paradise Publications (Attention: Newsletter Dept.) 8110 S.W. Wareham, Portland, OR 97223, and enclosing a self-addressed, stamped, #10 size envelope. Subscription is $10 annually.

MAUI, A PARADISE FAMILY GUIDE (Including the Island of Lana'i), by Greg & Christie Stilson. The island of Maui is one of Hawai'i's most popular. This guide is packed with information on over 150 condos & hotels, 200 restaurants, 50 great beaches, sights to see and travel tips for the valley island. All new! The island of Lana'i, as a part of the County of Maui, has been added to this popular guide. Lana'i recently joined the tourist industry with the opening of two fabulous new resorts. There is fine dining, local eateries, remote beaches, wonderful hikes and an enchantment unlike any other island. *"A down-to-earth, nuts-and-bolts companion with answers to most any question."* L.A Times. 320 pages, multi-indexed, maps, illustrations, $12.95. Fifth edition.

KAUA'I, A PARADISE FAMILY GUIDE, by Don & Bea Donohugh. Island accommodations, restaurants, secluded beaches, recreation and tour options, remote historical sites, an unusual and unique island tour, this guide covers it all. "If you need a 'how to do it' book to guide your next to Kaua'i, here's the one."..."*this guide may be the best available for the island. It has that personal touch of authors who have spent many happy hours digging up facts.*" Hawaii Gateway to the Pacific Magazine. 290 pages, multi-indexed, maps, illustrations, $12.95. Fourth edition.

HAWAI'I: THE BIG ISLAND, A PARADISE FAMILY GUIDE, by John Penisten. Outstanding for its completeness, this well-organized guide provides useful information for people of every budget and lifestyle. Each chapter features the author's personal recommendations and "best bets." Comprehensive information on more than 70 island accommodations and 150 restaurants. Sights to see, recreational activities, beaches, and helpful travel tips. 280 pages. Multiple indexes, maps and illustrations. 300 pages. $12.95. Third edition.

UPDATE NEWSLETTERS! *THE MAUI UPDATE, THE KAUA'I UPDATE,* and *HAWAI'I: THE BIG ISLAND UPDATE* are quarterly newsletters published by Paradise Publications that highlight the most current island events. Each features late breaking tips on the newest restaurants, island activities or special, not-to-be missed events. Each newsletter is available at the single issue price of $2.50 or a yearly subscription (four issues) rate of $10. Orders to Canada are $3 each or $12 per year.

Also available from Paradise Publications are books and videos to enhance your travel library and assist with your travel plans!

For a full listing of current titles send request to Paradise Publications. Prices are subject to change without notice.

BOOKS

MAUI, THE ROMANTIC ISLAND, and *KAUA'I, THE UNCONQUERABLE* by K.C. Publications. These two books present full color photographs depicting the most magnificent sights on each island. Brief descriptive text adds perspective. Highly recommended. 9 x 12, 48 pages, $5.95 each, paperback.

HALEAKALA and *HAWAII VOLCANOES* by K.C. Publications. Each fascinating and informative book is filled with vivid photographs depicting these natural volcanic wonders. A great gift or memento. 9 x 12, $5.95 each.

WHALES, DOLPHINS, PORPOISES OF THE PACIFIC by K.C. Publications. Enjoy the antics of these beautiful aquatic mammals through full color photographs and descriptive text. A great book for children!! 9 x 12, paperback, $5.95

SHARKS! by K.C. Publications. Loaded with incredible photography, this book describes the many varied predators of the deep. 9 x 12, paperback, $5.95.

HAWAIIAN HIKING TRAILS by Craig Chisholm. This very attractive and accurate guide details 49 of Hawaii's best hiking trails. Includes photography, topographical maps, and detailed directions. An excellent book for the outdoorsperson! 6 x 9, paperback, 152 pgs., $14.95. 1991.

KAUAI HIKING TRAILS by Craig Chisholm. New from Fernglen Press this 160 page book features color photographs, topographical maps and detailed directions to Kaua'i's best hiking trails. A quality publication. $12.95. 1991.

HIKING HAWAII (The Big Island) by Robert Smith. Over 40 hiking trails throughout the Island of Hawai'i. 5 x 8 paperback, 157 pages, $8.95. Also by Robert Smith. *HIKING MAUI*, discover 27 hiking areas all around Maui. 160 pages. $8.95. *HIKING KAUAI*, over 40 hiking trails, 116 pages, $8.95, and *HAWAI'I'S BEST HIKING TRAILS*, 250 pages, $12.95, all six islands are included with a total of 42 trails. Black & white photographs and maps.

COOKING WITH ALOHA by Elvira Monroe and Irish Margah. Discover the flavors and smells of the Hawaiian islands in your own kitchen with this beautiful illustrated and easy-to-follow cookbook. Delicacies range from exotic pickled Japanese seaweed or taro cakes to flavorful papaya sherbet or chicken 'ono niu. Drinks, appetizers, main courses and desserts are covered. 9 x 12, paperback, 184 pages, $7.95.

VIDEOS   (All Videos are VHS format)

FOREVER HAWAII
This 60 minute, video portrait features all six major Hawaiian islands. (Note: Does not include coverage of the new resorts on Lana'i.) It includes breathtaking views from the snowcapped peaks of Mauna Kea to the bustling city of Waikiki, from the magnificent Waimea Canyon to the spectacular Halakeala Crater. A lasting memento. $29.95

FOREVER MAUI
An in-depth visit to Maui with scenic shots and interesting stories about the Valley Isle. An excellent video for the first time, or even the returning Maui visitor. 30 minutes. $24.95

FLIGHT OF THE CANYON BIRD
An inspired view of the Garden Island of Kaua'i from a bird's eye perspective; an outstanding 30 minute piece of cineamatagraphy. This short feature presentation explores the lush tropical rainforests surrounding Waialeale (the wettest spot on earth), the awesome Waimea Canyon and the Napili Coastline. The narration explores the geologic beginnings of the island and its historical beginnings as well. An outstanding presentation and a valuable tool for vacation preparation, a lasting memento or a gift! $19.95.

EXPLORE HAWAII: A TRAVEL GUIDE
The scenes are similar to that of Forever Hawai'i, but this is a very fast paced 30-minute tour of all six islands. One helpful feature of this tape is the way place names of the areas being viewed are displayed on the screen. A great way to learn correct Hawaiian pronunciations! $19.95.

*KUMU HULUA: KEEPERS OF A CULTURE
This 85-minute tape was funded by the Hawaii State Foundation on Culture and Arts. If you enjoy the hula and culture of Hawai'i, then this is the tape for you. The tape includes hulas from various troupes on various islands, attired in their brilliantly colored costumes. It explores the unique qualities of hula as well as explaining the history. A documentary style production with many wonderfully performed dances. $29.95.

*TARGET: PEARL HARBOR
This historical documentary includes eyewitness accounts of survivors of the December 7, 1941 attack. Featuring a dramatic narrative with actual footage and modern reenactment. This tape was released to commemorate the 50th anniversary of the Pearl Harbor Attack. $29.95

*WHALE SONG
The majestic humpback whales have chosen Hawai'i as their winter paradise. Join Lloyd Bridges as he narrates this excellent video which explores the world of cetaceans. Dolphins and whales are intelligent mammals that are portrayed in their undersea home with rare footage. 40 minutes. $24.95.

*HULA - LESSONS ONE AND TWO
"Lovely Hula Hands" and "Little Brown Gal" are the two featured hulas taught by Carol "Kalola" Lorenzo. She explains the basic steps of the hula. Kalola, born on the island of Maui, has been singing and dancing since she was six. A fun and interesting video for the whole family. 30 minutes. $19.95.

SHIPPING

In the Continental U.S.-- Please add $4 for 1 to 4 items (books or videos). Each additional item over 4, please add $1. Orders shipped promptly by UPS (United Parcel Service). Addresses which are Post Office boxes will be shipped U.S. Mail, first class. If you'd prefer items shipped bookrate mail, we'll be happy to quote you shipping costs.

Hawai'i and Alaska -- Please add $4 for the first book/tape, $1 each additional book/tape when shipped to the same address. Orders shipped U.S. first class mail.

Canadian Orders -- Please add $4 for the first book and $1 each additional book/tape. Orders shipped U.S. airmail.

NOTE: UPS overnight or two-day airmail service is available. Call for quotes. For larger orders, we can ship by other means. Call for shipping quotes. Generally all books/tapes will be sent out within 24 hours. Those which are a special order item (indicated by an "*") may require additional shipping time; 4 -6 weeks in some cases.

A GIFT? We'd be happy to forward books as a gift. Simply supply us with the name and address. If you'd like to enclose a personal note, please do so, or we can provide one for you.

Please include your check or money order with your order. We can accept Visa or Mastercard orders also.

PARADISE PUBLICATIONS
8110 S.W. Wareham, Suite 202
Portland, Oregon 97223
Phone or FAX (503) 246-1555